Middle School 2-2

중간고사 완벽대비

적중100

영어 기출 문제집

중**2**

시사 | 송미정

Best Collection

구성과 특징

교과서의 주요 학습 내용을 중심으로 학습 영역별 특성에 맞춰 단계별로 다양한 학습 기회를 제공하여 단원별 학습능력 평가는 물론 중간 및 기말고사 시험 등에 완벽하게 대비할 수 있도록 내용을 구성

Words & Expressions

Step1	Key Words 단원별 핵심 단어 설명 및 풀이 Key Expression 단원별 핵심 숙어 및 관용어 설명 Word Power 반대 또는 비슷한 뜻 단어 배우기 English Dictionary 영어로 배우는 영어 단어
Step2	실력평가 단원별 수시평가 대비 주관식, 객관식 문제풀이
Step3	서술형 대비 학업성취도 및 수행능력평가 대비 서술형 문제풀이

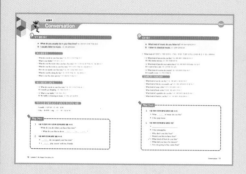

Conversation

Step1	핵심 의사소통 의사소통에 필요한 주요 표현 방법 요약 핵심 Check 기본적인 표현 방법 및 활용능력 확인
Step2	대화문 익히기 상황에 따른 대화문 활용 및 연습
Step3	기본평가 시험대비 기초 학습 능력 평가
Step4	실력평가 단원별 수시평가 대비 주관식, 객관식 문제풀이
Step5	서술형 대비 학업성취도 및 수행능력평가 대비 서술형 문제풀이

Grammar

Step1	주요 문법 단원별 주요 문법 사항과 예문을 알기 쉽게 설명 핵심 Check 기본 문법사항에 대한 이해 여부 확인
Step2	기본평가 시험대비 기초 학습 능력 평가
Step3	실력평가 단원별 수시평가 대비 주관식, 객관식 문제풀이
Step4	서술형 대비 학업성취도 및 수행능력평가 대비 서술형 문제풀이

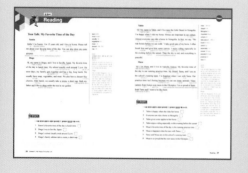

Reading

Step1	구문 분석 단원별로 제시된 문장에 대한 구문별 분석과 내용 설명 확인문제 문장에 대한 기본적인 이해와 인지능력 확인
Step2	확인학습A 빈칸 채우기를 통한 문장 완성 능력 확인
Step3	확인학습B 제시된 우리말을 영어로 완성하여 작문 능력 키우기
Step4	실력평가 단원별 수시평가 대비 주관식, 객관식 문제풀이
Step5	서술형 대비 학업성취도 및 수행능력평가 대비 서술형 문제풀이 교과서 구석구석 교과서에 나오는 기타 문장까지 완벽 학습

Composition

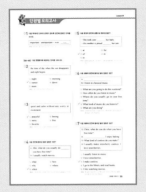

|영역별 핵심문제|
단어 및 어휘, 대화문, 문법, 독해 등 각 영역별 기출문제의 출제 유형을 분석하여 실전에 대비하고 연습할 수 있도록 문제를 배열

|서술형 실전 및 창의사고력 문제|
학교 시험에서 점차 늘어나는 서술형 시험에 집중 대비하고 고득점을 취득하는데 만전을 기하기 위한 학습 코너

|단원별 예상문제|
기출문제를 분석한 후 새로운 시험 출제 경향을 더하여 새롭게 출제될 수 있는 문제를 포함하여 시험에 완벽하게 대비할 수 있도록 준비

|단원별 모의고사|
영역별, 단계별 학습을 모두 마친 후 실전 연습을 위한 모의고사

INSIGHT on the textbook .... 교과서 파헤치기

- **단어Test1~2** 영어 단어 우리말 쓰기와 우리말을 영어 단어로 쓰기

- **대화문Test1~2** 대화문 빈칸 완성 및 전체 대화문 쓰기

- **본문Test1~5** 빈칸 완성, 우리말 쓰기, 문장 배열연습, 영어 작문하기 복습 등 단계별 반복 학습을 통해 교과서 지문에 대한 완벽한 습득

- **구석구석지문Test1~2** 지문 빈칸 완성 및 전문 영어로 쓰기

이책의 차례

Contents

Lesson **5** **We Love Baseball** 05～56

Lesson **6** **New Places, New Experiences** 57～108

Lesson **7** **Living in the AI World** 109～160

⟨Insight on the textbook⟩ 교과서 파헤치기 01～58

⟨책 속의 책⟩ 정답 및 해설 01～44

Lesson 5

We Love Baseball

의사소통 기능

- 선호하는 것 묻고 답하기
  A: Which story book do you like? *Peter Pan* or
  The Last Leaf?
  B: I like *Peter Pan*.

- 희망, 기대 표현하기
  A: What are you going to do on your vacation?
  B: I'm going to take a boat ride. I can't wait.

언어 형식

- 부가의문문
  Jian, this is your first time to come to the
  baseball stadium, **isn't it**?

- 수동태
  The numbers **were determined** by the players'
  batting order.

Words & Expressions

Key Words

- □ **anxious** [ǽŋkʃəs] 형 불안한
- □ **base** [beis] 명 (야구의) 루, 베이스
- □ **batter** [bǽtər] 명 타자
- □ **better** [bétər] 형 더 좋은, 더 나은 (**good**의 비교급)
- □ **competition** [kὰmpətíʃən] 명 대회
- □ **crack** [kræk] 명 찢어지는 듯한[날카로운] 소리
- □ **decide** [disáid] 동 결정하다
- □ **determine** [ditə́ːrmin] 동 결정하다
- □ **dirt** [dəːrt] 명 먼지, 때
- □ **either** [íːðər] 부 (부정문에서) ~도
- □ **fit** [fit] 동 맞다
- □ **forget** [fərgét] 동 잊다
- □ **get** [get] 동 획득하다, 사다
- □ **hide** [haid] 동 감추다, 숨기다
- □ **home run** 홈런
- □ **home team** 홈팀
- □ **international** [ìntərnǽʃənəl] 형 국제적인
- □ **match** [mætʃ] 명 경기, 성냥
- □ **mean** [miːn] 동 의미하다

- □ **miss** [mis] 동 놓치다, 그리워하다
- □ **order** [ɔ́ːrdər] 명 순서, 명령
- □ **past** [pæst] 명 과거
- □ **pet** [pet] 명 애완동물
- □ **pitch** [pitʃ] 명 투구
- □ **rock climbing** 암벽 등반
- □ **rule** [ruːl] 명 규칙
- □ **shorts** [ʃɔːrts] 명 반바지
- □ **sometime** [sʌmtàim] 부 언젠가
- □ **stadium** [stéidiəm] 명 경기장
- □ **support** [səpɔ́ːrt] 동 (특정 스포츠 팀을) 응원하다, 지원하다
- □ **team** [tiːm] 명 팀
- □ **then** [ðen] 부 (시간적·공간적으로) 그 뒤에, 그런 다음
- □ **thunder** [θʌ́ndər] 명 천둥
- □ **ticket** [tíkit] 명 티켓
- □ **vacation** [veikéiʃən] 명 휴가
- □ **visit** [vízit] 동 방문하다
- □ **visiting team** 원정 팀

Key Expressions

- □ **at bat** 타석에 서서
- □ **be a big fan of** ~의 열렬한 팬이다
- □ **be about to** 동사원형 막 ~하려고 하다
- □ **be excited about** ~에 신나다, ~에 들뜨다
- □ **between A and B** A와 B 사이에
- □ **can't wait to** 동사원형 ~을 몹시 기대하다
- □ **come back to** ~로 돌아오다
- □ **come out** 나오다
- □ **hurry up** 서둘러 ~하다
- □ **I can't wait** 너무 기다려져
- □ **in a hurry** 서둘러
- □ **in the past** 과거에
- □ **live in** ~에서 살다
- □ **look at** ~을 보다

- □ **look forward to** (동)명사 ~을 기대하다
- □ **over there** 저기, 저쪽에
- □ **think about** ~에 대해 생각하다
- □ **twice a week** 일주일에 두 번
- □ **wait for** ~을 기다리다
- □ **warm up** (스포츠나 활동 전에) 몸을 천천히 풀다, 준비 운동을 하다
- □ **Which** 명사 **do you like** (**better/more**), **A or B**? A나 B 중 어느 것이 (더) 좋습니까?
- □ **which** 명사 어느 명사
- □ **while**+동사**ing** ~하는 동안
- □ **Why don't you** ~? ~하는 게 어때?
- □ **Why not**? 좋아, 왜 아니겠어?
- □ **would like to** 동사원형 ~하고 싶다

Word Power

※ 동작 동사에 'er'을 붙여 동작의 행위자가 되는 단어 (어미가 e로 끝나면 r만 붙임)

- □ **bake**(굽다) – **baker**(제빵사)
- □ **bat**(공을 치다) – **batter**(타자)
- □ **drive**(운전하다) – **driver**(운전자)
- □ **lead**(지휘하다, 이끌다) – **leader**(지도자)
- □ **manage**(경영하다) – **manager**(경영자)

- □ **play**(경기를 하다) – **player**(선수)
- □ **run**(달리다) – **runner**((달리기) 주자)
- □ **sing**(노래하다) – **singer**(가수)
- □ **teach**(가르치다) – **teacher**(교사)
- □ **write**(쓰다) – **writer**(작가)

※ 'go' vs 'play'

- □ **go skiing** 스키 타러 가다
- □ **go surfing** 서핑하러 가다
- □ **go swimming** 수영하러 가다

- □ **play baseball** 야구를 하다
- □ **play soccer** 축구를 하다
- □ **play tennis** 테니스를 치다

English Dictionary

- □ **anxious** 불안한
  → very nervous or worried about something
  매우 긴장하거나 어떤 것에 대해 걱정을 하는
- □ **base** (야구의) 루, 베이스
  → each corner of the square that makes a baseball diamond
  (야구) 내야를 만드는 사각형의 각 모퉁이
- □ **competition** 대회
  → an event or contest in which people try to win something by defeating others
  사람들이 다른 사람들을 물리침으로써 어떤 것을 얻으려고 하는 행사나 경기
- □ **crack** 찢어지는 듯한[날카로운] 소리
  → the sudden loud explosive sound of something when it falls or bumps into itself or something else
  어떤 것이 떨어지거나 자체로 또는 다른 것과 부딪칠 때 나는 갑작스러운 큰 폭발음
- □ **determine** 결정하다
  → to decide or establish something conclusively
  최종적으로 어떤 것을 결정하거나 수립하다
- □ **either** (부정문에서) ~도
  → used in a negative sentence to indicate a similarity with a statement just made
  부정문에서 방금 언급된 진술에 대해 비슷함을 보여주기 위해 사용되는 것
- □ **fit** 맞다
  → to be the right size and shape for someone or something
  어떤 사람이나 사물에 알맞은 크기나 모양이 되다
- □ **hide** 감추다, 숨기다
  → to put something out of sight
  보이지 않는 곳에 무언가를 두다
- □ **home team** 홈팀
  → a sports team playing on its own ground
  홈그라운드에서 경기를 하는 스포츠 팀

- □ **international** 국제적인
  → relating to or involving different countries
  다른 나라들을 포함하거나 관련된
- □ **order** 순서
  → the arrangement or disposition of people or things in a list from first to last
  어떤 목록에서 처음부터 끝까지 사람이나 사물의 배열이나 배치
- □ **past** 과거
  → the time before the moment of speaking or writing
  말하거나 쓰는 순간 이전의 시간
- □ **pitch** 투구
  → a throw of the ball for the batter to hit it
  타자가 치도록 공을 던지는 것
- □ **stadium** 경기장
  → an athletic or sports ground used for playing and watching sports with rows of seats
  운동 경기를 하고 그 경기를 보기 위해 사용되는 여러 줄의 의자가 있는 육상경기나 운동경기장
- □ **team** 팀
  → a group of people who play a sport or game together against other groups of people
  다른 모임의 사람들에 대항해서 운동이나 경기를 함께 하는 사람들의 모임
- □ **thunder** 천둥
  → the loud noise in the sky heard after a lightning flash during a storm
  폭풍우 동안 번개가 번쩍인 후에 들리는 하늘에서 나는 큰 소리
- □ **ticket** 티켓
  → an official piece of paper or card that shows you have paid to enter a place or do something
  어느 장소에 들어가기 위해 또는 어떤 것을 하기 위해 당신이 돈을 지불했다는 것을 보여 주는 공식적인 종이나 카드
- □ **visiting team** 원정 팀
  → a sports team playing on the competing team's field or court
  경쟁하는 팀의 경기장이나 코트에서 경기를 하는 스포츠 팀

01 다음 중 낱말의 관계가 나머지와 <u>다른</u> 하나는?

① lead – leader   ② bake – baker
③ sing – singer   ④ teach – teacher
⑤ cook – cooker

서답형

02 다음 우리말을 주어진 어휘를 알맞게 배열하여 영작하시오.

내가 네게 막 전화를 걸려던 참인데 네가 전화했어.
(I, me, you, you, was, call, called, when, to, about) (I로 시작할 것)

➡ _____

03 다음 빈칸에 들어갈 말로 알맞은 것은?

Let's take the problems in a different _____.

① order   ② class
③ lesson   ④ kind
⑤ nature

서답형

04 다음 빈칸에 공통으로 들어갈 말을 쓰고 그 뜻을 쓰시오.

(1) Is there a particular baseball team that you _____?
(2) His parents wanted to _____ the community center.
(3) Without the _____ of your friends you will not succeed.

(1) _____ (2) _____ (3) _____

05 다음 빈칸에 공통으로 알맞은 말을 고르시오. (대·소문자 무시)

• You can go slow because this work is not _____ a hurry.
• _____ the past, doctors didn't know the reason.

① at   ② from   ③ to
④ in   ⑤ as

06 다음 중 밑줄 친 'miss'의 뜻이 〈보기〉와 <u>다른</u> 것을 고르시오.

┌─ 보기 ─┐
Hurry up or you'll <u>miss</u> the school bus.

① I hate to <u>miss</u> the beginning of a movie.
② Do not <u>miss</u> this exciting festival next year.
③ I'm sure you will <u>miss</u> your school days.
④ Don't <u>miss</u> this chance to learn and experience science!
⑤ It's a pity to <u>miss</u> the match.

07 다음 영영 풀이에 해당하는 단어를 고르시오.

the loud noise in the sky heard after a lightning flash during a storm

① earthquake   ② wave
③ hurricane   ④ thunder
⑤ typhoon

01 다음 〈보기〉와 같은 관계가 되도록 빈칸에 알맞은 말을 쓰시오.

┌─ 보기 ─
act – actor
└─

(1) bat – _____ (2) write – _____

02 다음 주어진 두 문장이 비슷한 의미가 되도록 빈칸을 알맞게 채우시오.

I'm looking forward to the New Year's Eve party.
➡ I _____ _____ for the New Year's Eve party.

03 다음 빈칸에 알맞은 단어를 〈보기〉에서 골라 쓰시오.

┌─ 보기 ─
home team   match   stadium   thunder
└─

(1) This _____ is so huge, isn't it?
(2) The _____ beat the visiting team 3 to 0.
(3) The alarm sounds like _____.
(4) The Spanish team is leading the soccer _____.

04 다음 대화의 빈칸에 공통으로 들어갈 말을 쓰시오.

A: _____ don't we go skiing together this afternoon?
B: _____ not?

[05~06] 다음 빈칸에 공통으로 들어갈 말을 쓰시오.

05
• He wanted to _____ back to Paris.
• New novels _____ out almost every day.

06
• Can you hurry _____? I don't have much time.
• Warm _____ before lifting heavy weights.

07 다음 주어진 우리말에 맞게 빈칸을 채우시오. (철자가 주어진 것도 있음)

(1) 나는 비틀즈의 열렬한 팬이다.
➡ I am _____ _____ _____ _____ the Beatles.
(2) 내가 가장 좋아하는 선수가 타석에 선다.
➡ My favorite player is _____ _____.
(3) 조용히 해 주세요. 영화가 곧 시작합니다.
➡ Be quiet, please. The movie _____ _____ _____ start.
(4) 저기 검정색 재킷을 입은 여자는 누구인가요?
➡ Who is that woman _____ _____ in the black jacket?
(5) 나는 일주일에 두 번 요가를 한다.
➡ I do yoga _____ _____ _____.
(6) 음악 클럽에 가입하고 싶어요.
➡ I would _____ _____ join a music club.

Conversation

교과서

① 선호하는 것 묻고 답하기

A Which story book do you like? *Peter Pan* or *The Last Leaf*?

너는 어느 이야기책을 좋아하니? "피터팬" 아니면 "마지막 잎새?"

B I like *Peter Pan*. "피터팬"을 좋아해.

■ 주어진 대상 가운데 어느 것을 더 좋아하는지를 물을 때는 'Which do you like better[more], A or B?' 또는 'Which do you prefer, A or B?' 등으로 표현한다. which는 뒤에 나오는 명사를 수식하는 의문형 용사로 쓰일 수 있다.

- Which (sport) do you like more[better], baseball or soccer?
- Which do you prefer, baseball or soccer?

■ 더 좋아하는 것에 대해 말할 때는 'I like A.', 'I like A better[more] than B.' 또는 'I prefer A to B.'로 표현한다. 이때 비교 대상이 되는 'than B'나 'to B'는 생략할 수 있다. 'prefer A to B'에서 to가 전치사 이므로 뒤에 (동)명사가 오는 것에 유의해야 한다.

- A: Which color do you prefer, red or blue?
- B: I prefer red (to blue). / I love red (more than blue). / I like red (more than blue).

선호 묻기

- Which (명사) do[would] you like better[more], A or B?
- Which (명사) do you prefer?
- Which (명사) do you prefer, A or B?

선호 대답하기

- I like A.
- I like A better[more] than B.
- I prefer A (to B).

핵심 Check

1. 다음 우리말과 일치하도록 빈칸에 알맞은 말을 쓰시오.

   A: _____ do you like better, meat _____ _____? (너는 어느 것을 더 좋아하니? 고기 아니면 생선?)

   B: I prefer _____ to fish. (나는 생선보다 고기를 더 좋아해.)

2. 다음 우리말과 일치하도록 주어진 단어를 배열하여 문장을 완성하시오.

   A: _____ _____ _____ _____ _____, _____ _____ _____?

   (cats, do, dogs, which, you, or, better, like)

   (너는 어느 것을 더 좋아하니, 개 아니면 고양이?)

   B: I like dogs. (나는 개를 좋아해.)

② 희망, 기대 표현하기

A What are you going to do on your vacation? 휴가 때 무엇을 할 예정이니?

B I'm going to take a boat ride. I can't wait. 나는 보트를 타러 갈 거야. 너무 기다려져.

■ 'I can't wait.'는 '너무 기다려져.' 또는 '나는 빨리 ~했으면 좋겠다.'라는 의미로 희망이나 기대를 나타내는 표현이다. 'I can't wait.' 뒤에는 'for+명사'나 'to+동사원형'을 덧붙여 쓸 수 있다. 'I'm going to take a boat ride. I can't wait.'에서 'I can't wait'를 'I can't wait for a boat ride.'나 'I can't wait to take a boat ride.'로 쓸 수 있다.

■ 유사한 표현으로는 'I'm looking forward to+(동)명사'가 있다. 'I can't wait' 다음의 to 다음에는 동사원형이 오는 것과 달리, 'I'm looking forward to'의 to는 전치사이므로, 뒤에는 (동)명사가 오는 것에 주의해야 한다.

희망, 기대 표현하기

• I can't wait. 너무 기다려져.   • I can't wait to 동사원형.

• I can't wait for 명사.   • I'm looking forward to (동)명사.

핵심 Check

3. 다음 대화의 순서를 바르게 배열하시오.

(A) That sounds great.

(B) What are your plans for this weekend?

(C) Yes. I'm looking forward to it.

(D) I'm going to go to the party this Saturday.

➡ _____

4. 다음 주어진 단어를 이용하여 대화의 밑줄 친 부분과 같은 의미의 문장을 쓰시오.

A: I heard that you are going to take the trip this summer.

B: Yeah! I'm looking forward to taking the trip.

➡ _____ (for, wait)

_____ (to, wait)

5. 다음 대화의 우리말과 일치하도록 빈칸에 알맞은 말을 쓰시오.

A: Do you want to watch *Harry Potter* with me this weekend? (나와 이번 주말에 해리 포터 볼래?)

B: Sure, I'd love to. I _____ wait _____ watch it. (물론, 그리고 싶어. 그것을 정말 보고 싶어.)

Listen & Speak 1 B-2

G: I'm ❶thinking about getting a pet. Do you have a pet?

B: Yes, I do. I have a dog and a cat.

G: ❷What do you think? ❸Which pet is better for me? A cat or a dog?

B: ❹Why don't you come to my house someday and play with my pets? ❺Then you can decide.

G: 나는 애완동물을 기르는 것에 대해 생각 중이야. 넌 애완동물을 기르니?

B: 응, 길러. 개와 고양이가 있어.

G: 어떻게 생각해? 어떤 애완동물이 나에게 더 나아? 고양이 아니면 개?

B: 어느 날 우리 집에 와서 내 애완동물과 놀아 보는 게 어때? 그런 다음 너는 결정할 수 있을 거야.

❶ think about: ~에 대해서 생각하다 (= think of)

❷ What do you think?: 어떻게 생각해? (의견을 묻는 표현) 대화의 흐름상 애완동물을 기르는 것에 대해 어떻게 생각하는지 상대방의 의견을 묻고 있다. (= What do you think about[of] getting a pet?)

❸ better는 good의 비교급으로 '더 좋은'의 의미를 가진다.

❹ Why don't you ~?: ~하는 게 어때? (상대방에게 권유) come과 play는 접속사 and로 연결되어 있다.

❺ then: (시간적·공간적으로) 그 뒤에, 그런 다음 decide 다음에 내용상 'which pet is better for you(어떤 동물이 더 나을지)'가 생략되어 있다.

Check(√) True or False

(1) The girl has a dog and a cat. T ☐ F ☐

(2) The boy advises the girl to come to his house and play with his pets. T ☐ F ☐

Listen & Speak 2 B-1

G: Do you ❶want to see my new mountain bike?

B: Sure. ❷When did you get it?

G: ❸Yesterday my father bought it for me. Can you come to my house this afternoon?

B: Of course. ❹I can't wait to see it.

G: 내 새 산악 자전거를 보고 싶니?

B: 물론이지. 언제 생긴 거야?

G: 어제 아빠가 나에게 사 주셨어. 오늘 오후에 우리 집에 올래?

B: 당연하지. 나는 그것을 빨리 보고 싶어.

❶ mountain bike: 산악 자전거 wants는 to부정사를 목적어로 갖는다.

❷ when: 언제 get: 얻다, 사다

❸ bought는 buy(사다)의 과거형이다. it은 my new mountain bike를 받는 대명사이다. buy+간접목적어(~에게)+직접목적어(~을, 를)[4형식] = buy+직접목적어+for+간접목적어[3형식]

❹ 'I can't wait.'는 '너무 기다려져.' 또는 '나는 빨리 ~했으면 좋겠다.'라는 의미로, 희망이나 기대를 표현할 때 사용한다. I can't wait to see it. = I'm looking forward to seeing it.

Check(√) True or False

(3) The girl bought a new mountain bike yesterday. T ☐ F ☐

(4) The boy is going to go to the girl's house this afternoon. T ☐ F ☐

Listen & Speak 1 A

M: ❶Which sport do you like? Soccer or basketball?

G: ❷I like soccer more. I play soccer ❸twice a week.

❶ Which 명사 do you like (better/more), A or B?: 어떤 ~가 더 좋아? A 아니면 B?
❷ 더 좋아하는 것에 대해 말할 때는 'I like A.', 'I like A better[more] than B.' 또는 'I prefer A to B.'로 표현한다. 이때 비교 대상이 되는 'than B'나 'to B'는 생략할 수 있다.
❸ twice a week: 일주일에 두 번

Listen & Speak 1 B-1

G: ❶What are you doing?

B: ❷I'm looking at a world map.

G: You checked two countries. ❸Which country would you like to visit first? The U.S. or Mexico?

B: I want to visit the U.S. I'd like to see a basketball game there.

❶ What are you doing?: 뭐 하고 있어?
❷ 대상의 동작이나 현재의 상태를 묘사할 때 현재진행형을 사용할 수 있다. look at: ~을 보다
❸ would like to 동사원형: ~하고 싶다 visit: 방문하다

Listen & Speak 2 A

G: Did you ❶get the tickets?

B: ❷Yes! ❸I can't wait to watch the game.

❶ get: 얻다, 사다
❷ Yes! 다음에 'I did.'가 생략되어 있다.
❸ can't wait to 동사원형: ~하기를 몹시 기대하다(희망, 기대 표현하기) 'can't wait for+명사'나 'can't wait to+동사원형'의 형태를 취할 수 있다. I can't wait to watch the game. = I'm looking forward to watching the game.)

Listen & Speak 2 B-2

B: ❶Don't forget that we're going rock climbing this weekend!

G: ❷Don't worry. ❸I won't forget.

B: I'm excited about going. I can't wait.

❶ 상대방에게 어떠한 일을 할 것을 상기시켜 줄 때는 'Don't forget that 주어+동사 ~.' 또는 'Don't forget to+동사원형 ~.'으로 말할 수 있다. 의미는 '~할 것을 잊지 마' 정도로 볼 수 있다.
❷ 'Don't worry.'는 '걱정 마.'의 의미로 상대방을 안심시킬 때 사용한다.
❸ won't는 will not을 줄여 쓴 말이다. forget 다음에 'that we're going rock climbing this weekend'가 생략되어 있다.

Listen & Speak 2 B-3

G: Did you hear about Jisu?

B: What about her? She ❶lives in Canada.

G: She ❷came back to Korea last month. She wants to see you.

B: Oh, ❸I can't wait to see her.

❶ live in: ~에서 살다
❷ come back to: ~로 돌아오다
❸ I can't wait: 너무 기다려져

Real-Life Zone A

B1: Jiho, why are you ❶in such a hurry?

B2: Hi, Alex! I ❷have to be home before 6:00. The game ❸between the Thunders and the Cobras starts at 6:00.

B1: Oh, are you a baseball fan? ❹Which team do you support? The Cobras or the Thunders?

B2: The Cobras.

B1: Me, too! ❺I don't want to miss the game either.

B2: ❻Hurry up! We only have thirty minutes ❼left.

B1: Okay. Maybe we can watch a game together ❽sometime.

B2: That's a great idea! ❾How about going to the next Cobras home game together?

B1: Okay. They have a game next Saturday. We can eat fried chicken ❿while watching the game!

B2: That sounds great. I can't wait!

❶ in a hurry: 서둘러
❷ have to 동사원형: ~해야 한다
❸ between A and B: A와 B 사이의
❹ support: (특정 스포츠 팀을) 응원하다
❺ miss: 놓치다 either: (부정문에서) ~도
❻ hurry up: 서두르다
❼ leave: 남아 있다 → left: 남겨진
❽ sometime: 언젠가
❾ How about (동)명사 ~?: ~하는 게 어때?, ~하지 않을래?(제안하기)
❿ while+동사ing: ~하는 동안

● 다음 우리말과 일치하도록 빈칸에 알맞은 말을 쓰시오.

Listen & Speak 1 A

M: _____ _____ do you like? Soccer _____ basketball?

G: I like soccer _____. I play soccer _____ a _____.

Listen & Speak 1 B

1. G: What are you _____?

   B: _____ looking _____ a world map.

   G: You checked two countries. _____ _____ would you like to visit first? The U.S. _____ Mexico?

   B: I want _____ _____ the U.S. I'd _____ _____ see a basketball game there.

2. G: _____ _____ about _____ a pet. Do you _____ a pet?

   B: Yes, I do. I have a dog and a cat.

   G: _____ do you think? _____ pet is _____ for me? A cat _____ a dog?

   B: _____ _____ you come to my house someday and _____ _____ my pets? Then you _____ _____.

Listen & Speak 2 A

G: _____ you get the tickets?

B: Yes! I _____ _____ _____ _____ the game.

Listen & Speak 2 B

1. G: Do you _____ _____ _____ my new mountain bike?

   B: Sure. _____ _____ you get it?

   G: Yesterday my father _____ _____ _____ _____. Can you _____ to my house this afternoon?

   B: Of course. I _____ _____ _____ _____ it.

M: 너는 어떤 운동을 좋아하니? 축구 아니면 농구?
G: 축구를 더 좋아해요. 저는 일주일에 두 번 축구를 해요.

1. G: 뭐 하고 있어?
   B: 세계 지도를 보고 있어.
   G: 두 나라에 표시를 했네. 어떤 나라를 먼저 방문하고 싶어? 미국 아니면 멕시코?
   B: 미국을 방문하고 싶어. 거기서 농구 경기를 보고 싶어.

2. G: 나는 애완동물을 기르는 것에 대해 생각 중이야. 넌 애완동물을 기르니?
   B: 응, 길러. 개와 고양이가 있어.
   G: 어떻게 생각해? 어떤 애완동물이 나에게 더 나아? 고양이 아니면 개?
   B: 어느 날 우리 집에 와서 내 애완동물과 놀아 보는 게 어때? 그런 다음 너는 결정할 수 있을 거야.

W: 너 티켓 구했니?
B: 응! 나는 경기를 빨리 보고 싶어.

G: 내 새 산악 자전거를 보고 싶니?
B: 물론이지. 언제 생긴 거야?
G: 어제 아빠가 나에게 사 주셨어. 오늘 오후에 우리 집에 올래?
B: 당연하지. 나는 그것을 빨리 보고 싶어.

2. **B:** Don't _____ _____ we're going rock climbing this weekend!

   G: Don't worry. I _____ _____.

   B: I'm _____ about going. _____ _____ _____.

3. **G:** Did you hear about Jisu?

   B: What _____ her? She lives _____ Canada.

   G: She _____ back to Korea last month. She _____ _____ _____ you.

   B: Oh, I _____ _____ _____ _____ her.

Real-Life Zone A

B1: Jiho, why are you in _____ a hurry?

B2: Hi, Alex! I have to be home _____ 6:00. The game _____ the Thunders and the Cobras _____ at 6:00.

B1: Oh, are you a baseball fan? _____ _____ do you _____? The Cobras or the Thunders?

B2: The Cobras.

B1: Me, too! I don't want to _____ the game _____.

B2: _____ up! We only have thirty minutes _____.

B1: Okay. Maybe we can watch a game together _____.

B2: That's a great idea! How _____ _____ _____ the next Cobras home game together?

B1: Okay. They have a game next Saturday. We can eat fried chicken _____ _____ the game!

B2: That sounds great. _____ _____ _____!

Wrap Up

B: Jimin, _____ _____ _____ _____ _____? Soccer _____ table tennis?

G: I love table tennis. How _____ you, Yunho?

B: I like soccer. I'm a _____ _____ _____ James Hood. He's a great soccer player.

G: Oh, really? There's a soccer match this weekend _____ Korea and Turkey. _____ you heard about it?

B: Of course. I already have a ticket. _____ _____ _____ _____ the game on Saturday. I _____ _____.

G: That's _____.

2. **B:** 이번 주말에 암벽 등반하러 가기로 한 거 잊지 마.
   G: 걱정 마. 잊지 않을게.
   B: 등반하러 가는 거 너무 신난다. 너무 기다려져.

3. **G:** 너 지수에 대해 들었니?
   B: 그녀에 대한 거 뭐? 그녀는 캐나다에 살고 있잖아.
   G: 지난달에 그녀는 한국에 돌아왔어. 너를 보고 싶어해.
   B: 오, 그녀를 빨리 보고 싶어.

B1: 지호야, 너 왜 그렇게 서두르니?
B2: 안녕, 알렉스! 나는 6시 전에 집에 있어야 해. 천둥 대 코브라의 경기가 6시에 시작돼.
B1: 오, 너 야구 팬이니? 어느 팀을 응원해? 코브라 아니면 천둥?
B2: 코브라.
B1: 나도야! 나도 이 경기를 놓치고 싶지 않아.
B2: 서둘러! 우리는 30분밖에 안 남았어.
B1: 알겠어. 언젠가 함께 경기를 볼 수도 있겠어.
B2: 좋은 생각이야! 다음 코브라 홈 경기를 함께 보러 가지 않을래?
B1: 좋아. 다음 주 토요일에 경기가 있어. 우리는 경기를 보면서 프라이드 치킨을 먹을 수 있어!
B1: 굉장해. 너무 기다려져!

B: 지민아, 너는 어떤 운동을 좋아하니? 축구 아니면 탁구?
G: 탁구를 좋아해. 윤호야, 너는 어때?
B: 축구가 좋아. 나는 제임스 후드의 열렬한 팬이야. 그는 위대한 축구 선수야.
G: 오, 정말? 이번 주말에 한국 대 터키의 축구 경기가 있어. 그것에 대해 들었니?
B: 물론이지. 나는 이미 표가 있어. 토요일에 경기를 보러 갈 거야. 너무 기다려져.
G: 환상적이다.

01 다음 대화의 밑줄 친 부분의 의도로 알맞은 것은?

> A: What are you going to do on your vacation?
> B: I'm going to take a boat ride. <u>I can't wait.</u>

① 관심 표현하기　　② 확신 표현하기　　③ 기대 표현하기
④ 거절 표현하기　　⑤ 불가능 표현하기

02 다음 대화의 빈칸에 알맞은 말은?

> A: Which sport do you like? Soccer or basketball?
> B: _____ I play soccer twice a week.

① I like basketball better.　　② I like soccer more.
③ I don't like sports.　　④ I like basketball more than baseball.
⑤ I prefer basketball.

03 다음 대화의 빈칸에 알맞은 말을 <u>모두</u> 고르시오.

> A: _____ *Peter Pan* or *The Last Leaf*?
> B: I like *Peter Pan*.

① Which shorts do you like?
② Which do you prefer?
③ Why don't we read a story book?
④ Which story book do you like?
⑤ How did you like the story book?

04 다음 대화의 밑줄 친 문장 대신 쓸 수 있는 것을 고르시오.

> A: Which sport do you like? Bowling or tennis?
> B: <u>I like tennis.</u> I'm going to play it with my friends this weekend.
>   I can't wait.

① I prefer bowling to tennis.
② I like bowling more than tennis.
③ I prefer tennis and bowling.
④ I like tennis more.
⑤ I like tennis and bowling.

[01~03] 다음 대화를 읽고 물음에 답하시오.

G: ⓐI'm thinking about getting a pet. Do you have a pet? (①)

B: Yes, I do. (②)

G: ⓑWhat do you think? (③) ⓒWhich pet is better for me? A cat or a dog? (④) ⓓI can't wait to play with your pets.

B: ⓔWhy don't you come to my house someday and play with my pets? (⑤) Then you can decide.

01 위 대화의 ①~⑤ 중 다음 주어진 말이 들어갈 알맞은 곳은?

I have a dog and a cat.

①   ②   ③   ④   ⑤

02 위 대화의 문장 ⓐ~ⓔ 중 흐름상 어색한 것을 고르시오.

① ⓐ   ② ⓑ   ③ ⓒ   ④ ⓓ   ⑤ ⓔ

03 위 대화를 읽고 알 수 없는 것을 고르시오.

① Does the boy have a pet?
② Why does the boy suggest that the girl come to his house someday?
③ Which animal does the girl like more? A dog or a cat?
④ How many dogs does the boy have?
⑤ What kind of pet does the boy have?

04 주어진 문장 이후에 이어질 대화의 순서가 바르게 배열된 것을 고르시오.

What are you doing?

(A) You checked two countries. Which country would you like to visit first? The U.S. or Mexico?
(B) I want to visit the U.S. I'd like to see a basketball game there.
(C) I'm looking at a world map.

① (A) – (C) – (B)   ② (B) – (A) – (C)
③ (B) – (C) – (A)   ④ (C) – (A) – (B)
⑤ (C) – (B) – (A)

05 다음 중 짝지어진 대화가 어색한 것은?

① A: Which do you like more, hotdogs or waffles?
   B: I like waffles more.
② A: Which do you prefer, dogs or cats?
   B: I prefer dogs to cats.
③ A: Which do you like more, to buy the books or to borrow them from the library?
   B: I like to borrow the books from the library more.
④ A: Which do you prefer, hiking or swimming?
   B: Of course I do.
⑤ A: Which shirt do you prefer, the red one or the yellow one?
   B: I think the red one is better.

[06~07] 다음 대화를 읽고 물음에 답하시오.

> G: Do you want to see my new mountain bike? (①)
> B: Sure. (②) When did you get it? (③)
> G: Yesterday my father bought it for me. (④)
> B: (⑤) Of course. 나는 그것을 빨리 보고 싶어.
> (wait, it, see, I, can't, to)

중요

06 위 대화의 ①~⑤ 중 다음 주어진 말이 들어갈 알맞은 곳은?

> Can you come to my house this afternoon?

①   ②   ③   ④   ⑤

서답형

07 위 대화의 밑줄 친 우리말 해석에 맞게 괄호 안의 단어를 배열하여 영작하시오.

➡ _____

[08~09] 다음 대화를 읽고 물음에 답하시오.

> B1: Jiho, why are you in such a hurry?
> B2: _____
> B1: _____
> B2: _____
> B1: _____
> B2: Hurry up! We only have thirty minutes left.
> B1: Okay. Maybe we can watch a game together sometime.
> B2: That's a great idea! How about going to the next Cobras home game together?
> B1: Okay. They have a game next Saturday. We can eat fried chicken while watching the game!
> B2: That sounds great. I can't wait!

08 위 대화의 빈 부분에 들어갈 순서가 올바른 것을 고르시오.

> (A) The Cobras.
> (B) Hi, Alex! I have to be home before 6:00. The game between the Thunders and the Cobras starts at 6:00.
> (C) Oh, are you a baseball fan? Which team do you support? The Cobras or the Thunders?
> (D) Me, too! I don't want to miss the game either.

① (B)–(A)–(C)–(D)   ② (B)–(C)–(A)–(D)
③ (B)–(D)–(A)–(C)   ④ (C)–(A)–(B)–(D)
⑤ (C)–(D)–(B)–(A)

09 위 대화를 읽고 질문에 답할 수 <u>없는</u> 것은?

① What time will the next Cobras home game start?
② What can they eat while watching the game?
③ When will the next Cobras home game be held?
④ Which team do they like more, the Cobras or the Thunders?
⑤ What time is it now?

서답형

10 다음 대화의 빈칸에 알맞은 말을 쓰시오.

> A: What are you going to do on your vacation?
> B: _____ I can't wait to go surfing.

➡ _____

[01~03] 다음 대화를 읽고 물음에 답하시오.

> B: Don't forget (A)[to / that] we're going rock climbing this weekend!
> G: Don't worry. I won't ___ⓐ___.
> B: I'm excited (B)[about / to] going. I can't wait.

01 (A)와 (B)에 알맞은 말을 골라 쓰시오.

(A) _____ (B) _____

02 위 대화의 빈칸 ⓐ에 알맞은 말을 대화에서 찾아 쓰시오.

➡ _____

03 위 대화의 내용과 일치하도록 주어진 질문에 대한 대답을 영어로 쓰시오. (9 단어, 주어진 단어를 이용할 것)

What is the boy looking forward to?

➡ _____
   (wait, to)

[04~05] 주어진 문장 다음에 이어질 대화의 순서를 바르게 배열 하시오.

04

Did you hear about Jisu?

(A) She came back to Korea last month. She wants to see you.
(B) Oh, I can't wait to see her.
(C) What about her? She lives in Canada.

➡ _____

05

Which sport do you like to play? Tennis or baseball?

(A) I like to play tennis.
(B) Why not?
(C) Why don't we play tennis together this afternoon?

➡ _____

[06~07] 다음 대화를 읽고 물음에 답하시오.

> B: Jimin, which sport do you like? Soccer or table tennis?
> G: I love table tennis. How about you, Yunho?
> B: I like soccer. I'm a big fan of James Hood. He's a great soccer player.
> G: Oh, really? There's a soccer match this weekend between Korea and Turkey. __(A)__ you heard about it?
> B: Of course. I already __(B)__ a ticket. I'm going to see the game on Saturday. (C)I can't wait.
> G: That's fantastic.

06 위 대화의 빈칸 (A)와 (B)에 공통으로 들어갈 말을 쓰시오.

(A) _____ (B) _____

07 밑줄 친 (C)의 뒤에 생략된 부분을 주어진 단어를 넣어 쓰시오. (6 단어)

➡ _____ (see)

Grammar

① 부가의문문

> • Jian, this is your first time to come to the baseball stadium, **isn't it**?
> 지안아, 네가 야구 경기장에 온 건 이번이 처음이야, 그렇지 않니?
>
> • You don't like English, **do you**? 너 영어를 싫어하지, 그렇지?

■ 문장의 끝에 붙은 의문문으로, 상대방의 동의를 구하거나 사실을 확인하기 위해 사용된다.

  • The post office is a few blocks from your office, **isn't it**?
  우체국은 네 사무실에서 몇 블록 떨어져 있잖아, 그렇지 않니?

  • She didn't tell a lie, **did she**? 그녀는 거짓말을 하지 않았어, 그렇지?

부가의문문을 만드는 법은 다음과 같다.

1. 앞 문장에 be동사나 조동사가 사용되었으면 be동사나 조동사를 사용하며 일반 동사가 사용된 경우에는 'do/does/did'를 사용한다.

2. 앞 문장이 긍정이면 부정, 부정이면 긍정으로 쓴다.

3. 주어는 반드시 인칭대명사로 받는다.

4. 부정형의 경우 반드시 축약형을 쓴다.

  • You aren't tired, **are you**? 너 피곤하지 않지, 그렇지?

  • You want to go to the amusement park, **don't you**? 너 놀이 공원에 가고 싶지, 그렇지 않니?

■ 명령문의 부가의문문은 will you?나 won't you?를 쓰고 권유문(Let's ~)의 경우에는 shall we?를 쓴다.

  • Clean your room, **won't you**? 네 방을 청소해, 그러지 않을래?

  • Let's work together, **shall we**? 함께 일하자, 그럴래?

핵심 Check

1. 다음 괄호 안에서 알맞은 말을 고르시오.

⑴ People usually buy presents to celebrate, (don't / aren't) they?

⑵ Ted wasn't at home yesterday, was (he / Ted)?

⑶ Your cellphone looks nice, (does / doesn't) it?

⑷ Mary felt happy, (did / didn't) she?

② 수동태

- Jake **made** this table. 〈능동태〉 Jake가 이 탁자를 만들었다.
- This table **was made** by Jake. 〈수동태〉 이 탁자는 Jake에 의해 만들어졌다.

■ 수동태는 '주어+be동사+동사의 과거분사+by+행위자'의 형식을 가지며 '…에 의해 ~되다[당하다]'라는 의미로 주어가 동작의 영향을 받거나 행위를 당할 때 사용한다.

능동태를 수동태로 만드는 법

1. 능동태의 목적어를 문장의 주어로 둔다.
2. 동사를 'be동사+과거분사'로 쓴다. 이때 be동사의 시제는 능동태 문장에 맞추고 수와 인칭은 수동태 문장의 주어에 맞춘다.
3. 능동태의 주어는 'by+행위자(목적격)'의 형태로 문장 끝에 쓴다. 이때 행위자가 중요치 않거나 확실하지 않은 경우 'by+행위자'는 생략한다. • The chair **was broken** by Jerry. 그 의자는 Jerry에 의해 부서졌다.

■ 4형식 문장의 수동태는 간접목적어와 직접목적어 각각을 주어로 하는 수동태가 가능하다. 직접목적어를 주어로 한 수동태에서는 간접목적어 앞에 특정한 전치사를 써야 한다. 전치사 to를 쓰는 동사는 'give, send, tell, teach, show, bring' 등이고, 전치사 for를 쓰는 동사는 'buy, make, choose, cook, get' 등이며, 전치사 of를 쓰는 동사에는 'ask' 등이 있다. 또한 make, buy, read, write 등은 직접목적어를 주어로 하는 수동태만 가능하다.

- Mom **bought** Jane a book. 엄마가 Jane에게 책을 사주셨다.
- A book **was bought** for Jane by Mom. 책이 엄마에 의해 Jane에게 사 주어졌다.

■ 조동사가 있는 문장의 수동태는 '조동사+be+p.p.' 형식을 갖는다.

- The work **will be finished** by me. 그 일은 나에 의해 끝내질 것이다.

■ 목적격보어가 원형부정사인 경우, 수동태 문장에서는 to부정사로 바뀐다.

- Harry **was made** to do the dishes by her. Harry는 그녀에 의해 설거지하도록 시켜졌다.

■ by 이외의 전치사를 사용하는 수동태에 유의한다.

- be interested in: ~에 흥미가 있다   be surprised at: ~에 놀라다
- be covered with: ~로 덮여 있다   be filled with: ~로 가득 차다
- be pleased with: ~로 기뻐하다   be satisfied with: ~에 만족하다
- be made of: ~로 만들어지다(물리적 변화)   be made from: ~로 만들어지다(화학적 변화)

핵심 Check

2. 다음 괄호 안에서 알맞은 말을 고르시오.

(1) Some nice presents were given (for / to) her by her friends.

(2) She is interested (in / with) working indoors.

01 다음 빈칸에 알맞은 것은?

> My cousin played the violin.
> ➡ The violin _____ by my cousin.

① plays ② played ③ is played
④ was played ⑤ has played

02 다음 빈칸에 들어갈 말로 적절한 것은?

> Visiting teams wear dark uniforms, _____?

① aren't they ② are they ③ don't they
④ do they ⑤ aren't them

03 다음 우리말에 맞게 빈칸에 알맞은 말을 쓰시오.

(1) 그 방은 Harold에 의해 청소되었다.
  ➡ The room _____ _____ by Harold.

(2) *Romeo and Juliet*은 William Shakespeare에 의해 쓰여졌다.
  ➡ *Romeo and Juliet* _____ _____ by William Shakespeare.

(3) 그녀는 그와 친구가 되고 싶어 해, 그렇지 않니?
  ➡ She wants to be friends with him, _____ _____?

(4) Sam은 운전할 수 없어, 그렇지?
  ➡ Sam cannot drive, _____ _____?

04 다음 문장에서 어법상 <u>어색한</u> 부분을 바르게 고쳐 쓰시오.

(1) The Golden Gate Bridge built in 1937.
  _____ ➡ _____

(2) Dorothy has a book, doesn't Dorothy?
  _____ ➡ _____

01 다음 빈칸에 알맞은 것은?

> The dirt _____ by the dark colors of the uniforms.

① hides   ② hid   ③ to hide
④ is hiding   ⑤ is hidden

02 다음 중 밑줄 친 부분의 쓰임이 올바른 것은?

① You can speak Japanese very well, <u>can you</u>?
② Yuna looks kind, <u>doesn't she</u>?
③ Yollanda gave the book to Petric, <u>doesn't she</u>?
④ Sophie bought a cell phone, <u>wasn't she</u>?
⑤ Mike isn't diligent, <u>doesn't he</u>?

03 다음 괄호 안에서 알맞은 것을 고르시오.

(1) Some flowers were given (to / for) her by Tim.
(2) The spaghetti was made (to / for) me by my mom.
(3) No questions were asked (to / of) us by the teacher.
(4) Laura likes roses, (does / is / doesn't / isn't) she?
(5) It is a kind of Korean traditional food, (does / is / doesn't / isn't) it?

04 다음 중 수동태로의 전환이 <u>어색한</u> 것은?

① Auguste Rodin made *the Thinker* in 1902.
→ *The Thinker* was made by Auguste Rodin in 1902.
② Harriot chose Grace a beautiful song.
→ A beautiful song was chosen for Grace by Harriot.
③ They built the Namdaemoon in 1398.
→ The Namdaemoon was built in 1398.
④ Emily gave me a nice pen.
→ A nice pen was given for me by Emily.
⑤ My teacher asked me to come to the library.
→ I was asked to come to the library by my teacher.

05 다음 중 어법상 옳은 것을 고르시오.

① Dorothy is wearing black shoes, doesn't she?
② My mom is going to make *gimbap* tonight, is she?
③ The children didn't play the violin, did they?
④ Angelina was kind to others last night, was not she?
⑤ Samanda bought a cute pink dress, didn't Samanda?

06 다음 우리말을 바르게 영작한 것은?

> 이 가방은 내 동생을 위해 엄마에 의해 만들어졌다.

① This bag was made for my sister by my mom.
② This bag was made to my sister by my mom.
③ This bag was made of my sister by my mom.
④ This bag was made to my mom by my sister.
⑤ My sister was made for this bag by my mom.

07 다음 문장의 빈칸에 알맞은 말은?

> You had dinner at the hotel last night, _____ you?

① hadn't   ② haven't   ③ have
④ didn't   ⑤ did

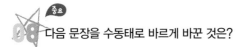

08 다음 문장을 수동태로 바르게 바꾼 것은?

> In the past, they determined the numbers by the players' batting order.

① In the past, the numbers determined the players' batting order.
② In the past, the numbers were determined the players' batting order.
③ In the past, the players' batting order was determined by the numbers.
④ In the past, the numbers was determined by the players' batting order.
⑤ In the past, the numbers were determined by the players' batting order.

09 다음 빈칸에 알맞은 것은?

> Kate looks friendly, _____?

① isn't she   ② does she
③ doesn't she   ④ does Kate
⑤ doesn't Kate

10 다음 중 어법상 틀린 것을 고르시오.

① In the early 1800s, soccer was invented in Newgate Prison in London by the prisoners.
② The article was wrote for the school newspaper by Harry.
③ A mouse was caught by a cat.
④ Is English spoken in many countries around the world?
⑤ A nice gift was given to Stephanie on her birthday by her dad.

11 다음 중 빈칸에 들어갈 말이 다른 하나는?

① A man was waiting for Jane outside, _____?
② Jim worked at the bank, _____?
③ He made Ann do the work, _____?
④ Chris went on a vacation, _____?
⑤ A boy played the piano, _____?

12 다음 빈칸에 공통으로 들어갈 알맞은 것은?

> • His heart was filled _____ pride at that time.
> • Does that mean that you're pleased _____ the present?

① at   ② with   ③ from
④ in   ⑤ of

서답형

13 주어진 어구를 이용하여 다음 우리말을 영어로 쓰시오.

(1) 이 편지가 David에 의해 배달되었나요?
   (deliver)

   ➡ _____

(2) 나의 삼촌 집이 홍수에 의해 무너졌다.
   (the flood, destroy)

   ➡ _____

(3) 그 탁자는 나무로 만들어졌다.
   (wood, make)

   ➡ _____

(4) 그 십대들은 유럽에 여행갈 거야, 그렇지 않니?
   (the teenagers, travel)

   ➡ _____

(5) 테니스 치러 가자, 그럴래? (let, to play)

   ➡ _____

서답형

14 다음 빈칸에 알맞은 부가의문문을 쓰시오.

(1) Sharon studies English very hard,
   _____ _____?

(2) You played computer games last night,
   _____ _____?

(3) Marylin can't play the guitar, _____
   _____?

(4) Alex wasn't angry, _____ _____?

(5) Always do the dishes after each meal,
   _____ _____?

(6) Let's take a walk after dinner, _____
   _____?

서답형

15 다음 문장에서 어법상 어색한 부분을 찾아 바르게 고치시오.

(1) The dress was chosen to her daughter
   for the party by Eveline.

   _____ ➡ _____

(2) Playing tennis is reduced my stress.

   _____ ➡ _____

(3) The changes will not be appeared
   immediately.

   _____ ➡ _____

(4) Mina finished washing the dishes, didn't
   Mina?

   _____ ➡ _____

(5) You will leave a message, will you?

   _____ ➡ _____

(6) She isn't going to go hiking tomorrow,
   does she?

   _____ ➡ _____

16 다음 밑줄 친 부분 중 어법상 어색한 것은?

He ①was known as a marathon winner at the Rome and Tokyo international sports competitions. When he ②was prepared to run the marathon in Rome, he found out that his shoes did not fit well, so he decided ③to run the race without shoes. He felt pain during the race, but he finished the race as the winner. He was ④one of the greatest runners in the world, ⑤wasn't he?

①   ②   ③   ④   ⑤

서답형

17 주어진 단어의 형태를 알맞게 바꿔 문장을 완성하시오.

Hana Middle School Sports Day _____ (hold) on the school playing field next week.

01 다음 문장을 수동태는 능동태로, 능동태는 수동태로 고치시오.

(1) Tino cleans the big house on Sundays.

➡ _____

(2) Sarang Middle School Sports Day will be held on the school playing field on Wednesday, June 15.

➡ _____

_____

(3) Jonathan made Judy delicious spaghetti.

➡ _____

_____

(4) Does your job as a tour guide satisfy you?

➡ _____

(5) Who painted *Water Lilies* in 1906?

➡ _____

(6) Cathy will make him take part in the science camp.

➡ _____

_____

(7) They are looking after the animals.

➡ _____

02 다음 빈칸에 공통으로 들어갈 말을 쓰시오.

• Mike studied hard, _____ _____?

• Joseph did his best at all times, _____ _____?

➡ _____

03 다음 빈칸에 알맞은 부가의문문을 쓰시오.

(1) These cars are really expensive, _____ _____?

(2) Her little son can't read the book, _____ _____?

(3) Matt didn't make his daughter a doll, _____ _____?

(4) Jenny isn't watching TV, _____ _____?

(5) The rock looks like a rabbit, _____ _____?

(6) Be careful when you drive a car at night, _____ _____?

(7) Let's go to the shop at which you bought your skirt, _____ _____?

04 다음 괄호 안에 주어진 어휘를 어법에 맞게 빈칸에 쓰시오.

(1) The computer _____ _____ by my father yesterday. (repair)

(2) The book _____ _____ _____ me by my father yesterday. (buy)

(3) Many smartphones _____ _____ in Korea. (make)

(4) Kathy _____ _____ _____ finish the report by her teacher. (make)

05 다음 그림을 보고 대화의 빈칸에 알맞은 말을 쓰시오.

A: She plays the game really well, _____
_____?

B: Yes, she does.

06 다음 그림을 보고 주어진 단어를 이용하여 빈칸을 알맞게 채우시오.

I and the Village _____ _____
by Marc Chagall in 1911. (paint)

07 다음 문장에서 어법상 어색한 부분을 바르게 고쳐 다시 쓰시오.

(1) The boy was bought the pens.

➡ _____
_____

(2) Soy sauce is made of soy beans and salt.

➡ _____

(3) Cloe was written a letter by Jack.

➡ _____
_____

(4) Vivian was heard open the window by her son.

➡ _____

(5) *Samgyupsal* is cooked to Emma by her husband next weekend.

➡ _____
_____

(6) Whom this table was made?

➡ _____

08 다음 우리말을 괄호 안에 주어진 어휘를 이용하여 영작하시오.

(1) 내 자전거는 지난 금요일에 도둑맞았다.
(bike, steal)

➡ _____

(2) 이 과자들은 나의 엄마에 의해 만들어졌다.
(these cookies, make, my mom)

➡ _____

(3) 그의 집은 책으로 가득 차 있었다. (fill)

➡ _____

(4) Jenny는 어젯밤에 파티에 없었어, 그렇지?
(at the party)

➡ _____

(5) 좋아하는 운동에 대해서 말해 보자, 그럴래?
(let's, our favorite sport, about)

➡ _____

Reading

A Day at the Baseball Stadium

Today the Thunders and the Cobras have a game. Jihun's family is at the baseball stadium.

Jihun: Jian, this is your first time to come to the baseball stadium, isn't it?

Jian: Yes, I'm so excited. I can't wait for the game to start.

Dad: Look, the players are coming out now!

Jian: Which team is the Thunders?

Jihun: Over there, behind third base. They are wearing dark gray uniforms because they are the visiting team.

Jian: Does the visiting team always wear a dark color?

Jihun: Yes, that's the rule. Home teams have bright uniforms and visiting teams have dark uniforms.

Jian: Why is that?

Mom: There is an interesting story about that. In the past, visiting teams could not wash their uniforms after every game. So they started wearing dark colors to hide the dirt.

Jian: Hahaha! That was a good idea!

base (야구의) 루, 베이스
visiting team 원정 팀
come out 나오다
dark 어두운
dirt 먼지, 때
hide 숨다, 숨기다
rule 규칙, 법칙

 확인문제

● 다음 문장이 본문의 내용과 일치하면 T, 일치하지 않으면 F를 쓰시오.

1 Jihun's family is at the baseball stadium. ☐

2 This is Jihun's first time to come to the baseball stadium. ☐

3 Jian is so excited that she can't wait for the game to start. ☐

4 The Cobras are the visiting team. ☐

5 Home teams have bright uniforms and visiting teams have dark uniforms. ☐

6 In the past, visiting teams could wash their uniforms after every game. ☐

The players are warming up.

Jian: Who's your favorite player?
Who is의 줄임말

Jihun: Number 77.

Jian: What does the number mean?

Jihun: Hmm…. Players choose a number they like.
관계대명사 which나 that 생략

Dad: You know what? In the past, the numbers were determined by
저 있잖아, 그거 알아?   수동태: be동사+과거분사
the players' batting order.

Jihun: That means there were no players with number 77!
앞 문장의 내용을 받는 지시대명사
Now, Jihun's favorite player is about to bat. Jihun looks anxious.
막 ~하려는 참이다   ~처럼 보이다

Jian: Your favorite player is at bat.
타석에 서서

Jihun: Yes. He has hit 21 home runs already this year. If he hits one
현재완료(완료)   접속사 if: ~라면   조건 부사절에서
                                              현재시제가 미래를 나타냄.
more today, he will be the home run leader this season.

The batter misses several balls. Now he has a full count. He is
놓치다   야구에서 스트라이크가 둘이고 볼이 셋인 상태
waiting for the next pitch.

Jihun: HOME RUN! HOME RUN!

Crack!

The ball flies fast. It is going, going, going, gone!

용어	뜻
warm up	준비 운동을 하다. 몸을 풀다
determine	결정하다
order	순서
anxious	불안해하는
be about to	막 ~하려고 하다
pitch	투구
wait for	~을 기다리다
crack	찢어지는 듯한 [날카로운] 소리
at bat	타석에 서서

확인문제

● 다음 문장이 본문의 내용과 일치하면 T, 일치하지 않으면 F를 쓰시오.

1 The players are warming up. ☐

2 In the past, players chose a number they liked. ☐

3 Jihun's favorite player is at bat. ☐

4 Jihun's favorite player has hit 20 home runs already this year. ☐

5 Jihun's favorite player misses several balls. ☐

6 Jihun's favorite player has a full count and he is out on a fly ball. ☐

● 우리말을 참고하여 빈칸에 알맞은 말을 쓰시오.

1 A Day at the _____ _____

2 Today the Thunders and the Cobras _____ _____ _____.

3 Jihun's family _____ _____ the baseball stadium.

4 Jihun: Jian, this is _____ _____ _____ to come to the baseball stadium, _____ _____?

5 Jian: Yes, I'm so excited. I _____ _____ _____ the game to start.

6 Dad: Look, the players _____ _____ _____ now!

7 Jian: _____ _____ is the Thunders?

8 Jihun: Over there, _____ _____ _____.

9 They are wearing dark gray uniforms because they are the _____ _____.

10 Jian: Does the visiting team always _____ _____ _____ _____?

11 Jihun: Yes, that's the _____.

12 Home teams _____ _____ _____ and visiting teams have dark uniforms.

13 Jian: _____ is that?

14 Mom: There is an _____ _____ about that.

15 In the past, visiting teams could not _____ _____ _____ after every game.

16 So they started wearing dark colors _____ _____ _____ _____.

17 Jian: Hahaha! That was _____ _____ _____!

1 야구 경기장에서의 하루

2 오늘 천둥 대 코브라 게임이 있다.

3 지훈이네 가족은 야구 경기장에 있다.

4 지훈: 지안아, 네가 야구 경기장에 온 건 이번이 처음이야, 그렇지 않니?

5 지안: 응, 나 아주 흥분돼. 나는 경기가 빨리 시작했으면 좋겠어.

6 아빠: 봐, 선수들이 지금 나오고 있어!

7 지안: 어떤 팀이 천둥이야?

8 지훈: 저기, 3루 뒤.

9 그들은 원정 팀이기 때문에 어두운 회색 유니폼을 입고 있어.

10 지안: 원정 팀은 항상 어두운 색을 입어?

11 지훈: 응, 그게 규칙이야.

12 홈팀은 밝은 유니폼을 입고 원정팀은 어두운 유니폼을 입어.

13 지안: 왜?

14 엄마: 그것에 대한 흥미로운 이야기가 있단다.

15 과거에는 원정 팀이 매 경기 후 유니폼을 세탁할 수가 없었어.

16 그래서 그들은 때를 숨기기 위해 어두운 색을 입기 시작했지.

17 지안: 하하하! 좋은 생각이었네요!

18 The players are _____ _____.

19 Jian: Who's your _____ _____?

20 Jihun: _____ 77.

21 Jian: _____ does the number _____?

22 Jihun: Hmm…. Players _____ a number _____ _____.

23 Dad: You know _____?

24 In the past, the numbers were determined _____ _____ _____ _____ _____.

25 Jihun: That means there were _____ players _____ number 77!

26 Now, Jihun's favorite player _____ _____ _____ bat.

27 Jihun looks _____.

28 Jian: Your favorite player is _____ _____.

29 Jihun: Yes. He _____ _____ 21 home runs already this year.

30 If he _____ _____ _____ today, he will be the home run leader this season.

31 The batter _____ several balls.

32 Now he has _____ _____ _____.

33 He is waiting for the _____ _____.

34 Jihun: HOME RUN! HOME RUN!

35 _____! The ball _____ fast.

36 It is going, going, going, _____!

---

18 선수들이 몸을 풀고 있다.

19 지안: 가장 좋아하는 선수가 누구야?

20 지훈: 77번.

21 지안: 그 숫자는 무엇을 의미해?

22 지훈: 음... 선수들이 원하는 번호를 선택해.

23 아빠: 그거 알아?

24 과거에는 번호가 선수들의 타순에 의해 결정되었단다.

25 지훈: 77번 선수가 없었다는 뜻이네요!

26 이제 지훈이의 가장 좋아하는 선수가 막 공을 치려고 한다.

27 지훈이는 불안해 보인다.

28 지안: 오빠가 가장 좋아하는 선수가 타석에 서네.

29 지훈: 응. 그는 올해 이미 21개의 홈런을 쳤어.

30 그가 오늘 하나를 더 치면, 그는 이번 시즌 홈런 리더가 될 거야.

31 타자는 여러 개의 공을 놓친다.

32 이제 그는 풀카운트가 되었다.

33 그는 다음 투구를 기다리고 있다.

34 지훈: 홈런! 홈런!

35 땅! 공은 빠르게 날아간다.

36 그것은 가고, 가고, 가고, 사라져 버렸다!

● 우리말을 참고하여 본문을 영작하시오.

1 야구 경기장에서의 하루

➡ _____

2 오늘 천둥 대 코브라 게임이 있다.

➡ _____

3 지훈이네 가족은 야구 경기장에 있다.

➡ _____

4 지훈: 지안아, 네가 야구 경기장에 온 건 이번이 처음이야, 그렇지 않니?

➡ _____

5 지안: 응, 나 아주 흥분돼. 나는 경기가 빨리 시작했으면 좋겠어.

➡ _____

6 아빠: 봐, 선수들이 지금 나오고 있어!

➡ _____

7 지안: 어떤 팀이 천둥이야?

➡ _____

8 지훈: 저기, 3루 뒤.

➡ _____

9 그들은 원정 팀이기 때문에 어두운 회색 유니폼을 입고 있어.

➡ _____

10 지안: 원정 팀은 항상 어두운 색을 입어?

➡ _____

11 지훈: 응, 그게 규칙이야.

➡ _____

12 홈팀은 밝은 유니폼을 입고 원정팀은 어두운 유니폼을 입어.

➡ _____

13 지안: 왜?

➡ _____

14 엄마: 그것에 대한 흥미로운 이야기가 있단다.

➡ _____

15 과거에는 원정 팀이 매 경기 후 유니폼을 세탁할 수가 없었어.

➡ _____

16 그래서 그들은 때를 숨기기 위해 어두운 색을 입기 시작했지.

➡ _____

17 지안: 하하하! 좋은 생각이었네요!

➡ _____

18 선수들이 몸을 풀고 있다.
➡ _____

19 지안: 가장 좋아하는 선수가 누구야?
➡ _____

20 지훈: 77번.
➡ _____

21 지안: 그 숫자는 무엇을 의미해?
➡ _____

22 지훈: 음... 선수들이 원하는 번호를 선택해.
➡ _____

23 아빠: 그거 알아?
➡ _____

24 과거에는 번호가 선수들의 타순에 의해 결정되었단다.
➡ _____

25 지훈: 77번 선수가 없었다는 뜻이네요!
➡ _____

26 이제 지훈이의 가장 좋아하는 선수가 막 공을 치려고 한다.
➡ _____

27 지훈이는 불안해 보인다.
➡ _____

28 지안: 오빠가 가장 좋아하는 선수가 타석에 서네.
➡ _____

29 지훈: 응. 그는 올해 이미 21개의 홈런을 쳤어.
➡ _____

30 그가 오늘 하나를 더 치면, 그는 이번 시즌 홈런 리더가 될 거야.
➡ _____

31 타자는 여러 개의 공을 놓친다.
➡ _____

32 이제 그는 풀카운트가 되었다.
➡ _____

33 그는 다음 투구를 기다리고 있다.
➡ _____

34 지훈: 홈런! 홈런!
➡ _____

35 땅! 공은 빠르게 날아간다.
➡ _____

36 그것은 가고, 가고, 가고, 사라져 버렸다!
➡ _____

[01~03] 다음 글을 읽고 물음에 답하시오.

Today the Thunders and the Cobras have a game. Jihun's family is at the baseball stadium.

Jihun: Jian, this is your first time ⓐto come to the baseball stadium, ___(A)___?

Jian: Yes, I'm so excited. I can't wait for the game to start.

Dad: Look, the players are coming out now!

Jian: Which team is the Thunders?

Jihun: Over there, behind third base. They are wearing dark gray uniforms because they are the visiting team.

01 위 글의 빈칸 (A)에 들어갈 알맞은 부가의문문을 고르시오.

① isn't this
② is it
③ doesn't it
④ isn't it
⑤ is this

02 위 글의 밑줄 친 ⓐto come과 to부정사의 용법이 같은 것을 모두 고르시오.

① He couldn't decide what to eat.
② It's time for you to finish your work.
③ She went there to meet her friend.
④ It's good for your health to jog every day.
⑤ She wanted to buy a book to read on the train.

03 위 글의 내용과 일치하지 않는 것은?

① 오늘 천둥 대 코브라 게임이 있다.
② 지훈이네 가족은 야구 경기장에 있다.
③ 지안이가 야구 경기장에 온 건 이번이 처음이 아니다.
④ 지안이는 경기가 빨리 시작하기를 바란다.
⑤ 천둥 팀은 어두운 회색 유니폼을 입고 있다.

[04~06] 다음 글을 읽고 물음에 답하시오.

Jian: Does the visiting team always wear a dark color?

Jihun: Yes, that's the rule. Home teams have ___(A)___ uniforms and visiting teams have dark uniforms.

Jian: Why is (B)that?

Mom: There is an interesting story about that. In the past, visiting teams could not wash their uniforms after every game. So they started wearing dark colors to hide the ___(C)___.

Jian: Hahaha! That was a good idea!

서답형
04 위 글의 빈칸 (A)에 문맥상 알맞은 말을 쓰시오.

➡ _____

서답형
05 위 글의 밑줄 친 (B)that이 가리키는 것을 본문에서 찾아 쓰시오.

➡ _____
_____

06 위 글의 빈칸 (C)에 들어갈 알맞은 말을 고르시오.

① pattern
② dirt
③ hole
④ shape
⑤ design

[07~10] 다음 글을 읽고 물음에 답하시오.

Abebe Bikila
Marathon Runner
Born: August 7, 1932
Nationality: Ethiopia
Speciality: He was known ___ⓐ___ a marathon winner at the Rome and Tokyo international sports competitions. When he was preparing (A)[to run / running] the marathon in Rome, he found out that his shoes did not fit well, so he decided (B)[to run / running] the race ___ⓑ___ shoes. He felt pain (C) [during / while] the race, but he finished the race ___ⓒ___ the winner. He was one of the greatest runners in the world, wasn't he?

07 위 글의 빈칸 ⓐ와 ⓒ에 공통으로 들어갈 알맞은 말을 고르시오.

① as ② to ③ for
④ by ⑤ in

서답형
08 위 글의 빈칸 ⓑ에 들어갈 알맞은 말을 쓰시오.

➡ _____

서답형
09 위 글의 괄호 (A)~(C)에서 문맥이나 어법상 알맞은 낱말을 골라 쓰시오.

(A) _____ (B) _____ (C) _____

10 Abebe Bikila에 대한 내용과 일치하지 <u>않는</u> 것을 고르시오.

① 에티오피아 출신의 마라톤 선수였다.
② 로마 국제 스포츠 대회의 마라톤 우승자로 알려졌다.
③ 도쿄 국제 스포츠 대회의 마라톤 우승자로 알려졌다.
④ 도쿄 국제 스포츠 대회에서 신발을 신지 않고 달렸다.
⑤ 경주 도중에 통증을 느꼈지만 우승자로 경주를 끝마쳤다.

[11~13] 다음 글을 읽고 물음에 답하시오.

(A)선수들이 몸을 풀고 있다.
Jian: Who's your favorite player?
Jihun: Number 77.
Jian: What does the number mean?
Jihun: Hmm.... Players choose a number they like.
Dad: You know what? In the past, the numbers were determined ___ⓐ___ the players' batting order.
Jihun: That means there were no players ___ⓑ___ number 77!

중요
11 위 글의 빈칸 ⓐ와 ⓑ에 들어갈 전치사가 바르게 짝지어진 것은?

① for – with ② by – in
③ in – from ④ for – in
⑤ by – with

서답형
12 위 글의 밑줄 친 (A)의 우리말에 맞게 주어진 어휘를 변형하여 5 단어로 영작하시오.

warm

➡ _____

서답형

13 등번호 7번의 과거와 현재의 의미를 우리말로 쓰시오.

과거: _____

현재: _____

[14~16] 다음 글을 읽고 물음에 답하시오.

Now, Jihun's favorite player is about to bat. Jihun looks anxious.

Jian: Your favorite player is at bat.

Jihun: Yes. He ⓐhas hit 21 home runs already this year. If he hits one more today, he will be the home run leader this season.

The batter misses several balls. Now he has a full count. He is waiting for the next pitch.

Jihun: HOME RUN! HOME RUN!

Crack!

The ball flies fast. It is going, going, going, gone!

14 아래 〈보기〉에서 위 글의 밑줄 친 ⓐhas hit과 현재완료의 용법이 다른 것의 개수는?

┌──── 보기 ────┐
① Tom has just eaten breakfast.
② Have you solved it yet?
③ I have worked for this company for two years.
④ He has already read the book.
⑤ She has lost her pen.
└─────────────┘

① 1개　② 2개　③ 3개　④ 4개　⑤ 5개

서답형

15 본문의 내용과 일치하도록 다음 빈칸에 알맞은 단어를 쓰시오.

It is likely that Jihun's favorite player will be the _____ _____ _____ this season because he finally hit a home run.

중요

16 위 글을 읽고 대답할 수 <u>없는</u> 질문은?

① Now, who is about to bat?
② How many home runs has Jihun's favorite player hit already this year?
③ Does Jihun's favorite player miss several balls?
④ How many foul balls has Jihun's favorite player hit today?
⑤ Does Jihun's favorite player hit a home run in this inning?

[17~19] 다음 글을 읽고 물음에 답하시오.

Seri Park
Professional golfer
Born: September 8, 1977
Nationality: South Korea
Speciality: She was the school's best ___(A)___ golfer when she was young. She turned ___(B)___ golfer in 1996. She played on the LPGA Tours from 1998 to 2016. She was inducted into the World Golf Hall of Fame in November 2007. She was great, ___(C)___ ?

17 위 글의 빈칸 (A)와 (B)에 들어갈 알맞은 말을 고르시오.

① professional – amateur
② mature – immature
③ amateur – professional
④ professional – expert
⑤ immature – mature

서답형

18 위 글의 빈칸 (C)에 들어갈 알맞은 부가의문문을 쓰시오.

➡ _____

19 위 글을 읽고 박세리에 대해 알 수 없는 것을 고르시오.

① 직업
② 골프를 시작한 나이
③ 프로 골프 선수가 된 시기
④ LPGA Tours에 참가한 시기
⑤ 세계 골프 영예의 전당에 가입한 시기

[20~22] 다음 글을 읽고 물음에 답하시오.

> A: Today the Thunders and the Cobras have a big game.
> B: Now, it is the Thunders' ⓐturn to hit the ball.
> A: The batter with number 77 is coming out to the field. He has hit 21 home runs this year.
> B: He is at bat. The Thunders' fans look very anxious. ⓑ누가 이길 것이라고 생각하시나요?
> (think, win, do, who, will, you, ?)
> A: Home run! Home run!
> B: ⓒHe will be the home run leader this year!

20 위 글의 밑줄 친 ⓐturn과 같은 의미로 쓰인 것을 고르시오.

① The wheels of the car began to turn.
② Please wait for your turn.
③ Turn the sweater inside out before you wash it.
④ Make a left turn into West Street.
⑤ The weather will turn cold.

서답형

21 위 글의 밑줄 친 ⓑ의 우리말에 맞게 주어진 어휘를 알맞게 배열하시오.

➡ _____

서답형

22 위 글의 밑줄 친 ⓒ와 같은 의미가 되도록 빈칸에 들어갈 알맞은 말을 서수로 쓰시오.

> The batter with number 77 succeeds in hitting his _____ home run.

[23~27] 다음 글을 읽고 물음에 답하시오.

> A: On today's show we are going to talk about fun facts in sports! We have here with us, sports reporter Dasom. Welcome, Dasom!
> B: Hi, I'm going to talk about baseball. Do you think catchers in the old days played the same role as catchers ⓐ _____ these days? ⓑHow do you think?
> A: Well.... I guess so.
> B: No. In the past, catchers stood about one meter behind home base and stopped the ball.
> A: ⓒThat's interesting!

서답형

23 위 글의 빈칸 ⓐ에 들어갈 알맞은 대동사를 쓰시오.

➡ _____

 24 위 글의 A와 B의 관계로 알맞은 것을 고르시오.

① announcer – newscaster
② newscaster – sports reporter
③ sports reporter – show host
④ newscaster – announcer
⑤ sports reporter – newscaster

25 위 글의 종류로 알맞은 것을 고르시오.

① summary ② article ③ essay
④ review ⑤ sports news script

서답형

26 위 글의 밑줄 친 ⓑ에서 어법상 틀린 부분을 찾아 고치시오.

_____ ➡ _____

서답형

27 위 글의 밑줄 친 ⓒ가 가리키는 것을 본문에서 찾아 쓰시오.

➡ _____
_____

[01~03] 다음 글을 읽고 물음에 답하시오.

Today the Thunders and the Cobras have a game. Jihun's family is at the baseball stadium.

Jihun: Jian, this is your first time to come to the baseball stadium, isn't it?

Jian: Yes, I'm so excited. ⓐI can't wait for the game to start.

Dad: Look, the players are coming out now!

Jian: Which team is the Thunders?

Jihun: Over there, behind third base. ⓑ그들은 원정 팀이기 때문에 어두운 회색 유니폼을 입고 있어.

01 위 글의 밑줄 친 ⓐ를 다음과 같이 바꿔 쓸 때 빈칸에 들어갈 알맞은 말을 쓰시오.

(1) I can't _____ to watch the game start.

(2) I'm _____ to watch the game start.

02 위 글의 밑줄 친 ⓑ의 우리말에 맞게 한 단어를 보충하여, 주어진 어휘를 배열하시오.

the / wearing / because / uniforms / gray / are / dark / they / they / team / are

➡ _____

_____

03 본문의 내용과 일치하도록 다음 빈칸 (A)와 (B)에 알맞은 단어를 쓰시오.

Jian has (A)_____ come to the baseball stadium before, so she is very (B)_____.

[04~06] 다음 글을 읽고 물음에 답하시오.

Jian: Does the visiting team always wear a dark color?

Jihun: Yes, that's ⓐthe rule. Home teams have bright uniforms and visiting teams have dark uniforms.

Jian: Why is that?

Mom: There is an interesting story about that. In the past, visiting teams could not wash their uniforms after every game. So they started wearing dark colors ⓑto hide the dirt.

Jian: Hahaha! That was a good idea!

04 위 글의 밑줄 친 ⓐthe rule의 내용을 우리말로 쓰시오.

➡ _____

05 위 글의 밑줄 친 ⓑ를 다음과 같이 바꿔 쓸 때 빈칸에 들어갈 알맞은 말을 쓰시오.

= _____ _____ to hide the dirt
= _____ _____ to hide the dirt
= _____ _____ _____ they _____ hide the dirt
= _____ _____ they _____ hide the dirt

06 다음 문장에서 위 글의 내용과 다른 부분을 찾아서 고치시오.

In the past, as visiting teams could not take a shower after every game, they started wearing dark colors to hide the dirt.

_____ ➡ _____

[07~09] 다음 글을 읽고 물음에 답하시오.

The players are warming up.

Jian: Who's your favorite player?

Jihun: Number 77.

Jian: What does the number mean?

Jihun: Hmm.... ⓐPlayers choose a number they like.

Dad: You know what? In the past, the numbers were determined by the players' batting order.

Jihun: ⓑThat means there were no players with number 77!

07 위 글의 밑줄 친 문장 ⓐ에 생략된 말을 넣어 문장을 다시 쓰시오.

➡ _____

08 본문의 내용과 일치하도록 다음 빈칸에 알맞은 숫자를 쓰시오.

> In the past, if a player was the fourth batter in the lineup, his uniform number was _____.
> *lineup: 타순

09 위 글의 밑줄 친 ⓑ의 이유를 우리말로 쓰시오.

➡ _____

_____

[10~12] 다음 글을 읽고 물음에 답하시오.

Now, Jihun's favorite player is about to bat. Jihun looks anxious.

Jian: ⓐ오빠가 가장 좋아하는 선수가 타석에 서네.

Jihun: Yes. He ___(A)___ 21 home runs already this year. If he ___(B)___ one more today, he will be the home run leader this season.

ⓑThe batter misses several balls. Now he has a full count. He is waiting for the next pitch.

Jihun: HOME RUN! HOME RUN!

Crack!

The ball flies fast. It is going, going, going, gone!

10 위 글의 빈칸 (A)와 (B)에 hit을 알맞은 형태로 각각 쓰시오.

(A) _____ (B) _____

11 위 글의 밑줄 친 ⓐ의 우리말에 맞게 주어진 어휘를 이용하여 6단어로 영작하시오.

> your, at

➡ _____

12 위 글의 밑줄 친 ⓑThe batter가 가리키는 것을 본문에서 찾아 쓰시오.

➡ _____

해석

Real-Life Zone B

A: Which sport do you like? Basketball or soccer?
어떤 ～을 좋아하니? A 아니면 B? Which는 의문형용사로 sport를 수식하며 '어느, 어떤'으로 해석한다
B: I like basketball. I'm going to play it with my friends this weekend. I can't wait.
= basketball 너무 기다려져(기대를 나타내는 표현)

구문해설 • be going to 동사원형: ～할 것이다

A: 너는 어떤 운동을 좋아하니? 농구 아니면 축구?
B: 농구를 좋아해. 이번 주말에 친구들이랑 농구를 할 거야. 너무 기다려져.

Writing Workshop

Abebe Bikila

Marathon Runner

Born: August 7, 1932

Nationality: Ethiopia

Speciality: He was known as a marathon winner at the Rome and Tokyo
be known as: ～로 알려져 있다
international sports competitions. When he was preparing to run the marathon
prepare는 목적어로 to부정사를 취한다.
in Rome, he found out that his shoes did not fit well, so he decided to run the
명사절을 이끄는 접속사 decide는 목적어로 to부정사를 취한다.
race without shoes. He felt pain during the race, but he finished the race as the
신발을 신지 않고, 신발 없이 ～ 중에 우승자로서
winner. He was one of the greatest runners in the world, wasn't he?
부가의문문은 앞 문장이 긍정이면 부정으로 만든다.

구문해설 • nationality: 국적 • speciality: 전문 (분야), 특별 사항 • competition: 경쟁, 대회, 시합
• prepare: 준비하다 • find out: 알아내다, 발견하다

Abebe Bikila
마라톤 선수
생일: 1932년 8월 7일
국적: 에티오피아
특별 사항: 그는 로마 국제 스포츠 대회와 도쿄 국제 스포츠 대회의 마라톤 우승자로 알려졌다. 그가 로마에서 달리기를 준비하던 도중에 자신의 신발이 잘 맞지 않는다는 것을 알고 그는 신발을 신지 않고 달리기로 결심했다. 그는 경주 도중에 통증을 느꼈지만 우승자로 경주를 끝마쳤다. 그는 세계에서 가장 위대한 달리기 선수들 중의 한 명이었다. 그렇지 않은가?

Wrap Up

Sarang Middle School Sports Day

Sarang Middle School Sports Day will be held on the school playing field on
조동사(will)+be+pp: 미래시제 수동태 요일 앞에 전치사 on
Wednesday, June 15. There will be various games such as baseball and soccer.
There will also be table tennis. It sounds like fun, doesn't it?
sound like+명사 부가의문문

구문해설 • various: 다양한, 여러 가지의

사랑 중학교 운동회
사랑 중학교 운동회가 학교 운동장에서 6월 15일 수요일에 열립니다. 야구와 축구 같은 여러 가지 게임이 있을 것입니다. 또한 탁구도 있을 것입니다. 재미있게 들리지요. 그렇지 않나요?

영역별 핵심문제

01 다음 중 밑줄 친 부분의 뜻풀이가 바르지 <u>않은</u> 것은?

① After the party Tommy will clean the living room and <u>then</u> do his homework. (그런 다음)

② There are some tips for making the perfect <u>pitch</u>. (투구)

③ I heard a <u>crack</u> when the vase fell over. (날카로운 소리)

④ It's important that you follow the <u>order</u> when adding liquids. (주문)

⑤ Do you think it will <u>fit</u> me? (맞다)

02 다음 밑줄 친 부분과 의미가 가장 가까운 것을 고르시오.

> She seemed <u>anxious</u> about the interview.

① excited   ② pleased   ③ bored
④ nervous   ⑤ interested

03 다음 빈칸에 공통으로 들어갈 말을 쓰시오.

> • The batter _____ed several balls.
> • I don't want to _____ the game.

04 다음 빈칸에 들어갈 말로 적절한 것은?

> He was covered with dust _____ walking along the road.

① for   ② when   ③ unless
④ while   ⑤ therefore

[05~07] 다음 대화를 읽고 물음에 답하시오.

B: Jimin, _____(A)_____ (①)
G: I love table tennis. (②)
B: I like soccer. I'm a big fan of James Hood. He's a great soccer player. (③)
G: Oh, really? There's a soccer match this weekend between Korea and Turkey. Have you heard about it? (④)
B: Of course. I already have a ticket. I'm going to see the game on Saturday. I can't wait. (⑤)
G: That's fantastic.

05 위 대화의 ①~⑤ 중 다음 주어진 말이 들어갈 알맞은 곳은?

> How about you?

①   ②   ③   ④   ⑤

06 그림을 참고하여 빈칸 (A) 들어갈 말을 다음 조건에 맞게 쓰시오.

> ┤ 조건 ├
> • 대화에 나온 단어를 이용할 것
> • 선호하는 것을 물을 것
> • 두 문장으로 쓸 것
> • 총 9 단어

➡ _____

07 다음 영영풀이에 해당하는 단어를 대화에서 찾아 쓰시오.

> an official piece of paper or card that shows you have paid to enter a place or do something

➡ _____

08 다음 대화의 밑줄 친 ⓐ~ⓔ 중 어법상 **틀린** 개수를 고르시오.

> G: What are you doing?
> B: ⓐI looked at a world map.
> G: You checked two countries. ⓑWhat country ⓒwould you like to visiting first? The U.S. ⓓor Mexico?
> B: I want to visit the U.S. ⓔI'd like to seeing a basketball game there.

① 1개　② 2개　③ 3개　④ 4개　⑤ 5개

[09~10] 다음 대화를 읽고 물음에 답하시오.

> A: 너는 어떤 야구 선수를 좋아하니? Mike Hans or Daniel Parker?
> B: (A)I like Mike Hans.

09 위 대화의 밑줄 친 우리말을 영작하시오. (6 words)

➡ _____

10 위 대화의 밑줄 친 (A)의 문장 뒤에 생략된 말을 쓰시오. (4 words)

➡ _____

[11~12] 다음 대화를 읽고 물음에 답하시오.

> G: ⓐDo you want to see my new mountain bike?
> B: ⓑSure. When did you get it?
> G: ⓒMy father bought it for me. ⓓCan you come to my house this afternoon?
> B: ⓔOf course. (A)I can't wait to see it.

11 문장 ⓐ~ⓔ 중에서 대화의 흐름상 어색한 것을 고르시오.

① ⓐ　② ⓑ　③ ⓒ　④ ⓓ　⑤ ⓔ

12 밑줄 친 (A)를 주어진 단어를 이용해 같은 뜻이 되도록 영작하시오.

➡ _____ (looking)

Grammar

13 다음 중 어법상 올바른 것은?

① James teaches math, isn't he?
② She was great, didn't she?
③ The door was open by Tom.
④ A cake was made for him by his mom.
⑤ The wall is painted by the painters tomorrow.

14 다음 빈칸에 들어갈 말을 바르게 짝지은 것을 고르시오.

> • Our house _____ by Mrs. Green every Thursday.
> • Jejudo has some beautiful scenery, _____ ?

① are cleaned – does it
② is cleaned – isn't it
③ is cleaned – doesn't it
④ are cleaning – doesn't it
⑤ is cleaning – isn't it

15 다음 문장에서 틀린 것을 고쳐 다시 쓰시오.

(1) At last the thief caught the police last Saturday.

➡ _____

_____

(2) We don't know exactly when the accident was happened.

➡ _____

_____

(3) Delicious *galbitang* is being made to him by Anna.

➡ _____

_____

(4) Your love can show to your partner by saying "I love you."

➡ _____

_____

(5) Mariel was seen go out with her friend by Andy.

➡ _____

_____

(6) The festival put off by the city on account of the bad weather.

➡ _____

_____

(7) She didn't say good-bye, was she?

➡ _____

(8) She can play soccer very well, doesn't she?

➡ _____

(9) Tino is wearing a blue shirt, doesn't Tino?

➡ _____

(10) The hotel where we stayed was near the city hall, didn't there?

➡ _____

_____

16 다음 두 문장을 부가의문문을 써서 한 문장으로 바꿔 쓰시오.

(1) Tino likes eating ice cream. Doesn't he like eating ice cream?

➡ _____

(2) It was an interesting movie. Wasn't it an interesting movie?

➡ _____

17 다음 빈칸에 들어갈 전치사가 나머지와 다른 것은?

① He was covered _____ dust while walking along the road.

② I'm interested _____ Switzerland.

③ You should be satisfied _____ what you have.

④ The president was pleased _____ the news.

⑤ The boxes were filled _____ chocolate bars for the children.

18 다음 우리말을 괄호 안에 주어진 어휘를 이용하여 영작하시오.

(1) 네 개는 어제 어디에서 발견되었니? (your dog, find, 6단어)

➡ _____

(2) 프랑스어는 아프리카에 있는 많은 국가들에서 말해진다. (Africa, speak , 8단어)

➡ _____

(3) 박씨는 매주 일요일마다 쇼핑을 해, 그렇지 않니? (Mr. Park, go, every, 8단어)

➡ _____

Reading

[19~21] 다음 글을 읽고 물음에 답하시오.

Today the Thunders and the Cobras have a game. Jihun's family is at the baseball stadium.

Jihun: Jian, this is your first time ⓐto come to the baseball stadium, isn't it?

Jian: Yes, I'm so excited. I (A)[can / can't] wait for the game to start.

Dad: Look, the players are coming out now!

Jian: Which team (B)[is / are] the Thunders?

Jihun: Over there, behind third base. ⓑThey are wearing dark gray uniforms because they are the (C)[visiting / visited] team.

19 위 글의 괄호 (A)~(C)에서 문맥이나 어법상 알맞은 낱말을 골라 쓰시오.

(A) _____ (B) _____ (C) _____

20 위 글의 밑줄 친 ⓐcome과 to부정사의 용법이 같은 것을 고르시오.

① He stopped his car to check the engine.
② She needs someone to talk with.
③ They hope to visit us next year.
④ He grew up to be a famous singer.
⑤ It is difficult to solve this problem.

21 위 글의 밑줄 친 ⓑThey가 가리키는 것을 영어로 쓰시오.

➡ _____

[22~24] 다음 글을 읽고 물음에 답하시오.

Jian: Does the visiting team always wear a dark color?

Jihun: Yes, that's the rule. Home teams have _____ⓐ_____ uniforms and visiting teams have _____ⓑ_____ uniforms.

Jian: Why is that?

Mom: There is an interesting story about that. In the past, visiting teams could not wash their uniforms after every game. So they started ⓒwearing dark colors to hide the dirt.

Jian: Hahaha! That was a good idea!

22 위 글의 빈칸 ⓐ와 ⓑ에 들어갈 알맞은 말을 고르시오.

① dark – bright   ② bright – light
③ bright – dark   ④ strong – dark
⑤ light – strong

23 아래 〈보기〉에서 위 글의 밑줄 친 ⓒwearing과 문법적 쓰임이 같은 것의 개수를 고르시오.

① I'm fond of wearing a pink dress.
② She is wearing a pink dress today.
③ Do you know the girl wearing a pink dress?
④ Wearing a pink dress makes me happy.
⑤ She came to the party wearing a pink dress.

① 1개   ② 2개   ③ 3개   ④ 4개   ⑤ 5개

24 위 글의 내용과 일치하지 <u>않는</u> 것은?

① 홈팀은 밝은 유니폼을 입는다.
② 원정 팀은 어두운 유니폼을 입는다.
③ 과거에는 원정 팀이 매 경기 후 유니폼을 세탁할 수가 없었다.
④ 원정 팀은 때를 숨기기 위해 어두운 색을 입기 시작했다.
⑤ 원정 팀의 유니폼은 더러웠을 것이라고 지안이는 말한다.

[25~26] 다음 글을 읽고 물음에 답하시오.

> The players are warming up.
> Jian: Who's your favorite player?
> Jihun: Number 77.
> Jian: What does the number mean?
> Jihun: Hmm.... Players choose a number they like.
> Dad: You know what? In the past, the numbers were determined by the players' batting ⓐorder.
> Jihun: That means there were no players with number 77!

25 위 글의 밑줄 친 ⓐorder와 같은 의미로 쓰인 것을 고르시오.

① I would like to place an order for ten copies of this book.
② The names are listed in alphabetical order.
③ When did the officer order them to fire?
④ The house was kept in good order.
⑤ He will order a new suit for his son.

26 위 글을 읽고 대답할 수 <u>없는</u> 질문은?

① What are the players doing now?
② Who's Jihun's favorite player?
③ Why does Jihun like the player?
④ What does the number 77 mean?
⑤ In the past, by what were the players' numbers determined?

[27~30] 다음 글을 읽고 물음에 답하시오.

> Now, Jihun's favorite player ⓐis about to bat. Jihun looks anxious.
> Jian: Your favorite player is ___(A)___ bat.
> Jihun: Yes. He has hit 21 home runs already this year. If he hits one more today, he will be the home run leader this season.
> The batter misses several balls. Now he has a full count. He is waiting ___(B)___ the next pitch.
> Jihun: HOME RUN! HOME RUN!
> Crack!
> The ball flies fast. It is going, going, going, ___(C)___ !

27 위 글의 빈칸 (A)와 (B)에 들어갈 전치사가 바르게 짝지어진 것은?

① on – for   ② at – by   ③ in – to
④ on – to   ⑤ at – for

28 다음과 같은 뜻이 되도록 위 글의 빈칸 (C)에 go를 알맞은 형태로 쓰시오.

> Jihun's favorite player hits a home run.

➡ _____

29 위 글의 밑줄 친 ⓐ를 다음과 같이 바꿔 쓸 때 빈칸에 들어갈 알맞은 말을 쓰시오.

> is on the point of _____

30 다음 문장에서 위 글의 내용과 <u>다른</u> 부분을 찾아서 고치시오.

> When Jihun's favorite player hits a ball, it falls to the ground.

_____ ➡ _____

01 다음 빈칸에 알맞은 말이 순서대로 바르게 나열된 것은?

출제율 95%

- My favorite player is _____ bat.
- The film is about _____ .
- He also takes English lessons _____ a week.

① on – to begin – two
② on – to beginning – twice
③ at – to begin – twice
④ at – to beginning – twice
⑤ at – beginning – two

출제율 95%

02 우리말 해석에 맞게 빈칸을 완성하시오.

(1) 선수는 1루로 걸어갔다.
 ➡ The player walked to _____ _____ .
(2) 그는 대회에서 우승하기 위해 열심히 노력했다.
 ➡ He tried hard to win the _____ .
(3) 나도 초콜릿을 좋아하지 않는다.
 ➡ I don't like chocolate, _____ .
(4) 반드시 순서를 지켜 주세요.
 ➡ Be sure to follow the _____ .

출제율 90%

03 〈보기〉에 주어진 단어를 이용해 빈칸 (A)와 (B)를 채우시오.

A: What are you going to do on your vacation?
B: I'm going _____(A)_____ a boat ride. I can't _____(B)_____ .

┌─ 보기 ┐
go play take wait
└──────────┘

(A) _____ (B) _____

출제율 100%

04 다음 중 밑줄 친 부분의 뜻풀이가 바르지 않은 것을 모두 고르시오.

① My daughter hid the ring under her bed. (숨겼다)
② Don't forget to check that your helmet fits properly. (맞다)
③ He can't go and I can't, either. (둘 중 하나)
④ It's not easy to decide what to eat. (결정하다)
⑤ Which team do you support? (지원하다)

출제율 90%

05 다음 단어와 영영풀이의 연결이 잘못된 것을 고르시오.

① pitch: a throw of the ball for the batter to hit it
② anxious: very nervous or worried about something
③ fit: to be the right size and shape for someone or something
④ home team: a sports team playing on the competing team's field or court
⑤ base: each corner of the square that makes a baseball diamond

[06~08] 다음 대화를 읽고 물음에 답하시오.

B1: Jiho, why are you _____ⓐ_____ such a hurry?
B2: Hi, Alex! I have to be home before 6:00. (①) The game between the Thunders _____ⓑ_____ the Cobras starts at 6:00.
B1: Oh, are you a baseball fan? Which team do you _____(A)_____ ? The Cobras or the Thunders?
B2: The Cobras. (②)
B1: Me, too! (③)

B2: Hurry ___©___ ! We only have thirty minutes left. (④)

B1: Okay. Maybe we can watch a game together sometime. (⑤)

B2: That's a great idea! How about going to the next Cobras home game together?

B1: Okay. They have a game next Saturday. We can eat fried chicken while watching the game!

B2: That sounds great. I can't wait!

출제율 90%
06 위 대화의 ①~⑤ 중 다음 주어진 말이 들어갈 알맞은 곳은?

> I don't want to miss the game either.

①   ②   ③   ④   ⑤

출제율 95%
07 위 대화의 빈칸 (A)에 들어갈 알맞은 단어를 고르시오.

① provide   ② support   ③ make
④ enjoy   ⑤ play

출제율 100%
08 위 대화의 빈칸 ⓐ~ⓒ에 알맞은 말을 〈보기〉에서 골라 쓰시오.

┌ 보기 ┐
and   at   for   in   or   to   up

ⓐ _____   ⓑ _____   ⓒ _____

[09~10] 다음 대화를 읽고 물음에 답하시오.

G: What are you doing?

B: I'm looking at a world map.

G: You checked two countries. 어떤 나라에 먼저 방문하고 싶어? 미국 아니면 멕시코?

B: I want to visit the U.S. I'd like to see a basketball game there.

출제율 85%
09 밑줄 친 우리말을 주어진 단어를 이용하여 영작하시오.

> (Mexico, would, country, like, The U.S.)

➡ _____

_____

출제율 95%
10 위 대화를 읽고 답할 수 없는 질문을 고르시오.

① What countries did the boy check on a world map?
② What does the boy want to do in Mexico?
③ What is the boy doing now?
④ Which country does the boy want to go first? Mexico or the U.S.?
⑤ What would the boy like to do when he visits the U.S.?

[11~12] 다음 대화를 읽고 물음에 답하시오.

B: Jimin, which sport do you like? Soccer or table tennis?

G: I love table tennis. How about you, Yunho?

B: I like soccer. I'm a big fan of James Hood. He's a great soccer player.

G: Oh, really? 이번 주말에 한국 대 터키의 축구 경기가 있어. (Korea, between, a, match, Turkey, soccer, there's, weekend, and, this) Have you heard about it?

B: Of course. I already have a ticket. I'm going to see the game on Saturday. I can't wait.

G: That's fantastic.

11 위 대화의 밑줄 친 우리말에 맞게 괄호 안의 단어를 알맞게 배열하여 영작하시오.

➡ _____

_____

12 위 대화의 내용과 일치하는 것을 고르시오.

① Jimin does not like soccer.

② Jimin and Yunho like table tennis.

③ Yunho has heard about the soccer match this weekend.

④ Yunho is going to see the final baseball game.

⑤ Jimin already has the soccer match ticket.

13 다음 밑줄 친 부분을 생략할 수 있는 것은?

① A lot of waste is thrown away in big cities by people.

② This picture was drawn by Lio.

③ The photos were not taken by my brother.

④ Math was taught to us by Mr. Lee.

⑤ This report was written by the student.

14 다음 주어진 문장과 같은 뜻이 되도록 빈칸을 채우시오.

(1) Simon will read his son the book tonight.

➡ The book _____

_____ .

(2) Peter fixed the car this morning.

➡ The car _____ .

15 다음 빈칸을 두 단어로 채워 상대방의 동의를 구하는 문장으로 완성하시오.

(1) She had her hair cut, _____ _____ ?

(2) The boys can play the violin, _____ _____ ?

(3) The movie wasn't interesting at all, _____ _____ ?

[16~18] 다음 글을 읽고 물음에 답하시오.

> Today the Thunders and the Cobras have a game. Jihun's family is at the baseball stadium.
>
> Jihun: Jian, this is your first time to come to the baseball stadium, ___ⓐ___ ?
>
> Jian: Yes, I'm so (A)[exciting / excited]. I can't wait for the game (B)[starting / to start].
>
> Dad: Look, the players are coming out now!
>
> Jian: Which team is the Thunders?
>
> Jihun: Over there, behind (C)[three bases / third base]. They are wearing dark gray uniforms because they are the visiting team.

16 위 글의 빈칸 ⓐ에 들어갈 알맞은 부가의문문을 쓰시오.

➡ _____

17 위 글의 괄호 (A)~(C)에서 문맥이나 어법상 알맞은 것을 골라 쓰시오.

(A) _____ (B) _____ (C) _____

18 위 글을 읽고 대답할 수 없는 질문은?

① What teams have a game today?

② Where is Jihun's family now?

③ Has Jian come to the baseball stadium before?

④ How does Jian feel to be in the baseball stadium?

⑤ Why are the players of the visiting team wearing dark gray uniforms?

[19~21] 다음 글을 읽고 물음에 답하시오.

Jian: Does the visiting team always wear a dark color?

Jihun: Yes, that's the rule. Home teams have bright uniforms and visiting teams have dark uniforms.

Jian: Why is that?

Mom: There is an interesting story about that. In the past, visiting teams could not wash their uniforms after every game. So they started wearing dark colors ⓐto hide the dirt.

Jian: Hahaha! That was a good idea!

출제율 100%

19 위 글의 주제로 알맞은 것을 고르시오.

① the reason why home teams like bright uniforms

② the reason why visiting teams wear dark uniforms

③ the difficulties that visiting teams experienced

④ the strong points of bright uniforms

⑤ the weak points of dark uniforms

출제율 90%

20 Why did visiting teams start wearing dark colors? Fill in the blanks with the suitable words.

> Because visiting teams could not _____ _____ _____ after every game in the past, they started wearing dark colors _____ _____ the dirt.

출제율 95%

21 위 글의 밑줄 친 ⓐto hide와 to부정사의 용법이 다른 것을 모두 고르시오.

① He studied hard to pass the exam.

② I didn't expect to see you here.

③ Tom needed someone to help him.

④ It's fun to teach the students.

⑤ I have come here to learn English.

[22~24] 다음 글을 읽고 물음에 답하시오.

The players are warming up.

Jian: Who's your favorite player?

Jihun: Number 77.

Jian: What does the number mean?

Jihun: Hmm.... Players choose a number they like.

Dad: ⓐYou know what? In the past, the numbers were determined by the players' batting order.

Jihun: That means there were no players with number 77!

출제율 95%

22 What is the number that Jihun's favorite player likes? Answer in English in a full sentence. (3 words)

➡ _____

출제율 90%

23 위 글의 밑줄 친 ⓐYou know what?과 바꿔 쓸 수 있는 말을 모두 고르시오.

① You know something?

② How do you feel about it?

③ How would you like it?

④ Guess what!

⑤ What do you think about it?

출제율 95%

24 위 글의 내용과 일치하지 않는 것은?

① 선수들이 몸을 풀고 있다.

② 지안이가 가장 좋아하는 선수는 77번 선수이다.

③ 지훈이는 선수들이 원하는 번호를 선택한다고 말한다.

④ 과거에는 번호가 선수들의 타순에 의해 결정되었다.

⑤ 과거에는 77번 선수가 없었다.

[01~02] 다음 대화의 흐름상 어색한 부분을 찾아 고치시오.

01

B: Don't forget that we're going rock climbing this weekend!
G: Don't worry. I will forget.
B: I'm excited about going. I can't wait.

_____ ➡ _____

02

A: Which sport do you like? Bowling or baseball?
B: I like baseball. I'm going to play it with my friends this weekend. I can wait.

_____ ➡ _____

03 대화의 밑줄 친 부분과 같은 의미가 되도록 주어진 단어를 이용하여 문장을 완성하시오.

G: Did you get the tickets?
B: Yes! I can't wait to watch the game.

➡ _____ (forward)

04 다음 주어진 문장을 능동태는 수동태로, 수동태는 능동태로 바꾸시오.

(1) What did she cook for her family last night?

➡ _____

(2) Dabotap was built in the eighth century by Kimdaesung.

➡ _____

(3) The plants are watered by Kevin every morning.

➡ _____

(4) My friend gave me some flowers two days ago.

➡ _____
_____
_____

05 다음 문장에서 틀린 것을 고쳐 다시 쓰시오.

(1) The light bulb invented Edison.

➡ _____
_____

(2) Sue was made a dress by her mom.

➡ _____

(3) You aren't paying attention, do you?

➡ _____

(4) You forgot to bring your umbrella, were not you?

➡ _____

Today the Thunders and the Cobras have a game. Jihun's family is at the baseball stadium.

Jihun: Jian, this is your first time to come to the baseball stadium, isn't it?

Jian: Yes, I'm so ___(A)___ . ⓐ나는 경기가 빨리 시작했으면 좋겠어.

Dad: Look, the players are coming out now!

Jian: Which team is the Thunders?

Jihun: Over there, behind third base. They are ___(B)___ dark gray uniforms because they are the visiting team.

06 위 글의 빈칸 (A), (B)에 알맞은 말을 주어진 어휘를 이용하여 쓰시오.

> (A) excite, (B) wear

(A) _____ (B) _____

07 위 글의 밑줄 친 ⓐ의 우리말에 맞게 주어진 어구를 이용하여 8단어로 영작하시오.

> can't wait, start

➡ _____

08 Why are the Thunders wearing dark gray uniforms? Fill in the blank with the suitable words.

➡ Because _____ .

09 다음 문장에서 위 글의 내용과 <u>다른</u> 부분을 찾아서 고치시오.

> Jian has come to the baseball stadium before.

_____ ➡ _____

The players are (A)[warming / warmed] up.

Jian: (B)[Whose / Who's] your favorite player?

Jihun: Number 77.

Jian: What does the number mean?

Jihun: Hmm.... ⓐPlayers choose a number they like.

Dad: You know (C)[how / what]? In the past, ⓑthe numbers were determined by the players' batting order.

Jihun: ⓒThat means there were no players with number 77!

10 위 글의 괄호 (A)~(C)에서 문맥이나 어법상 알맞은 낱말을 골라 쓰시오.

(A) _____ (B) _____ (C) _____

11 위 글의 밑줄 친 ⓐ를 수동태로 고치시오.

➡ _____

_____

12 위 글의 밑줄 친 ⓑ를 능동태로 고치시오.

➡ _____

_____

13 위 글의 밑줄 친 ⓒThat이 가리키는 것을 본문에서 찾아 쓰시오.

➡ _____

_____

창의사고력 서술형 문제

01 주어진 동사의 수동태를 사용하여 다양한 문장을 쓰시오.

> **보기**
>
> choose, donate, turn off, make, write

(1) _____

(2) _____

(3) _____

(4) _____

(5) _____

02 다음 내용을 바탕으로 선수의 프로필을 작성하시오.

> Seri Park
>
> Professional golfer
>
> Born: September 8, 1977
>
> Nationality: South Korea
>
> Speciality: • When young: the best amateur golfer
>
> • in 1996: turned professional golfer
>
> • from 1998 to 2016: played on the LPGA Tours
>
> • in November 2007: inducted into the World Golf Hall of Fame
>
> *induct: (조직에) 가입시키다

> Seri Park
>
> Professional golfer
>
> Born: September 8, 1977
>
> Nationality: South Korea
>
> Speciality: She was the best (A)_____ golfer when she was young. She turned (B)_____ golfer in 1996. She played on the (C)_____ from 1998 to 2016. She was inducted into the (D)_____ in November 2007. She was great, wasn't she?

단원별 모의고사

01 다음 밑줄 친 부분과 의미가 가까운 것을 고르시오.

> The price is <u>determined</u> by supply and demand.

① decided   ② got

③ agreed   ④ made

⑤ discussed

02 다음 제시된 의미에 맞는 단어를 주어진 철자로 시작하여 빈칸에 쓰고 알맞은 것을 골라 문장을 완성하시오. (필요하면 어형 변화를 할 것)

> • c_____ : an event or contest in which people try to win something by defeating others
> • c_____ : the sudden loud explosive sound of something when it falls or bumps into itself or something else
> • p_____ : the time before the moment of speaking or writing
> • h_____ : to put something out of sight

(1) The dog _____ the bone in the ground yesterday.

(2) There were huge _____ of thunders all night long.

(3) The _____ is heating up.

(4) In the _____, people traveled on horseback.

03 다음 우리말에 맞게 빈칸에 알맞은 말을 쓰시오.

(1) 제 차는 저기 주차장에 주차되어 있습니다.

➡ My car is in the parking lot _____ _____.

(2) 그녀는 급해서 빨간 불을 무시하고 지나갔다.

➡ She was _____ _____ _____ and drove through a red light.

(3) 언제 그의 새로운 소설이 나오나요?

➡ When will his new novel _____ _____?

(4) 남자는 수하물을 기다리고 있다.

➡ The man is _____ _____ his luggage.

04 다음 중 동사와의 연결이 <u>어색한</u> 것을 고르시오.

① go surfing   ② play soccer

③ go swimming   ④ go tennis

⑤ play baseball

[05~06] 다음 대화를 읽고 물음에 답하시오.

> A: Which shorts do you like? The green ones or the red ones?
> B: (A)<u>I like the green ones.</u>

05 위 대화의 밑줄 친 문장 (A)에서 생략된 부분을 쓰시오.

➡ _____

06 밑줄 친 문장 (A)와 같은 의미가 되도록 주어진 단어를 이용해 문장을 완성하시오.

➡ _____ (to, 9단어)

[07~11] 다음 대화를 읽고 물음에 답하시오.

> B1: Jiho, why are you in such a hurry?
>
> B2: Hi, Alex! I have to be home before 6:00. The game between the Thunders and the Cobras (A)[start / starts] at 6:00. (①)
>
> B1: Oh, are you a baseball fan? ____ⓐ____ The Cobras or the Thunders?
>
> B2: The Cobras. (②)
>
> B1: Me, too! I don't want to miss the game (B)[either / too]. (③)
>
> B2: Hurry up! We only have thirty minutes (C)[left / leaving].
>
> B1: Okay. Maybe we can watch a game together sometime. (④)
>
> B2: That's a great idea! (⑤)
>
> B1: Okay. They have a game next Saturday. We can eat fried chicken while watching the game!
>
> B2: That sounds great. I can't wait!

07 위 대화의 ①~⑤ 중 다음 주어진 문장이 들어갈 알맞은 곳은?

> How about going to the next Cobras home game together?

①   ②   ③   ④   ⑤

08 위 대화의 빈칸 ⓐ에 들어갈 알맞은 표현을 고르시오.

① Where can we watch the game?
② Which team do you support?
③ Do you like baseball?
④ What are they going to do at 6:00?
⑤ What do you want to eat while watching TV?

09 위 대화의 (A)~(C)에서 알맞은 말을 골라 쓰시오.

(A) _____ (B) _____ (C) _____

10 다음 영영풀이에 해당하는 단어를 대화에서 찾아 쓰시오.

> a group of people who play a sport or game together against other groups of people

➡ _____

11 위 대화의 내용과 일치하지 않는 것을 고르시오.

① It is five-thirty now.
② They watched the Cobras home game together.
③ Jiho is a baseball fan.
④ There is a baseball game at 6:00.
⑤ Jiho is in a hurry to watch a baseball game.

12 다음 대화의 흐름상 어색한 부분을 찾아 고치시오. (밑줄 친 부분에서 고를 것)

> G: I'm thinking about getting a pet. Do you have a pet?
>
> B: Yes, I do. I have a dog and a cat.
>
> G: What do you think? Which pet is more for me? A cat or a dog?
>
> B: Why don't you come to my house someday and play with my pets? Then you can decide.

_____ ➡ _____

13 다음 중 어법상 바른 것은?

① Cheesecake bakes for Scott every day.
② Mr. Lee was written a letter.
③ My computer was fixed my brother.
④ Mastering English in a year or two is really difficult, isn't it?
⑤ You have a pen, do you?

14 다음 중 능통태를 수동태로 잘못 바꾼 것은?

① People living near the river have eaten fish.
  = Fish have been eaten by people living near the river.
② His teacher made him study English every day.
  = He was made to study English every day by his teacher.
③ They gave up the plan because of the heavy costs.
  = The plan was given because of the heavy costs.
④ Sam gave Alicia a present.
  = A present was given to Alicia by Sam.
⑤ Amedeo Modigliani painted *Woman with Blue Eyes* in 1918.
  = *Woman with Blue Eyes* was painted by Amedeo Modigliani in 1918.

15 다음 문장에서 틀린 것을 고치시오.

(1) This house is made from stone.
  _____ ➡ _____
(2) William was bought a new computer by her mother.
  _____ ➡
  _____
(3) The Olympic Games are taken place every four years.
  _____ ➡ _____
(4) They are doctors, don't they?
  _____ ➡ _____
(5) Come home by 8 o'clock tonight, can't you?
  _____ ➡ _____

16 다음 밑줄 친 부분의 쓰임이 나머지 넷과 다른 것은?

① The station was <u>built</u> in 1894.
② His words often <u>made</u> no sense.
③ The roof of my house was <u>covered</u> with snow.
④ These cookies were <u>cooked</u> for him by Joanna.
⑤ The greetings are <u>used</u> to welcome people.

17 다음 빈칸에 알맞은 부가의문문을 쓰시오.

(1) You like dogs, _____ _____?
(2) Emily is tired, _____ _____?
(3) He was one of the greatest runners in the world, _____ _____?
(4) The man always parks his car on the street, _____ _____?
(5) You will go there, _____ _____?
(6) You looked so busy, _____ _____?
(7) Be good to yourself, _____ _____?
(8) Let's help that child, _____ _____?

[18~19] 다음 글을 읽고 물음에 답하시오.

Today the Thunders and the Cobras have a game. Jihun's family is at the baseball stadium.

Jihun: Jian, this is your first time to come to the baseball stadium, isn't it?
Jian: Yes, I'm so excited. I can't wait for the game to start.
Dad: Look, the players are coming out now!
Jian: Which team is the Thunders?
Jihun: Over there, behind third base. They are wearing dark gray uniforms because they are the ⓐvisiting team.

18 아래 〈보기〉에서 위 글의 밑줄 친 ⓐvisiting과 문법적 쓰임이 다른 것의 개수를 고르시오.

> ① I came home running all the way from school.
> ② He enjoyed studying with his friends.
> ③ Mastering foreign languages is not easy.
> ④ The boy sitting under the tree is my brother.
> ⑤ Thank you for showing me the way to the subway station.

① 1개 ② 2개 ③ 3개 ④ 4개 ⑤ 5개

19 Which team is the home team, the Thunders or the Cobras? Answer in English. (2 words)

➡ _____

[20~21] 다음 글을 읽고 물음에 답하시오.

Jian: Does the visiting team always wear a dark color?

Jihun: Yes, that's the rule. Home teams have bright uniforms and visiting teams have dark uniforms.

Jian: Why is that?

Mom: There is an interesting story about that. In the past, visiting teams could not wash their uniforms after every game. So they started wearing dark colors to hide the dirt.

Jian: Hahaha! ⓐThat was a good idea!

20 위 글의 밑줄 친 ⓐThat이 가리키는 것을 본문에서 찾아 쓰시오.

➡ _____

21 위 글을 읽고 대답할 수 없는 질문은?

① Does the home team always wear a bright color?
② What's the rule about the color of the uniforms?
③ Why did visiting teams have dark uniforms in the past?
④ What team started wearing dark colors for the first time?
⑤ What does Jian think about the origin of dark uniforms?

[22~23] 다음 글을 읽고 물음에 답하시오.

The players are warming up.

Jian: Who's your favorite player?

Jihun: Number 77.

Jian: What does the number mean?

Jihun: Hmm.... Players choose a number they like.

Dad: You know what? In the past, ⓐ번호가 선수들의 타순에 의해 결정되었단다.

Jihun: That means there were no players with number 77!

22 위 글의 밑줄 친 ⓐ의 우리말에 맞게 한 단어를 보충하여, 주어진 어휘를 알맞게 배열하시오.

> order / were / the numbers / batting / determined / the players'

➡ _____

_____

23 다음 빈칸 (A)와 (B)에 알맞은 단어를 넣어 현재 등번호가 결정되는 방법에 대한 설명을 완성하시오.

> At present, the number is chosen by (A)_____ themselves, which is a number they (B)_____.

Lesson 6

New Places, New Experiences

🎙 의사소통 기능

- 경험 묻기

  A: Have you ever traveled to another country?

  B: Yes, I have. It was a wonderful experience.

- 만족이나 불만족에 대해 묻기

  A: How do you like this shirt?

  B: It's colorful. I like it.

🎙 언어 형식

- 원인과 결과를 나타내는 'so ... that'

  It was **so** delicious **that** I asked for more.

- 목적격 관계대명사

  It was from the *khorkhog* **that** she was cooking for us.

교과서
Words & Expressions

Key Words

- **abroad**[əbrɔ́ːd] 부 해외에
- **airport**[ɛ́ərpɔrt] 명 공항
- **amazing**[əméiziŋ] 형 굉장한, 놀라운
- **arrive**[əráiv] 동 도착하다
- **asleep**[əslíːp] 형 잠이 든
- **barbecue**[báːrbikjùː] 명 바비큐
- **beginning**[bigíniŋ] 명 시작, 처음
- **bright**[brait] 형 밝은
- **camel**[kǽməl] 명 낙타
- **capital**[kǽpətl] 명 수도
- **chance**[tʃæns] 명 기회
- **cheerful**[tʃíərfəl] 형 쾌활한, 유쾌한
- **coastline**[kóustlain] 명 해안선
- **colorful**[kʌ́lərfəl] 형 화려한, (색이) 다채로운
- **cozy**[kóuzi] 형 아늑한
- **culture**[kʌ́ltʃər] 명 문화
- **during**[djúəriŋ] 전 ~ 동안[내내]
- **enough**[inʌ́f] 부 ~할 만큼 (충분히)
- **expect**[ikspékt] 동 기대하다, 예상하다
- **flight**[flait] 명 비행
- **guest**[gest] 명 손님
- **imagine**[imǽdʒin] 동 상상하다

- **kid**[kid] 동 농담하다
- **lamb**[læm] 명 양고기
- **language**[lǽŋgwidʒ] 명 언어
- **magical**[mǽdʒikəl] 형 아주 멋진, 마법의, 마술의
- **modern**[mádərn] 형 현대의
- **moment**[móumənt] 명 순간
- **Mongolian**[maŋgóuliən] 형 몽골의 명 몽골 사람
- **moved**[muːvd] 형 가슴 뭉클한
- **once**[wʌns] 접 ~하자마자
- **part**[paːrt] 명 부분, 일부
- **rise**[raiz] 동 (해가) 뜨다, 일어나다
- **scared**[skɛərd] 형 겁먹은, 무서워하는
- **serve**[səːrv] 동 제공하다
- **shooting star** 유성
- **station**[stéiʃən] 명 역, 정거장
- **sweet**[swiːt] 형 달콤한, 단
- **tasty**[téisti] 형 맛있는
- **traditional**[trədíʃənl] 형 전통적인
- **TV station** 텔레비전 방송국
- **view**[vjuː] 명 경관, 전망
- **wedding**[wédiŋ] 명 결혼(식)
- **whole**[houl] 명 전체, 모든

Key Expressions

- **at first** 처음에는
- **be cooked with** ~으로 요리되다
- **be full of** ~로 가득하다
- **be made of** ~로 만들어지다
- **be made with** ~로 만들어지다
- **can't wait to** 빨리 ~하면 좋겠다
- **feel like**+주어+동사 ~인 것처럼 느끼다
- **from A to B** A에서 B로
- **get used to** ~에 익숙해지다

- **Have you been (to)** ~? ~에 가 본 적 있니?
- **Have you ever**+과거분사 ~? 너는 ~해 본 적 있니?
- **How did you like** ~? ~는 어땠어?
- **How do you like** ~? ~는 어떠니?
- **How was** ~? ~는 어땠어?
- **show A around B** …에게 ~을 둘러보도록 안내하다
- **smell**+형용사 ~한 냄새가 나다
- **so** 형용사/부사 **that** 주어+동사 매우 ~해서 …하다
- **wake up** 잠에서 깨다

Word Power

※ 동사 – 동사ing – 동사ed

감정을 나타내는 동사에 '-ing'를 붙이면 '~한 감정을 일으키는'의 의미가 되고, '-ed'를 붙이면 '~한 감정을 느끼는'의 의미가 된다.

- ☐ **amaze**(놀라게 하다) – **amazing**(놀라운) – **amazed**(놀란)
- ☐ **annoy**(짜증나게 하다) – **annoying**(짜증나게 하는) – **annoyed**(짜증이 난)
- ☐ **bore**(지루하게 만들다) – **boring**(재미없는, 지루하게 하는) – **bored**(지루해 하는)
- ☐ **disappoint**(실망시키다) – **disappointing**(실망시키는) – **disappointed**(실망한)
- ☐ **excite**(신나게 하다) – **exciting**(신나게 하는) – **excited**(신난)
- ☐ **interest**(흥미를 갖게 하다) – **interesting**(흥미로운) – **interested**(흥미를 느끼는)
- ☐ **relax**(느긋이 쉬다) – **relaxing**(느긋하게 해 주는) – **relaxed**(느긋함을 느끼는)
- ☐ **satisfy**(만족시키다) – **satisfying**(만족감을 주는) – **satisfied**(만족하는)
- ☐ **surprise**(놀라게 하다) – **surprising**(놀라운) – **surprised**(놀란)
- ☐ **tire**(피곤하게 만들다) – **tiring**(피곤하게 만드는) – **tired**(피곤한)

English Dictionary

- ☐ **abroad** 해외에
  → in or to a different country or countries
  다른 나라에서 또는 다른 나라로

- ☐ **airport** 공항
  → a place where planes take off and land with facilities for passengers
  승객들을 위한 시설을 갖춘 곳으로 비행기가 이륙하고 착륙하는 장소

- ☐ **asleep** 잠이 든
  → not awake 깨어 있지 않은

- ☐ **bright** 밝은
  → shining strongly 강하게 빛나는

- ☐ **chance** 기회
  → an opportunity to do something
  어떤 것을 할 기회

- ☐ **cheerful** 쾌활한, 유쾌한
  → noticeably happy 현저히 행복한

- ☐ **expect** 기대하다, 예상하다
  → to believe or think that something will happen
  어떤 것이 발생할 것이라고 믿거나 생각하다

- ☐ **get used to** ~에 익숙해지다
  → to become familiar with something or someone
  어떤 사람이나 사물과 친숙해지다

- ☐ **guest** 손님
  → someone who is invited to visit you
  당신을 방문하도록 초대된 사람

- ☐ **kid** 농담하다
  → to make a joke 농담을 하다

- ☐ **language** 언어
  → the method of human communication used by the people of a country or region for talking or writing
  한 나라나 지역의 사람들에 의해 말하거나 쓰기 위해서 사용되는 의사소통 방법

- ☐ **magical** 마법의
  → seems to use special powers
  특별한 힘을 사용하는 것처럼 보이는

- ☐ **modern** 현대의
  → designed and made using the latest ides or methods
  가장 최신의 생각이나 방법을 사용하여 디자인되고 만들어진

- ☐ **Mongolian** 몽골의
  → relating to Mongolia or its people
  몽골 혹은 몽골 사람들과 관련된

- ☐ **part** 부분, 일부
  → one of the pieces, sections, or elements that makes the whole of something
  어떤 것의 전체를 만드는 조각, 부분품 또는 요소들 중의 하나

- ☐ **rise** (해가) 뜨다
  → appear above the horizon in the sky
  지평선 위로 하늘에 나타나다

- ☐ **station** 역, 정거장
  → a place where trains or buses stop so that people can get on or off
  사람들이 타거나 내릴 수 있도록 지하철이나 버스가 멈추는 장소

- ☐ **view** 경관, 전망
  → everything that can be seen from a particular place
  특정한 장소로부터 보여지는 모든 것

서답형

01 다음 괄호 안의 단어를 문맥에 맞게 빈칸에 써 넣으시오.

(1) The soccer game last night was really _____. (excite)

(2) He was _____ with the test results. (disappoint)

02 〈보기〉에 주어진 단어를 이용해 빈칸을 채울 때 들어갈 말이 다른 하나를 고르시오.

┌─ 보기 ─┐

interest

① Math is the most _____ subject to me.

② The subject in which I'm _____ is computer technology.

③ This is the most _____ part in this movie.

④ Is there any _____ news in the paper?

⑤ I watched a very _____ show last weekend.

중요

03 밑줄 친 부분과 의미가 가장 가까운 것을 고르시오.

As soon as he went to bed, he fell asleep.

① Since   ② Until

③ Once   ④ In case

⑤ After

04 빈칸에 알맞은 단어를 고르시오.

I was surprised because I didn't _____ to see him there.

① expect   ② arrive

③ allow   ④ encourage

⑤ decide

중요

05 다음 밑줄 친 부분의 의미로 알맞지 <u>않은</u> 것은?

① The coach called the whole team over. (전체)

② Do you mean I don't practice enough? (충분히)

③ Many people were moved by his songs and his beautiful voice. (움직였다)

④ I've waited a long time for a moment like this. (순간)

⑤ Cars have become an important part of our modern lifestyle. (현대의)

서답형

06 다음 주어진 우리말에 맞게 빈칸을 채우시오. (철자가 주어진 것도 있음)

(1) 나는 곧 그 일에 익숙해질 거라고 생각한다.

➡ I think I will soon g_____ the work.

(2) 우리 삼촌은 내게 그 도시 곳곳을 안내하기로 약속했다.

➡ My uncle promised to _____ me _____ the city.

01 다음 괄호 안의 단어를 문맥에 맞게 고쳐 쓰시오.

(1) The movie was so _____ that I fell asleep while watching it. (bore)

(2) We were all _____ at his speed of working. (amaze)

02 두 문장이 같은 의미가 되도록 빈칸을 채우시오.

I think that you are familiar with my accent now.
= I think that you _____ my accent now.

03 다음 우리말에 맞도록 빈칸에 알맞은 말을 쓰시오. (철자가 주어진 경우 주어진 철자로 시작할 것)

(1) 유성은 사실 전혀 별이 아니다.
➡ A _____ is not actually a star at all.

(2) 그는 너무 무서워서 결국 남은 하루를 차 속에서 머무르는 것으로 끝냈다.
➡ He was _____ s_____ _____ he ended up staying in the car for the rest of the day.

(3) 네가 만약 쉽게 잠들 수 없다면, 지루한 것을 해라.
➡ If you can't fall _____ easily, do something b_____.

(4) 캔버라는 호주의 수도이다.
➡ Canberra is the _____ city of Australia.

04 다음 빈칸에 공통으로 들어갈 말을 쓰시오.

• Do you know what dish is made _____ red beans, milk and ice?
• Usually, spaghetti is cooked _____ tomato sauce.

05 다음 빈칸에 들어갈 말을 〈보기〉에서 찾아 쓰시오.

보기
at   for   like   up

(1) She set a clock but she didn't wake _____.

(2) _____ first, I thought I understood what you said

(3) He can't wait _____ the party.

(4) I feel _____ I am much taller.

06 다음 우리말에 맞게 주어진 단어를 바르게 배열하시오.

(1) 올해에 기쁨이 가득하길 바란다.
(be, joy, hope, I, of, will, this, full, year)
➡ _____

(2) 이 장소는 아주 멋져서 나는 여기서 살고 싶다.
(this, magical, here, is, want, I, so, live, place, that, to)
➡ _____

Conversation

① **경험 묻기**

> **A** Have you ever traveled to another country? 다른 나라로 여행 가 본 적 있니?
>
> **B** Yes, I have. It was a wonderful experience. 응. 있어. 그것은 멋진 경험이었어.

- 'Have you ever+과거분사 ~?'는 '너는 ~해 본 적 있니?'의 뜻으로, 상대방에게 경험을 묻는 표현으로 ever 다음에는 동사의 과거분사형을 써야 한다. 보통 before나 ever 등의 부사가 자주 함께 사용된다. 상대방에게 경험을 묻는 질문을 되물을 때는 Have you?만 써서 물을 수 있다.

- 'Have you ever+과거분사 ~?'로 물었을 때 'Yes, I have.'로 응답하는 경우 구체적인 설명을 덧붙이면 좋다. 해 본 적이 없으면 'No, I haven't.'로 답한다.

경험을 물어보는 표현들

- Have you (ever) 과거분사 ~? 너는 ~해 본 적 있니?
- Do you have any experience of 동명사 ~? 너는 ~해 본 경험이 있니?

경험을 묻는 말에 답하는 표현

- I have 과거분사 ~. 나는 ~해 본 적이 있어요.
- I have a lot of experience. 나는 경험이 풍부해요.
- I have never 과거분사 ~. 나는 ~해 본 적이 없어요.
- I don't have any experience of ~. 나는 ~해 본 경험이 전혀 없어요.

핵심 Check

1. 다음 우리말과 일치하도록 빈칸에 알맞은 말을 쓰시오.

   (1) **A:** _____ a marathon? (너는 마라톤을 뛰어 본 적 있니?)

      B: Yes, I have. (응, 있어.)

   (2) **A:** Do you have any experience of meeting a famous actor?

      (너는 유명한 배우를 만나 본 경험이 있니?)

      B: No, _____. (아니, 난 전에 유명한 배우를 만나 본 적이 전혀 없어.)

2. 대화의 순서를 바르게 배열하시오.

   (A) I hope you have a chance to do that some time.

   (B) No, I haven't.

   (C) Have you been to Africa before?

   ➡ _____

2 만족이나 불만족에 대해 묻기

A How do you like this shirt? 이 셔츠가 마음에 드니?

B It's colorful. I like it. 그것은 색이 화려하구나. 마음에 들어.

■ 'How do you like ~?'는 어떤 것에 대한 만족이나 불만족에 대해 물을 때 사용하며 '~는 어떠니?'라는 의미이다. 유사한 표현으로 'What do you think of[about] ~?', 'What is your opinion of[on] ~?' 등의 표현을 사용한다.

■ 'What do you think of[about] ~?'의 경우 우리말로 '어떻게'라는 말이 들어간다고 What 대신 How를 쓰지 않도록 유의한다.

■ 과거의 경험에 대한 의견을 물을 때는 'How did you like ~?'라고 한다. 묻는 사람이 상대방의 경험에 대해 알고자 할 때 쓰는 표현으로 '~가 어땠니?'라는 의미이다. 'How was ~?'로 바꾸어 쓸 수 있다.

> **만족이나 불만족에 대해 묻기**
>
> • How do you like ~? ~는 어떠니?
>
> • How is ~? ~는 어떠니?

■ 'How do you like ~?'의 대답으로 긍정의 경우에는 'Great!'이나 'Terrific!' 등으로, 부정의 대답은 'It was terrible.'이나 'It was not so good.' 등으로 할 수 있다.

✎ 핵심 Check

3. 다음 우리말과 일치하도록 빈칸에 알맞은 말을 쓰시오.

(1) A: _____ as your present? (너의 선물로 이 책 어떠니?)

　　 B: It is wonderful. (훌륭해.)

(2) A: _____ (영화 어땠어?)

　　 B: It was great. I love the scene with the festival. (매우 좋았어. 나는 축제 장면이 정말 좋았어.)

4. 다음 대화에서 <u>어색한</u> 부분을 찾아 바르게 고치시오.

　 A: What did you like the dance festival?

　 B: It was really nice.

➡ _____

A. Listen & Speak 1 B-1

G: ❶You look excited, Inho. ❷What's up?

B: I'm going to Jejudo with my family this weekend. ❸Have you ever been there?

G: Yes, ❹many times. I love the coastline. How about you?

B: It'll be my first visit to Jejudo. ❺I can't wait for this weekend!

G: 인호야, 너 신나 보인다. 무슨 일이니?

B: 이번 주말에 가족들과 함께 제주도에 가거든. 넌 가 본 적 있니?

G: 응. 여러 번 가 봤어. 나는 그 해안선을 좋아해. 너는 어떠니?

B: 난 이번이 제주도 첫 방문이야. 이번 주말이 빨리 왔으면 좋겠다!

❶ look+형용사: ~하게 보이다 excited: 신난

❷ 상대방이 신난 이유를 'What's up?'으로 물어보고 있다.

❸ 'Have you ever+과거분사 ~?'는 '너는 ~ 해 본 적 있니?'의 뜻으로, 상대방에게 경험을 묻는 표현이다.

❹ many times 앞에 I have been there가 생략되어 있다.

❺ 'I can't wait for ~.'는 원하던 일이 다가오고 있어 빨리하고 싶은 기대감을 나타내는 표현이며, '~하는 것을 기다릴 수 없다' 또는 '당장 ~하고 싶다, 빨리 ~했으면 좋겠다' 정도로 해석한다.

Check(√) True or False

(1) The girl has never been to Jejudo.　　　　T ☐ F ☐

(2) The boy will go to Jejudo this weekend.　　　T ☐ F ☐

B. Listen & Speak 2 B-1

G: ❶How was your vacation?

B: Great. I went to Dokdo with my family.

G: ❷How did you like it?

B: It was ❸amazing. I want to visit ❹there again.

G: 방학 잘 보냈니?

B: 좋았어. 가족과 함께 독도에 다녀왔어.

G: 어땠어?

B: 굉장했어. 다시 한 번 가 보고 싶어.

❶ 'How was ~?'는 묻는 사람이 상대방의 의견에 대해 알고자 할 때 쓰는 표현으로 '~가 어땠니?'라는 의미이다. 'How did you like ~?'로 바꾸어 쓸 수 있다.

❷ 'How do you like ~?'는 어떤 것에 대해 만족하는지를 물을 때 사용하며 '~는 어떠니?'라는 의미이다. 유사한 표현으로 'What do you think of[about] ~?', 'What is your opinion of[on] ~?' 등의 표현을 사용한다.

❸ amazing: 굉장한, 놀라운

❹ there는 장소 부사로 여기서는 Dokdo를 나타낸다.

Check(√) True or False

(3) The boy went to Dokdo with his family.　　　T ☐ F ☐

(4) The boy wants to visit Dokdo again.　　　　T ☐ F ☐

Listen & Speak 1 A

B: ❶Have you ever tried Spanish food?

G: ❷Yes, I have. It's really ❸tasty.

❶ Have you ever+과거분사 ~?: 너는 ~해 본 적 있니?
❷ 'Yes, I have tried Spanish food.'가 원래의 문장으로, 경험을 묻는 질문에 긍정으로 답할 때는 보통 질문과 중복되는 부분은 생략하고 'Yes, I have.'로 답한다.
❸ tasty: 맛있는

Listen & Speak 1 B-2

B: ❶Have you ever watched the sun rise over the ocean?

G: ❷No. ❸How about you?

B: ❹I watched the sun rise in Gangneung on New Year's Day. It was great.

G: I ❺tried several times, but I just couldn't ❻ wake up early ❼enough.

❶ Have you ever+과거분사 ~?: 너는 ~해 본 적 있니?
❷ 'No, I haven't watched the sun rise over the ocean.'이 원래의 문장으로 질문과 중복되는 부분은 생략되었다.
❸ 경험을 묻는 질문을 되물을 때 사용하는 'Have you?'를 'How about you?' 대신에 사용해도 된다.
❹ 'on New Year's Day'가 과거의 시점이므로 'watched'라고 동사의 과거형을 사용하였다. New Year's Day는 날짜 관련 표현이므로 날짜 앞에 쓰는 전치사 on을 사용하였다.
❺ try: 시도하다
❻ wake up: 잠에서 깨다
❼ enough: ~할 만큼 (충분히)

Listen & Speak 2 A

G: ❶How do you like your new house?

B: ❷It's great. I have a bigger room now.

❶ 'How do you like ~?'는 어떤 것에 대한 만족이나 불만족에 대해 물을 때 사용하며 '~는 어떠니?'라는 의미이다.
❷ It은 앞에서 나온 'my new house'를 가리킨다.

Listen & Speak 2 B-2

B: ❶Have you been to the new Chinese restaurant?

G: ❷Yes. ❸I had dinner there last Saturday.

B: ❹How did you like it?

G: The ❺service was bad. I ❻won't go back there again.

❶ 어떤 장소에 다녀온 적이 있는지 경험을 물어볼 때는, 'Have you gone ~?'이 아닌 'Have you been (to) ~?'의 표현을 사용하는 것에 유의해야 한다.
❷ 경험을 묻는 질문에 긍정으로 답할 때 'Yes, I have.'로 대답할 수 있다. 'I have'가 생략되어 있다.
❸ 'last Saturday(지난주 토요일)'가 과거를 나타내는 부사구로, 과거동사 'had'를 사용하였다.
❹ 여기서 it은 앞에 나온 the new Chinese restaurant을 의미하고, 'How did you like it?'은 새로 생긴 중국 음식점에 대해 어떻게 생각하는지를 묻는 표현이다.
❺ service: 서비스
❻ won't = will not

Real-Life Zone

B: ❶Have you ever traveled abroad, Sujin?

G: Yes, I went to Cambodia last summer.

B: Wow. ❷How did you like it?

G: It was really hot, but I enjoyed the trip.

B: Tell me some ❸interesting experiences you had during the trip.

G: Hmm... ❹let me think. I ate fried spiders!

B: What? ❺You're kidding. ❻How did you like them?

G: They were really big, so I was a little ❼scared at first. But the taste was okay.

B: Really? I cannot ❽imagine eating spiders.

❶ Have you ever+과거분사 ~?: 너는 ~해 본 적 있니? abroad: 해외에
❷ 과거의 일에 대해 만족하는지를 물을 때 'How did you like ~?'로 표현한다.
❸ interesting은 동사 'interest(흥미를 갖게 하다)'에서 파생된 현재분사형 형용사로 '흥미로운'의 뜻이다.
❹ 대화 중에 질문을 받았을 때, 생각할 시간이 필요하면 'Let me think'나 'Let me see'를 말할 수 있다
❺ 'You're kidding.'은 '설마, 농담이지.'라는 뜻으로, 상대방이 방금 한 말이 믿기지 않아서 놀람을 나타낼 때 쓰는 표현이다.
❻ How did you like ~?: ~는 어땠어?
❼ scared 겁먹은, 무서워하는 at first: 처음에는
❽ imagine: 상상하다

● 다음 우리말과 일치하도록 빈칸에 알맞은 말을 쓰시오.

Listen & Speak 1 A

B: _____ _____ _____ tried Spanish food?

G: Yes, I _____ . It's really _____ .

Listen & Speak 1 B

1. G: You _____ excited, Inho. What's up?

   B: I'm _____ to Jejudo _____ my family this weekend. _____ you ever _____ there?

   G: Yes, many times. I love the _____ . How about you?

   B: It'll be my first visit to Jejudo. I _____ wait _____ this weekend!

2. B: _____ you _____ watched the sun _____ over the ocean?

   G: No. How about you?

   B: I _____ the sun rise in Gangneung _____ New Year's Day. It was great.

   G: I _____ several times, but I just couldn't _____ up _____ enough.

Listen & Speak 1 C

1. A: _____ _____ _____ traveled to another country?

   B: Yes, I have. It was a wonderful _____ .

2. A: Have _____ _____ _____ a horse?

   B: Yes, I have. It was a wonderful _____ .

Listen & Speak 2 A

G: _____ _____ _____ like your new house?

B: It's great. I have a _____ room now.

해석

B: 스페인 음식을 먹어 본 적 있니?
G: 응, 먹어 봤어. 매우 맛있어.

1. G: 인호야, 너 신나 보인다. 무슨 일이니?
   B: 이번 주말에 가족들과 함께 제주도에 가거든. 넌 가 본 적 있니?
   G: 응. 여러 번 가 봤어. 나는 그 해안선을 좋아해. 너는 어떠니?
   B: 난 이번이 제주도 첫 방문이야. 이번 주말이 빨리 왔으면 좋겠다!

2. B: 바다 위로 해가 뜨는 것을 본 적 있니?
   G: 아니. 너는?
   B: 나는 새해 첫날에 강릉에서 해돋이를 봤어. 멋지더라.
   G: 나는 몇 번 시도해 봤는데 일찍 일어나지 못했어.

1. A: 다른 나라로 여행 가 본 적 있니?
   B: 응, 있어. 그것은 멋진 경험이었어.

2. A: 말을 타 본 적 있니?
   B: 응, 있어. 그것은 멋진 경험이었어.

G: 새 집은 어때?
B: 좋아. 나는 이제 더 큰 방을 가졌어.

Listen & Speak 2 B

1. **G:** _____ was your _____?

   B: Great. I _____ to Dokdo with my family.

   G: _____ _____ you like it?

   B: It was _____. I want to visit there again.

2. **B:** _____ _____ _____ _____ the new Chinese restaurant?

   G: Yes. I _____ dinner there last Saturday.

   B: _____ _____ _____ like it?

   G: The service was bad. I _____ go back there again.

Listen & Speak 2 C

1. **A:** _____ do you like this shirt?

   B: It's _____. I like it.

2. **A:** How _____ _____ _____ your ice cream?

   B: It's _____. I like it.

Real-Life Zone A

B: _____ _____ _____ _____ _____ _____, Sujin?

G: Yes, I _____ to Cambodia last summer.

B: Wow. _____ did you like it?

G: It was really hot, but I _____ the trip.

B: Tell me some _____ experiences you _____ during the trip.

G: Hmm... _____ me think. I ate _____ spiders!

B: What? You're kidding. _____ did you _____ _____?

G: They were really big, _____ I was a little _____ _____ _____. But the taste was okay.

B: Really? I cannot _____ eating spiders.

Communication Task

A: _____ _____ _____ _____ tacos?

B: Yes, I have. They were _____.

  / No, I _____. I want to _____ some someday.

해석

1. G: 방학 잘 보냈니?
   B: 좋았어. 가족과 함께 독도에 다녀
   왔어.
   G: 어땠어?
   B: 굉장했어. 다시 한 번 가 보고 싶
   어.

2. B: 새로 생긴 중국 음식점에 가 봤
   니?
   G: 응. 지난주 토요일에 거기서 저녁
   을 먹었어.
   B: 어땠어?
   G: 서비스가 형편없었어. 그곳에 다
   시는 가지 않을 거야.

1. A: 이 셔츠가 마음에 드니?
   B: 그것은 색이 화려하구나. 마음에
   들어.

2. A: 너의 아이스크림은 어떠니?
   B: 그것은 달콤해. 마음에 들어.

B: 수진아 해외여행 가 본 적 있니?
G: 응, 지난여름에 캄보디아에 다녀왔
   어.
B: 와. 여행은 어땠니?
G: 날씨가 너무 더웠지만 여행은 즐거
   웠어.
B: 여행하면서 재미있었던 경험 좀 이야
   기해 줘.
G: 음… 생각 좀 해 볼게. 거미 튀김을
   먹었어!
B: 뭐라고? 진짜로? 거미 튀김은 어땠
   는데?
G: 너무 커서 처음엔 조금 무서웠는데.
   맛은 괜찮았어.
B: 정말? 난 내가 거미를 먹는 걸 상상
   할 수가 없어.

A: 타코를 먹어본 적 있니?
B: 응, 먹어 봤어. 맛있었어.
   / 아니, 안 먹어 봤어. 언젠간 한 번
   먹어 보고 싶어.

[01~02] 다음 대화의 빈칸에 알맞은 것을 고르시오.

01

> B: _____
>
> G: Yes, I have. It's really tasty.

① Did you have tacos?

② How is the new Chinese restaurant?

③ Have you ever traveled to another country?

④ Have you ever tried Spanish food?

⑤ Have you ever seen the picture before?

02

> A: How do you like this song?
>
> B: _____

① I listened to it on my cell phone.　② It's cheerful. I like it.

③ I like pop songs.　④ It was played at the concert.

⑤ Yes, it does. It sounds like a song.

03 대화 순서를 바르게 배열하시오

> (A) Yes, many times. I love the coastline. How about you?
>
> (B) I'm going to Jejudo with my family this weekend. Have you ever been there?
>
> (C) You look excited, Inho. What's up?
>
> (D) It'll be my first visit to Jejudo. I can't wait for this weekend!

➡ _____

04 다음 대화의 밑줄 친 부분과 바꾸어 쓸 수 있는 것을 고르시오.

> G: <u>How did you like it?</u>
>
> B: It was amazing. I want to visit there again.

① What did you do?

② What did you think of it?

③ What was an amazing experience?

④ What do you like?

⑤ What is your view about it?

[01~02] 다음 대화를 읽고 물음에 답하시오.

B: _____
G: No. How about you?
B: I watched the sun rise in Gangneung on New Year's Day. It was great.
G: I tried several times, but I just couldn't wake up early enough.

01 빈칸 (A)에 알맞은 말을 고르시오.

① Have you ever been to Jejudo?
② Have you ever watched the sun rise over the ocean?
③ Have you ever had *tteokguk* on New Year's Day?
④ Have you ever woken up early in the morning?
⑤ Have you ever traveled to another country?

02 위의 대화를 읽고 답할 수 <u>없는</u> 질문은?

① Has the girl watched the sun rise?
② Has the boy watched the sun rise?
③ When did the boy watch the sun rise?
④ How many times has the boy watched the sun rise?
⑤ Where did the boy watch the sun rise?

03 다음 중 짝지어진 대화가 <u>어색한</u> 것은?

① A: How did you like the new movie?
   B: It was okay. The story was good, but the acting was bad.

② A: How was the English test today?
   B: I didn't do well. I was sleepy during the test.
③ A: Have you ever made a pizza?
   B: Yes, I have. I have only eaten it many times.
④ A: Have you ever been to the Mexican food restaurant?
   B: Yes, I have. The food was delicious and the service was good.
⑤ A: How do you like this restaurant?
   B: The food is okay, but the service is terrible.

04 대화의 순서를 바르게 배열한 것을 고르시오.

(A) It was amazing. I want to visit there again.
(B) How did you like it?
(C) How was your vacation?
(D) Great. I went to Dokdo with my family.

① (B) – (A) – (C) – (D)
② (B) – (C) – (A) – (D)
③ (C) – (A) – (B) – (D)
④ (C) – (B) – (A) – (D)
⑤ (C) – (D) – (B) – (A)

[05~06] 다음 대화를 읽고 물음에 답하시오.

B: Have you ___(A)___ to the new Chinese restaurant?
G: Yes. I had dinner there last Saturday.
B: ___(B)___ did you like it?
G: The service was bad. I won't go back there again.

05 빈칸 (A)에 알맞은 말을 고르시오.

① watched ② had ③ went
④ gone ⑤ been

06 빈칸 (B)에 알맞은 것을 고르시오.

① How ② Who ③ When
④ What ⑤ Where

07 다음 대화의 빈칸에 들어갈 말을 〈보기〉에서 골라 순서대로 옳게 배열한 것은?

B: Have you ever traveled abroad, Sujin?
G: _____
B: _____
G: _____
B: _____
G: _____
B: What? You're kidding. How did you like them?
G: They were really big, so I was a little scared at first. But the taste was okay.
B: Really? I cannot imagine eating spiders.

─── 보기 ───
(A) Hmm... let me think. I ate fried spiders!
(B) Wow. How did you like it?
(C) Yes, I went to Cambodia last summer.
(D) It was really hot, but I enjoyed the trip.
(E) Tell me some interesting experiences you had during the trip.

① (B) – (A) – (E) – (D) – (C)
② (B) – (E) – (D) – (A) – (C)
③ (C) – (A) – (B) – (E) – (D)
④ (C) – (B) – (D) – (E) – (A)
⑤ (C) – (D) – (A) – (E) – (B)

[08~09] 다음 대화를 읽고 물음에 답하시오.

G: (A)   was your weekend, Tony?
B: It was great. I went to the International Food Festival with my parents.
G: (B)   food did you try?
B: I had a traditional Chinese dessert, *tangyuan*.
G: (C)   did you like it?
B: I enjoyed it. It's made with sweet rice balls. Chinese people usually serve it to guests at a wedding.

08 빈칸 (A)~(C)에 알맞은 말로 짝지어진 것을 고르시오.

(A)   (B)   (C)
① How – How – How
② How – What – How
③ How – What – What
④ What – How – What
⑤ What – What – How

09 대화의 내용과 일치하지 <u>않는</u> 것을 고르시오.

① Tony는 주말에 탕위안을 먹었다.
② 중국 사람들은 보통 결혼식에서 손님들에게 탕위안을 대접한다.
③ 탕위안은 중국의 전통 후식이다.
④ Tony는 국제 음식 축제에 친구들과 다녀왔다.
⑤ 탕위안은 달콤한 맛이 난다.

[01~03] 다음 대화를 읽고 물음에 답하시오.

G: You look ___(A)___ (excite), Inho. What's up?

B: I'm going to Jejudo with my family this weekend. ⓐ넌 거기 가 본 적 있니?

G: Yes, many times. I love the coastline. How about you?

B: It'll be my first visit to Jejudo. I can't wait ___(B)___ this weekend!

01 빈칸 (A)를 괄호 안의 주어진 단어를 이용하여 채우시오.

➡ _____

02 밑줄 친 ⓐ의 우리말을 주어진 단어를 이용해 영작하시오.

➡ _____

(there, ever)

03 빈칸 (B)에 알맞은 전치사를 쓰시오.

➡ _____

04 괄호 안에 주어진 단어를 알맞게 배열하시오.

G: _____(new, like, how, do, your, you, house)

B: It's great. I have a bigger room now.

➡ _____

[05~06] 다음 대화를 읽고 물음에 답하시오.

A: I have ___(A)___ (ride) a water slide.

B: _____(B)_____

A: It was really exciting. It was faster than I expected.

05 빈칸 (A)를 괄호 안의 주어진 단어를 이용해 채우시오.

➡ _____

06 빈칸 (B)에 적절한 말을 주어진 단어를 이용하여 채우시오.

➡ _____ (like)

[07~08] 다음 대화를 읽고 물음에 답하시오.

B: (A)해외여행 가 본 적 있니(traveled, have, abroad, you, ever), Sujin?

G: Yes, ⓐI have been to Cambodia last summer.

B: Wow. ⓑHow did you like it?

G: It was really hot, but I enjoyed the trip.

B: ⓒTell me some interesting experiences you had during the trip.

G: Hmm... let me think. ⓓI ate fried spiders!

B: What? You're kidding. How did you like them?

G: They were really big, ⓔso I was a little scared at first. But the taste was okay.

B: Really? I cannot imagine eating spiders.

07 괄호 안의 주어진 단어를 알맞게 배열하여 밑줄 친 (A)의 우리말을 영작하시오.

➡ _____

08 ⓐ~ⓔ 중 어법상 어색한 것을 바르게 고치시오.

_____ ➡ _____

Grammar

1 원인과 결과를 나타내는 'so ... that'

> • It was **so** delicious **that** I asked for more. 그것은 너무 맛있어서 나는 더 달라고 했다.

- **형태**: so+형용사/부사+that+주어+동사

  의미: 매우 …해서 (주어가) ~하다

- 'that' 앞의 내용은 원인을 나타내고, 'that' 이하는 결과를 나타내며 'so+형용사/부사+that+주어+동사'의 어순이 된다.

- (원인) Julie is so kind / (결과) that everybody likes her. (Julie는 매우 친절해서 모든 사람이 그녀를 좋아한다.)

- 'so+형용사/부사+that+주어+can+동사원형'은 '형용사/부사+enough+to부정사'로 바꿔 쓸 수 있다.

  • He is **so** rich **that** he **can** buy the building. 그는 매우 부자여서 그 건물을 살 수 있다.

  = He is rich **enough to** buy the building.

- 'so+형용사/부사+that+주어+cannot[can't]+동사원형'은 'too+형용사/부사+to부정사'로 바꿔 쓸 수 있다.

  • She is **so** poor **that** she **can't** buy the house. 그녀는 너무 가난해서 그 집을 살 수 없다.

  = She is **too** poor **to** buy the house.

- 'so that 주어+동사'는 '~하기 위해서'라는 의미로 목적을 나타낸다.

  • She ran fast **so that** she could catch the thief. 그녀는 그 도둑을 잡기 위해서 빨리 뛰었다.

핵심 Check

1. 다음 우리말에 맞게 빈칸에 알맞은 말을 고르시오.

   (1) 바람이 매우 강해서 나는 문을 열 수 없었다.

   ➡ The wind was (too / so) strong that I couldn't open the door.

   (2) 그 반지는 매우 커서 그녀는 그 반지를 낄 수 없었다.

   ➡ The ring was so big (because / that) she couldn't wear it.

② 목적격 관계대명사

• It was from the *khorkhog* **that** she was cooking for us.
그것은 그녀가 우리를 위해 요리하고 있던 호르호그에서 나는 냄새였다.

■ **형태**: 사람 who(m)/that 주어+동사
　　　 사물, 동물 which/that 주어+동사

　 의미: '~하는, ~하고 있는'

■ 목적격 관계대명사는 관계사절에서 선행사가 목적어 역할을 할 때 사용하며 관계사절은 선행사를 '~하는, ~하고 있는'으로 뒤에서 꾸며준다.

　 • She is the doctor **who(m)[that]** I respect. 그녀는 내가 존경하는 의사이다.
　　　　　선행사　　목적격 관계대명사

　 • The cake **which[that]** he made was delicious. 그가 만든 케이크는 맛있었다.
　　　　선행사　　목적격 관계대명사

■ 목적격 관계대명사는 흔히 생략할 수 있다.

　 • She is the girl (**whom**) I told you about. 그녀는 내가 너에게 말했던 소녀야.

　 • This is the book (**which**) I borrowed yesterday. 이것은 내가 어제 빌렸던 책이야.

■ 관계대명사가 전치사의 목적어인 경우 전치사를 빠뜨리지 않는다.

　 • The lady is very considerate. + I always talk about her.

　 → The lady **who** I always talk **about** is very considerate. 내가 항상 이야기하는 그 여성분은 매우 사려 깊다.

■ 목적격 관계대명사는 흔히 생략할 수 있지만 그것이 전치사의 목적어이고 그 전치사가 관계대명사 앞에 위치하는 경우는 생략할 수 없고 선행사가 사람은 'whom', 사물은 'which'를 쓴다.

　 • The girl **with whom** he is talking is Sue. 그가 함께 이야기를 하고 있는 소녀는 Sue이다.

　 • The tent **in which** they lived was very big. 그들이 살고 있는 텐트는 매우 컸다.

핵심 Check

2. 다음 우리말에 맞게 빈칸을 알맞게 채우시오.

(1) 우리가 만난 남자는 배우였다.

➡ The man ＿＿＿＿＿＿ we met was an actor.

(2) 이것은 할머니가 나를 위해 만들어 주신 케이크이다.

➡ This is the cake ＿＿＿＿＿ Grandma made for me.

Grammar 시험대비 기본평가

01 다음 빈칸에 들어갈 말로 알맞지 <u>않은</u> 것은? (2개)

> • This is the author _____ I wanted to meet.

① who ② what ③ that
④ whom ⑤ whose

02 다음 문장에서 어법상 <u>어색한</u> 부분을 바르게 고쳐 쓰시오.

(1) The music is so loud which I cannot sleep.

_____ ➡ _____

(2) The question is very difficult that nobody can answer it.

_____ ➡ _____

(3) The mirror who you broke is my sister's.

_____ ➡ _____

(4) Did you see the book which I left it on the desk?

_____ ➡ _____

03 다음 우리말에 맞게 괄호 안에 주어진 어휘에 한 단어를 추가하여 바르게 배열하시오. (필요하면 어형을 바꿀 것)

(1) 그가 너무 빨리 말해서 나는 그의 말을 이해할 수 없었다. (he, fast, I, him, could not, spoke, that, understand)

➡ _____

(2) Eric이 사고 싶은 자전거는 매우 비싸다. (the bike, wants, expensive, is, to buy, Eric, very)

➡ _____

04 빈칸에 공통으로 들어갈 말로 알맞은 것은?

> • The village _____ I was born in was very small.
> • Julie is so kind _____ everybody likes her.

① which ② who ③ that
④ what ⑤ whom

01 다음 빈칸에 들어갈 수 있는 말이 <u>다른</u> 하나는?

① The man _____ is playing with the dogs is my husband.

② This is the teacher _____ everyone respects.

③ We want to see the movie _____ you chose.

④ I want to eat fruit _____ I grew in my garden.

⑤ I'm looking for the car _____ color is purple.

02 다음 중 어법상 바르지 <u>않은</u> 것은?

① The boy who the teacher is waiting for is my classmate.

② The car which Ms. Kim wants to buy is expensive.

③ This is the dog that I found in the park.

④ He is so strong that he can lift the box.

⑤ He was so young that he can't drive.

03 다음 밑줄 친 부분의 쓰임이 나머지 넷과 <u>다른</u> 하나는?

① The students <u>that</u> she invited couldn't come to the class.

② The vase <u>that</u> you broke is my mom's.

③ The old lady <u>that</u> Jimin helped is my grandmother.

④ This is the cap <u>that</u> I bought last month.

⑤ The computer <u>that</u> makes a lot of noise is Tom's.

04 다음 밑줄 친 that의 성격이 나머지 넷과 <u>다른</u> 것은?

① It is surprising <u>that</u> he knows the answer.

② I asked my mom to buy me a dress <u>that</u> I wanted to wear.

③ This is the pig <u>that</u> my grandfather raises.

④ It is the question <u>that</u> nobody solved.

⑤ This is the movie <u>that</u> we produced.

서답형
05 주어진 어휘를 이용하여 다음 우리말을 영어로 쓰시오.

> 그 의자는 매우 편안해서 그녀는 잠이 들었다.
> (comfortable, fell, asleep)

➡ _____

서답형
06 다음 괄호 안에서 알맞은 말을 고르시오.

(1) I will join the camp (which / who) I have been interested in.

(2) Penguins are birds (who / which) cannot fly.

(3) Look at the boy and his dog (that / which) are running.

(4) The boxes which you placed on the table (is / are) very heavy.

(5) She spoke so (clear / clearly) that I could understand her.

(6) She is (so / enough) tall that she can reach the ceiling.

07 다음 중 생략할 수 있는 것을 찾아 쓰시오.

(1) He teaches me the things that I never knew before.

➡ _____

(2) I have seen the boy who is wearing a blue jacket.

➡ _____

08 다음 중 어법상 어색한 문장을 고르시오.

① Diana was too young to be a driver.

② The car is too expensive for us to buy.

③ This book is enough easy for your kids to understand.

④ She's so wise that she doesn't make any trouble.

⑤ This juice is so cold that I can't drink it.

09 다음 중 어법상 올바른 문장을 고르시오.

① Is he enough strong to lift it?

② The dinner yesterday was too awful to eat it.

③ This watch is so expensive that I can't buy.

④ The box is so heavy that we can't carry it.

⑤ I got up too late that I couldn't have breakfast this morning.

10 밑줄 친 부분을 생략할 수 있으면 O표, 그렇지 않으면 X표를 하시오.

(1) This is all that I can give you. ( )

(2) Do you know the girl who is singing loudly? ( )

(3) I lost the watch of which my father was fond. ( )

(4) Jin is a student who everyone likes. ( )

(5) I want smartphone apps that translate English sentences into Korean. ( )

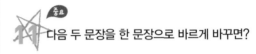
다음 두 문장을 한 문장으로 바르게 바꾸면?

• The woman is a famous writer.
• You met her at Dan's party.

① The woman is a famous writer who you met her at Dan's party.

② The woman who you met at Dan's party is a famous writer.

③ The woman who you met her at Dan's party is a famous writer.

④ The woman is a famous writer that you met her at Dan's party.

⑤ The woman whose you met at Dan's party is a famous writer.

12 다음 괄호 안에 주어진 어구들을 바르게 배열하여 문장을 완성하시오.

• She is wearing (which, the wedding dress, left, her mother) her.

➡ _____
_____

13 우리말에 맞게 괄호 안의 어휘를 바르게 배열하시오.

그는 매우 일찍 일어나서 아침 내내 졸렸다. (he, early, that, he, sleepy, got up, so, was, all morning)

➡ _____

서답형

14 다음 그림을 보고 괄호 안에 주어진 어휘를 이용하여 빈칸을 알맞게 채우시오.

➡ The _____ _____ so heavy _____ the man _____ carry _____. (bag)

서답형

15 다음 두 문장이 같은 뜻이 되도록 빈칸에 알맞은 말을 쓰시오.

(1) They are too strong for us to defeat.
　　→ They are so strong that _____ _____ defeat _____.

(2) She was so slow that she couldn't win the race.
　　→ She was _____ _____ _____ _____ the race.

(3) Sean was so cute that I could fall in love with him.
　　→ Sean was _____ _____ for me _____ fall in love with.

중요

16 주어진 문장의 밑줄 친 부분과 동일한 역할을 하는 것을 고르시오.

• Every doctor that I've ever seen is kind.

① That is my house.
② That book is mine.
③ I think that she can take care of you.
④ This is the movie that I am interested in.
⑤ That she went out with James is not true.

17 다음 중 주어진 문장의 밑줄 친 ~~that~~과 쓰임이 같은 것은?

• The advice that he gave me was useful.

① Do you know the girl that is dancing on the stage?
② That is not similar with me.
③ I knew that she was there yesterday.
④ That you're doing very well is true.
⑤ The book that I bought is not the best seller.

중요

18 빈칸에 들어갈 말을 순서대로 바르게 연결한 것은?

• My house is _____ small for all of us to live in together.
• My house is _____ small that all of us can't live in together.

① too – enough
② so – enough
③ too – so
④ enough – so
⑤ so – too

서답형

19 관계대명사를 이용하여 만든 다음 문장을 원래의 두 문장으로 쓰시오.

(1) The boy band that I like most is BTS.
　　➡ _____

(2) This is the picture which I took three days ago.
　　➡ _____

(3) I know some people who work for Google.
　　➡ _____

01 다음 두 문장을 관계대명사를 이용하여 한 문장으로 연결하시오. (that을 사용하지 말 것)

(1) • The story was surprising.
  • She told me the story.

  ➡ _____

(2) • This is the money.
  • I really need it.

  ➡ _____

(3) • I have a friend.
  • She lives in Canada.

  ➡ _____

(4) • This is the movie.
  • It has a sad ending.

  ➡ _____

(5) • I met a person.
  • Her hobby is mountain climbing.

  ➡ _____

02 다음 문장에서 관계대명사가 생략된 곳에 써넣으시오. (필요하면 be동사도 추가할 것)

(1) This is the apartment she lives in.

  ➡ _____

(2) I like the jacket my wife bought for me.

  ➡ _____

(3) Aladdin is the movie I like best.

  ➡ _____

(4) Look at the cloud floating in the sky.

  ➡ _____

03 다음 두 문장의 뜻이 같도록 빈칸에 알맞은 말을 쓰시오.

(1) I am too young to take care of myself.
  → I am _____ young _____ _____ _____ take care of myself.

(2) The book that I bought yesterday is hard to read.
  → The book _____ I bought yesterday is hard to read.

04 잘못된 부분을 바르게 고쳐 문장을 다시 쓰시오.

(1) The boy has no toys with that he can play.

  ➡ _____
  _____

(2) He is the mechanic which I want to introduce to you.

  ➡ _____
  _____

(3) The girls who I took care of was my nieces.

  ➡ _____
  _____

(4) The pen that I'm writing is Mike's.

  ➡ _____
  _____

(5) Everything what I told you was true.

  ➡ _____
  _____

05 다음 그림을 보고 주어진 어휘를 이용하여 문장의 빈칸에 알맞은 말을 쓰시오.

(1) (cook, well)

• My mother _____ _____ _____

_____ everybody loves her food.

(2) (run, fast)

• Kelly _____ _____ _____

_____ no one can win her in a race.

(3) (smart, get)

• He is _____ _____ _____ _____

always _____ A in math.

06 다음은 "Can You Guess What It Is?" 퀴즈 문제이다. 빈칸에 적절한 말을 써 넣어 퀴즈 문제를 완성하시오.

(1)
1. It is something _____ _____

_____. (3 points)

2. Its color is white. (2 points)

3. It comes from cows. (1 point)

→ Answer: milk

(2)

1. It is _____ _____ _____

_____. (3 points)

2. It is usually written in European countries. (2 points)

3. Mozart and Bach are the most well-known composers of it. (1 point)

→ Answer: classical music

⭐ 중요

07 다음 우리말을 주어진 어휘를 이용하여 영어로 옮기시오.

(1) 나는 매우 피곤해서 더 이상 일을 할 수 없었다. (tired, that, work, any more)

➡ _____

(2) 그 고양이는 너무 조용히 움직여서 아무도 그것을 눈치채지 못했다. (move, quietly, no one, notice)

➡ _____

(3) 그 계단은 매우 높고 가팔라서 나는 어지러움을 느꼈다. (stairs, high and steep, feel, dizzy)

➡ _____

🏠 고난이도

08 다음 중 어법상 <u>어색한</u> 것을 바르게 고쳐 다시 쓰시오.

(1) This game console is so small that you can take anywhere.

➡ _____

_____

(2) The bags are too heavy for you to carry them to the airport.

➡ _____

_____

Reading

A Trip to Mongolia

This year, I had a special summer <u>because</u> I visited Mongolia for the
= as
first time. My friend Altan <u>is from</u> Mongolia. His grandmother invited
= comes from
me to <u>Ulaanbaatar, the capital of Mongolia.</u>
동격

After a <u>four-hour</u> flight from Seoul, Altan and I arrived at Chinggis
'숫자+단위 명사'가 하나의 낱말로 형용사처럼 쓰일 경우에 하이픈으로 연결
Khaan International Airport in Ulaanbaatar. It took thirty minutes

by taxi from the airport to Altan's grandmother's house.
교통, 통신 수단을 나타낼 때: by+무관사 명사
Her house is a *ger*, <u>a traditional Mongolian house.</u> It is a big tent,
동격
but it is cozy inside. When we entered, <u>something</u> <u>smelled</u> <u>wonderful</u>.
S   V   C
It was from the *khorkhog* <u>that</u> she was cooking for us. *Khorkhog* is a
목적격 관계대명사
Mongolian barbecue. It is <u>made of</u> lamb and cooked with hot stones.
수동태(be동사+pp): ~로 만들어지다
I was <u>moved</u> when Altan said Mongolians serve *khorkhog* to special
= touched
guests. It was <u>so</u> delicious <u>that</u> I asked for more. After dinner, Altan
매우 …해서 ~하다
and I went outside <u>to see</u> the night sky. The sky was <u>full of</u> bright stars.
to부정사의 부사적 용법(목적)   ~로 가득했다
I <u>felt like</u> I was in a magical place.
~인 것처럼 느꼈다

capital: 수도
flight: 비행
arrive: 도착하다
airport: 공항
Mongolian: 몽골의; 몽골 사람
barbecue: 바비큐
lamb: 양고기
moved: 감동한
guest: 손님
magical: 마법의, 신비한

확인문제

● 다음 문장이 본문의 내용과 일치하면 T, 일치하지 <u>않으면</u> F를 쓰시오.

1 Altan comes from Mongolia. ☐

2 Altan's parents invited the writer to Ulaanbaatar, the capital of Mongolia. ☐

3 It took four hours by plane from Seoul to Chinggis Khaan International Airport in
   Ulaanbaatar. ☐

4 A ger is a modern Mongolian house. ☐

5 *Khorkhog* is a Mongolian barbecue. ☐

6 *Khorkhog* is made of beef and cooked with hot stones. ☐

During the next three days, Altan showed me around and helped me
during+특정 기간을 나타내는 명사   (목적어)가 ~하도록 돕다

experience Mongolian culture. Every moment was fun and exciting,

but I had the most fun when I rode a camel in the Gobi Desert. At first,
　　　　형용사(much)의 최상급   처음에

I was scared because the camel was taller than I expected. But once
　　　　　　　　　　　　　　　형용사의 비교급+than   ~하자마자(접속사)

I sat on its back, I soon got used to its movement. From the camel's
　　　　　　　　　　　　get used to: ~에 익숙해지다

back, the view of the desert was truly amazing.
　　　　　　　　　　　　감정을 나타내는 동사는 감정을 유발할 때 현재분사를 쓰는 것이 적절하다.

My visit to Mongolia was a special experience in many ways. It gave

me a great chance to get to know my friend's country and culture. I
　　　　　　　　　to부정사의 형용사적 용법

want to visit Mongolia again someday!
to부정사의 명사적 용법

experience: 경험	
culture: 문화	
moment: 순간	
fun: 재미있는; 재미	
scared: 겁먹은	
have fun: 재미있게 놀다	
ride: 타다	
camel: 낙타	
expect: 기대하다, 예상하다	
once: ~하자마자	
special: 특별한	
chance: 기회	
get to 원형동사: ~하게 되다	

확인문제

● 다음 문장이 본문의 내용과 일치하면 T, 일치하지 않으면 F를 쓰시오.

1　During the next three days, Altan showed the writer around.　☐

2　The writer didn't like to ride a camel in the Gobi Desert.　☐

3　The writer was scared because the camel was taller than the writer expected.　☐

4　The writer couldn't get used to the camel's movement.　☐

5　From the camel's back, the view of the desert was truly amazing.　☐

6　The writer's visit to Mongolia was a terrible experience in many ways.　☐

● 우리말을 참고하여 빈칸에 알맞은 말을 쓰시오.

1 A _____ to Mongolia

2 This year, I had a special summer because I visited Mongolia _____ _____ _____ _____.

3 My friend Altan _____ _____ Mongolia.

4 His grandmother _____ me _____ Ulaanbaatar, the capital of Mongolia.

5 After _____ _____ _____ from Seoul, Altan and I _____ _____ Chinggis Khaan International Airport in Ulaanbaatar.

6 _____ _____ thirty minutes _____ _____ from the airport to Altan's grandmother's house.

7 Her house is a *ger*, a _____ Mongolian house.

8 It is a big tent, but it is _____ _____.

9 When we entered, something _____ _____.

10 It was _____ the *khorkhog* that she was _____ _____ us.

11 *Khorkhog* is a _____ _____.

12 It _____ _____ _____ lamb and cooked _____ hot stones.

13 I _____ _____ when Altan said Mongolians _____ *khorkhog* _____ special guests.

1 몽골 여행

2 나는 올해 몽골을 처음으로 방문해서 특별한 여름을 보냈다.

3 내 친구 알탕은 몽골 출신이다.

4 그의 할머니께서는 몽골의 수도인 울란바토르에 나를 초대하셨다.

5 서울에서 네 시간 비행 후 알탕과 나는 울란바토르의 칭기즈 칸 국제공항에 도착했다.

6 공항에서 알탕의 할머니 댁까지 택시로 30분이 걸렸다.

7 할머니의 집은 몽골 전통 가옥인 게르이다.

8 큰 텐트이지만 내부는 아늑하다.

9 우리가 들어갔을 때, 뭔가 좋은 냄새가 났다.

10 그녀가 우리를 위해 요리하고 있던 호르호그에서 나는 냄새였다.

11 호르호그는 몽골식 바비큐이다.

12 그것은 양고기로 만들어졌으며 뜨거운 돌로 요리되었다.

13 나는 알탕이 몽골인들은 특별한 손님에게 호르호그를 대접한다고 말했을 때 감동을 받았다.

14 It was _____ delicious _____ I asked for more.

15 After dinner, Altan and I _____ _____ to see the night sky.

16 The sky _____ _____ _____ bright stars.

17 I _____ _____ I was in a magical place.

18 _____ the next three days, Altan _____ _____ _____

and helped me experience Mongolian culture.

19 Every moment was fun and exciting, but I _____ _____

_____ _____ when I rode a camel in the Gobi Desert.

20 _____ _____, I was scared because the camel was _____

_____ I expected.

21 But _____ I sat on its back, I soon _____ _____ _____

its movement.

22 From the camel's back, _____ _____ _____ _____

_____ was truly amazing.

23 My visit to Mongolia was a special experience _____ _____

_____.

24 It gave me a great chance _____ _____ _____ _____

my friend's country and culture.

25 I want to visit Mongolia _____ _____!

14 그것은 너무 맛있어서 나는 더 달라고 했다.

15 저녁 식사 후, 알탕과 나는 밤하늘을 보기 위해 밖으로 나갔다.

16 하늘은 밝은 별들로 가득했다.

17 나는 신비한 장소에 있는 것처럼 느꼈다.

18 그 후 3일 동안, 알탕은 나를 구경시켜 주었고 몽골 문화를 경험할 수 있게 도와주었다.

19 매 순간이 재미있고 흥미진진했지만, 고비 사막에서 낙타를 탈 때가 가장 재미있었다.

20 처음에는 내가 예상했던 것보다 낙타의 키가 커서 무서웠다.

21 그러나 낙타 등에 앉자 곧 움직임에 익숙해졌다.

22 낙타의 등에서 보는 사막의 경치는 정말로 놀라웠다.

23 내가 몽골을 방문한 것은 여러 면에서 특별한 경험이었다.

24 내 친구의 나라와 문화를 알 수 있는 좋은 기회가 되었다.

25 나는 언젠가 몽골을 다시 방문하고 싶다!

● 우리말을 참고하여 본문을 영작하시오.

1 몽골 여행

➡ _____

2 나는 올해 몽골을 처음으로 방문해서 특별한 여름을 보냈다.

➡ _____

3 내 친구 알탕은 몽골 출신이다.

➡ _____

4 그의 할머니께서는 몽골의 수도인 울란바토르에 나를 초대하셨다.

➡ _____

5 서울에서 네 시간 비행 후 알탕과 나는 울란바토르의 칭기즈 칸 국제공항에 도착했다.

➡ _____

6 공항에서 알탕의 할머니 댁까지 택시로 30분이 걸렸다.

➡ _____

7 할머니의 집은 몽골 전통 가옥인 게르이다.

➡ _____

8 큰 텐트이지만 내부는 아늑하다.

➡ _____

9 우리가 들어갔을 때, 뭔가 좋은 냄새가 났다.

➡ _____

10 그녀가 우리를 위해 요리하고 있던 호르호그에서 나는 냄새였다.

➡ _____

11 호르호그는 몽골식 바비큐이다.

➡ _____

12 그것은 양고기로 만들어졌으며 뜨거운 돌로 요리되었다.

➡ _____

13 나는 알탕이 몽골인들은 특별한 손님에게 호르호그를 대접한다고 말했을 때 감동을 받았다.

➡ _____

14 그것은 너무 맛있어서 나는 더 달라고 했다.

➡ _____

15 저녁 식사 후, 알탕과 나는 밤하늘을 보기 위해 밖으로 나갔다.

➡ _____

16 하늘은 밝은 별들로 가득했다.

➡ _____

17 나는 신비한 장소에 있는 것처럼 느꼈다.

➡ _____

18 그 후 3일 동안, 알탕은 나를 구경시켜 주었고 몽골 문화를 경험할 수 있게 도와주었다.

➡ _____

19 매 순간이 재미있고 흥미진진했지만, 고비 사막에서 낙타를 탈 때가 가장 재미있었다.

➡ _____

20 처음에는 내가 예상했던 것보다 낙타의 키가 커서 무서웠다.

➡ _____

21 그러나 낙타 등에 앉자 곧 움직임에 익숙해졌다.

➡ _____

22 낙타의 등에서 보는 사막의 경치는 정말로 놀라웠다.

➡ _____

23 내가 몽골을 방문한 것은 여러 면에서 특별한 경험이었다.

➡ _____

24 내 친구의 나라와 문화를 알 수 있는 좋은 기회가 되었다.

➡ _____

25 나는 언젠가 몽골을 다시 방문하고 싶다!

➡ _____

[01~04] 다음 글을 읽고 물음에 답하시오.

This year, I had a special summer because I visited Mongolia for the first time. My friend Altan is ___ⓐ___ Mongolia. His grandmother invited me ___ⓑ___ Ulaanbaatar, the capital of Mongolia.

ⓒ서울에서 네 시간 비행 후, Altan and I arrived at Chinggis Khaan International Airport in Ulaanbaatar. ⓓIt took thirty minutes by a taxi from the airport to Altan's grandmother's house.

01 위 글의 빈칸 ⓐ와 ⓑ에 들어갈 전치사가 바르게 짝지어진 것은?

① from – for
② in – for
③ in – at
④ from – to
⑤ for – to

서답형

02 위 글의 밑줄 친 ⓒ의 우리말에 맞게 주어진 어휘를 이용하여 6 단어로 영작하시오.

> flight, from

➡ _____

서답형

03 위 글의 밑줄 친 ⓓ에서 어법상 틀린 부분을 찾아 고치시오.

_____ ➡ _____

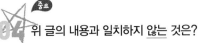

04 위 글의 내용과 일치하지 않는 것은?

① This year, the writer visited Mongolia for the first time.
② Altan's mother invited the writer to Ulaanbaatar.
③ Ulaanbaatar is the capital of Mongolia.

④ It took four hours by plane from Seoul to Chinggis Khaan International Airport.
⑤ After a thirty-minute taxi ride from the airport, Altan and the writer arrived at Altan's grandmother's house.

[05~07] 다음 글을 읽고 물음에 답하시오.

Her house is a *ger*, a traditional Mongolian house. ⓐIt is a big tent, but it is cozy inside. When we entered, something smelled wonderful. ⓑ그녀가 우리를 위해 요리하고 있던 호르호그에서 나는 냄새였다. *Khorkhog* is a Mongolian barbecue. It is made of lamb and cooked with hot stones. I was moved when Altan said Mongolians serve *khorkhog* to special guests. ⓒIt was so delicious that I asked for more. After dinner, Altan and I went outside to see the night sky. ⓓThe sky was full of bright stars. I felt like I was in a magical place.

서답형

05 위 글의 밑줄 친 ⓐIt과 ⓒIt이 가리키는 것을 본문에서 각각 찾아 쓰시오.

➡ ⓐ _____ ⓒ _____

서답형

06 위 글의 밑줄 친 ⓑ의 우리말에 맞게 한 단어를 보충하여, 주어진 어휘를 알맞게 배열하시오.

> the *khorkhog* / for us / it / was cooking / was / she / that

➡ _____

서답형

07 위 글의 밑줄 친 ⓓ를 다음과 같이 바꿔 쓸 때 빈칸에 들어갈 알맞은 말을 쓰시오.

➡ The sky was _____ _____ bright stars.

[08~10] 다음 글을 읽고 물음에 답하시오.

During the next three days, Altan showed me around and helped me experience Mongolian culture. Every moment was fun and exciting, but I had the most fun when I rode a camel in the Gobi Desert. At first, I was scared because the camel was taller than I expected. But ⓐonce I sat on its back, I soon got used to its movement. From the camel's back, the view of the desert was truly amazing.

My visit to Mongolia was a special experience in many ways. It gave me a great chance to ___(A)___ know my friend's country and culture. I want to visit Mongolia again someday!

08 위 글의 빈칸 (A)에 들어갈 알맞은 말을 모두 고르시오.

① get to   ② arrive at   ③ reach
④ come to   ⑤ go to

09 위 글의 밑줄 친 ⓐonce와 같은 의미로 쓰인 것을 고르시오.

① I've only been there once.
② There was once a giant.
③ The water is fine once you're in!
④ He cleans his car once a week.
⑤ He once lived in Zambia.

10 위 글의 주제로 알맞은 것을 고르시오.

① how to enjoy every exciting moment
② the scary experience of riding a camel
③ the view of the desert from the camel's back
④ the mystery of the Gobi Desert
⑤ a special experience in Mongolia

[11~12] 다음 글을 읽고 물음에 답하시오.

A Trip to Suncheon

My family took a trip to Suncheon last summer. We visited the National Garden. It was so large that we could not see the whole garden. After three hours' walking, we were really hungry. For dinner, we had Gukbap ⓐthat my parents like. Suncheon is famous for Gukbap and we enjoyed it.

This trip was so good that I would never forget it for a long time.

11 아래 〈보기〉에서 위 글의 밑줄 친 ⓐthat과 문법적 쓰임이 같은 것의 개수를 고르시오.

┌─── 보기 ├───
① Are you mad that you should do such a thing?
② It is natural that he should say so.
③ There's a man that you want to meet.
④ It's true that we were a little late.
⑤ This is the pen that I bought yesterday.
└──────────────

① 1개   ② 2개   ③ 3개   ④ 4개   ⑤ 5개

12 위 글의 내용과 일치하지 않는 것은?

① 글쓴이의 가족은 작년 여름에 순천으로 여행을 갔다.
② 글쓴이의 가족은 순천 국가 정원을 방문했다.
③ 세 시간에 걸쳐 글쓴이의 가족은 국가 정원 전체를 다 볼 수 있었다.
④ 저녁 식사로 글쓴이의 가족은 국밥을 먹었다.
⑤ 순천은 국밥으로 유명하다.

[13~15] 다음 글을 읽고 물음에 답하시오.

(①) This year, I had a special summer because I visited Mongolia for the first time. (②) His grandmother invited me to Ulaanbaatar, the capital of Mongolia. (③) After a four-hour ____ⓐ____ from Seoul, Altan and I arrived at Chinggis Khaan International Airport in Ulaanbaatar. (④) It took thirty minutes by taxi from the airport to Altan's grandmother's house. (⑤)

서답형

13 위 글의 빈칸 ⓐ에 fly를 알맞은 형태로 쓰시오.

➡ _____

14 위 글의 흐름으로 보아 주어진 문장이 들어가기에 가장 적절한 곳은?

My friend Altan is from Mongolia.

①   ②   ③   ④   ⑤

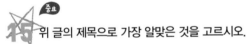 위 글의 제목으로 가장 알맞은 것을 고르시오.

① How to Spend a Summer Vacation
② A Special Summer I Spent in Mongolia
③ Altan, My friend, Is from Mongolia.
④ Let Me Introduce Chinggis Khaan International Airport!
⑤ Altan's Grandmother's House Is Only a Thirty-Minute Taxi Ride Away.

[16~18] 다음 글을 읽고 물음에 답하시오.

Her house is a *ger*, a traditional Mongolian house. It is a big tent, but it is cozy inside. When we entered, something smelled wonderful. It was from the *khorkhog* that she was cooking for us. *Khorkhog* is a Mongolian barbecue. It is made of lamb and cooked with hot stones. I was moved when Altan said Mongolians serve *khorkhog* to special guests. It was ____ⓐ____ delicious ____ⓑ____ I asked for more. After dinner, Altan and I went outside ⓒto see the night sky. The sky was full of bright stars. I felt like I was in a magical place.   *she: Altan's grandmother

서답형

16 위 글의 빈칸 ⓐ와 ⓑ에 들어갈 알맞은 말을 쓰시오.

➡ ⓐ _____   ⓑ _____

17 위 글의 밑줄 친 ⓒto see와 to부정사의 용법이 같은 것을 모두 고르시오. (3개)

① Ann has no one to love her.
② She studied hard to pass the exam.
③ How stupid she was to marry such a man!
④ He promised me to be here at ten o'clock.
⑤ He got up early to catch the first train.

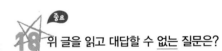 위 글을 읽고 대답할 수 없는 질문은?

① What is a *ger*?
② Who was cooking *khorkhog*?
③ What is *khorkhog* made of?
④ Why is *khorkhog* cooked with hot stones?
⑤ To whom do Mongolians serve *khorkhog*?

[19~22] 다음 글을 읽고 물음에 답하시오.

During the next three days, Altan showed me around and helped me experience Mongolian culture. Every moment was fun and exciting, but I had the most fun when I rode a camel in the Gobi Desert. At first,

I was scared because the camel was taller than I expected. But once I sat on its back, I soon got used to its movement. From the camel's back, the view of the desert was truly amazing.

My visit ___ⓐ___ Mongolia was a special experience ___ⓑ___ many ways. It gave me a great chance to get to know my friend's country and culture. I want to visit Mongolia again someday!

19 위 글의 빈칸 ⓐ와 ⓑ에 들어갈 전치사가 바르게 짝지어진 것은?

① to – in
② in – by
③ in – for
④ for – in
⑤ to – for

20 At first, when the writer rode a camel in the Gobi Desert, why was the writer scared? Fill in the blank with a suitable word.

➡ It was because the camel was _____ than the writer expected.

21 다음 문장에서 위 글의 내용과 <u>다른</u> 부분을 찾아서 고치시오.

> After sitting on the camel's back, the writer couldn't get used to the camel's movement.

_____ ➡ _____

22 위 글의 마지막 부분에서 알 수 있는 'I'의 심경으로 가장 알맞은 것을 고르시오.

① bored
② disappointed
③ satisfied
④ self-confident
⑤ upset

[23~24] 다음 글을 읽고 물음에 답하시오.

A Trip to Ulleungdo

Last summer, my parents and I went to Ulleungdo. Ulleungdo is an island ___ⓐ___ I always wanted to visit. We walked along the road around the island. ⓑ<u>This trip was so great that I would never forget for a long time.</u>

23 위 글의 빈칸 ⓐ에 들어갈 알맞은 말을 <u>모두</u> 고르시오.

① which
② where
③ when
④ that
⑤ what

24 위 글의 밑줄 친 ⓑ에서 어법상 <u>어색한</u> 것을 고치시오.

_____ ➡ _____

[25~26] 다음 글을 읽고 물음에 답하시오.

This is your captain speaking. We ⓐ<u>have just arrived</u> at the airport. Welcome to Mongolia, a country full of the beauty of nature and culture. The time in Ulaanbaatar is now ⓑ4:30 p.m. and there is a chance of rain. We hope you had a nice flight. Thank you for flying with us. We hope to see you again.

25 위 글의 밑줄 친 ⓐhave just arrived와 현재완료의 용법이 같은 것을 <u>모두</u> 고르시오.

① She <u>hasn't washed</u> the dishes yet.
② <u>Have</u> you ever <u>been</u> to Japan?
③ I <u>have</u> never <u>seen</u> a koala before.
④ We <u>have known</u> her for a long time.
⑤ I <u>have</u> already <u>seen</u> it.

26 위 글의 ⓑ의 읽는 법을 영어로 쓰시오.

➡ _____

[01~03] 다음 글을 읽고 물음에 답하시오.

This year, I had a (A)[general / special] summer because I visited Mongolia for the first time. My friend Altan is from Mongolia. His grandmother (B)[invited / visited] me to Ulaanbaatar, the capital of Mongolia.

After a (C)[four-hour / four-hours] flight from Seoul, Altan and I arrived at Chinggis Khaan International Airport in Ulaanbaatar. It took thirty minutes by taxi from the airport to Altan's grandmother's house.

01 위 글의 괄호 (A)~(C)에서 문맥이나 어법상 알맞은 낱말을 골라 쓰시오.

➡ (A) _____ (B) _____ (C) _____

02 How long did it take from Seoul to Chinggis Khaan International Airport in Ulaanbaatar by airplane? Answer in English in a full sentence. (4 words)

➡ _____

03 본문의 내용과 일치하도록 다음 빈칸 (A)와 (B)에 알맞은 단어를 쓰시오.

This summer, the writer visited (A)_____ for the first time. Altan and the writer went to Altan's (B)_____ house.

[04~06] 다음 글을 읽고 물음에 답하시오.

Her house is a *ger*, a traditional Mongolian house. It is a big tent, but it is cozy inside. When we entered, something smelled wonderful. ⓐIt was from the *khorkhog* that she was cooking for us. *Khorkhog* is a Mongolian barbecue. It is made of lamb and cooked with hot stones. I was moved when Altan said Mongolians serve *khorkhog* to special guests. It was so delicious that I asked for more. After dinner, Altan and I went outside to see the night sky. The sky was full of bright stars. I felt like I was in a magical place.   *she: Altan's grandmother

04 위 글에서 주어진 영영풀이에 해당하는 단어를 찾아 쓰시오.

comfortable and warm

➡ _____

05 위 글의 밑줄 친 ⓐIt이 가리키는 내용을 우리말로 쓰시오.

➡ _____

06 본문의 내용과 일치하도록 다음 빈칸 (A)와 (B)에 알맞은 단어를 쓰시오.

Altan's grandmother cooked delicious (A)_____ for Altan and the writer. After eating it, Altan and the writer went outside to see the (B)_____ _____ which was full of bright stars.

[07~09] 다음 글을 읽고 물음에 답하시오.

During the next three days, ⓐAltan showed me around and helped me experience Mongolian culture. Every moment was fun and exciting, but I had the most fun when I rode a camel in the Gobi Desert. At first, ⓑ내가 예상했던 것보다 낙타의 키가 커서 무서웠다. But once I sat on its back, I soon got used to its movement. From the camel's back, the view of the desert was truly amazing.

My visit to Mongolia was a special experience in many ways. ⓒIt gave me a great chance to get to know my friend's country and culture. I want to visit Mongolia again someday!

07 위 글의 밑줄 친 ⓐ를 다음과 같이 바꿔 쓸 때 빈칸에 들어갈 알맞은 말을 쓰시오.

➡ Altan showed me around and helped me _____ _____ Mongolian culture.

08 위 글의 밑줄 친 ⓑ의 우리말에 맞게 한 단어를 보충하여, 주어진 어휘를 알맞게 배열하시오. (I로 시작할 것)

expected / the camel / scared / was / I / because / was / taller / I

➡ _____
_____

09 위 글의 밑줄 친 ⓒit이 가리키는 것을 본문에서 찾아 쓰시오.

➡ _____

[10~12] 다음 글을 읽고 물음에 답하시오.

Her house is a *ger*, a traditional Mongolian house. It is a big tent, but it is cozy inside. When we entered, something smelled wonderful. It was from the *khorkhog* that she was cooking for us. *Khorkhog* is a Mongolian barbecue. It is made of lamb and cooked with hot stones. I ___ⓐ___ when Altan said Mongolians serve *khorkhog* to special guests. It was so delicious that I asked for more. After dinner, Altan and I went outside ⓑto see the night sky. The sky was full of bright stars. I felt like I was in a magical place.

10 위 글의 빈칸 ⓐ에 move를 알맞은 형태로 쓰시오.

➡ _____

11 위 글의 밑줄 친 ⓑ를 다음과 같이 바꿔 쓸 때 빈칸에 들어갈 알맞은 말을 쓰시오.

➡ in order that _____ see the night sky
= _____ we could[might] see the night sky

12 다음 빈칸 (A)와 (B)에 알맞은 단어를 넣어 *ger*에 대한 소개를 완성하시오.

It is a (A)_____ _____ house. Though it is a big tent, it is (B)_____ inside.

Writing Workshop - Step 2

A Trip to Suncheon

My family took a trip to Suncheon last summer. We visited the National
~으로 여행을 갔다

Garden. It was so large that we could not see the whole garden. After three
The National Garden   so ~ that+주어+can't … = too ~ to …: 너무 ~해서 …할 수 없다

hours' walking, we were really hungry. For dinner, we had Gukbap that my
= which(목적격 관계대명사)

parents like. Suncheon is famous for Gukbap and we enjoyed it.
= Gukbap

This trip was so good that I would never forget it for a long time.
= This trip

구문해설 · take a trip: 여행하다 · whole: 전체[전부]의 · be famous for: ~으로 유명하다
· for a long time: 오랫동안

순천으로의 여행

나의 가족은 작년 여름에 순천으로 여행을 갔다. 우리는 순천 국가 정원을 방문했다. 그곳은 너무 넓어서 우리는 정원 전체를 다 볼 수 없었다. 세 시간 동안 걸은 후, 우리는 정말 배가 고팠다. 저녁 식사로 우리는 부모님들이 좋아하시는 국밥을 먹었다. 순천은 국밥으로 유명하고, 우리는 그것을 즐겼다.

이번 여행은 너무 좋아서 나는 오랫동안 그것을 결코 잊지 않을 것이다.

Wrap Up 1-2

G: How was your weekend, Tony?
'~가 어땠니?'라는 의미이다. 'How did you like ~?'로 바꾸어 쓸 수 있다.

B: It was great. I went to the International Food Festival with my parents.
=My weekend

G: What food did you try?
의문 형용사: 어떤, 무슨

B: I had a traditional Chinese dessert, *tangyuan*.
= eat

G: How did you like it?
How did you like ~?: ~는 어땠어?

B: I enjoyed it. It's made with sweet rice balls. Chinese people usually serve it
= tangyuan   be made with: ~로 만들어지다

to guests at a wedding.

구문해설 · traditional: 전통적인 · serve: 제공하다, 대접하다

G: 토니야, 주말 잘 보냈니?
B: 좋았어. 부모님과 함께 국제 음식 축제에 다녀왔어.
G: 무슨 음식 먹어 봤니?
B: 중국 전통 후식인 탕위안을 먹었어.
G: 어땠어?
B: 맛있었어. 그건 달콤하고 동그란 떡으로 만들었어. 중국 사람들은 보통 결혼식에서 손님들에게 이것을 대접해.

Wrap Up 7

How was the restaurant that just opened around the corner?
주격 관계대명사

└ The restaurant was so crowded that I had to wait for an hour to get in.
so+형용사(원인)   that+주어+동사(결과)   부사적 용법(목적)

└ The cheese cake tasted so good that I ate all of it.
=the cheese cake

└ The restaurant was so noisy that I couldn't talk with my friends.

구문해설 · crowed: 붐비는 · get in: ~에 들어가다

모퉁이에 막 오픈한 그 식당은 어땠나요?

└ 그 식당은 매우 붐벼서 나는 안에 들어가기 위해 한 시간 동안 기다려야 했어요.

└ 그 치즈 케이크는 매우 맛있어서 나는 전부 먹어 치웠어요.

└ 그 식당은 매우 시끄러워서 나는 친구와 이야기할 수 없었어요.

01 다음 대화의 빈칸 (A)와 (B)에 들어갈 말로 알맞은 것끼리 짝지어진 것을 고르시오.

> A: Wow! It's a new movie. When did you watch it?
> B: I watched it last Monday.
> A: It looks really interesting. Are you ___(A)___ with it?
> B: No, I am not. It's ___(B)___ .

	(A)	(B)
①	satisfied	interesting
②	satisfied	bored
③	satisfied	boring
④	satisfying	interesting
⑤	satisfying	bored

02 다음 우리말에 맞도록 빈칸에 알맞은 말을 쓰시오.

(1) 이 탁자는 나무로 만들어졌다.
➡ This table _____ of wood.

(2) 박물관 가이드는 우리에게 둘러보도록 안내해 줄 것이다.
➡ The guide at the museum will _____ us _____.

(3) 내 방은 현대식 스타일로 꾸며져 있다.
➡ My room is decorated in a _____ style.

03 빈칸에 알맞은 말을 고르시오.

> Take a look at this picture _____ right to left.

① from　　② for　　③ with
④ in　　⑤ by

04 다음 영영풀이가 나타내는 말을 고르시오.

> an opportunity to do something

① chance　　② experience
③ effort　　④ effect
⑤ purpose

05 다음 대화의 빈칸에 들어갈 말을 고르시오.

> A: Have you _____ won a prize?
> B: Yes, I have.

① always　　② still　　③ yet
④ just　　⑤ ever

[06~08] 다음 대화를 읽고 물음에 답하시오.

> G: How was your weekend, Tony?
> B: It was great. I went to the International Food Festival with my parents.
> G: What food did you try?
> B: I had a traditional Chinese dessert, *tangyuan*.
> G: How did you like it?
> B: I enjoyed it. It's made _____ sweet rice balls. Chinese people usually serve it to guests at a wedding.

06 빈칸에 들어갈 말을 고르시오.

① by　　② about　　③ as
④ for　　⑤ with

07 대화에서 다음 영영풀이에 해당하는 단어를 찾아 쓰시오.

> someone who is invited to visit you

➡ _____

08 위의 대화를 읽고 답할 수 있는 질문을 〈보기〉에서 모두 고르시오.

┌─ 보기 ─
ⓐ Has the girl ever eaten *tangyuan*?
ⓑ Who did Tony go to the International Food Festival with?
ⓒ What is *tangyuan*?
ⓓ Where did Tony go on weekend?
ⓔ What did Tony have at the International Food Festival?

➡ _____

09 대화의 흐름상 어색한 것을 고르시오.

B: ⓐHave you been to the new Chinese restaurant?
G: ⓑNo. I had dinner there last Saturday.
B: ⓒHow did you like it?
G: ⓓThe service was bad. ⓔI won't go back there again.

① ⓐ   ② ⓑ   ③ ⓒ   ④ ⓓ   ⑤ ⓔ

[10~12] 다음 대화를 읽고 물음에 답하시오.

B: Have you ever traveled abroad, Sujin?
G: Yes, I went to Cambodia last summer. (①)
B: Wow. How did you like it?
G: It was really hot, but I enjoyed the trip. (②)
B: Tell me some interesting experiences you had during the trip.
G: Hmm... let me think. (③)

B: What? You're kidding. (④)_____
G: They were really big, so I was a little scared at first. But the taste was okay. (⑤)
B: Really? I cannot imagine eating spiders.

10 ①~⑤ 중 주어진 문장이 들어갈 곳은?

┌──────────────────────┐
│ I ate fried spiders! │
└──────────────────────┘

①   ②   ③   ④   ⑤

11 위 대화의 표현을 이용해 흐름에 맞게 빈칸을 채우시오.

➡ _____

12 대화의 내용과 일치하지 않는 것을 고르시오.

① 수진이가 캄보디아 여행을 갔을 때 날씨가 너무 더웠다.
② 수진이는 해외여행을 간 경험이 있다.
③ 남자아이는 수진이가 거미를 먹는 걸 상상할 수 없었다.
④ 수진이는 지난여름에 캄보디아에 다녀왔다.
⑤ 수진이는 거미 튀김이 맛이 없다고 생각했다.

Grammar

13 다음 괄호 안에서 알맞은 말을 고르시오.

(1) Is it (warm enough / enough warm) to go swimming?
(2) This black tea is (too / so) hot that you can't drink it.
(3) The shoes are too big (to / for) me to wear.

14 주어진 문장의 밑줄 친 that과 용법이 <u>다른</u> 하나는?

> • The cheese cake tasted so good that I ate all of it.

① He studied hard so that he could pass the test.
② The tea is so hot that I can't drink it.
③ She was so beautiful that I couldn't take my eyes off her.
④ This book was so interesting that I read it all day.
⑤ I was so tired that I slept all day.

15 다음 중 어법상 <u>어색한</u> 문장을 고르시오.

① This is the game I really want to play.
② The doctor you visited is my aunt.
③ The song the cellist is playing is Verdi's.
④ The road which he was driving was not safe.
⑤ The woman who is shaking hands with my teacher is my mom.

16 다음 우리말을 주어진 어휘를 이용하여 영어로 옮기시오.

(1) 내가 초대한 소녀들이 나의 생일 파티에 오지 않았다. (girls, invite)

➡ _____

(2) 내가 보고 싶었던 TV 프로그램이 있었다. (there, a TV program, watch)

➡ _____

(3) 네가 먹을 수 있는 쿠키가 좀 있어. (there, some cookies)

➡ _____

(4) 그 가방은 매우 튼튼해서 나는 많은 책을 넣고 다닐 수 있어. (bag, strong, that, a lot of, carry, in)

➡ _____

(5) 나는 매우 바빠서 쇼핑을 갈 수 없었다. (busy, shopping)

➡ _____

(6) 그건 매우 쉬워서 누구든지 그것을 할 수 있어. (anyone, it, can)

➡ _____

17 다음 빈칸에 공통으로 알맞은 말을 쓰시오.

> • The skirt _____ you are wearing is mine. Take it off right now!
> • I can't decide _____ to buy. All the skirts you showed me are awesome.

➡ _____

18 관계대명사를 이용하여 만든 다음 문장을 원래의 두 문장으로 쓰시오.

(1) The radio which I bought isn't working.

➡ _____

(2) That's the coach who I saw at the soccer match.

➡ _____

19 다음 중 두 문장을 한 문장으로 만들 때 의미가 <u>다른</u> 하나는?

① The traffic was very heavy. + We were late.
→ The traffic was so heavy that we were late.

② I missed you very much. + I could do anything to see you.
→ I missed you so much that I could do anything to see you.

③ It was raining very hard. + We had to stop playing soccer.
→ It was raining too hard for us to play soccer.

④ I worked very hard. + I was promoted to director.
→ I worked hard enough to be promoted to director.

⑤ I got up late. + I couldn't catch the bus.
→ I got up too late to miss the bus.

Reading

[20~21] 다음 글을 읽고 물음에 답하시오.

This year, I had a special summer because I visited Mongolia for the first time. ⓐMy friend Altan is from Mongolia. His grandmother invited me to Ulaanbaatar, the capital of Mongolia.

After a four-hour flight from Seoul, Altan and I arrived at Chinggis Khaan International Airport in Ulaanbaatar. ⓑIt took thirty minutes by taxi from the airport to Altan's grandmother's house.

20 위 글의 밑줄 친 ⓐ를 다음과 같이 바꿔 쓸 때 빈칸에 들어갈 알맞은 말을 쓰시오.

➡ My friend Altan _____ from Mongolia.

21 위 글의 밑줄 친 문장 ⓑ에서 생략할 수 있는 한 단어를 생략하여 문장을 다시 쓰시오.

➡ _____

[22~24] 다음 글을 읽고 물음에 답하시오.

Her house is a *ger*, a traditional Mongolian house. (①) It is a big tent, but it is cozy inside. (②) When we entered, something smelled wonderful. (③) *Khorkhog* is a Mongolian barbecue. (④) It is made of lamb and cooked with hot stones. (⑤) I was moved when Altan said Mongolians serve *khorkhog* to special guests. ⓐ그것은 너무 맛있어서 나는 더 달라고 했다. After dinner, Altan and I went outside to see the night sky. The sky was full of bright stars. I felt like I was in a magical place.

22 위 글의 흐름으로 보아, 주어진 문장이 들어가기에 가장 적절한 곳은?

It was from the *khorkhog* that she was cooking for us.

①　　②　　③　　④　　⑤

23 다음 문장에서 위 글의 내용과 다른 부분을 찾아서 고치시오.

A *ger* is a big tent, so it isn't cozy inside.

_____ ➡ _____

24 위 글의 밑줄 친 ⓐ의 우리말에 맞게 주어진 어휘를 이용하여 9단어로 영작하시오.

so, that, for, more

➡ _____

[25~27] 다음 글을 읽고 물음에 답하시오.

During the next three days, Altan showed me around and helped me experience Mongolian culture. Every moment was fun and exciting, but I had the most fun when I rode a camel in the Gobi Desert. At first, I was scared because the camel was taller than I expected. But once I sat on its back, I soon got used to its movement. From the camel's back, the view of the desert was truly amazing.

My visit to Mongolia was a special experience in many ways. ⓐ그것은 내 친구의 나라와 문화를 알 수 있는 좋은 기회가 되었다. I want to visit Mongolia again someday!

25 위 글의 밑줄 친 ⓐ의 우리말에 맞게 주어진 어휘를 알맞게 배열하시오.

> my friend's country and culture / me / to know / it / a great chance / gave / to get

➡ _____

_____

26 위 글의 제목으로 가장 알맞은 것을 고르시오.

① My Visit to Mongolia, a Special Experience
② A Special Mongolian Culture
③ Enjoy Riding a Camel!
④ Let Me Introduce Mongolia to You!
⑤ When Can I Visit Mongolia Again?

27 위 글을 읽고 대답할 수 <u>없는</u> 질문은?

① How long did Altan show the writer around?
② What did the writer experience with Altan?
③ When was the most fun moment to the writer during the trip?

④ How long did the writer ride a camel in the Gobi Desert?
⑤ What gave the writer a great chance to get to know Mongolia and its culture?

[28~30] 다음 글을 읽고 물음에 답하시오.

(A)[I am / This is] your captain speaking. We have just arrived at the airport. 자연과 문화의 아름다움으로 가득 찬 나라 몽골에 오신 것을 환영합니다. The time in Ulaanbaatar is now 4:30 p.m. and there is a chance of rain. We hope you (B) [had / will have] a nice flight. Thank you for flying with us. We hope (C)[seeing / to see] you again.

28 위 글의 괄호 (A)~(C)에서 문맥이나 어법상 알맞은 낱말을 골라 쓰시오.

➡ (A) _____ (B) _____ (C) _____

29 위 글의 종류로 알맞은 것을 고르시오.

① live broadcast   ② boarding call
③ travel essay   ④ traffic report
⑤ in-flight announcement

30 위 글의 밑줄 친 우리말을 주어진 어휘를 알맞게 배열하여 영작하시오.

> Mongolia, the beauty, a country, nature and culture, welcome, full of, of, to

➡ _____

_____

01 제시된 영영풀이의 단어로 대화의 빈칸을 채우시오. (주어진 철자로 시작할 것)

> c_____: noticeably happy

> **A:** How do you like this song?
> **B:** It's c_____. I like it.

02 다음 빈칸에 공통으로 들어갈 말을 쓰시오.

> • It was full _____ animals waiting for their new owner.
> • This pink dress is made _____ silk.

03 다음 중 〈보기〉에 있는 단어를 사용하여 자연스러운 문장을 만들 수 없는 것은?

> ┤ 보기 ├
> abroad   bright   modern   whole

① The moon was very _____ last night.
② You must see many small dots in order to see the _____ painting.
③ From ancient buildings to _____ works of art, you can find them.
④ I'm planning to travel _____.
⑤ After a busy day, he falls _____.

04 다음 영영풀이에 해당하는 단어를 고르시오.

> to believe or think that something will happen

① wait
② require
③ decide
④ expect
⑤ explain

[05~07] 다음 대화를 읽고 물음에 답하시오.

> **B:** 바다 위로 해가 뜨는 것을 본 적 있니?
> **G:** ⓐNo. ⓑHow about you?
> **B:** ⓒI watched the sun rise in Gangneung on New Year's Day. It was great.
> **G:** ⓓI tried several times, ⓔso I just couldn't wake up early enough.

05 밑줄 친 우리말과 일치하도록 주어진 단어를 이용해 문장을 만드시오.

➡ _____
_____ (over, ever, watch, rise)

06 위 대화에서 다음 영영풀이에 해당하는 단어를 찾아 쓰시오.

> to appear above the horizon in the sky

➡ _____

07 위 대화의 문맥상 어색한 것을 고르시오.

① ⓐ   ② ⓑ   ③ ⓒ   ④ ⓓ   ⑤ ⓔ

08 다음 대화의 빈칸에 알맞은 말을 고르시오.

> **A:** Have you ever gone camping?
> **B:** _____ It was a wonderful experience.

① Yes, I have.
② No, I haven't.
③ Of course, I did.
④ No, I didn't.
⑤ I have never had it.

09 빈칸 (A)와 (B)에 어울리는 의문사를 각각 쓰시오.

> G: (A)_____ was your vacation?
> B: Great. I went to Dokdo with my family.
> G: (B)_____ did you like it?
> B: It was amazing. I want to visit there again.

[10~12] 다음 대화를 읽고 물음에 답하시오.

> B: Have you ever traveled abroad, Sujin?
> G: (A)[No, I haven't. / Yes, I have.] I went to Cambodia last summer.
> B: Wow. How did you like it?
> G: It was really hot, but I enjoyed the trip.
> B: Tell me some ____ⓐ____ (interest) experiences you had (B)[during / while] the trip.
> G: Hmm... let me think. I ate fried spiders!
> B: What? You're kidding. How did you like them?
> G: They were really big, so I was a little ____ⓑ____ (scare) at first. ____(C)____ the taste was okay.
> B: Really? I cannot imagine eating spiders.

10 위 대화의 괄호 (A), (B)에서 적절한 것을 고르시오.

➡ (A) _____ (B) _____

11 괄호 안에 주어진 단어를 이용해 빈칸 ⓐ와 ⓑ를 채우시오.

➡ ⓐ _____ ⓑ _____

12 빈칸 (C)에 알맞은 말을 고르시오.

① Because ② When ③ But
④ Therefore ⑤ Since

13 잘못된 부분을 바르게 고치시오.

(1) He teaches me new things that I have never tried them before.

➡ _____

(2) Jack is the boy who she is in love.

➡ _____

(3) My sister likes the cake who I baked.

➡ _____

(4) I know the boys which she is talking to.

➡ _____

(5) This is the tablet PC that I really want to buy it.

➡ _____

(6) I was too tired that I couldn't work out.

➡ _____

(7) The girl is enough fast that she can catch the bus.

➡ _____

(8) The man is very smart that he solves any problem.

➡ _____

14 다음 중 어법상 어색한 문장을 고르시오.

① The house in which we lived was beautiful.
② This is the issue that everyone is talking about.
③ The city I visited is called the windy city.
④ The women I talked with just a minute ago are my aunts.
⑤ That is the cousin whom played with me when I was young.

15 빈칸에 공통으로 알맞은 말을 쓰시오.

> • It was raining, _____ we didn't go to the park.
> • It was _____ cold that we couldn't go outside.

16 다음 중 어법상 올바른 문장을 고르시오.

① This is the video camera who he lent me.
② I'm listening to the music who you recommended.
③ I know a boy which speaks English very well.
④ This is the book I read last year.
⑤ I don't like people whom tells a lie.

17 다음 문장을 어법에 맞게 고쳐 쓰시오.

(1) This report was so difficult that you can't read it.
➡ _____

(2) I was so tired to finish my task.
➡ _____

(3) I was stupid enough for believe what you said.
➡ _____

(4) The rings that she was wearing was fantastic.
➡ _____

(5) I've found the dog whom you lost.
➡ _____

[18~20] 다음 글을 읽고 물음에 답하시오.

ⓐThis year, I had a special summer though I (A)[invited / visited] Mongolia for the first time. My friend Altan is from Mongolia. His grandmother invited me to Ulaanbaatar, the (B)[capital / capitol] of Mongolia.

After a four-hour flight from Seoul, Altan and I arrived at Chinggis Khaan International Airport in Ulaanbaatar. It (C)[spent / took] thirty minutes by taxi from the airport to Altan's grandmother's house.

18 위 글의 괄호 (A)~(C)에서 문맥이나 어법상 알맞은 낱말을 골라 쓰시오.

➡ (A) _____ (B) _____ (C) _____

19 위 글의 밑줄 친 ⓐ에서 흐름상 어색한 부분을 찾아 고치시오.

_____ ➡ _____

20 위 글을 읽고 대답할 수 없는 질문은?

① When did the writer take a trip to Mongolia?
② Has the writer ever been to Mongolia before?
③ Who invited the writer to Ulaanbaatar?
④ Why was the writer invited to Ulaanbaatar?
⑤ How long did it take from the airport to Altan's grandmother's house by taxi?

[21~23] 다음 글을 읽고 물음에 답하시오.

Her house is a *ger*, a traditional Mongolian house. It is a big tent, but it is cozy inside. When we entered, something smelled wonderful. It was ①from the *khorkhog* that she was cooking ②for us. *Khorkhog* is a Mongolian barbecue. It is made ③of lamb and cooked ④with hot stones. I was moved when Altan said Mongolians serve *khorkhog* to special guests. It was so delicious that I asked ⑤of more. After dinner, Altan and I went outside to see the night sky. The sky was full of bright stars. I felt like I was in a magical place.

21 *출제율 90%*
밑줄 친 전치사 ①~⑤ 중에서 그 쓰임이 알맞지 <u>않은</u> 것을 고르시오.

① ② ③ ④ ⑤

22 *출제율 100%*
위 글의 제목으로 알맞은 것을 고르시오.

① What Is a *Ger*?
② Have you Ever Eaten *Khorkhog*?
③ I Enjoyed a *Ger* and *Khorkhog*
④ Serve *Khorkhog* to Special Guests
⑤ The Night Sky Full of Bright Stars

23 *출제율 95%*
위 글의 내용과 일치하지 <u>않는</u> 것은?

① 게르는 큰 텐트이지만 내부는 아늑하다.
② 호르호그는 몽골식 바비큐이다.
③ 호르호그는 양고기로 만들어졌다.
④ 몽골인들은 저녁식사로 주로 호르호그를 먹는다.
⑤ 글쓴이는 호르호그가 너무 맛있어서 더 달라고 했다.

[24~26] 다음 글을 읽고 물음에 답하시오.

During the next three days, Altan showed me around and helped me experience _____ⓐ_____ culture. (①) Every moment was fun and exciting, but I had the most fun when I rode a camel in the Gobi Desert. (②) At first, I was scared because the camel was taller than I expected. (③) From the camel's back, the view of the desert was truly amazing. (④)

My visit to Mongolia was a special experience in many ways. (⑤) It gave me a great chance ⓑto get to know my friend's country and culture. I want to visit Mongolia again someday!

24 *출제율 95%*
본문의 한 단어를 변형하여 위 글의 빈칸 ⓐ에 들어갈 알맞은 말을 쓰시오.

➡ _____

25 *출제율 100%*
위 글의 흐름으로 보아, 주어진 문장이 들어가기에 가장 적절한 곳은?

> But once I sat on its back, I soon got used to its movement.

① ② ③ ④ ⑤

26 *출제율 90%*
위 글의 밑줄 친 ⓑto get과 to부정사의 용법이 <u>다른</u> 것을 <u>모두</u> 고르시오.

① The house <u>to spend</u> the night in was cozy.
② You will find it difficult <u>to read</u> the novel.
③ He is the man <u>to blame</u> for the mistake.
④ Literature is not something <u>to study</u>.
⑤ He is rich enough <u>to buy</u> a plane of his own.

01 대화의 흐름상 또는 어법상 어색한 것을 하나 찾아서 고치시오.

> B: Have you been to the new Chinese restaurant?
> G: Yes. I had dinner there last Saturday.
> B: How did you like it?
> G: The service was good. I won't go back there again.
> B: Really? I wanted to go there, but I won't go, either.

_____ ➡ _____

02 밑줄 친 부분 앞에 생략된 부분을 대화에서 찾아 완전한 문장으로 쓰시오.

> G: You look excited, Inho. What's up?
> B: I'm going to Jejudo with my family this weekend. Have you ever been there?
> G: Yes, <u>many times</u>. I love the coastline. How about you?
> B: It'll be my first visit to Jejudo. I can't wait for this weekend!

➡ _____

_____

03 대화의 밑줄 친 부분과 같은 뜻이 되도록 주어진 단어를 이용해 문장을 완성하시오.

> A: <u>How do you like your ice cream?</u>
> B: It's sweet. I like it.

➡ (1) _____
   (think)
  (2) _____
   (opinion)

04 다음 두 문장을 'so ... that' 구문을 이용하여 한 문장으로 연결하여 쓰시오.

(1) • Jack was very sleepy.
   • Jack couldn't work any more.

➡ _____

_____

(2) • Mason is very short.
   • Mason can't ride a roller coaster.

➡ _____

(3) • The man is very busy.
   • He can't play with his daughter.

➡ _____

_____

(4) • It was too hot.
   • Children couldn't play outside.

➡ _____

_____

05 다음 두 문장을 관계대명사를 이용하여 한 문장으로 연결하여 쓰시오.

(1) • I want a robot.
   • I can control the robot.

➡ _____

_____

(2) • Look at the picture.
   • My classmate drew the picture.

➡ _____

_____

(3) • Daniel is the boy.
   • I met the boy at the concert.

➡ _____

_____

(4) • The cathedral was beautiful.
   • We visited the cathedral last year.

➡ _____

_____

06 우리말과 일치하도록 주어진 단어를 바르게 배열하시오.

(1) 그는 매우 정직해서 거짓말을 못한다.
→ He is (so, he, honest, that, tell, can't) a lie.

⇒ _____

(2) 그는 나이가 들어 대학교에 입학할 수 있다.
→ He is (that, old, enter, he, can, so) a university.

⇒ _____

[07~09] 다음 글을 읽고 물음에 답하시오.

Her house is a *ger*, a traditional Mongolian house. It is a big tent, but it is cozy inside. When we entered, something smelled (A)[wonderful / wonderfully]. It was from the *khorkhog* that she was cooking for us. *Khorkhog* is a Mongolian barbecue. It is made of lamb and (B)[cooking / cooked] with hot stones. I was moved when Altan said Mongolians serve *khorkhog* to special guests. It was (C)[so / such] delicious that I asked for more. After dinner, Altan and I went outside to see the night sky. The sky was full of bright stars. I felt ___ⓐ___ I was in a magical place.

07 위 글의 빈칸 ⓐ에 들어갈 알맞은 한 단어를 쓰시오.

⇒ _____

08 위 글의 괄호 (A)~(C)에서 어법상 알맞은 낱말을 골라 쓰시오.

⇒ (A) _____ (B) _____ (C) _____

09 다음 빈칸 (A)와 (B)에 알맞은 단어를 넣어 *khorkhog*에 대한 소개를 완성하시오.

> *Khorkhog* is a (A)_____ _____ which is made of lamb and cooked with hot stones. Mongolians serve it to (B)_____ _____ .

[10~12] 다음 글을 읽고 물음에 답하시오.

During the next three days, Altan showed me around and helped me experience Mongolian culture. Every moment was fun and exciting, but I had the most fun when I rode a camel in the Gobi Desert. At first, I was scared because the camel was taller than I expected. But once I sat on its back, I soon ⓐ익숙해졌다 its movement. From the camel's back, the view of the desert was truly amazing.

My visit to Mongolia was a special experience in many ways. ⓑIt gave me a great chance to get to know my friend's country and culture. I want to visit Mongolia again someday!

10 위 글의 밑줄 친 ⓐ의 우리말을 got을 사용하여 세 단어로 쓰시오.

⇒ _____

11 위 글의 밑줄 친 ⓑ를 3형식 문장으로 고치시오.

⇒ _____

_____

12 본문의 내용과 일치하도록 다음 빈칸 (A)와 (B)에 알맞은 단어를 쓰시오.

> Altan helped the writer experience (A)_____ _____ , and the visit to Mongolia was a (B)_____ _____ in many ways.

01 그림과 관련된 경험을 해 본 적이 있는지 묻고 대답하는 대화를 완성하시오.

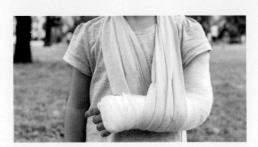

조건
- break를 이용할 것

A: _____

B: _____

02 과거의 자신의 모습을 생각하며 할 수 있었던 것과 할 수 없었던 것을 'so … that ∼' 구문을 이용하여 〈보기〉와 같이 쓰시오.

보기

I was so young that I couldn't ride a bike.

(1) I _____ I couldn't _____ .
(2) I _____ I couldn't _____ .
(3) I _____ I could _____ .
(4) I _____ I could _____ .

03 다음 내용을 바탕으로 기행문을 쓰시오.

My trip
Where: Ulleungdo
When: Last summer
Who With: My parents
What I Did:
- walked along the road around the island

A Trip to Ulleungdo
(A)_____, my parents and I went to (B)_____. Ulleungdo is an island that I always wanted to visit. We (C)_____ along the road around (D)_____.
This trip was so great that I would never forget it for a long time.

단원별 모의고사

01 빈칸에 알맞은 말을 〈보기〉에서 골라 쓰시오. (2번 사용 가능)

┌─ 보기 ─┐
at   for   to   about   in   of

(1) The room was full _____ smoke. So I opened the windows.

(2) _____ first, his accent was difficult to understand. But soon, we got used _____ it.

(3) *Feijoada* is a Brazilian national dish. It is made _____ black beans and meat.

02 우리말과 일치하도록 주어진 단어를 알맞게 배열하시오.

(1) 내 친구는 지금 유학 중입니다.

➡ _____

(now, friend, studying, abroad, my, is)

(2) 우리는 서로 다시 만날 것을 기대했다.

➡ _____

(expected, again, see. we, other, to, each)

03 다음 빈칸에 공통으로 들어갈 말을 쓰시오.

• Let's talk more about snowboarding _____ the break.

• I have traveled _____ the winter vacation.

04 단어와 영영풀이의 연결이 잘못된 것을 고르시오.

① get used to: to become familiar with something or someone

② kid: to make a joke

③ station: a place where trains or buses stop so that people can get on or off

④ part: one of the pieces, sections, or elements that makes the whole of something

⑤ modern: designed and made using the oldest ides or methods

05 다음 대화의 문맥상 어색한 것을 고르시오.

B: ⓐHave you ever watched the sun rise over the ocean?

G: No. ⓑHow about you?

B: ⓒI watched the sun rise in Gangneung on New Year's Day. It was great.

G: ⓓI tried several times, ⓔbut I just couldn't wake up late enough.

① ⓐ　　② ⓑ　　③ ⓒ　　④ ⓓ　　⑤ ⓔ

[06~07] 다음 대화를 읽고 물음에 답하시오.

G: 방학은 어땠니?

B: Great. I went to Dokdo with my family.

G: How did you like it?

B: It was ___(A)___ (amaze). I want to visit there again.

06 밑줄 친 우리말을 how를 사용해 두 가지로 영작하시오.

➡ (1) _____
　 (2) _____

07 빈칸 (A)에 알맞은 말을 주어진 단어를 이용해 쓰시오.

➡ _____

08 다음 대화의 빈칸에 들어갈 말을 〈보기〉에서 골라 순서대로 바르게 배열한 것은?

G: How was your weekend, Tony?

B: _____

G: _____

B: _____

G: _____

B: I enjoyed it. It's made with sweet rice balls. Chinese people usually serve it to guests at a wedding.

┌─── 보기 ───┐

(A) What food did you try?

(B) I had a traditional Chinese dessert, *tangyuan*.

(C) It was great. I went to the International Food Festival with my parents.

(D) How did you like it?

① (B) – (A) – (C) – (D)

② (B) – (C) – (D) – (A)

③ (C) – (A) – (B) – (D)

④ (C) – (B) – (A) – (D)

⑤ (C) – (D) – (B) – (A)

[09~10] 다음 대화를 읽고 물음에 답하시오.

B: 새로 생긴 중국 음식점에 가 봤니?

G: Yes. I had dinner there last Saturday.

B: _____(A)_____

G: The service was bad. I won't go back there again.

09 빈칸 (A)에 알맞은 말을 고르시오.

① Why did you go there?

② How did you like it?

③ What did you like?

④ What didn't you like about it?

⑤ Why do you think so?

10 밑줄 친 우리말을 영작하시오.

➡ _____

[11~12] 다음 대화를 읽고 물음에 답하시오.

B: Have you ever traveled abroad, Sujin?

G: Yes, I went to Cambodia last summer. (①)

B: Wow. (②)

G: It was really hot, but I enjoyed the trip.

B: Tell me some interesting experiences you had during the trip. (③)

G: Hmm... let me think. I ate fried spiders! (④)

B: What? You're kidding. How did you like them?

G: They were really big, so I was a little scared at first. But the taste was okay. (⑤)

B: Really? I cannot imagine eating spiders.

11 ①~⑤ 중 주어진 문장이 들어갈 곳은?

┌─────────────────────────────┐
│   How did you like it?   │
└─────────────────────────────┘

①   ②   ③   ④   ⑤

12 위 대화를 읽고 대답할 수 없는 질문을 고르시오.

① How was the weather when Sujin went to Cambodia?

② Where did Sujin travel last summer?

③ Who did Sujun travel to Cambodia with?

④ Has Sujin ever been abroad before?

⑤ What did Sujin eat in Cambodia?

13 다음 중 어법상 <u>어색한</u> 것은?

① Give me a pen I can write with.

② There are many products which are made in China.

③ The boy who playing the violin is my son.

④ The movie I watched yesterday was fantastic.

⑤ I haven't heard the language which is spoken in that country.

14 빈칸에 공통으로 들어갈 알맞은 것은?

> • It is the notebook _____ you lent me.
> • Look at the boys and their bikes _____ are under the tree.

① who   ② which   ③ that
④ what   ⑤ whose

15 두 문장을 관계대명사를 사용하여 한 문장으로 쓰시오.

(1) There is a shop in front of my office.
   + It sells good coffee.

   ➡ _____

   _____

(2) I like the game.
   + The boys are downloading the game now.

   ➡ _____

   _____

16 다음 문장에서 생략된 말이 있는 곳은?

> The man ① I sat ② next to ③ on the train ④ slept ⑤ all the way.

17 다음 우리말에 맞게 괄호 안에 주어진 어휘를 바르게 배열하시오.

(1) 네가 가장 존경하는 사람에 대해 얘기해 봐라. (most, tell, about, me, the man, you, whom, admire)

   ➡ _____

(2) 그녀는 옆집에 사는 여자이다. (she, next door, is, the woman, lives, who)

   ➡ _____

(3) Mandy는 매우 빠르게 수영해서 금메달을 딸 수 있었다. (swam, that, won, so, Mandy, fast, the gold medal, she)

   ➡ _____

[18~19] 다음 글을 읽고 물음에 답하시오.

> This year, I had a special summer because I visited Mongolia for the first time. My friend Altan is from Mongolia. His grandmother invited me to Ulaanbaatar, the capital of Mongolia.
>
> After a four-hour flight from Seoul, Altan and I arrived at Chinggis Khaan International Airport in Ulaanbaatar. ⓐ<u>공항에서 알탕의 할머니 댁까지 택시로 30분이 걸렸다.</u>

18 What's the capital of Mongolia? Answer in English in a full sentence. (2 words)

   ➡ _____

19 위 글의 밑줄 친 ⓐ의 우리말에 맞게 한 단어를 보충하여, 주어진 어휘를 알맞게 배열하시오.

> to Altan's grandmother's house / took / taxi / from the airport / it / thirty minutes

   ➡ _____

   _____

[20~22] 다음 글을 읽고 물음에 답하시오.

Her house is a *ger*, a traditional Mongolian house. It is a big tent, but it is cozy inside. When we entered, something smelled wonderful. It was from the *khorkhog* ⓐ_____ she was cooking for us. *Khorkhog* is a Mongolian barbecue. It is made of lamb and cooked with hot stones. I was ⓑmoved when Altan said Mongolians serve *khorkhog* to special guests. It was so delicious that I asked for more. After dinner, Altan and I went outside to see the night sky. The sky was full of bright stars. I felt like I was in a magical place.

20 위 글의 빈칸 ⓐ에 들어갈 알맞은 말을 모두 고르시오.

① who
② that
③ whom
④ what
⑤ which

21 위 글의 밑줄 친 ⓑmoved와 바꿔 쓸 수 있는 단어를 쓰시오.

➡ _____

22 위 글의 주제로 알맞은 것을 고르시오.

① a special Mongolian house
② the Mongolians who like lamb
③ a traditional Mongolian house and food
④ a special recipe using hot stones
⑤ the Mongolian night sky full of bright stars

[23~25] 다음 글을 읽고 물음에 답하시오.

During the next three days, Altan showed me around and helped me (A)[experience / experiencing] Mongolian culture. Every moment was fun and exciting, but I had the most fun when I rode a camel in the Gobi Desert. At first, I was (B)[scared / scary] because the camel was taller than I expected. But once I sat on its back, I soon got used to its movement. From the camel's back, the view of the desert was truly (C)[amazing / amazed].

My visit to Mongolia was a special experience in many ways. It gave me a great chance to get to know my friend's country and culture. I want ⓐto visit Mongolia again someday!

23 위 글의 괄호 (A)~(C)에서 어법상 알맞은 낱말을 골라 쓰시오.

➡ (A) _____ (B) _____ (C) _____

24 〈보기〉에서 위 글의 밑줄 친 ⓐto visit와 문법적 쓰임이 같은 것의 개수를 고르시오.

┤ 보기 ├
① It was impossible to solve the problem.
② He is the last man to tell a lie.
③ To hear him talk, you would take him for a fool.
④ My goal is to become a great doctor.
⑤ She tried not to weep at the sad news.

① 1개 ② 2개 ③ 3개 ④ 4개 ⑤ 5개

25 위 글의 내용과 일치하지 않는 것은?

① 알탄은 3일 동안 글쓴이를 구경시켜 주었다.
② 글쓴이는 고비 사막에서 낙타를 탈 때가 가장 재미있었다.
③ 처음에 글쓴이는 예상했던 것보다 낙타의 키가 커서 무서웠다.
④ 낙타의 등에서 보는 사막의 경치는 정말로 무서웠다.
⑤ 글쓴이는 언젠가 몽골을 다시 방문하고 싶다.

Lesson 7

Living in the AI World

🔊 **의사소통 기능**

- 의견 표현하기

  A: I'm going to fly a drone.

  B: That sounds like fun.

- 가능 여부 표현하기

  A: Is it possible for you to text with your eyes closed?

  B: Sure. I can do that.

🔊 **언어 형식**

- 지각동사

  I **see** a cat **crossing** the street.

- 가주어 'it'

  It is hard **to believe** that you can understand us.

Words & Expressions

Key Words

- **AI** 인공지능(artificial intelligence)
- **amusement**[əmjúːzmənt] 몡 즐거움, 오락
- **animated**[ǽnəmèitid] 혱 동영상의, 생기 있는
- **beat**[biːt] 동 이기다
- **beatbox**[bíːtbɑks] 동 비트박스를 하다
- **bedroom**[bédrùːm] 몡 침실
- **burn**[bəːrn] 동 불타다
- **chance**[tʃæns] 몡 기회
- **check**[tʃek] 동 확인하다, 점검하다
- **closet**[klɑ́zit] 몡 옷장
- **cloudy**[kláudi] 혱 구름의, 흐린
- **cross**[krɔːs] 동 건너다
- **danger**[déindʒər] 몡 위험
- **dictionary**[díkʃənèri] 몡 사전
- **easily**[íːzili] 부 쉽게
- **else**[els] 부 그 밖의
- **exciting**[iksáitiŋ] 혱 흥미진진한, 신나는
- **freeze**[friːz] 동 얼리다, 얼다
- **impossible**[impɑ́səbl] 혱 불가능한
- **intelligent**[intélədʒənt] 혱 똑똑한
- **interesting**[íntərəstiŋ] 혱 재미있는, 흥미로운
- **like**[laik] 전 ~같이, ~처럼
- **lucky**[lʌ́ki] 혱 행운의
- **machine**[məʃíːn] 몡 기계
- **mean**[miːn] 동 의미하다
- **off**[ɔːf] 부 할인되어
- **perfect**[pə́ːrfikt] 혱 완벽한
- **point**[pɔint] 동 돌리다, 향하게 하다
- **possible**[pɑ́səbl] 혱 가능한
- **predict**[pridíkt] 동 예측하다
- **project**[prɑ́dʒekt] 몡 과제
- **replace**[ripléis] 동 대체하다
- **select**[silékt] 동 선택하다
- **sense**[sens] 동 감지하다
- **situation**[sìtʃuéiʃən] 몡 상황
- **space**[speis] 몡 공간, 우주
- **strange**[streindʒ] 혱 이상한
- **take**[teik] 동 선택하다, 사다
- **teleport**[téləpɔ̀ːrt] 동 순간 이동하다
- **text**[tekst] 동 (휴대전화로) 문자를 보내다
- **theater**[θíːətər] 몡 극장
- **through**[θruː] 부 ~을 통해, ~ 사이로
- **translate**[trænsléit] 동 번역하다
- **translator**[trænsléitər] 몡 번역가
- **unbelievable**[ʌnbilívəbəl] 혱 믿기 어려운, 놀랄만한
- **without**[wiðáut] 전 ~ 없이

Key Expressions

- **based on** ~에 근거하여
- **be able to 동사원형** ~할 수 있다
- **because of** ~ 때문에
- **by the way** 그런데, 그건 그렇고
- **by 동사ing** ~함으로써
- **don't have to** ~할 필요가 없다(need not)
- **face to face** (~와) 서로 얼굴을 맞대고
- **free from** ~의 염려가 없는
- **get in** ~에 타다
- **get off** ~에서 내리다, ~에서 떨어지다
- **get to** ~에 도착하다
- **get 비교급** 점점 더 ~해지다
- **go with** 같이 가다, 어울리다
- **in danger** 위험에 처한, 위험에 빠진
- **Is it possible (for 목적격) to 동사원형 ~?**
  (…가) ~하는 것이 가능할까?
- **keep 동사ing** 계속 ~하다
- **look for** ~을 찾다
- **look ~ up** (사전·참고 자료·컴퓨터 등에서 정보를) 찾아보다
- **look 형용사** ~하게 보이다
- **move on** ~로 이동하다
- **not just** 단지 ~뿐이 아니다
- **no longer** 더 이상 ~하지 않다
- **out of** (원천·출처) ~에서, ~으로부터
- **over there** 저쪽에
- **see if 주어 동사** ~인지 아닌지 확인하다
- **slow down** 속도를 늦추다
- **sound like 명사** ~처럼 들리다
- **sound 형용사** ~하게 들리다
- **try to 동사원형** 노력하다
- **watch out** 조심하다

Word Power

※ 명사 + 접미사 -y → 형용사

- □ **dust**(먼지) – **dusty**(먼지가 많은)
- □ **ease**(쉬움) – **easy**(쉬운)
- □ **fun**(재미) – **funny**(재미있는)
- □ **greed**(욕심) – **greedy**(욕심 많은)

- □ **health**(건강) – **healthy**(건강한)
- □ **luck**(행운) – **lucky**(운이 좋은)
- □ **noise**(소음) – **noisy**(시끄러운)
- □ **sleep**(잠) – **sleepy**(졸린)

※ 날씨 관련 명사에 y가 붙어 형용사가 되는 경우

- □ **cloud**(구름) – **cloudy**(흐린)
- □ **rain**(비) – **rainy**(비가 오는)
- □ **snow**(눈) – **snowy**(눈이 내리는)

- □ **sun**(태양) – **sunny**(맑은)
- □ **wind**(바람) – **windy**(바람이 부는)
- □ **fog**(안개) – **foggy**(안개가 낀)

※ 음식 관련 명사에 y가 붙어 형용사가 되는 경우

- □ **oil**(기름) – **oily**(기름기가 있는)
- □ **salt**(소금) – **salty**(짠)

- □ **taste**(맛) – **tasty**(맛있는)

English Dictionary

- □ **amusement** 즐거움, 오락
  → the enjoyment that you get from being entertained
  즐겁게 되는 것에서 얻는 기쁨

- □ **beat** 이기다
  → to defeat someone in a game
  경기에서 누군가를 패배시키다

- □ **beatbox** 비트박스를 하다
  → to create the sounds of powerful rhythm with the voice and the hands
  목소리와 손으로 강력한 리듬의 소리를 만들다

- □ **burn** 불타다
  → to be destroyed by fire 불에 의해서 파괴되다

- □ **closet** 옷장
  → a large piece of furniture with a door used for storing clothes 의복을 저장하기 위해 만들어진 문이 있는 큰 가구

- □ **cloudy** 구름의, 흐린
  → when the sky is covered with a lot of clouds
  하늘이 많은 구름으로 덮인

- □ **cross** 건너다
  → to go from one side to the other side of an area
  한 지역의 한쪽에서 다른 쪽으로 가다

- □ **dictionary** 사전
  → a book that contains a list of words and phrases alphabetically with their meanings or their translations in another language
  알파벳순으로 그것의 의미 또는 다른 언어로의 번역이 있는 일련의 단어와 구를 포함하는 책

- □ **lucky** 행운의
  → having desirable things unexpectedly happen to you
  바람직한 상황이 예기치 않게 일어난

- □ **perfect** 완벽한
  → the best possible 가능한 최고의

- □ **possible** 가능한
  → able to happen or be done
  일어나거나 발생할 수 있는

- □ **predict** 예측하다
  → to say that an event will happen in the future
  미래에 어떤 일이 발생할 것이라고 말하다

- □ **replace** 대체하다
  → to take the place of …에 대신하다, …을 대리하다

- □ **select** 선택하다
  → to choose something from a number of things
  많은 것들 중에서 어떤 것을 고르다

- □ **sense** 감지하다
  → to perceive or realize something
  어떤 것을 인지하거나 깨닫다

- □ **situation** 상황
  → what is happening at a particular time and place
  특정한 시간과 장소에서 발생하는 것

- □ **translate** 번역하다
  → to change words in another language
  말들을 다른 언어로 바꾸다

01 다음 중 밑줄 친 부분의 뜻풀이가 바르지 <u>않은</u> 것은?

① Some animals have the ability to <u>predict</u> earthquakes. (예측하다)

② I hope my water pipes in the house don't <u>freeze</u>. (얼다)

③ I can <u>teleport</u> through time and space. (전화하다)

④ Please <u>check</u> the password and try again. (확인하다)

⑤ I <u>selected</u> a toy for a child. (선택했다)

02 주어진 단어를 이용해 빈칸을 완성하시오.

> Your story is so _____ that I can't stop laughing. (fun)

[03~04] 다음 빈칸에 알맞은 것을 고르시오.

03

> Do you know anyone who can _____ French into English?

① translate ② transform ③ prevent
④ select   ⑤ mean

04

> In the first match against Greece, the South Korean team _____ the Greek team.

① fell   ② hit   ③ beat
④ broke   ⑤ predicted

05 다음 밑줄 친 단어의 성격이 다른 하나를 고르시오.

① Doesn't it sound <u>like</u> fun to learn in a forest?

② You look <u>like</u> a totally new person in that suit.

③ Why do you <u>like</u> it so much?

④ Doesn't it seem <u>like</u> a chess game of some sort?

⑤ They are sad for a long time <u>like</u> humans.

06 다음 밑줄 친 부분과 의미가 가장 가까운 것은?

> After the test, the people were asked if they saw anything <u>strange</u>.

① natural   ② unusual
③ expected   ④ familiar
⑤ necessary

07 다음 주어진 우리말에 맞게 빈칸을 채우시오. (철자가 주어진 것도 있음)

(1) 우리는 Oliver가 이 마을에 더 이상 살지 않기 때문에 그를 자주 볼 수 없다.
➡ We cannot see Oliver very often because he _____ _____ lives in this town.

(2) 더 이상 저를 걱정할 필요 없어요. 전 괜찮아요.
➡ You _____ h_____ to worry about me. I'm fine.

01 다음 〈보기〉의 단어를 골라 문맥에 맞게 고쳐 쓰시오.

┌─ 보기 ┤

cloud fun greed luck sun

(1) Scrooge was a _____ old man.

(2) I like this book because the story is _____.

(3) It was _____ today, but it will be _____ tomorrow. You will have to bring your umbrella.

(4) I met my favorite movie star by chance. It's my _____ day!

02 두 문장이 같은 의미가 되도록 빈칸을 채우시오. (주어진 철자로 시작할 것)

The new cells take the place of the old cells. = The new cells r_____ the old cells.

03 다음 빈칸에 공통으로 들어갈 말을 쓰시오.

• _____ the way, are you still working at the public library? • You can learn time management skills _____ doing it.

04 다음 우리말에 맞도록 빈칸에 알맞은 말을 쓰시오. (철자가 주어진 경우 주어진 철자로 시작할 것)

(1) 영어를 한국어로 번역할 수 있나요?
➡ Can you _____ English into Korean?

(2) 마감 시간 전에 숙제를 끝내는 것이 가능한가요?
➡ Is it p_____ to _____ your homework before deadline?

(3) 그 밖에 또 필요한 것이 있나요?
➡ Do you need anything e_____?

(4) 그것은 완벽할 필요는 없다.
➡ It doesn't h_____ to be _____.

05 다음 빈칸에 들어갈 말을 〈보기〉에서 찾아 쓰시오.

┌─ 보기 ┤

in off to

(1) Get _____ the car right now, or you'll be late.

(2) When I got _____ the top of the mountain, it was very dark.

(3) We will see him soon. Passengers are getting _____ the plane now.

06 다음 우리말에 맞게 주어진 단어를 바르게 배열하시오.

(1) 나는 그가 길을 건너는 것을 봤다.
(saw, the, crossing, I, him, street)
➡ _____

(2) 그는 국내 총 생산량이 오를 것이라고 예측했다.
(he, up, go, that, would, the, predicted, GDP)
➡ _____

Conversation

1 의견 표현하기

> **A** I'm going to fly a drone. 난 드론을 날릴 거야.
> **B** That sounds like fun. 그거 재미있겠다.

■ 의견을 물어 보는 질문에 대한 답으로 동사 'sound(~하게 들리다)'를 사용해 의견을 표현할 수 있다. 'sound+형용사'를 사용하거나, 'sound+like+명사'를 이용하여 말할 수 있다.

  • It sounds interesting. 그거 재미있겠다.

  • It sounds like fun. 그거 재미있겠다.

■ 'It'이나 'That'을 생략해서 'Sounds interesting/good/terrible.'로도 말할 수 있다.

■ 의견을 나타내는 다른 표현들로는 'I think ~.', 'It seems that ~.', 'In my opinion, ~.' 등이 있다.

■ 자신의 의견을 나타낸 뒤, 자신의 생각을 뒷받침하는 이유나 근거를 함께 언급하기도 한다. 또는 'How about you?(너는 어때?)'를 사용해 상대방의 의견을 다시 물어볼 수도 있다.

의견 표현하기

  • (That) Sounds (very) interesting.
  • How interesting!
  • I think (that) it's interesting.
  • In my opinion, it's interesting.

핵심 Check

1. 다음 우리말과 일치하도록 빈칸에 알맞은 말을 쓰시오.

   A: I will go swimming with my friends. (내 친구들과 수영하러 갈 거야.)

   B: _____ like fun. (재미있겠다.)

2. 다음 우리말과 일치하도록 주어진 단어를 바르게 배열하시오.

   A: Why don't we make a movie together? (함께 영화를 만드는 것은 어때?)

   B: _____ _____ _____. (good, that, sounds) How about you? (좋아. 너는 어때?)

   C: _____ _____ _____ _____. (exciting, it's, I, think)
   (나는 그것이 재미있다고 생각해.)

② 가능 여부 표현하기

A Is it possible for you to text with your eyes closed?

눈 감고 문자 메시지 보내는 것이 가능하니?

B Sure. I can do that. 물론이지. 할 수 있어.

- 'Is it possible for 목적격 to 동사원형 ~?'은 상대방에게 어떤 것을 하는 것이 가능한지 물어볼 때 쓰는 표현이다. 여기서 it은 가주어이며 to 동사원형이 to부정사로 진주어이며 for 목적격은 to부정사의 의미상 주어이다. to부정사 대신에 that절을 사용해서 말할 수도 있다.

  · Is it possible for you to text with your eyes closed?
   = Is it possible that you text with your eyes closed?

- possible 대신에 likely(~할 것 같은)나 probable((현실로) 있음직한, 가망이 있는)을 사용할 수도 있다.

- 조동사 'can(~할 수 있다)'을 사용해서 'Can+주어+동사원형 ~?(~을 할 수 있니?)'으로 질문할 수 있다.

가능 여부 표현하기

· Is it possible[probable/likely] that 주어 동사 ~?

· Is it possible[probable/likely] for 목적격 to 동사원형 ~?

· Can 주어 동사원형 ~?

핵심 Check

3. 다음 우리말과 일치하도록 빈칸에 알맞은 말을 쓰시오.

A: _____ _____ _____ _____ I can carry that box?

(제가 저 상자를 운반할 수 있을까요?)

B: I think it's possible with some help. I'll help you.

(전 약간의 도움으로 가능하다고 생각해요. 제가 도와드릴게요.)

A: Thanks. (고마워요.)

4. 다음 대화에서 밑줄 친 부분과 같은 의미가 되도록 주어진 단어를 이용해 문장을 만드시오.

A: <u>Is it possible that he can finish this marathon?</u>

B: Yes, it's possible.

➡ _____ (possible, to)

➡ _____ (can)

5. 다음 우리말과 일치하도록 주어진 어구를 빈칸에 알맞게 배열하시오.

A: _____ (a cake, it, you, to, is, possible, for, make)

(케이크를 만들 수 있니?)

B: Yes, it is. (응. 할 수 있어.)

Listen & Speak 1 B-1

B: Do you have any ideas for our group project?

G: No. What about you?

B: ❶I'm thinking we should talk about future jobs. ❷What do you think?

G: ❸That sounds perfect for our project. ❹Let's look for some information on the Internet.

B: 우리 조별 프로젝트에 대한 좋은 생각이 있니?

G: 아니. 너는 어때?

B: 나는 미래 직업에 대해 이야기하면 좋겠다고 생각하고 있어. 너는 어떻게 생각해?

G: 우리 프로젝트에 완벽한 것 같아. 인터넷에서 정보를 찾아보자.

❶ 'we should talk about future jobs'는 think의 목적어이며 앞에 접속사 that이 생략되어 있다. talk about: ~에 대해서 이야기하다

❷ 'What do you think?'는 자신의 의견을 말한 뒤, 상대방의 의견을 물어볼 때 쓰며 '너는 어떻게 생각하니?'의 의미이다. 바꿔서 쓸 수 있는 표현으로 'How about you?', 'What about you?' 등이 있다.

❸ sound 형용사: ~하게 들리다 perfect: 완벽한

❹ 'Let's 동사원형'은 '~하자'라는 의미로 어떤 것을 제안하고자 할 때 사용한다. 'Why don't we ~?'로 바꿔 쓸 수 있다.

Check(√) True or False

(1) They are going to look for some information for their group project in the book.   T ☐ F ☐

(2) They will look for some information about future jobs.   T ☐ F ☐

Listen & Speak 2 B-1

G: This computer ❶looks nice. ❷How much is it?

M: ❸It's 500 dollars. It's ❹the newest one.

G: ❺Is it possible to use this coupon?

M: Let me ❻check. Yes, you can. So, you'll get 30 dollars ❼off.

G: Perfect. I'll ❽take it.

G: 이 컴퓨터가 좋아 보이네요. 얼마예요?

M: 500달러예요. 가장 최신 컴퓨터예요.

G: 이 쿠폰을 사용하는 것이 가능한가요?

M: 확인해 볼게요. 네, 사용할 수 있어요. 그러면, 30달러 할인돼요.

G: 좋아요. 이걸로 살게요.

❶ look 형용사: ~하게 보이다

❷ 가격을 묻고자 할 때 'How much ~?(~은 얼마인가요?)' 표현을 사용한다.

❸ 'How much ~?'의 질문에 'It's+가격.'으로 대답한다.

❹ the newest는 형용사 new의 최상급으로 '가장 최신의'의 의미이다. one = computer

❺ 'Is it possible to+동사원형 ~?'은 '~하는 것이 가능한가요?'라는 의미로 가능 여부를 물을 때 사용하는 표현이다. 이때 it은 가주어이고 to부정사구가 진주어이다.

❻ check: 확인하다, 점검하다

❼ off: 할인되어

❽ take: 선택하다, 사다

Check(√) True or False

(3) The girl has a coupon which cannot be used.   T ☐ F ☐

(4) The girl will buy the newest computer.   T ☐ F ☐

Listen & Speak 1 A

B: ❶Why don't we try a new VR game?
G: ❷That sounds interesting.

❶ '~을 하자'라는 제안을 하고자 할 때 'Why don't we ~?' 외에도 'Let's ~'의 표현을 쓸 수 있다.
❷ 'That sounds interesting.' 상대방이 한 말에 대하여 '재미있겠다'라는 표현으로 'How interesting!'이나 'Sounds interesting!'으로 바꾸어 사용할 수 있다.

Listen & Speak 1 B-2

G: The Robot Expo begins next week. ❶Why don't you go with me?
B: ❷Yes, I'd love to. ❸That sounds exciting.
G: We'll have ❹a chance to meet robotics engineers.
B: ❺That'll be great.

❶ Why don't you ~?: ~하는 게 어때? (= What about ~? = How about ~?)
go with: 같이 가다, 어울리다
❷ 상대방의 제안에 응할 때는 'Yes, I'd love to.', 그렇지 않을 때는 'Sorry, but I can't.'로 대답할 수 있다.
❸ sound 형용사: ~하게 들리다 exciting: 흥미진진한
❹ to meet이 a chance(기회)를 수식하는 형용사적 용법으로 사용되고 있다.
robotics: 로봇 공학 engineer: 기술자
❺ That'll be great.: 그러면 아주 좋겠다.

Listen & Speak 2 A

G: ❶Is it possible for you to live without your smartphone?
B: No, it's ❷not possible.

❶ Is it possible (for 목적격) to 동사원형 ~?: (…가) ~하는 것이 가능할까?
without: ~ 없이
❷ 'not possible'을 'impossible(불가능한)'로 바꿔 쓸 수 있다.

Listen & Speak 2 B-2

B: ❶We took lots of pictures during our trip.
G: We sure ❷did. We have more than 500 pictures.
B: ❸Is it possible to make an animated photo album out of them?
G: Yes, it's ❹possible. I have an app for that.

❶ take a picture: 사진을 찍다 lots of: 많은 during: ~ 동안
❷ did는 'took lots of pictures'를 의미한다.
❸ Is it possible (for 목적격) to 동사원형 ~?: (…가) ~하는 것이 가능할까? 'it'은 가주어, 'to make an animated photo album out of them'은 진주어이다.
out of: (원천·출처) ~에서, ~으로부터
❹ possible: 가능한

Listen & Speak 2 C-1

A: ❶Is it possible for you to text ❷with your eyes closed?
B: Sure. I can ❸do that.

❶ Is it possible (for 목적격) to 동사원형 ~?: (…가) ~하는 것이 가능할까? text: (휴대전화로) 문자를 보내다
❷ with+명사구(your eyes)+과거분사(closed): 너의 눈을 감은 채로 / 명사구가 과거분사된 채로(부대상황)
❸ do = text with my eyes closed

Real-Life Zone

G: Look at those words on the board.
B: ❶What do they mean? Let's ❷look them up in the dictionary.
G: ❸What about using the AI translator?
B: How do I use ❹it?
G: ❺You point your smartphone camera at the words and ask AI to translate. You will get an answer.
B: ❻Is it possible for AI to read those words?
Speaker: Sure. I can read any language and translate it.
B: ❼Wow, that sounds unbelievable. So, AI, what do those words mean?
Speaker: ❽They mean "Dreams come true!"
B: ❾That's amazing.

❶ 'What do they mean?'은 '그 말들은 무슨 뜻이지?'란 의미로 의미를 묻는 말이다.
❷ look ~ up: (사전·참고 자료·컴퓨터 등에서 정보를) 찾아보다
❸ What about 동명사 ~?: ~하는 게 어때? translator: 번역가
❹ it은 앞에 나온 'the AI translator'를 가리킨다.
❺ point: 돌리다, 향하게 하다 point와 ask는 접속사 and로 연결된 병렬 관계이다. translate: 번역하다
❻ Is it possible (for 목적격) to 동사원형 ~?: (…가) ~하는 것이 가능할까?
❼ sound 형용사: ~하게 들리다 unbelievable: 믿기 어려운, 놀랄만한
❽ 'What does[do] it[they] mean?'으로 의미를 물었을 때 'mean(의미하다)'을 이용해 'It/They mean(s) ~.(~라는 뜻이에요.)'로 대답할 수 있다.
❾ 놀람을 표현할 때는 'That's surprising.', 'That's amazing.', 'I can't believe it.' 등으로 말할 수 있다.

● 다음 우리말과 일치하도록 빈칸에 알맞은 말을 쓰시오.

Listen & Speak 1 A

B: Why _____ we try a new VR game?

G: That _____ interesting.

해석

B: 우리 새로운 VR 게임을 해 보는 게 어때?

G: 그거 재미있겠다.

Listen & Speak 1 B

1. B: Do you _____ _____ ideas _____ our group _____?

   G: No. _____ _____ you?

   B: I'm thinking we should _____ _____ _____ jobs. _____ do you _____?

   G: That _____ _____ for our project. Let's _____ _____ some information on the Internet.

2. G: The Robot Expo _____ next week. _____ don't you go _____ me?

   B: Yes, I'd love _____. That _____ exciting.

   G: We'll have a _____ _____ _____ _____ engineers.

   B: That'll be _____.

1. B: 우리 조별 프로젝트에 대한 좋은 생각이 있니?

   G: 아니. 너는 어때?

   B: 나는 미래 직업에 대해 이야기하면 좋겠다고 생각하고 있어. 너는 어떻게 생각해?

   G: 우리 프로젝트에 완벽한 것 같아. 인터넷에서 정보를 찾아보자.

2. G: 로봇 박람회가 다음 주에 시작돼. 나와 함께 가는 게 어때?

   B: 응, 가고 싶어. 그거 재미있겠는데.

   G: 우리는 로봇 공학자를 만날 기회가 있을 거야.

   B: 그거 아주 좋겠다.

Listen & Speak 1 C

1. A: I'm _____ to fly a _____.

   B: That sounds _____ _____.

2. A: I'm _____ to _____ a model car.

   B: That sounds _____ _____.

1. A: 난 드론을 날릴 거야.

   B: 그거 재미있겠다.

2. A: 난 모형 자동차를 조립할 거야.

   B: 그거 재미있겠다.

Listen & Speak 2 A

G: It is _____ for you _____ _____ _____ your smartphone?

B: No, it's not _____.

G: 네가 스마트폰 없이 사는 것이 가능할까?

B: 아니, 그건 불가능해.

Listen & Speak 2 B

1. **G:** This computer _____ nice. _____ _____ is it?

   M: It's 500 dollars. It's the _____ one.

   G: _____ _____ _____ _____ _____ this coupon?

   M: Let me _____. Yes, you can. So, you'll get 30 dollars _____.

   G: _____. I'll take it.

2. **B:** We _____ lots of _____ _____ our trip.

   G: We sure _____. We have more _____ 500 pictures.

   B: Is _____ _____ _____ _____ an animated photo album _____ _____ them?

   G: Yes, it's possible. I _____ an app for that.

Listen & Speak 2 C

1. **A:** _____ _____ _____ for you _____ _____ _____ your eyes _____?

   B: Sure. I can do that.

2. **A:** Is it _____ _____ _____ to travel around Gangwondo _____ bicycle?

   B: Sure. I can do that.

Real-Life Zone A

G: Look _____ those words on the board.

B: _____ do _____ _____? Let's _____ _____ _____ in the _____.

G: What _____ _____ the AI translator?

B: _____ do I use it?

G: You _____ your smartphone camera at the words and ask AI to _____. You will _____ an answer.

B: Is it _____ _____ _____ _____ _____ those words?

Speaker: Sure. I can _____ any language and _____ it.

B: Wow, that sounds _____. So, AI, what do those words _____?

Speaker: They mean "Dreams come true!"

B: That's _____.

해석

1. **G:** 이 컴퓨터가 좋아 보이네요. 얼마예요?
   M: 500달러예요. 가장 최신 컴퓨터예요.
   G: 이 쿠폰을 사용하는 것이 가능한가요?
   M: 확인해 볼게요. 네, 사용할 수 있어요. 그러면, 30달러 할인돼요.
   G: 좋아요. 이걸로 살게요.

2. **B:** 우리는 여행 동안 사진을 많이 찍었어.
   G: 진짜 그랬어. 500장 넘게 있어.
   B: 그 사진들로 동영상 앨범을 만드는 것이 가능하니?
   G: 응, 가능해. 나는 그것을 위한 앱이 있어.

1. **A:** 눈 감고 문자 메시지 보내는 것이 가능하니?
   B: 물론이지. 할 수 있어.

2. **A:** 자전거로 강원도를 여행하는 것이 가능하니?
   B: 물론이지. 할 수 있어.

G: 저기 칠판에 있는 글자 좀 봐.
B: 무슨 뜻이지? 사전에서 찾아보자.
G: AI 번역기를 사용하는 게 어때?
B: 어떻게 사용하는 거니?
G: 스마트폰 카메라를 글자 위에 댄 후에 AI에게 번역해 달라고 해 봐. 아마 답을 해 줄 거야.
B: AI가 저런 글자를 읽는 것이 가능해?
Speaker: 물론이에요. 저는 어떤 언어도 읽을 수 있고 번역할 수 있어요.
B: 오, 정말 놀라워. 그럼 AI, 이 글자는 뜻이 뭐니?
Speaker: "꿈은 이루어진다."라는 뜻이에요.
B: 정말 대단하구나.

Conversation 시험대비 기본평가

01 다음 대화의 밑줄 친 부분과 바꿔 쓸 수 있는 것을 고르시오.

> A: <u>Is it possible for you to read 50 novels during summer vacation?</u>
>
> B: Sure. I can do that.

① Should you read 50 novels during summer vacation?

② Are you going to read 50 novels during summer vacation?

③ Is it possible that you read 50 novels during summer vacation?

④ Is it unlikely for you to read 50 novels during summer vacation?

⑤ Are you thinking of reading 50 novels during summer vacation?

02 다음 대화의 빈칸에 알맞은 것을 고르시오.

> B: Do you have any ideas for our group project?
>
> G: No. What about you?
>
> B: I'm thinking we should talk about future jobs. What do you think?
>
> G: _____ Let's look for some information on the Internet.

① That sounds perfect for our project.

② I have a different idea about our project.

③ I think it's too small for us.

④ In my opinion, that's not true.

⑤ I agree with you. That sounds bad.

03 주어진 문장 뒤에 올 대화의 순서가 바르게 배열된 것을 고르시오.

> The Robot Expo begins next week. Why don't you go with me?

> (A) We'll have a chance to meet robotics engineers.
>
> (B) Yes, I'd love to. That sounds exciting.
>
> (C) That'll be great.

① (A) – (C) – (B)   ② (B) – (A) – (C)

③ (B) – (C) – (A)   ④ (C) – (A) – (B)

⑤ (C) – (B) – (A)

[01~02] 다음 대화를 읽고 물음에 답하시오.

G: The Robot Expo begins next week. Why don't you go with me?

B: Yes, I'd love to. _____ (A) _____

G: We'll have a chance to meet robotics engineers.

B: That'll be great.

01 위 대화의 빈칸 (A)에 알맞은 말을 고르시오.

① I think it's very boring.

② That sounds exciting.

③ In my opinion, it will be crowded.

④ It doesn't sound like fun.

⑤ I'm not interested in robots.

02 위 대화를 읽고 답할 수 <u>없는</u> 질문은?

① What does the boy think about the Robot Expo?

② Who can they meet at the Robot Expo?

③ Where does the girl want to go with the boy?

④ Where will they meet to go to the Robot Expo?

⑤ When does the Robot Expo begin?

[03~04] 다음 대화를 읽고 물음에 답하시오.

G: Look at those words on the board.

B: What do they mean? Let's look them up in the dictionary. (①)

G: What about using the AI translator?

B: How do I use it? (②)

G: You point your smartphone camera at words and ask AI to translate. (③) You will get an answer. (④)

B: Is it possible for AI to read those words?

Speaker: Sure. I can read any language and translate it.

B: Wow, that sounds unbelievable. So, AI! (⑤)

Speaker: They mean "Dreams come true!"

B: That's amazing.

03 위 대화의 ①~⑤ 중 주어진 문장이 들어갈 곳은?

> What do those words mean?

① ② ③ ④ ⑤

04 위 대화의 내용과 일치하지 <u>않는</u> 것을 고르시오.

① AI 번역기는 모든 언어를 읽을 수 있고 번역할 수 있다.

② 여자아이는 AI 번역기를 사용하는 방법을 알고 있다.

③ 칠판에 있는 글자는 "꿈은 이루어진다."라는 뜻을 가지고 있다.

④ 여자아이와 남자아이는 칠판 위의 모르는 글자를 사전에서 찾아봤다.

⑤ AI 번역기를 사용하기 위해서 먼저 스마트폰 카메라를 글자 위에 대야 한다.

[05~07] 다음 대화를 읽고 물음에 답하시오.

G: Minseok, there is a smart food-ordering machine over there. (①) Why don't we try it?

B: _____(A)_____ We'll be able to order easily and fast by using it.

G: I hope so. (②) By the way, do you think maybe it will be possible for robots to replace humans someday?

B: I'm not sure. (③) But we will be free from danger because of robots.

G: What do you mean?

B: (④) Robots can do the dangerous work so humans don't have to.

G: You're right. We should always try to look on the bright side. (⑤)

05 위 대화의 ①~⑤ 중 주어진 문장이 들어갈 곳은?

> Robots can help people in danger.

①   ②   ③   ④   ⑤

06 위 대화의 빈칸 (A)에 알맞은 말을 고르시오.

① I think that it is delicious.
② In my opinion, robots are necessary in our lives.
③ I don't want to try it.
④ We don't have to use it.
⑤ That sounds interesting.

07 위 대화의 내용과 일치하지 <u>않는</u> 것을 고르시오.

① 민석이는 로봇 덕분에 사람들이 위험한 일을 하지 않을 것이라고 생각한다.
② 민석이는 로봇이 인간을 대체할 수 있을 거라고 생각한다.
③ 민석이는 스마트 음식 주문 자판기가 주문을 쉽고 빠르게 해 줄 것이라고 생각한다.
④ 여자아이는 항상 좋은 면을 봐야 한다고 말하고 있다.
⑤ 그들은 스마트 음식 주문 자판기를 사용할 것이다.

[08~09] 다음 중 짝지어진 대화가 <u>어색한</u> 것은?

08 ① A: I go to the farm with my family on weekends.
    B: That sounds interesting.
② A: Is it possible that I finish my homework by tomorrow?
    B: Sure. You can.
③ A: Is it possible that I keep a pet?
    B: Yes, I can.
④ A: Do you know that ice cream is from China?
    B: No. That sounds interesting.
⑤ A: Is it possible that you go abroad alone?
    B: Of course. I can.

09 ① A: Is it possible to drink juice in space?
    B: Sure, it's possible.
② A: What do you think about this place?
    B: I like it. I think it's very comfortable.
③ A: Why don't we join the Mozart Club?
    B: That sounds like fun. I love music.
④ A: Why don't we watch a movie tonight?
    B: I don't think so. It sounds like fun.
⑤ A: Is it possible that a dog solves a math problem?
    B: No. That sounds impossible.

01 다음 대화의 밑줄 친 문장과 의미가 같도록 빈칸에 알맞은 말을 쓰시오.

> G: Is it possible for you to live without your smartphone?
> B: No, it's not possible.

> _____ _____ live without your smartphone?

[02~03] 다음 대화를 읽고 물음에 답하시오.

> G: This computer looks nice. How much is it?
> M: It's 500 dollars. It's the newest one.
> G: 이 쿠폰을 사용하는 것이 가능한가요?
> M: Let me check. Yes, you can. So, you'll get 30 dollars off.
> G: Perfect. I'll take it.

02 다음 밑줄 친 우리말을 주어진 단어를 이용해 영작하시오.

> (possible, use)

➡ _____

03 다음 질문에 주어진 단어를 이용해 완전한 문장으로 대답하시오.

> How much will the girl pay for the computer?

➡ _____ (will)

[04~05] 다음 대화를 읽고 물음에 답하시오.

> G: Look at those words on the board.
> B: What do they mean? Let's look them ___(A)___ in the dictionary.
> G: What ___(B)___ using the AI translator?
> B: How do I use it?
> G: You point your smartphone camera at the words and ask AI to translate. You will get an answer.
> B: Is it possible for AI to read those words?
> Speaker: Sure. I can read any language and translate it.
> B: Wow, that sounds (C)believe. So, AI, what do those words mean?
> Speaker: They mean "Dreams come true!"

04 위 대화의 빈칸 (A)와 (B)에 알맞은 것을 쓰시오.

(A) _____ (B) _____

05 위 대화의 밑줄 친 believe를 알맞은 형으로 고치시오.

➡ _____

06 다음 괄호 안에 주어진 단어를 알맞게 배열하시오.

> G: _____
> (Gangwondo, travel, is, bicycle, for, to, possible, you, it, by, around)
> B: Sure. I can do that.

➡ _____
_____

Grammar

① 지각동사

> • I **see** a cat **crossing** the street. 고양이가 길을 건너고 있는 게 보여.
> • I **heard** him **sing**. 나는 그가 노래하는 소리를 들었다.

■ 지각동사는 감각 기관을 통하여 인지하는 것을 나타내는 동사로, '보다, 듣다, 느끼다' 등의 의미를 갖는 see, look at, watch, hear, listen to, feel 등의 동사를 말한다. 'see/hear/feel+목적어+원형부정사/현재분사'의 형태로 '목적어가 ~하는 것을[~하는 중인 것을] 보다/듣다/느끼다'라는 의미를 갖는다. 목적격보어 자리에 원형부정사와 현재분사를 모두 사용할 수 있으나 의미상 그 동작이 진행 중인 것을 나타낼 때에는 주로 현재분사를 사용한다.

  • They **saw** him **read** a book. 그들은 그가 책을 읽는 것을 보았다.

  • Did you **hear** the baby **crying**? 너는 그 아기가 울고 있는 소리를 들었니?

■ '지각동사+목적어+원형부정사[현재분사]'로 쓰이는 경우, 목적어와 목적격보어는 능동 관계가 된다. '지각동사+목적어+과거분사'로 쓰이는 경우 목적어와 목적격보어의 관계는 수동 관계이다.

  • She **felt** him **touch** her hand. 그녀는 그가 손을 만지는 것을 느꼈다.

  • I **heard** my name **called**. 나는 내 이름이 불리는 소리를 들었다.

■ 사역동사 make, have, let과 혼동하지 않도록 한다. 사역동사도 5형식 동사로 목적어와 목적격보어를 취하지만, 사역동사의 목적격보어로는 동사원형이 나온다. have나 make는 목적격보어로 과거분사를 취할 때도 있다.

  • The teacher **made** me **do** my homework. 선생님은 나에게 숙제를 하도록 시키셨다.

  • I **had** my computer **fixed** yesterday. 나는 어제 내 컴퓨터가 수리되도록 했다.

핵심 Check

1. 다음 괄호 안에서 알맞은 말을 고르시오.

  (1) She saw him (to do / doing) his homework.

  ➡ _____

  (2) I heard my sister (sing / sang) in her room.

  ➡ _____

  (3) He had his car (washing / washed).

  ➡ _____

② 가주어 'it'

> • **It** is hard **to believe** that you can understand us.
> 네가 우리를 이해할 수 있다는 것을 믿기 힘들어.
>
> • **It** is interesting **to play** soccer. 축구하는 것은 재미있다.

■ 비교적 긴 to부정사 부분이 문장의 주어로 쓰일 때 그 to부정사 부분을 보통의 주어 자리인 문장의 맨 앞에 두지 않고 문장 뒤에 두고, 대신 그 주어 자리에 it을 넣어주는데 그것이 가주어 it이며 뒤로 간 to부정사 부분은 진주어라고 한다. 이때 쓰인 가주어 'it'은 해석하지 않는다.

- • **It** is not easy **to study** hard every day. 매일 열심히 공부하는 것은 쉽지 않다.
  = **To study** hard every day is not easy.
- • **It** is a lot fun **to draw** cartoons. 만화를 그리는 것은 아주 재미있다.
  = **To draw** cartoons is a lot fun.

■ to부정사의 의미상 주어

'to부정사'가 행하는 동작의 주체를 to부정사의 의미상 주어라고 한다. to부정사의 의미상 주어를 나타낼 때는 to부정사 바로 앞에 'for+목적격'의 형태로 쓴다. 문장에 쓰인 형용사가 kind, foolish, rude, careless, wise 등과 같이 사람의 성질을 나타내는 말일 때는 'of+목적격'을 쓴다. 또한 to부정사의 부정은 to부정사 앞에 not[never]을 써서 'not[never]+to V'로 나타낸다.

- • **It** is necessary **for you to be** careful all the time. 너는 항상 조심할 필요가 있다.
- • **It** is kind **of you to show** me the way. 길을 가르쳐 주셔서 감사합니다.
- • **It** was difficult **for him not to smoke**. 그가 담배를 피우지 않는 것은 힘들었다.

■ 주어로 쓰인 'that'절의 경우에도 보통 가주어 'it'을 쓰고 'that'절을 문장 뒤로 보낸다.

- • **That** he should attend the meeting every day is important. 그가 매일 회의에 참석하는 것이 중요하다.
  = **It** is important **that** he should attend the meeting every day.

핵심 Check

2. 다음 괄호 안에서 알맞은 말을 고르시오.

(1) It is fun (play / to play) basketball.

➡ _____

(2) It was hard for him (solve / to solve) the problem.

➡ _____

(3) (It / That) is necessary for you to exercise.

➡ _____

01 다음 문장에서 어법상 <u>어색한</u> 부분을 바르게 고쳐 쓰시오.

(1) The girl heard the birds sang.

_____ ➡ _____

(2) He saw a drone to fly.

_____ ➡ _____

(3) It is important choose good friends.

_____ ➡ _____

(4) That is necessary to learn a new language.

_____ ➡ _____

02 주어진 단어를 어법에 맞게 빈칸에 쓰시오.

(1) I heard her _____ in the room. (cry)
(2) They saw the room _____. (clean)
(3) People came to watch them _____ the game. (play)
(4) Helen felt the water _____ with her hands. (flow)

03 다음 우리말을 영어로 바르게 옮긴 것은?

> 그 여행 가방들을 들고 다니는 것은 불가능하다.

① That is impossible to carry the suitcases.
② That is impossible carrying the suitcases.
③ It is impossible carry the suitcases.
④ It is impossible to carry the suitcases.
⑤ It is impossible carries the suitcases.

04 주어진 어구를 바르게 배열하여 다음 우리말을 영어로 쓰시오. 필요하다면 단어를 추가하거나 변형하시오.

> 당신은 쉬는 것이 필요하다.
> (a rest, you, it, take, is, necessary, to)

➡ _____

01 다음 빈칸에 알맞은 말이 순서대로 바르게 짝지어진 것은?

> • I saw a cat _____ the street.
> • It is a lot of fun _____ cartoons.

① cross – drawing
② crossed – draw
③ crossed – to draw
④ crossing – draw
⑤ crossing – to draw

02 다음 빈칸에 들어갈 말로 가장 적절한 것은?

> David felt the dog _____ his clothes.

① pulls   ② pulled
③ pulling   ④ to pull
⑤ to pulling

03 다음 빈칸에 알맞은 말로 바르게 짝지어진 것을 고르시오.

> _____ is very exciting _____ the soccer game in the stadium.

① It – to watch
② It – watch
③ That – watching
④ That – watch
⑤ That – to watch

서답형
04 주어진 단어를 이용하여 다음 우리말을 영어로 쓰시오. (10단어)

> 주말에 재미로 자전거를 타는 것은 좋다. (it, for fun, good, ride bicycles)

➡ _____

05 다음 중 어법상 바르지 않은 것은?

① I saw a boy helping an old lady cross the road.
② They listened to Michelle singing on the stage.
③ Jekyll heard someone coming up the stairs.
④ At times, Nora felt him to stare at her.
⑤ She watched her father come toward her.

서답형
06 다음 괄호 안에서 알맞은 말을 고르시오.

(1) Did you see many people (to wait / waiting) in a line?
(2) I heard Jack (played / playing) the guitar.
(3) I watched the game (played / playing) from beginning to end.
(4) Why are you making him (listening / listen) to Wayne?
(5) (That / It) is not easy to speak in front of many people.
(6) It is dangerous (swims / to swim) in the sea.
(7) It's so kind (for / of) you to show me the way to the station.

07 다음 중 어법상 바르지 <u>않은</u> 것은?

> Max ①sat ②in front of the oven and ③ watched her ④to bake ⑤the cookies.

①   ②   ③   ④   ⑤

08 다음 문장에서 어법상 <u>틀린</u> 부분을 찾아 바르게 고쳐 쓰시오.

> This isn't true that Ella likes to speak in front of people.

_____ ➡ _____

[09~10] 다음 우리말을 영어로 바르게 옮긴 것을 <u>모두</u> 고르시오.

09

> 나는 누군가 내 어깨를 만지는 것을 느꼈다.

① I felt someone touches my shoulder.
② I felt someone touched my shoulder.
③ I felt someone touch my shoulder.
④ I felt someone touching my shoulder.
⑤ I felt someone to touch my shoulder.

> 여름에 선글라스를 쓰는 것은 도움이 된다.

① It is helpful wears sunglasses in summer.
② It is helpful wore sunglasses in summer.
③ It is helpful wear sunglasses in summer.
④ It is helpful to wear sunglasses in summer.
⑤ It is helpful to wearing sunglasses in summer.

11 다음 대화의 빈칸에 알맞은 말을 4단어로 쓰시오.

> **A:** It is cold here. Who turned off the stove?
> **B:** Bill did. I saw _____.

➡ _____

12 다음 중 어법상 올바른 문장을 <u>모두</u> 고르시오.

① Jane heard the dog barking at a stranger.
② I saw a boy to solve math problems.
③ By the way, do you think it will be possible of robots to replace humans someday?
④ Is it possible to flying through a rainbow?
⑤ It is not dangerous to do bungee jumping.

13 다음 중 (A)～(C)에서 어법상 옳은 것끼리 바르게 짝지은 것은?

> • I heard the boy (A)(shouting / to shout).
> • We can see the sky (B)(turn / turned) yellow with dust.
> • He was almost asleep when he heard his name (C)(calling / called).

① to shout – turn – calling
② to shout – turned – called
③ shouting – turn – called
④ shouting – turn – calling
⑤ shouting – turned – calling

14 다음 중 밑줄 친 부분의 쓰임이 <u>다른</u> 하나는?

① Is <u>it</u> possible for AI to read those words?
② Look! <u>It</u> is going up that tree.
③ <u>It</u> is hard to believe that you can understand us.
④ <u>It</u> is difficult to remember all my friends' birthdays.
⑤ Of course <u>it</u> was not easy to break my old habit.

15 다음 주어진 문장의 밑줄 친 부분과 쓰임이 같은 것은?

> Jekyll's friend saw Jekyll <u>drinking</u> strange water.

① <u>Watching</u> the movie, we had some popcorn.
② The smell was from the soup that she was <u>cooking</u> for us.
③ We all heard a baby <u>crying</u> loudly.
④ <u>Driving</u> a smart car was not so difficult.
⑤ When I was standing in front of the screen on the smart closet door, my clothes kept <u>changing</u>.

서답형

16 다음 문장을 it을 이용하여 바꿔 쓰시오.

(1) To make her laugh is not easy.

➡ _____

(2) To read 10 books during winter vacation is my plan.

➡ _____

_____

서답형

17 다음 문장에서 어법상 어색한 부분을 바르게 고치시오.

(1) Stephanie watched her husband to paint the wall.

_____ ➡ _____

(2) It is safer wears a helmet when riding a bike.

_____ ➡ _____.

(3) Is it possible of you to live without your smartphone?

_____ ➡ _____.

서답형

18 다음 괄호 안에 주어진 단어를 이용하여 우리말을 영어로 옮기시오.

(1) 민수는 그 집을 지나갈 때마다 개가 짖는 소리를 듣는다. (Minsu로 시작할 것)
(a dog, bark, hear, pass by, whenever)

➡ _____

_____

(2) 나는 새가 하늘 높이 나는 것을 봤다.
(see, a bird, fly, high)

➡ _____

(3) 내가 친구들과 함께 야구 경기를 관람하는 것은 재미있다.
(my friends, exciting, watch, baseball games, it) (12 단어)

➡ _____

_____

(4) 종이를 불 근처에 두는 것은 위험하다.
(dangerous, near the fire, put, it) (9 단어)

➡ _____

01 다음 문장에서 어법상 <u>어색한</u> 부분을 찾아 바르게 고쳐 다시 쓰시오.

(1) I saw them to play soccer in the playground.

➡ _____

(2) Barbara felt her heart beaten faster.

➡ _____

(3) Aaron looked at Sylvia came with Alex hand in hand.

➡ _____

_____

(4) A farmer bought 43 sheep at the market and saw them steal 24 hours later.

➡ _____

_____

(5) It is hard take care of a baby.

➡ _____

(6) That is a lot of fun to go on a picnic.

➡ _____

(7) It is difficult of me to learn a new language.

➡ _____

02 〈보기〉와 같이 다음 두 문장을 하나의 문장으로 쓰시오.

┌─ 보기 ─────────────────────┐
• I saw a boy. • He was reading a book.
➡ I saw a boy reading a book.
└───────────────────────────┘

┌───────────────────────────┐
• I heard Sam.
• Sam was baking some cookies.
└───────────────────────────┘

➡ _____

03 다음 문장을 It으로 시작하여 다시 쓰시오.

(1) To answer the math questions was very difficult.

➡ _____

(2) To swim in the blue sea was a great experience.

➡ _____

(3) To exercise regularly is good for your health.

➡ _____

(4) To learn English is not easy for me.

➡ _____

(5) That a friend in need is a friend indeed is true.

➡ _____

04 〈보기〉에서 의미상 적절한 단어를 골라 빈칸에 알맞은 형태로 쓰시오.

┌─ 보기 ─────────────────────┐
pull / stay / take / sing
└───────────────────────────┘

(1) The doctor told me _____ _____ in bed for one more day.

(2) He saw the building _____ down by the workers.

(3) Can you hear my sister _____ upstairs?

(4) She made him _____ off his shirt.

05 다음 빈칸에 적절한 말을 쓰시오.

Is it possible for you _____ _____ _____ _____ during summer vacation? (50 novels)

06 두 문장이 같은 뜻이 되도록 (1)~(3)은 to부정사를 이용하여, (4)는 that절을 이용하여 빈칸을 완성하시오.

(1) I have difficulty in passing the driver's test.

➡ It is difficult _____.

(2) Watching the view as we went higher and higher was so exciting.

➡ It was so exciting _____

_____

(3) You are kind to help that old woman.

➡ It is kind _____.

(4) In fact, Annabelle didn't tell him a lie.

➡ It is true _____.

07 다음 빈칸에 적절한 말을 쓰시오.

I saw Jane _____ a website.

08 다음 두 문장을 〈보기〉와 같이 한 문장으로 고쳐 쓰시오.

┤ 보기 ├

I saw him. + He was running with his dog.

= I saw him running with his dog.

(1) He heard them.

+ They were playing the drums.

➡ _____

(2) Suhan looked at AI Speaker.

+ AI Speaker was playing a movie.

➡ _____

09 to부정사를 진주어로 하여 주어진 문장과 같은 의미가 되도록 쓰시오.

(1) She is very smart to solve that problem.

➡ _____

(2) This river is not safe to swim in as it is very deep.

➡ _____

_____

Grammar **131**

Reading

교과서

A Day at the AI Expo

Jina and Suhan are at the World AI Expo. They are entering the AI
현재진행형(be+~ing): ~하고 있다
home.

Suhan: Look at this! It's a house of the future.

Jina: Let's go into the bedroom first. Look, there's a smart closet.
~으로 들어가다

Suhan: I'm standing in front of this screen on the closet door and my
~ 앞에
clothes keep changing.
keep -ing: 계속 ~하다

Jina: The screen suggests clothes that suit the weather.
주격 관계대명사

Suhan: That's amazing! We no longer have to worry about dressing for
더 이상 ~하지 않다   ~에 대해 걱정하다
the weather.

Jina: Right. Let's move on to the living room.
~로 이동하다

Suhan: Oh, I like this music speaker.

AI Speaker: I'm not just a music speaker. I can do more than you can
단지 ~이 아닌   ~ 이상
imagine.

Jina: It's hard to believe that you can understand us. What can you do?
가주어   진주어

AI Speaker: How about watching a movie? I'll play one for you.
제안, 권유: ~하는 것이 어때?   = a movie

Suhan: Look, those smart windows are getting darker. I feel like I'm in
get+비교급: 점점 ~해지다   ~인 것 같다
a movie theater.

AI 인공 지능
Expo 박람회
enter 들어가다
future 미래
bedroom 침실
closet 옷장
suggest 제안하다
dress 옷을 입다; 옷, 드레스
imagine 상상하다
window 창문
theater 극장
dark 어두운

📎 확인문제

● 다음 문장이 본문의 내용과 일치하면 T, 일치하지 않으면 F를 쓰시오.

1 Jina and Suhan are at the World AI Expo. ☐

2 Suhan actually keeps changing his clothes. ☐

3 AI Speaker can do more than people can imagine. ☐

4 Jina and Suhan are in a movie theater now. ☐

Jina: What else can you do?
그 밖의

AI Speaker: I can beatbox, too. Here comes, "cats and boots and cats and boots."

Suhan: You're funny. Good job!
잘했어!

Jina: Hurry! There's a smart car station outside! Let's go and ride in that red car.

Suhan: This car is so cool. Let's get in.
타다

AI Car: Welcome. Are you ready to go?
be ready to: ~할 준비가 되다

Jina: Yes, what should we do now? It's my first time to ride in a smart car.
to부정사의 형용사적 용법

AI Car: You don't need to do anything. I will drive and take you to the
~할 필요가 없다   아무것도   데리고 가다
next station.

Suhan: Watch out! I see a cat crossing the street.
조심해!   지각동사+목적어+목적격보어(원형부정사/현재분사)

AI Car: Don't worry. I have just sensed it. When I sense dangerous
have+pp: 현재완료의 완료 용법(막 ~했다)
situations, I slow down or stop.
속도를 늦추다

Jina: How can you do that?
= slow down or stop

AI Car: I'm a very intelligent robotic car. I know all about driving. I can predict danger based on knowledge and experience.
~에 근거하여

Suhan: How smart! You think and act like a person. You are really like
감탄문 How+형용사(+주어+동사)!   ~처럼   ~와 같은
a human.

else 그 밖의

beatbox 비트박스를 하다

boot 부츠, 목이 긴 신발

funny 재미있는

station 정류장

outside 밖에

cross 건너다

sense 감지하다

dangerous 위험한

situation 상황

intelligent 지능적인, 똑똑한

predict 예측하다

person 사람, 개인

human 인간, 인간의

📎 **확인문제**

● 다음 문장이 본문의 내용과 일치하면 T, 일치하지 않으면 F를 쓰시오.

1 AI Speaker can beatbox, too. ☐

2 Jina has ridden in a smart car before. ☐

3 When AI Car senses dangerous situations, it slows down or stops. ☐

4 AI Car can't drive as well as humans. ☐

● 우리말을 참고하여 빈칸에 알맞은 말을 쓰시오.

1 A Day _____ the AI Expo

2 Jina and Suhan are _____ _____ _____ _____ _____.

3 They are _____ the AI home.

4 Suhan: Look at this! It's a house _____ _____ _____.

5 Jina: Let's _____ _____ the bedroom first. Look, there's a smart closet.

6 Suhan: I'm standing in front of this screen _____ _____ _____ _____ and my clothes _____ _____.

7 Jina: The screen suggests clothes _____ _____ _____ _____.

8 Suhan: That's amazing! We _____ _____ have to worry about _____ _____ _____ _____.

9 Jina: Right. Let's _____ _____ _____ the living room.

10 Suhan: Oh, I like _____ _____ _____.

11 AI Speaker: _____ _____ _____ a music speaker.

12 I can do _____ _____ you can imagine.

13 Jina: _____ _____ _____ _____ that you can understand us. What can you do?

14 AI Speaker: _____ _____ watching a movie?

15 I'll _____ _____ for you.

16 Suhan: Look, those smart windows are _____ _____.

17 I _____ _____ I'm in a movie theater.

1	인공 지능 박람회에서의 하루
2	진아와 수한이가 세계 인공 지능 박람회에 있다.
3	그들은 인공 지능 집으로 들어가고 있다.
4	수한: 이것 봐! 미래의 집이야.
5	진아: 침실 먼저 들어가 보자. 이거 봐, 스마트 옷장이 있어.
6	수한: 옷장 문에 있는 스크린 앞에 서 있으니까 내 옷이 계속해서 바뀌어.
7	진아: 스크린이 날씨에 적합한 옷을 제안하는 거야.
8	수한: 놀라워! 우린 더 이상 날씨 때문에 무슨 옷을 입을지 걱정할 필요가 없겠다.
9	진아: 맞아. 이제 거실로 가 보자.
10	수한: 오, 이 음악 스피커 마음에 들어.
11	인공 지능 스피커: 저는 그냥 음악 스피커가 아니에요.
12	저는 당신이 상상하는 것 이상의 것을 할 수 있어요.
13	진아: 네가 우리를 이해한다니 믿기 어려운 걸! 넌 뭘 할 수 있어?
14	인공 지능 스피커: 영화 보는 건 어때요?
15	하나 틀어 줄게요.
16	수한: 이것 봐, 스마트 창문이 점점 어두워지고 있어.
17	마치 내가 영화관 안에 있는 것 같아.

18 Jina: _____ _____ can you do?

19 AI Speaker: I can beatbox, too. _____ _____, "cats and boots and cats and boots."

20 Suhan: You're funny. _____ _____!

21 Jina: _____! There's a smart car station outside!

22 Let's go and _____ _____ that red car.

23 Suhan: This car is _____ _____. Let's _____ _____.

24 AI Car: Welcome. Are you _____ _____ _____?

25 Jina: Yes, _____ _____ we do now?

26 It's _____ _____ _____ to ride in a smart car.

27 AI Car: You _____ _____ _____ do anything.

28 I will drive and _____ _____ _____ the next station.

29 Suhan: Watch out! I see a cat _____ the street.

30 AI Car: Don't worry. I _____ _____ _____ it.

31 When I _____ _____ _____, I slow down or stop.

32 Jina: _____ can you do that?

33 AI Car: I'm a very _____ _____ car.

34 I know _____ _____ _____.

35 I can predict danger _____ _____ knowledge and experience.

36 Suhan: _____ smart! You think and act _____ a person.

37 You are really _____ a human.

18 진아: 또 뭘 할 수 있어?

19 인공 지능 스피커: 비트박스도 할 수 있어요. "북치기 박치기 북치기 박치기."

20 수한: 넌 정말 재미있구나. 잘했어!

21 진아: 서둘러! 밖에 스마트 자동차 정류장이 있어.

22 가서 저 빨간 차를 타 보자.

23 수한: 이 차 정말 멋지다. 차에 타자.

24 인공 지능 자동차: 어서 오세요. 갈 준비 됐나요?

25 진아: 응. 우린 이제 뭘 해야 하지?

26 스마트 자동차에 타는 건 처음이야.

27 인공 지능 자동차: 아무 것도 하지 않아도 돼요.

28 제가 운전해서 다음 정류장까지 데려다줄 거니까요.

29 수한: 조심해! 고양이가 길을 건너고 있는 게 보여.

30 인공 지능 자동차: 걱정 말아요. 이미 감지했어요.

31 저는 어떤 위험 상황을 감지하면 속도를 늦추거나 멈춰요.

32 진아: 어떻게 그렇게 할 수 있어?

33 인공 지능 자동차: 전 아주 지능적인 로봇 차예요.

34 저는 운전에 대한 모든 걸 알고 있어요.

35 저는 제 지식과 경험을 바탕으로 위험을 예측할 수 있어요.

36 수한: 정말 똑똑하구나! 사람처럼 생각하고 행동하는구나.

37 정말 인간 같아.

● 우리말을 참고하여 본문을 영작하시오.

1 인공 지능 박람회에서의 하루
➡ _____

2 진아와 수한이가 세계 인공 지능 박람회에 있다.
➡ _____

3 그들은 인공 지능 집으로 들어가고 있다.
➡ _____

4 수한: 이것 봐! 미래의 집이야.
➡ _____

5 진아: 침실 먼저 들어가 보자. 이거 봐, 스마트 옷장이 있어.
➡ _____

6 수한: 옷장 문에 있는 스크린 앞에 서 있으니까 내 옷이 계속해서 바뀌어.
➡ _____

7 진아: 스크린이 날씨에 적합한 옷을 제안하는 거야.
➡ _____

8 수한: 놀라워! 우린 더 이상 날씨 때문에 무슨 옷을 입을지 걱정할 필요가 없겠다.
➡ _____

9 진아: 맞아. 이제 거실로 가 보자.
➡ _____

10 수한: 오, 이 음악 스피커 마음에 들어.
➡ _____

11 인공 지능 스피커: 저는 그냥 음악 스피커가 아니에요.
➡ _____

12 저는 당신이 상상하는 것 이상의 것을 할 수 있어요.
➡ _____

13 진아: 네가 우리를 이해한다니 믿기 어려운 걸! 넌 뭘 할 수 있어?
➡ _____

14 인공 지능 스피커: 영화 보는 건 어때요?
➡ _____

15 하나 틀어 줄게요.
➡ _____

16 수한: 이것 봐, 스마트 창문이 점점 어두워지고 있어.
➡ _____

17 마치 내가 영화관 안에 있는 것 같아.
➡ _____

18 진아: 또 뭘 할 수 있어?

➡ _____

19 인공 지능 스피커: 비트박스도 할 수 있어요. "북치기 박치기 북치기 박치기."

➡ _____

20 수한: 넌 정말 재미있구나. 잘했어!

➡ _____

21 진아: 서둘러! 밖에 스마트 자동차 정류장이 있어.

➡ _____

22 가서 저 빨간 차를 타 보자.

➡ _____

23 수한: 이 차 정말 멋지다. 차에 타자.

➡ _____

24 인공 지능 자동차: 어서 오세요. 갈 준비 됐나요?

➡ _____

25 진아: 응, 우린 이제 뭘 해야 하지?

➡ _____

26 스마트 자동차에 타는 건 처음이야.

➡ _____

27 인공 지능 자동차: 아무 것도 하지 않아도 돼요.

➡ _____

28 제가 운전해서 다음 정류장까지 데려다줄 거니까요.

➡ _____

29 수한: 조심해! 고양이가 길을 건너고 있는 게 보여.

➡ _____

30 인공 지능 자동차: 걱정 말아요. 이미 감지했어요.

➡ _____

31 저는 어떤 위험 상황을 감지하면 속도를 늦추거나 멈춰요.

➡ _____

32 진아: 어떻게 그렇게 할 수 있어?

➡ _____

33 인공 지능 자동차: 전 아주 지능적인 로봇 차예요.

➡ _____

34 저는 운전에 대한 모든 걸 알고 있어요.

➡ _____

35 저는 제 지식과 경험을 바탕으로 위험을 예측할 수 있어요.

➡ _____

36 수한: 정말 똑똑하구나! 사람처럼 생각하고 행동하는구나.

➡ _____

37 정말 인간 같아.

➡ _____

[01~03] 다음 글을 읽고 물음에 답하시오.

Jina and Suhan are at the World AI Expo. ⓐ They are entering the AI home.

Suhan: Look at this! It's a house of the future.

Jina: Let's go into the bedroom first. Look, there's a smart closet.

Suhan: I'm ⓑstanding in front of this screen on the closet door and my clothes keep changing.

Jina: The screen suggests clothes that suit the weather.

Suhan: That's amazing! We no longer have to worry about dressing for the weather.

Jina: Right. Let's move on to the living room.

서답형

01 위 글의 밑줄 친 ⓐThey가 가리키는 것을 본문에서 찾아 쓰시오.

➡ _____

02 위 글의 밑줄 친 ⓑstanding과 문법적 쓰임이 같은 것을 고르시오. (3개)

① You must stop smoking for your health.

② I smelled something burning.

③ My plan is going to Paris.

④ Kids are playing on the sand.

⑤ I saw him playing tennis.

중요

03 위 글의 내용과 일치하지 <u>않는</u> 것은?

① 진아와 수한이는 세계 인공 지능 박람회에 있다.

② 수한이는 침실에 먼저 들어가 보자고 말한다.

③ 옷장 문에 있는 스크린 앞에 서 있으면 옷이 계속해서 바뀐다.

④ 옷장 문에 있는 스크린이 날씨에 적합한 옷을 제안해 준다.

⑤ 수한이는 더 이상 날씨 때문에 무슨 옷을 입을지 걱정할 필요가 없겠다고 말한다.

[04~06] 다음 글을 읽고 물음에 답하시오.

Suhan: Oh, I like this music speaker. (①)

AI Speaker: (②) I'm not just a music speaker. (③) I can do more than you can imagine. (④)

Jina: (⑤) What can you do?

AI Speaker: How about watching a movie? I'll play (A)[it / one] for you.

Suhan: Look, those smart windows are getting darker. ⓐ마치 내가 영화관 안에 있는 것 같아.

Jina: (B)[What / What else] can you do?

AI Speaker: I can beatbox, too. Here (C)[come / comes], "cats and boots and cats and boots."

Suhan: You're funny. Good job!

04 위 글의 흐름으로 보아, 주어진 문장이 들어가기에 가장 적절한 곳은?

It's hard to believe that you can understand us.

① ② ③ ④ ⑤

서답형

05 위 글의 괄호 (A)~(C)에서 문맥이나 어법상 알맞은 낱말을 골라 쓰시오.

(A) _____ (B) _____ (C) _____

서답형

06 위 글의 밑줄 친 ⓐ의 우리말에 맞게 주어진 어휘를 이용하여 8단어로 영작하시오.

feel like

➡ _____

[07~09] 다음 글을 읽고 물음에 답하시오.

Jina: Hurry! There's a smart car station outside! Let's go and ride in that red car.

Suhan: This car is so ⓐcool. Let's get in.

AI Car: Welcome. Are you ready to go?

Jina: Yes, what should we do now? It's my first time to ride in a smart car.

AI Car: You don't need to do anything. I will drive and take you to the next station.

Suhan: Watch out! I see a cat ___(A)___ the street.

AI Car: Don't worry. I have just sensed it. When I sense dangerous situations, I slow down or stop.

Jina: How can you do that?

AI Car: I'm a very intelligent robotic car. I know all about driving. I can predict danger based on knowledge and experience.

Suhan: How smart! You think and act like a person. You are really like a human.

07 위 글의 빈칸 (A)에 들어갈 알맞은 말을 고르시오. (2개)

① cross   ② to cross

③ crosses   ④ crossing

⑤ crossed

08 위 글의 밑줄 친 ⓐcool과 같은 의미로 쓰인 것을 모두 고르시오.

① I like a cool breeze in autumn.

② You look pretty cool with that new haircut.

③ How did you keep cool in the moment of danger?

④ Store lemons in a cool dry place.

⑤ How cool my new smart phone is!

09 위 글의 제목으로 가장 알맞은 것을 고르시오.

① Let's Go and Ride in a Smart Car

② My First Time to Ride in a Smart Car

③ Don't Worry! I Know All about Driving

④ Watch Out! A Cat Is Crossing the Street

⑤ I've Already Sensed a Dangerous Situation!

[10~12] 다음 글을 읽고 물음에 답하시오.

Jina and Suhan are at the World AI Expo. They are entering the AI home.

Suhan: Look at this! It's a house of the future.

Jina: Let's go into the bedroom first. Look, there's a smart closet.

Suhan: I'm standing in front of this screen on the closet door and my clothes keep ___ⓐ___ .

Jina: The screen suggests clothes that suit the weather.

Suhan: That's amazing! We no longer have to ⓑworry about dressing for the weather.

Jina: Right. Let's move on to the living room.

10 위 글의 빈칸 ⓐ에 change를 알맞은 형태로 쓰시오.

➡ _____

11 위 글의 밑줄 친 ⓑworry about과 바꿔 쓸 수 없는 것을 모두 고르시오.

① be concerned about

② be anxious for

③ be worried about

④ be anxious about

⑤ be concerned with

12 위 글을 읽고 대답할 수 <u>없는</u> 질문은?

① Where are Jina and Suhan entering?

② Where do Jina and Suhan enter first at the AI home?

③ Where is Suhan standing?

④ How does Suhan's clothes keep changing?

⑤ What does the screen on the closet door suggest?

[13~16] 다음 글을 읽고 물음에 답하시오.

> Suhan: Oh, I like this music speaker.
>
> AI Speaker: I'm not just a music speaker. ①I can do more than you can imagine.
>
> Jina: It's hard to believe that you can understand us. What can ②you do?
>
> AI Speaker: How about watching a movie? I'll play one for ③you.
>
> Suhan: Look, those smart windows are getting darker. I feel ⓐlike I'm in a movie theater.
>
> Jina: What else can you do?
>
> AI Speaker: ④I can beatbox, too. Here comes, "cats and boots and cats and boots."
>
> Suhan: ⑤You're funny. Good job!

13 다음 밑줄 친 ①~⑤ 중에서 가리키는 대상이 나머지 넷과 <u>다른</u> 것은?

①   ②   ③   ④   ⑤

14 위 글의 밑줄 친 ⓐlike와 문법적 쓰임이 같은 것을 고르시오. (2개)

① No one sings the blues <u>like</u> she did.

② I <u>like</u> my coffee strong.

③ Cut the cabbage <u>like</u> this.

④ It looks <u>like</u> her bed wasn't slept in.

⑤ She responded in <u>like</u> manner.

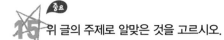

15 위 글의 주제로 알맞은 것을 고르시오.

① the speaker that Suhan likes most at the World AI Expo

② the reason why Jina can't believe that the speaker can understand them

③ how to watch a movie using AI Speaker

④ AI Speaker that can beatbox

⑤ what AI Speaker can do besides playing its original role

서답형

16 본문의 내용과 일치하도록 다음 빈칸 (A)와 (B)에 알맞은 단어를 쓰시오.

> AI Speaker not only is a (A)_____ _____ but also can play a movie and (B)_____.

[17~19] 다음 글을 읽고 물음에 답하시오.

> Jina: Hurry! There's a smart car station outside! Let's go and ride in that red car.
>
> Suhan: This car is so cool. Let's get in.
>
> AI Car: Welcome. Are you ready ⓐto go?
>
> Jina: Yes, what should we do now? It's my first time to ride in a smart car.
>
> AI Car: You don't need to do anything. I will drive and take you ___(A)___ the next station.
>
> Suhan: Watch out! I see a cat crossing the street.
>
> AI Car: Don't worry. I have just sensed it. When I sense dangerous situations, I slow down or stop.

Jina: How can you do that?

AI Car: I'm a very intelligent robotic car. I know all about driving. I can ____(B)____ based ____(C)____ knowledge and experience.

Suhan: How smart! You think and act like a person. You are really like a human.

17 위 글의 빈칸 (A)와 (C)에 들어갈 전치사가 바르게 짝지어진 것은?

① to – on
② in – by
③ in – from
④ to – by
⑤ for – on

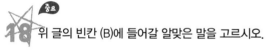

18 위 글의 빈칸 (B)에 들어갈 알맞은 말을 고르시오.

① predict safety
② protect cats
③ decide routes
④ predict danger
⑤ generate danger

19 위 글의 밑줄 친 ⓐto go와 to부정사의 용법이 다른 것을 고르시오. (2개)

① I have nothing particular to do today.
② He must be a liar to say such a thing.
③ He is rich enough to buy large house.
④ I told him to clean the room.
⑤ I am sorry to have to leave so early.

[20~23] 다음 글을 읽고 물음에 답하시오.

DAILY NEWS

AI Beats Human!

An AI program has ____(A)____ a human in a baduk match. The AI had a match with Lee Sedol, ⓐ그는 가장 위대한 바둑기사들 중의 한 명이다.

Baduk is a board game, and the rules are difficult to understand. Many people believed ____(B)____ would be impossible for an AI to beat a human player. However, the AI was able to predict Lee's play, and it finally won the game. People are shocked that an AI can be more intelligent than a human.

서답형

20 본문의 한 단어를 변형하여 위 글의 빈칸 (A)에 들어갈 알맞은 말을 쓰시오.

➡ _____

서답형

21 위 글의 빈칸 (B)에 들어갈 알맞은 말을 쓰시오.

➡ _____

서답형

22 위 글의 밑줄 친 ⓐ의 우리말에 맞게 주어진 어휘를 이용하여 8단어로 영작하시오.

who, baduk players

➡ _____

23 위 글의 내용과 일치하지 <u>않는</u> 것은?

① 바둑 대국에서 AI 프로그램이 인간을 이겼다.
② 바둑은 보드 게임이고, 그 규칙은 이해하기 어렵다.
③ 많은 사람들은 AI가 인간 기사를 이기는 것은 불가능할 것이라고 믿었다.
④ 이세돌은 경기를 예측할 수 있었고, 그리고 마침내 AI와의 경기에서 이겼다.
⑤ 사람들은 AI가 인간보다 더 똑똑할 수 있다는 것에 충격을 받았다.

[01~03] 다음 글을 읽고 물음에 답하시오.

Jina and Suhan are at the World AI Expo. ⓐ <u>They are entering into the AI home.</u>

Suhan: Look at this! It's a house of the future.

Jina: Let's go into the bedroom first. Look, there's a smart closet.

Suhan: I'm standing in front of this screen on the closet door and my clothes keep changing.

Jina: (A)<u>The screen</u> suggests clothes that suit the weather.

Suhan: That's amazing! ⓑ우린 더 이상 날씨 때문에 무슨 옷을 입을지 걱정할 필요가 없겠다.

Jina: Right. Let's move on to the living room.

01 위 글의 밑줄 친 ⓐ에서 어법상 틀린 부분을 찾아 고치시오.

_____ ➡ _____

02 위 글의 밑줄 친 ⓑ의 우리말에 맞게, 주어진 어휘를 알맞게 배열하시오.

> the weather / dressing / have to / we / about / no longer / for / worry

➡ _____
_____

03 다음 빈칸 (a)와 (b)에 알맞은 단어를 넣어 위 글의 밑줄 친 (A)The screen에 대한 소개를 완성하시오.

> It is the screen on the smart (a)_____ _____ and suggests clothes that suit (b)_____ _____ to the person who is standing in front of it.

[04~07] 다음 글을 읽고 물음에 답하시오.

Suhan: Oh, I like this music speaker.

AI Speaker: I'm not just a music speaker. I can do more ⓐ_____ you can imagine.

Jina: It's hard to believe that you can understand us. What can you do?

AI Speaker: ⓑ<u>How about watching a movie?</u> I'll play one for you.

Suhan: Look, those smart windows are ⓒ <u>getting</u> darker. I feel like I'm in a movie theater.

Jina: What else can you do?

AI Speaker: I can beatbox, too. Here comes, "cats and boots and cats and boots."

Suhan: You're funny. Good job!

04 위 글의 빈칸 ⓐ에 들어갈 알맞은 말을 쓰시오.

➡ _____

05 위 글의 밑줄 친 ⓑ를 다음과 같이 바꿔 쓸 때 빈칸에 들어갈 알맞은 말을 쓰시오.

> _____ _____ watching a movie?
> = _____ _____ _____ watch a movie?

06 위 글의 밑줄 친 ⓒgetting과 바꿔 쓸 수 있는 단어를 쓰시오.

➡ _____

07 위 글을 읽고 '음악 스피커의 역할' 외에 AI Speaker가 할 수 있는 일 두 가지를 우리말로 쓰시오.

(1) _____
(2) _____

[08~11] 다음 글을 읽고 물음에 답하시오.

Jina: Hurry! There's a smart car station outside! Let's go and ride in that red car.

Suhan: This car is so cool. Let's get in.

ⓐAI Car: Welcome. Are you ready to go?

Jina: Yes, what should we do now? It's my first time to ride in a smart car.

AI Car: ⓑYou don't need to do anything. I will drive and take you to the next station.

Suhan: Watch out! I see a cat crossing the street.

AI Car: ⓒDon't worry. I have just sensed ⓓit. When I sense dangerous situations, I slow down or stop.

Jina: How can you do that?

AI Car: I'm a very intelligent robotic car. I know all about driving. I can predict danger based on knowledge and experience.

Suhan: How smart! You think and act like a person. You are really like a human.

08 다음 빈칸에 본문의 한 단어를 알맞은 형태로 바꿔 넣어, 위 글의 밑줄 친 ⓐAI의 줄이지 않은 형태를 완성하시오.

Artificial _____

09 위 글의 밑줄 친 ⓑ를 다음과 같이 바꿔 쓸 때 빈칸에 들어갈 알맞은 말을 쓰시오.

(1) You _____ _____ _____ do anything.

(2) You _____ _____ do anything.

10 위 글에서 AI Car가 밑줄 친 ⓒ처럼 말한 이유를 우리말로 쓰시오.

➡ _____

_____

_____

11 위 글의 밑줄 친 ⓓit이 가리키는 것을 본문에서 찾아 쓰시오.

➡ _____

[12~14] 다음 글을 읽고 물음에 답하시오.

Jina and Suhan are at the World AI Expo. They are entering the AI home.

Suhan: Look at this! It's a house of the future.

Jina: Let's go into the bedroom first. Look, there's a smart closet.

Suhan: I'm standing in front of this screen on the closet door and my clothes keep changing.

Jina: The screen suggests clothes that suit the weather.

Suhan: ⓐThat's amazed! We no longer have to worry about dressing for the weather.

Jina: Right. Let's move on to the living room.

12 위 글의 본문의 내용과 일치하도록 다음 빈칸 (A)와 (B)에 알맞은 단어를 쓰시오.

(A)_____ doesn't actually keep changing his clothes. He is only standing in front of the screen on the closet door and (B)_____ _____ keep changing.

13 위 글의 밑줄 친 ⓐ에서 어법상 틀린 부분을 찾아 고치시오.

_____ ➡ _____

14 Why does Suhan say that they no longer have to worry about dressing for the weather? Fill in the blanks with suitable words.

Because the screen on the closet door _____ _____ that suit the weather.

해석

Before You Read

DAILY NEWS

AI Beats Human!

An AI program has beaten a human in a baduk match. The AI had a match
with Lee Sedol, who is one of the greatest baduk players.
Baduk is a board game, and the rules are difficult to understand. Many people
believed it would be impossible for an AI to beat a human player. However,
the AI was able to predict Lee's play, and it finally won the game.
People are shocked that an AI can be more intelligent than a human.

구문해설 · **beat**: 이기다 · **match**: 경기, 시합 · **board game**: 보드 게임(판을 놓고 그 위에서 말을 이
동시켜 가며 하는 모든 게임) · **intelligent**: 총명한, 똑똑한 · **shocked**: 충격을 받은

Focus on Expressions

In 2099, people get in a flying car to get to the moon. Kids love to go to the
moon because the greatest amusement park is there. Above all, horse-riding is
their favorite activity. They don't want to get off the horses.

구문해설 · **get in**: ~에 들어가다, ~에 타다 · **get to**: ~에 도착하다 · **above all**: 다른 무엇보다도 특
히, 우선 첫째로 · **get off**: ~에서 내리다, ~에서 떨어지다

Wrap Up 1-2

G: Minseok, there is a smart food-ordering machine over there. Why don't we
try it?

B: That sounds interesting. We'll be able to order easily and fast by using it.

G: I hope so. By the way, do you think maybe it will be possible for robots to
replace humans someday?

B: I'm not sure. But we will be free from danger because of robots.

G: What do you mean?

B: Robots can help people in danger. Robots can do the dangerous work so
humans don't have to.

G: You're right. We should always try to look on the bright side.

구문해설 · **machine**: 기계 · **over there**: 저쪽에 · **be able to**: ~할 수 있다(= can) · **by the
way**: 그런데, 그건 그렇고 (대화에서 화제를 바꿀 때 씀) · **possible**: 가능한 · **replace**: 대체
하다 · **free from**: ~이 없는 · **danger**: 위험 · **because of**: ~ 때문에

데일리 뉴스
AI가 인간을 이기다!
바둑 대국에서 AI 프로그램이
인간을 이겼다. AI가 이세돌과
대국을 벌였는데, 그는 가장
위대한 바둑기사들 중의 한 명
이다.
바둑은 보드 게임이고, 그 규
칙은 이해하기 어렵다. 많은
사람들은 AI가 인간 기사를 이
기는 것은 불가능할 것이라고
믿었다. 그러나, AI는 이세돌의
경기를 예측할 수 있었고, 그
리고 마침내 경기에서 이겼다.
사람들은 AI가 인간보다 더 똑
똑할 수 있다는 것에 충격을
받았다.

2099년에 사람들은 달에 가
기 위해 날아다니는 차를 탑
니다. 아이들은 가장 멋진 놀
이공원이 그곳에 있기 때문에
달에 가는 것을 좋아합니다.
다른 무엇보다도, 말타기는
그들이 가장 좋아하는 활동입
니다. 그들은 말에서 내리기
를 원하지 않습니다.

G: 민석아, 저쪽에 스마트 음
식 주문 자판기가 있어.
가서 해 보지 않을래?

B: 재미있겠다. 저걸 사용하
면 우린 쉽고 빠르게 주문
할 수 있을 거야.

G: 그러길 바라. 그건 그렇
고, 너는 로봇이 언젠가
인간을 대체할 수 있을 거
라고 생각하니?

B: 잘 모르겠어. 하지만 우리
는 로봇 덕분에 위험이 없
어질 거야.

G: 무슨 뜻이야?

B: 로봇은 위험에 처한 사람
들을 도울 수 있어. 로봇
이 위험한 일을 할 수 있
어서 사람들이 그 일을 하
지 않아도 되지.

G: 네 말이 맞아. 우리는 항상
좋은 면을 보도록 해야 해.

영역별 핵심문제

01 다음 빈칸에 공통으로 들어갈 말을 쓰시오.

> • He will give you enough time to _____ them up on the Internet.
> • These whales _____ for their food as a team.

02 다음 빈칸에 알맞은 말을 고르시오.

> She is never free _____ worry.

① from ② for ③ at
④ in ⑤ on

03 다음 문장의 빈칸에 알맞은 것을 〈보기〉에서 찾아 쓰시오.

> ┌─── 보기 ───
> if   just   longer   on

(1) The movie is based _____ a famous novel.
(2) It's not _____ about the money.
(3) She is no _____ a child.
(4) Go and see _____ the door is locked.

04 다음 우리말에 맞도록 빈칸에 알맞은 말을 쓰시오. (주어진 철자로 시작할 것.)

(1) 이 경기에선 우리 팀이 너희 팀을 이길 것이다.
   ➡ Our team will b_____ your team in this match.
(2) Dave는 잘생겼을 뿐만 아니라 똑똑하기까지 하다.
   ➡ Dave is not only handsome but also i_____.
(3) 너는 쉽게 전구를 교체할 수 있다.
   ➡ You can easily r_____ the bulb.

[05~06] 다음 대화를 읽고 물음에 답하시오.

> B: We took lots of pictures during our trip.
> G: We sure ___(A)___. We have more than 500 pictures.
> B: Is it possible ___(B)___ an animated photo album out of them?
> G: _____(C)_____ I have an app for that.

05 빈칸 (A)와 (B)에 들어갈 말이 순서대로 바르게 짝지어진 것은?

① do – making ② do – to make
③ did – make ④ did – to make
⑤ can – making

06 빈칸 (C)에 알맞은 말을 고르시오.

① No, I think it's impossible.
② Yes, I am able to take many pictures.
③ Yes, it's possible.
④ Yes, it sounds interesting.
⑤ That sounds perfect.

07 다음 대화의 빈칸 (A)와 (B)에 들어갈 말이 순서대로 바르게 짝지어진 것은?

> B: ___(A)___ don't we try a new VR game?
> G: That ___(B)___ interesting.

① What – sounds   ② What – was

③ Why – thinks   ④ Why – was

⑤ Why – sounds

[08~10] 다음 대화를 읽고 물음에 답하시오.

> B: Do you have any ideas for our group project? (①)
> G: No. (②) What about you?
> B: I'm thinking we should talk about future jobs. (③)
> G: That sounds perfect ___(A)___ our project. (④) Let's look ___(B)___ some information on the Internet. (⑤)

08 ①~⑤ 중 주어진 문장이 들어갈 알맞은 곳은?

> What do you think?

①   ②   ③   ④   ⑤

09 다음 빈칸 (A)와 (B)에 공통으로 들어갈 말을 쓰시오.

➡ _____

10 위 대화의 내용과 일치하지 <u>않는</u> 것을 고르시오.

① The girl doesn't have any ideas about the group project.

② Their group project will be about future jobs.

③ The girl disagrees with the boy's idea about the group project.

④ They are talking about their group project.

⑤ They will use the Internet to find some information.

11 다음 대화의 빈칸에 들어갈 말을 고르시오.

> G: The Robot Expo begins next week. Why don't you go with me?
> B: _____ That sounds exciting.
> G: We'll have a chance to meet robotics engineers.
> B: That'll be great.

① Yes, I'd love to.

② Really? Me, too.

③ That's too bad.

④ I think it's not perfect.

⑤ I don't want to go with you.

12 다음 대화의 빈칸에 들어갈 말을 고르시오.

> A: Is it possible (A)[for / of] you to read 50 novels during summer vacation?
> B: (B)[Sure not / Sure]. I can (C)[do / be] that.

(A) _____ (B) _____ (C) _____

Grammar

[13~14] 다음 빈칸에 알맞은 말이 순서대로 짝지어진 것은?

13

- I can smell the bread _____ .
- I watched the people _____ in the river.

① bake – to swim
② bakes – swimming
③ baked – swam
④ to bake – swims
⑤ baking – swim

14

_____ is good for both body and mind _____ every day.

① This – exercising
② That – exercise
③ That – to exercise
④ It – exercise
⑤ It – to exercise

15 다음 그림을 보고 괄호 안에 주어진 어휘를 이용하여 빈칸에 알맞은 말을 쓰시오.

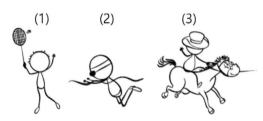

(1)　　　(2)　　　(3)

(1) I saw a person _____ badminton. (play)
(2) I saw a person _____ in the pool. (swim)
(3) I saw a person _____ a horse. (ride)

16 다음 중 어법상 올바르지 <u>않은</u> 것은?

① It is impossible to finish the work in time.
② It was interesting that compare their situation and ours.
③ It is hard to believe that he knows all the answers to the problems.
④ It is true that nature itself is a teacher and a school.
⑤ Is it possible to make energy from waste?

17 다음 중 어법상 올바르지 <u>않은</u> 것은?

① She had him throw away the trash yesterday.
② I often watch her talking on the phone.
③ It is important to wash your hands before doing an experiment.
④ Now it is not hard to see AI robots to serve dishes in the school cafeteria.
⑤ Is it possible to drink while standing on your head?

18 괄호 안에 주어진 어휘를 이용하여 다음을 영작하시오.

(1) 나는 그가 공원에서 자전거를 타고 있는 것을 보았다. (ride, see, a bike)
➡ _____

(2) 나는 부엌에서 무언가 타고 있는 냄새를 맡았다. (smell, something, burn)
➡ _____

(3) 달에서 말하는 것은 가능하지 않다. (not, talk, the moon, it)
➡ _____

(4) 친구들과 농구하는 것은 흥미롭다. (it, exciting, with friends)
➡ _____

19 다음 문장에서 어법상 <u>어색한</u> 부분을 바르게 고치시오.

(1) We saw him danced on the street.

＿＿＿＿＿＿ ➡ ＿＿＿＿＿＿

(2) Hyde smells something burns in the room.

＿＿＿＿＿＿ ➡ ＿＿＿＿＿＿

(3) I felt my heart tearing to pieces by regret.

＿＿＿＿＿＿ ➡ ＿＿＿＿＿＿

(4) It is dangerous of you to swim in the sea.

＿＿＿＿＿＿ ➡ ＿＿＿＿＿＿

(5) Many people believed it would be impossible for an AI beating a human player.

＿＿＿＿＿＿ ➡ ＿＿＿＿＿＿

(6) Is it possible make an animated photo album out of them?

＿＿＿＿＿＿ ➡ ＿＿＿＿＿＿

Reading

[20~22] 다음 글을 읽고 물음에 답하시오.

Jina and Suhan are at the World AI Expo. They are entering the AI home.

Suhan: Look at this! It's a house of the future.

Jina: Let's go into the bedroom first. Look, there's a smart closet.

Suhan: I'm standing in front of this screen on the closet door and my clothes keep changing.

Jina: The screen suggests clothes ___ⓐ___ suit the weather.

Suhan: That's amazing! We no longer have to worry about dressing for the weather.

Jina: Right. Let's move on to the living room.

20 위 글의 빈칸 ⓐ에 들어갈 알맞은 말을 <u>모두</u> 고르시오.

① that   ② who

③ what   ④ whom

⑤ which

21 위 글의 제목으로 가장 알맞은 것을 고르시오.

① The World AI Expo

② The House of the Future

③ There's a Screen on the Closet Door!

④ The Screen Which Suggests Clothes

⑤ How to Wear Clothes Suitable for the Weather

22 주어진 영영풀이에 해당하는 단어를 위 글에서 찾아 쓰시오.

a small room or cabinet used for storage space

➡ ＿＿＿＿＿＿＿＿＿＿＿＿

[23~24] 다음 글을 읽고 물음에 답하시오.

Suhan: Oh, I like this music speaker.

AI Speaker: I'm not just a music speaker. ⓐ저는 당신이 상상하는 것 이상의 것을 할 수 있어요.

Jina: ⓑIt's hard to believe that you can understand us. What can you do?

AI Speaker: How about watching a movie? I'll play one for you.

Suhan: Look, those smart windows are getting darker. I feel like I'm in a movie theater.

Jina: What else can you do?

AI Speaker: I can beatbox, too. Here comes, "cats and boots and cats and boots."

Suhan: You're funny. Good job!

23 위 글의 밑줄 친 ⓐ의 우리말에 맞게 주어진 어휘를 알맞게 배열하시오.

> more / can / you / do / than / imagine / can / I

➡ _____

24 위 글의 밑줄 친 ⓑit과 문법적 쓰임이 같은 것을 고르시오.

① It was raining this morning.
② It's impossible to get there in time.
③ I find it strange that she doesn't want to go.
④ It's two miles from here to the beach.
⑤ Look! It's going up that tree.

[25~27] 다음 글을 읽고 물음에 답하시오.

Jina: Hurry! There's a smart car station outside! Let's go and ride in that red car.
Suhan: This car is so cool. Let's get in.
AI Car: Welcome. Are you ready to go?
Jina: Yes, what should we do now? It's my first time to ride in a smart car.
AI Car: You don't need to do anything. I will drive and take you to the next station.
Suhan: ⓐWatch out! I see a cat crossing the street.
AI Car: Don't worry. I ⓑhave just sensed it. When I sense dangerous situations, I slow down or stop.
Jina: How can you ⓒdo that?
AI Car: I'm a very intelligent robotic car. I know all about driving. I can predict danger based on knowledge and experience.
Suhan: How smart! You think and act like a person. You are really like a human.

25 위 글의 밑줄 친 ⓐWatch out!과 바꿔 쓸 수 있는 말을 쓰시오.

➡ _____

26 아래 〈보기〉에서 위 글의 밑줄 친 ⓑhave just sensed와 현재완료의 용법이 다른 것의 개수를 고르시오.

> ① We have already done it.
> ② I have never read the book.
> ③ They have lived in Seoul for ten years.
> ④ He has gone to Busan.
> ⑤ She has waited for you since last night.

① 1개   ② 2개   ③ 3개   ④ 4개   ⑤ 5개

27 위 글의 밑줄 친 ⓒdo that이 가리키는 것을 본문에서 찾아 영어로 쓰시오.

➡ _____
_____

[28~29] 다음 글을 읽고 물음에 답하시오.

> Messi Is Playing at Our School!
> Scientists have developed a soccer robot ___ⓐ___ "Alpha-Foot." Alpha-Foot is almost human looking and is programmed as Messi. Next week, Alpha-Foot will play in his first soccer match with our soccer team. We are all excited to see the AI robot play for our school.

28 위 글의 빈칸 ⓐ에 call을 알맞은 형태로 쓰시오.

➡ _____

29 위 글의 종류로 알맞은 것을 고르시오.

① review   ② book report
③ essay   ④ diary
⑤ a school paper article

출제율 90%

01 제시된 영영풀이의 단어로 빈칸을 채우시오. (주어진 철자로 시작할 것)

> b_____ : to be destroyed by fire

> Lower the heat, or it'll _____.

출제율 95%

02 다음 밑줄 친 부분을 알맞은 형태로 고치시오.

> The next night was dark and <u>cloud</u>.

➡ _____

출제율 100%

03 다음 중 〈보기〉에 있는 단어를 사용하여 자연스러운 문장을 만들 수 없는 것은?

> ┌── 보기 ──┐
> point   take   text   freeze

① It takes all day just to _____ a tray of ice cubes.

② It is widely used to _____ down aging.

③ Do you like _____ or talking to your friends online?

④ It's not polite to _____ at strangers in public.

⑤ I'll _____ two adult tickets, please.

출제율 95%

04 주어진 우리말에 맞게 빈칸을 채우시오.

(1) 얼마나 많은 공장 노동자들이 일자리를 잃을 위험에 처해 있는가?

➡ How many factory workers are _____ _____ of losing their jobs?

(2) 너의 성적은 네 개의 과제물과 기말 고사를 기준으로 매겨질 것이다.

➡ Your grade will be _____ _____ four papers and a final exam.

[05~08] 다음 대화를 읽고 물음에 답하시오.

> G: Look at those words on the board.
> B: What do they mean? Let's look them up in the dictionary.
> G: What about using the AI __(A)__ ?
> B: _____(B)_____
> G: You point your smartphone camera at the words and ask AI to translate. You will get an answer.
> B: <u>AI가 저 글자들을 읽는 것이 가능해?</u>
> Speaker: Sure. I can read any language and translate it.
> B: Wow, that sounds unbelievable. So, AI, what do those words mean?
> Speaker: They mean "Dreams come true!"
> B: That's amazing.

출제율 90%

05 위의 대화에 나온 단어를 이용해 빈칸 (A)에 알맞은 말을 쓰시오. (주어진 철자로 시작할 것)

➡ t_____

출제율 95%

06 위 대화의 빈칸 (B)에 알맞은 말을 고르시오.

① What do you think?

② Why don't you use those words?

③ What about you?

④ Do you have any ideas for those words?

⑤ How do I use it?

07 밑줄 친 우리말과 일치하도록 주어진 단어를 이용해 문장을 만드시오.

> (AI, possible, those)

➡ _____

08 위 대화에서 다음 영영풀이에 해당하는 단어를 찾아 쓰시오.

> a book that contains a list of words and phrases alphabetically with their meanings or their translations in another language

➡ _____

[09~10] 문장을 대화의 흐름에 맞게 배열하시오.

09

(A) That sounds perfect for our project. Let's look for some information on the Internet.

(B) I'm thinking we should talk about future jobs. What do you think?

(C) Do you have any ideas for our group project?

(D) No. What about you?

➡ _____

10

(A) We sure did. We have more than 500 pictures.

(B) Yes, it's possible. I have an app for that.

(C) Is it possible to make an animated photo album out of them?

(D) We took lots of pictures during our trip.

➡ _____

[11~12] 다음 대화를 읽고 물음에 답하시오.

> A: Let's see (A)[which / if / what] we can answer these science questions.
> B: That sounds like fun.
> A: <u>불을 얼리는 것이 가능할까?</u>
> B: Yes, I think it's possible.

11 위 대화의 괄호 (A)에서 적절한 것을 고르시오.

➡ _____

12 밑줄 친 우리말과 일치하도록 주어진 단어를 이용하여 영작하시오. (6단어)

> (possible)

➡ _____

13 다음 빈칸에 들어갈 말이 바르게 짝지어진 것은?

> _____ is possible _____ a robot _____ me how to play the piano.

① It – of – teach

② It – for – to teach

③ That – of – teach

④ That – for – to teach

⑤ This – of – to teach

14 다음 빈칸에 들어갈 말이 바르게 짝지어진 것은?

> • I noticed the man _____ slowly toward me.
> • It is fun _____ together with Ella and Jaden every day.

① coming – get   ② coming – to get
③ to come – get   ④ to come – to get
⑤ come – get

[15~16] 다음 중 어법상 올바른 문장을 모두 고르시오.

15 ① Alice saw him running toward her.
② I heard my name calling repeatedly.
③ Jenny felt somebody pulling her hair.
④ Mick watched them fought each other.
⑤ He was looking at the dog to eat the bones.

16 ① That is necessary to come early in the morning.
② It is good to go for a walk on holidays.
③ It is helpful read many kinds of books.
④ It was really boring of me to memorize English words.
⑤ It is important that you follow the rules.

[17~19] 다음 글을 읽고 물음에 답하시오.

> Jina and Suhan are at the World AI Expo. They are entering the AI home.
> Suhan: Look at this! It's a house of the future.
> Jina: Let's go into the bedroom first. Look, there's a smart closet.
> Suhan: I'm standing in front of this screen on the closet door and my clothes keep changing.

> Jina: ⓐThe screen suggests clothes that suits the weather.
> Suhan: That's amazing! We no longer have to worry __(A)__ dressing __(B)__ the weather.
> Jina: Right. Let's move on to the ⓑliving room.

17 위 글의 빈칸 (A)와 (B)에 들어갈 전치사가 바르게 짝지어진 것은?

① for – from   ② about – for
③ at – for   ④ for – to
⑤ about – to

18 위 글의 밑줄 친 ⓐ에서 어법상 틀린 부분을 찾아 고치시오.

_____ ➡ _____

19 위 글의 밑줄 친 ⓑliving과 문법적 쓰임이 다른 것을 모두 고르시오.

① a sleeping car   ② a waiting lady
③ a walking stick   ④ a waiting room
⑤ a walking dictionary

[20~22] 다음 글을 읽고 물음에 답하시오.

> Suhan: Oh, I like this music speaker.
> AI Speaker: I'm not just a music speaker. I can do more than ⓐyou can imagine.
> Jina: It's hard (A)to believe that ⓑyou can understand ⓒus. What can you do?
> AI Speaker: How about watching a movie? ⓓI'll play one for you.

Suhan: Look, those smart windows are getting darker. I feel like I'm in a movie theater.

Jina: What else can ⓔyou do?

AI Speaker: How

Suhan: You're funny. Good job!

출제율 95%

20 위 글의 밑줄 친 ⓐ~ⓔ 중 가리키는 대상이 같은 것끼리 짝지어진 것은?

① ⓐ – ⓑ   ② ⓐ – ⓓ   ③ ⓑ – ⓒ
④ ⓑ – ⓓ   ⑤ ⓒ – ⓔ

출제율 90%

21 아래 보기에서 위 글의 밑줄 친 (A)to believe와 to부정사의 용법이 다른 것의 개수를 고르시오.

① This plan leaves nothing to be desired.
② To read these books is important.
③ He was too foolish to solve it.
④ Would you like to leave a message?
⑤ To read is to feed the mind.

① 1개   ② 2개   ③ 3개   ④ 4개   ⑤ 5개

출제율 100%

22 위 글의 내용과 일치하지 않는 것은?

① 수한이는 음악 스피커가 마음에 든다.
② 인공 지능 스피커는 사람들이 상상하는 것 이상의 것을 할 수 있다고 말한다.
③ 화면이 점점 어두워지고 있다.
④ 수한이는 마치 영화관 안에 있는 것 같이 느낀다.
⑤ 인공 지능 스피커는 비트박스도 할 수 있다.

[23~25] 다음 글을 읽고 물음에 답하시오.

Jina: Hurry! There's a smart car station outside! Let's go and ride in that red car.

Suhan: This car is so cool. Let's get in.

AI Car: Welcome. Are you ready to go?

Jina: Yes, what should we do now? It's my first time to ride in a smart car.

AI Car: You don't need to do anything. I will drive and take you to the next station.

Suhan: Watch out! I see a cat crossing the street.

AI Car: Don't worry. (①) I have just sensed it. (②)

Jina: How can you do that? (③)

AI Car: I'm a very intelligent robotic car. (④) I know all about driving. (⑤) I can predict danger based on knowledge and experience.

Suhan: How smart! You think and act like a person. You are really like a human.

출제율 95%

23 위 글의 흐름으로 보아, 주어진 문장이 들어가기에 가장 적절한 곳은?

When I sense dangerous situations, I slow down or stop.

①   ②   ③   ④   ⑤

출제율 100%

24 위 글의 주제로 알맞은 것을 고르시오.

① People want to ride in a cool smart car.
② People share the experience to ride in a smart car.
③ What should we do to ride in a smart car?
④ The AI car knows all about driving.
⑤ How does a smart car sense dangerous situations?

출제율 90%

25 다음 빈칸 (A)와 (B)에 알맞은 단어를 넣어 '인공 지능 자동차'에 대한 소개를 완성하시오.

It's a very intelligent (A)_____ _____ which knows all about driving. People don't need to (B)_____ _____ while they are riding in this smart car.

01 대화의 흐름상 또는 어법상 어색한 것을 하나 찾아서 고치시오.

> A: Do you have any questions?
> B: Yes. Is that possible to communicate face to face with other people without speaking?
> A: Not now. But maybe someday.

_____ ➡ _____

02 대화의 밑줄 친 부분과 같은 뜻이 되도록 주어진 단어를 이용하여 문장을 완성하시오.

> B: Do you have any ideas for our group project?
> G: No. What about you?
> B: I'm thinking we should talk about future jobs. What do you think?
> G: That sounds perfect for our project. Let's look for some information on the Internet.

➡ _____ (think)

03 밑줄 친 우리말과 일치하도록 주어진 단어를 이용하여 문장을 만드시오.

> A: 눈 감고 문자 메시지 보내는 것이 가능하니?
> B: Sure. I can do that.

(it. for, close, with)

➡ _____

04 주어진 어휘를 이용하여 다음 우리말을 (1) to부정사 주어를 써서, (2) 가주어를 써서 영작하시오.

> 우리 일상생활에서 에너지를 절약하는 것이 중요하다. (save, our daily lives)

(1) _____
(2) _____

> 퇴근 후 피곤함을 느끼는 것은 당연하다.
> (natural, tired, after work)

(1) _____
(2) _____

05 다음 그림을 보고 괄호 안에 주어진 어휘를 이용하여 빈칸을 알맞게 채우시오.

> I watched Jane _____ _____ _____.
> (ride)

Jina and Suhan are at the World AI Expo. They are entering the AI home.

Suhan: Look at this! It's a house of the future.

Jina: Let's ⓐgo into the bedroom first. Look, there's a smart closet.

Suhan: I'm standing in front of this screen on the closet door and my clothes keep changing.

Jina: ⓑ스크린이 날씨에 적합한 옷을 제안하는 거야.

Suhan: That's amazing! ⓒWe no longer have to worry about dressing for the weather.

Jina: Right. Let's move on to the living room.

06 위 글의 밑줄 친 ⓐgo into와 바꿔 쓸 수 있는 한 단어를 본문에서 찾아 알맞은 형태로 쓰시오.

➡ _____

07 위 글의 밑줄 친 ⓑ의 우리말에 맞게 주어진 어휘를 이용하여 8단어로 영작하시오.

suggests, suit, weather

➡ _____

_____

08 위 글의 밑줄 친 ⓒ를 다음과 같이 바꿔 쓸 때 빈칸에 들어갈 알맞은 말을 쓰시오.

We don't have to worry about dressing for the weather _____ _____.

Jina: Hurry! There's a smart car station outside! Let's go and ride in that red car.

Suhan: This car is so cool. Let's get in.

AI Car: Welcome. Are you ready to go?

Jina: Yes, (A)[how / what] should we do now? It's my first time to ride in a smart car.

AI Car: You don't need to do anything. I will drive and take you to the next station.

Suhan: Watch out! I see a cat crossing the street.

AI Car: Don't worry. I have just sensed it. ⓐ When I sense dangerous situations, I speed up or stop.

Jina: (B)[How / What] can you do that?

AI Car: I'm a very intelligent robotic car. I know all about driving. I can predict danger (C)[basing / based] on knowledge and experience.

Suhan: ⓑHow smart! You think and act like a person. You are really like a human.

09 위 글의 괄호 (A)~(C)에서 어법상 알맞은 낱말을 골라 쓰시오.

(A) _____ (B) _____ (C) _____

10 위 글의 밑줄 친 ⓐ에서 흐름상 어색한 부분을 찾아 고치시오.

_____ ➡ _____

11 위 글의 밑줄 친 ⓑHow smart!를 What을 사용하여 고치시오.

➡ _____

01 가능 여부를 묻고 대답하는 다음 대화를 완성하시오.

조건
- 더운 날 길 위에서 계란을 부치는 것이 가능한지에 대해 이야기할 것.
- possible을 이용할 것.

A: _____

B: _____

02 지각동사 see를 이용하여 다음 그림을 묘사하는 문장을 완성하시오. (괄호 안에 주어진 어휘를 이용할 것.)

(1) I can see a man and a woman _____ a song together. (sing)

(2) I can see _____ an ice corn with her left arm raised. (girl, eat)

(3) I can see _____ the shirts in the store. (boy, look)

03 다음 내용을 바탕으로 기획한 제품을 쇼핑 호스트가 되어 홍보하는 대본을 쓰시오.

AI Cook
- It selects vegetables and meat from the refrigerator.
- It cooks a delicious meal with these vegetables and meat.

Today, I'll tell you about the "(A)_____." It can select (B)_____ from the refrigerator for you. It can cook (C)_____ with these (D)_____ _____. When the meal is ready, it'll let you know. Now, please call 800-1234-8282 if you'd like to buy one of these AI Cooks.

단원별 모의고사

01 다음 문장에 공통으로 들어갈 말을 고르시오.

> • The story is _____ more and more interesting.
> • He is _____ in the front seat of the taxi.

02 다음 빈칸에 알맞은 말을 〈보기〉에서 골라 쓰시오.

> ┌ 보기 ┐
> of   on   to

(1) They are sitting face _____ face and looking at each other.

(2) Now, let's move _____ to the next story.

(3) They make plastics out _____ plant materials such as corn and soybeans.

03 다음 빈칸에 알맞은 말을 고르시오.

> We are offering 25% _____ all furniture purchased on the day of our grand opening.

① on   ② in   ③ off
④ from   ⑤ to

[04~05] 다음 대화를 읽고 물음에 답하시오.

> G: 네가 스마트폰 없이 사는 것이 가능할까?
> B: No, it's (A)not possible.

04 밑줄 친 우리말과 일치하도록 주어진 단어를 이용하여 영작하시오.

> (possible)

➡ _____

05 위 대화의 밑줄 친 (A)를 한 단어로 바꾸시오.

➡ _____

[06~08] 다음 대화를 읽고 물음에 답하시오.

> G: This computer looks nice. How much is ⓐit?
> M: ⓑIt's 500 dollars. ⓒIt's the newest one.
> G: Is ⓓit possible to use this coupon?
> M: Let me check. Yes, you can. ___(A)___, you'll get 30 dollars off.
> G: Perfect. I'll take ⓔit.

06 위 대화의 ⓐ~ⓔ 중 대상이 다른 하나를 고르시오.

① ⓐ   ② ⓑ   ③ ⓒ   ④ ⓓ   ⑤ ⓔ

07 위 대화의 빈칸 (A)에 알맞은 말을 고르시오.

① So   ② However
③ Unfortunately   ④ Also
⑤ In addition

08 위 대화를 읽고 대답할 수 없는 질문을 고르시오.

① Is the coupon which the girl has available to use?
② Will the girl pay in cash or credit card?
③ Where are they?
④ How much discount does the girl get?
⑤ What does the girl want to buy?

[09~12] 다음 대화를 읽고 물음에 답하시오.

> G: Minseok, there is a smart food-ordering machine over there. ⓐWhy don't we try it?
> B: That sounds ___(A)___ (interest). ⓑWe'll be able to order easily and fast by using it.
> G: ⓒI hope so. By the way, do you think maybe it will be possible for robots ___(B)___ (replace) humans someday?
> B: I'm not sure. But we will be free ___(C)___ danger because ___(D)___ robots.
> G: ⓓWhat do you mean?
> B: Robots can help people in danger. Robots can do the dangerous work so humans don't have to.
> G: You're right. ⓔWe should always try to look on the dark side.

09 위 대화의 괄호 안에 주어진 단어를 이용하여 빈칸 (A)와 (B)를 채우시오.

　　(A) _____ (B) _____

10 위 대화의 빈칸 (C), (D)에 알맞은 전치사를 쓰시오.

　　(C) _____ (D) _____

11 위 대화의 문맥상 어색한 것을 고르시오.

　　① ⓐ　　② ⓑ　　③ ⓒ　　④ ⓓ　　⑤ ⓔ

12 위 대화에서 다음 영영풀이에 해당하는 단어를 찾아 쓰시오.

able to happen or be done

　　➡ _____

13 다음 문장을 it을 주어로 하여 다시 쓰시오.

　　(1) To eat a lot of vegetables is good for your health.

　　➡ _____

　　(2) That people may not want to talk to each other anymore is possible.

　　➡ _____
　　_____

14 다음 중 어법상 어색한 것은?

　　① Mike heard his phone ringing.
　　② It is my plan to read 10 books during the winter vacation.
　　③ It was exciting to watch them singing and dancing to the music.
　　④ She watched him to cut the paper.
　　⑤ Is it possible for you to text with your eyes closed?

15 다음 중 어법상 어색한 것은?

　　① She heard someone crying.
　　② I saw the boy singing in the classroom.
　　③ She watched him helping the lady get into the bus.
　　④ Is it possible to freeze fire?
　　⑤ It is very kind for you to help us.

16 주어진 단어를 이용하여 다음 우리말을 영어로 쓰시오.

(1) 민아는 양파가 튀겨지는 냄새를 맡았다.
(smell, fry)

➡ _____

(2) 우리는 그들이 서로에게 속삭이고 있는 것을 들었다. (whisper, each other)

➡ _____

(3) 새로운 것들을 찾아서 만드는 것은 흥미롭다.
(new things, interesting, find and create, it)

➡ _____

(4) 당신이 이메일을 보내는 것은 쉽다.
(it, send e-mails)

➡ _____

17 다음 어법상 틀린 문장의 개수는?

ⓐ I saw my brother singing a song.
ⓑ We heard Yena played the violin.
ⓒ She noticed him shaking his head.
ⓓ Jeniffer felt him came closer.
ⓔ It is good to volunteer at the community center.
ⓕ I think it's possible that a spacecraft can be controlled by a computer program.
ⓖ Is it safe swim in this river?

① 1개　② 2개　③ 3개　④ 4개　⑤ 5개

[18~20] 다음 글을 읽고 물음에 답하시오.

Jina and Suhan are at the World AI Expo. They are entering the AI home.

Suhan: Look at this! It's a house of the future.
Jina: Let's go into the bedroom first. Look, there's a smart closet.
Suhan: I'm standing in front of this screen on the closet door and my clothes keep changing.
Jina: The screen suggests clothes ⓐthat suit the weather.
Suhan: ⓑThat's amazing! We no longer have to worry about dressing for the weather.
Jina: ⓒRight. Let's move on to the living room.

18 아래 보기에서 위 글의 밑줄 친 ⓐthat과 문법적 쓰임이 다른 것의 개수를 고르시오.

① I believe that you'll pass the exam.
② He is the only man that I love.
③ I'm glad that you like it.
④ I was so busy that I could not help him.
⑤ This is the pen that he bought yesterday.

① 1개　② 2개　③ 3개　④ 4개　⑤ 5개

19 위 글의 밑줄 친 ⓑThat이 가리키는 것을 본문에서 찾아 쓰시오.

➡ _____

20 위 글의 밑줄 친 ⓒRight과 바꿔 쓸 수 없는 말을 고르시오.

① You got it.
② You can say that again.
③ I agree with you.
④ That's all right.
⑤ You said it.

[21~22] 다음 글을 읽고 물음에 답하시오.

Suhan: Oh, I __(A)__ this music speaker.

AI Speaker: I'm not just a music speaker. I can do more than you can imagine.

Jina: It's hard to believe that you can understand us. What can you do?

AI Speaker: How about watching a movie? I'll play one for you.

Suhan: Look, ⓐthat smart windows are getting darker. I feel __(B)__ I'm in a movie theater.

Jina: What else can you do?

AI Speaker: I can beatbox, too. Here comes, "cats and boots and cats and boots."

Suhan: You're funny. Good job!

21 위 글의 빈칸 (A)와 (B)에 공통으로 들어갈 알맞은 말을 쓰시오.

➡ _____

22 위 글의 밑줄 친 ⓐ에서 어법상 틀린 부분을 찾아 고치시오.

_____ ➡ _____

[23~25] 다음 글을 읽고 물음에 답하시오.

Jina: Hurry! There's a smart car station outside! Let's go and ride in that red car.

Suhan: This car is so cool. Let's get in.

AI Car: Welcome. Are you ready to go?

Jina: Yes, what should we do now? It's my first time ⓐto ride in a smart car.

AI Car: You don't need to do anything. I will drive and take you to the next station.

Suhan: Watch out! I see a cat crossing the street.

AI Car: Don't worry. I have just sensed it. When I sense dangerous situations, I slow down or stop.

Jina: How can you do that?

AI Car: I'm a very intelligent robotic car. I know all about driving. ⓑ저는 제 지식과 경험을 바탕으로 위험을 예측할 수 있어요.

Suhan: How smart! You think and act like a person. You are really like a human.

23 위 글의 밑줄 친 ⓐto ride와 to부정사의 용법이 같은 것을 모두 고르시오.

① I don't know when to begin the work.
② Does she have a house to live in?
③ I had an opportunity to see him last year.
④ It is best not to make him angry.
⑤ You must work hard to succeed in the examination.

24 위 글의 밑줄 친 ⓑ의 우리말에 맞게 한 단어를 보충하여, 주어진 어휘를 알맞게 배열하시오.

| and / predict / experience / can / based / I / knowledge / danger |

➡ _____
_____

25 위 글의 내용과 일치하지 않는 것은?

① 진아는 스마트 자동차 정류장에 가서 빨간 차를 타 보기를 원한다.
② 진아는 스마트 자동차에 처음 타 본다.
③ 인공 지능 자동차는 고양이가 길을 건너고 있는 것을 감지했다.
④ 인공 지능 자동차는 어떤 위험 상황을 감지하면 속도를 늦추거나 멈춘다.
⑤ 인공 지능 자동차는 자신의 학습 능력을 바탕으로 위험을 예측할 수 있다.

INSIGHT
on the textbook

교과서 파헤치기

Lesson **5** **We Love Baseball**

Lesson **6** **New Places, New Experiences**

Lesson **7** **Living in the AI World**

※ 다음 영어를 우리말로 쓰시오.

01 competition _____

02 fit _____

03 hide _____

04 crack _____

05 rule _____

06 miss _____

07 home team _____

08 anxious _____

09 shorts _____

10 determine _____

11 pitch _____

12 sometime _____

13 dirt _____

14 either _____

15 stadium _____

16 base _____

17 batter _____

18 international _____

19 decide _____

20 forget _____

21 pet _____

22 visiting team _____

23 better _____

24 ticket _____

25 match _____

26 order _____

27 then _____

28 vacation _____

29 mean _____

30 thunder _____

31 past _____

32 rock climbing _____

33 support _____

34 can't wait to 동사원형 _____

35 between A and B _____

36 wait for _____

37 be a big fan of _____

38 hurry up _____

39 look forward to (동)명사 _____

40 twice a week _____

41 be excited about _____

42 come back to _____

43 in a hurry _____

※ 다음 우리말을 영어로 쓰시오.

01 감추다, 숨기다	
02 (부정문에서) ~도	
03 티켓	
04 휴가	
05 경기장	
06 (야구의) 루, 베이스	
07 규칙	
08 방문하다	
09 타자	
10 경기, 성냥	
11 순서	
12 결정하다	
13 투구	
14 암벽 등반	
15 의미하다	
16 천둥	
17 찢어지는 듯한 소리	
18 불안한	
19 대회	
20 맞다	
21 애완동물	

22 원정 팀	
23 반바지	
24 과거	
25 잊다	
26 국제적인	
27 놓치다, 그리워하다	
28 언젠가	
29 먼지	
30 획득하다, 사다	
31 더 좋은, 더 나은	
32 (특정 스포츠 팀을) 응원하다	
33 그 뒤에, 그런 다음	
34 막 ~하려고 하다	
35 A와 B 사이에	
36 서둘러 ~하다	
37 ~의 열렬한 팬이다	
38 ~을 몹시 기대하다	
39 일주일에 두 번	
40 서둘러	
41 ~에 신나다, ~에 들뜨다	
42 ~을 기대하다	
43 ~을 기다리다	

※ 다음 영영풀이에 알맞은 단어를 <보기>에서 골라 쓴 후, 우리말 뜻을 쓰시오.

1 _____ : to put something out of sight: _____

2 _____ : very nervous or worried about something: _____

3 _____ : to be the right size and shape for someone or something: _____

4 _____ : a sports team playing on its own ground: _____

5 _____ : the time before the moment of speaking or writing: _____

6 _____ : a throw of the ball for the batter to hit it: _____

7 _____ : relating to or involving different countries: _____

8 _____ : each corner of the square that makes a baseball diamond: _____

9 _____ : to decide or establish something conclusively: _____

10 _____ : a sports team playing on the competing team's field or court: _____

11 _____ : an event or contest in which people try to win something by defeating

others: _____

12 _____ : the arrangement or disposition of people or things in a list from first to

last: _____

13 _____ : the loud noise in the sky heard after a lightning flash during a storm:

_____

14 _____ : used in a negative sentence to indicate a similarity with a statement just

made: _____

15 _____ : the sudden loud explosive sound of something when it falls or bumps

into itself or something else: _____

16 _____ : an athletic or sports ground used for playing and watching sports with

rows of seats: _____

보기	anxious	determine	home team	pitch
	base	either	international	stadium
	competition	fit	order	thunder
	crack	hide	past	visiting team

※ 다음 우리말과 일치하도록 빈칸에 알맞은 말을 쓰시오.

Listen & Speak 1 A

M: _____ _____ do you like? Soccer _____ basketball?

G: I like soccer _____. I play soccer _____ _____ _____.

M: 너는 어떤 운동을 좋아하니? 축구 아니면 농구?

G: 축구를 더 좋아해요. 저는 일주일에 두 번 축구를 해요.

Listen & Speak 1 B

1. G: What _____ you _____?

   B: _____ _____ _____ a world map.

   G: You _____ two countries. _____ _____ would you like _____ _____ first? The U.S. _____ Mexico?

   B: I want _____ _____ the U.S. I'd _____ _____ see a basketball game there.

2. G: _____ _____ about _____ a pet. Do you _____ a pet?

   B: Yes, I do. I have a dog and a cat.

   G: _____ _____ you _____? _____ pet is _____ _____ me? A cat _____ a dog?

   B: _____ _____ _____ _____ _____ my house someday and _____ _____ my pets? Then you _____ _____.

1. G: 뭐 하고 있어?

   B: 세계 지도를 보고 있어.

   G: 두 나라에 표시를 했네. 어떤 나라를 먼저 방문하고 싶어? 미국 아니면 멕시코?

   B: 미국을 방문하고 싶어. 거기서 농구 경기를 보고 싶어.

2. G: 나는 애완동물을 기르는 것에 대해 생각 중이야. 넌 애완동물을 기르니?

   B: 응, 길러. 개와 고양이가 있어.

   G: 어떻게 생각해? 어떤 애완동물이 나에게 더 나아? 고양이 아니면 개?

   B: 어느 날 우리 집에 와서 내 애완동물과 놀아 보는 게 어때? 그런 다음 너는 결정할 수 있을 거야.

Listen & Speak 2 A

G: _____ you get the tickets?

B: Yes! I _____ _____ _____ _____ the game.

W: 너 티켓 구했니?

B: 응! 나는 경기를 빨리 보고 싶어.

Listen & Speak 2 B

1. G: Do you _____ _____ _____ my new mountain bike?

   B: Sure. _____ _____ you get it?

   G: Yesterday my father _____ _____ _____ _____ _____. Can you _____ _____ _____ _____ this afternoon?

   B: Of _____. I _____ _____ _____ _____ _____ it.

G: 내 새 산악 자전거를 보고 싶니?

B: 물론이지. 언제 생긴 거야?

G: 어제 아빠가 나에게 사 주셨어. 오늘 오후에 우리 집에 올래?

B: 당연하지. 나는 그것을 빨리 보고 싶어.

2. B: _____ _____ _____ we're going _____ _____ this weekend!

   G: Don't _____ . I _____ _____ .

   B: I'm _____ _____ going. _____ _____ _____ .

3. G: Did you _____ _____ Jisu?

   B: What _____ her? She _____ _____ Canada.

   G: She _____ _____ to Korea last month. She _____ _____ _____ you.

   B: Oh, I _____ _____ _____ _____ _____ her.

2. B: 이번 주말에 암벽 등반하러 가기로 한 거 잊지 마.
G: 걱정 마. 잊지 않을게.
B: 등반하러 가는 거 너무 신난다. 너무 기다려져.

3. G: 너 지수에 대해 들었니?
B: 그녀에 대한 거 뭐? 그녀는 캐나다에 살고 있잖아.
G: 지난달에 그녀는 한국에 돌아왔어. 너를 보고 싶어해.
B: 오, 그녀를 빨리 보고 싶어.

Real-Life Zone A

B1: Jiho, why are you in _____ _____ _____ ?

B2: Hi, Alex! I _____ _____ be home _____ 6:00. The game _____ the Thunders _____ the Cobras _____ at 6:00.

B1: Oh, are you a baseball fan? _____ _____ do you _____ ? The Cobras _____ the Thunders?

B2: The Cobras.

B1: Me, too! I don't want _____ _____ the game _____ .

B2: _____ _____ ! We only have thirty minutes _____ .

B1: Okay. _____ we can watch a game together _____ .

B2: That's a great idea! How _____ _____ _____ the next Cobras _____ _____ _____ ?

B1: Okay. They have a game next Saturday. We _____ _____ _____ _____ _____ _____ the game!

B2: That _____ great. _____ _____ _____ !

Wrap Up

B: Jimin, _____ _____ _____ _____ _____ ? Soccer _____ table tennis?

G: I love table tennis. _____ _____ you, Yunho?

B: I like soccer. I'm a _____ _____ _____ James Hood. He's a great soccer player.

G: Oh, really? There's a _____ _____ this weekend _____ Korea and Turkey. _____ you _____ _____ it?

B: Of course. I _____ _____ a ticket. _____ _____ _____ the game on Saturday. I _____ _____ .

G: That's _____ .

B1: 지호야, 너 왜 그렇게 서두르니?
B2: 안녕, 알렉스! 나는 6시 전에 집에 있어야 해. 천둥 대 코브라의 경기가 6시에 시작돼.
B1: 오, 너 야구 팬이니? 어느 팀을 응원해? 코브라 아니면 천둥?
B2: 코브라.
B1: 나도야! 나도 이 경기를 놓치고 싶지 않아.
B2: 서둘러! 우리는 30분밖에 안 남았어.
B1: 알겠어. 언젠가 함께 경기를 볼 수도 있겠다.
B2: 좋은 생각이야! 다음 코브라 홈 경기를 함께 보러 가지 않을래?
B1: 좋아. 다음 주 토요일에 경기가 있어. 우리는 경기를 보면서 프라이드 치킨을 먹을 수 있어!
B1: 굉장해. 너무 기다려져!

B: 지민아, 너는 어떤 운동을 좋아하니? 축구 아니면 탁구?
G: 탁구를 좋아해. 윤호야, 너는 어때?
B: 축구가 좋아. 나는 제임스 후드의 열렬한 팬이야. 그는 위대한 축구 선수야.
G: 오, 정말? 이번 주말에 한국 대 터키의 축구 경기가 있어. 그것에 대해 들었니?
B: 물론이지. 나는 이미 표가 있어. 토요일에 경기를 보러 갈 거야. 너무 기다려져.
G: 환상적이다.

대화문 Test

※ 다음 우리말에 맞도록 대화를 영어로 쓰시오.

Listen & Speak 1 A

M: _____

G: _____

M: 너는 어떤 운동을 좋아하니? 축구 아니면 농구?
G: 축구를 더 좋아해요. 저는 일주일에 두 번 축구를 해요.

Listen & Speak 1 B

1. G: _____

   B: _____

   G: _____

   _____

   B: _____

2. G: _____

   B: _____

   G: _____

   B: _____

1. G: 뭐 하고 있어?
   B: 세계 지도를 보고 있어.
   G: 두 나라에 표시를 했네. 어떤 나라를 먼저 방문하고 싶어? 미국 아니면 멕시코?
   B: 미국을 방문하고 싶어. 거기서 농구 경기를 보고 싶어.

2. G: 나는 애완동물을 기르는 것에 대해 생각 중이야. 넌 애완동물을 기르니?
   B: 응, 길러. 개와 고양이가 있어.
   G: 어떻게 생각해? 어떤 애완동물이 나에게 더 나아? 고양이 아니면 개?
   B: 어느 날 우리 집에 와서 내 애완동물과 놀아 보는 게 어때? 그런 다음 너는 결정할 수 있을 거야.

Listen & Speak 2 A

G: _____

B: _____

W: 너 티켓 받았니?
B: 응! 나는 경기를 빨리 보고 싶어.

Listen & Speak 2 B

1. G: _____

   B: _____

   G: _____

   B: _____

G: 내 새 산악 자전거를 보고 싶니?
B: 물론이지. 언제 생긴 거야?
G: 어제 아빠가 나에게 사 주셨어. 오늘 오후에 우리 집에 올래?
B: 당연하지. 나는 그것을 빨리 보고 싶어.

2. **B:** _____

   G: _____

   B: _____

3. **G:** _____

   B: _____

   G: _____

   B: _____

2. **B:** 이번 주말에 암벽 등반하러 가기로 한 거 잊지 마.
   G: 걱정 마. 잊지 않을게.
   B: 등반하러 가는 거 너무 신난다. 너무 기다려져.

3. **G:** 너 지수에 대해 들었니?
   B: 그녀에 대한 거 뭐? 그녀는 캐나다에 살고 있잖아.
   G: 지난 달에 그녀는 한국에 돌아왔어. 너를 보고 싶어해.
   B: 오, 그녀를 빨리 보고 싶어.

Real-Life Zone A

B1: _____

B2: _____

_____

B1: _____

B2: _____

B1: _____

B2: _____

B1: _____

B2: _____

B1: _____

_____

B2: _____

B1: 지호야, 너 왜 그렇게 서두르니?
B2: 안녕, 알렉스! 나는 6시 전에 집에 있어야 해. 천둥 대 코브라의 경기가 6시에 시작돼.
B1: 오, 너 야구 팬이니? 어느 팀을 응원해? 코브라 아니면 천둥?
B2: 코브라.
B1: 나도야! 나도 이 경기를 놓치고 싶지 않아.
B2: 서둘러! 우리는 30분밖에 안 남았어.
B1: 알겠어. 언젠가 함께 경기를 볼 수도 있겠다.
B2: 좋은 생각이야! 다음 코브라 홈 경기를 함께 보러 가지 않을래?
B1: 좋아. 다음 주 토요일에 경기가 있어. 우리는 경기를 보면서 프라이드 치킨을 먹을 수 있어!
B1: 굉장해. 너무 기다려져!

Wrap Up

B: _____

G: _____

B: _____

G: _____

_____

B: _____

G: _____

B: 지민아, 너는 어떤 운동을 좋아하니? 축구 아니면 탁구?
G: 탁구를 좋아해. 윤호야, 너는 어때?
B: 축구가 좋아. 나는 제임스 후드의 열렬한 팬이야. 그는 위대한 축구 선수야.
G: 오, 정말? 이번 주말에 한국 대 터키의 축구 경기가 있어. 그것에 대해 들었니?
B: 물론이지. 나는 이미 표가 있어. 토요일에 경기를 보러 갈 거야. 너무 기다려져.
G: 환상적이다.

※ 다음 우리말과 일치하도록 빈칸에 알맞은 것을 골라 쓰시오.

1   A _____ at the _____ _____.
    A. Day   B. Stadium   C. Baseball

2   Today the Thunders _____ the Cobras _____ a _____.
    A. game   B. have   C. and

3   Jihun's family _____ _____ the baseball _____.
    A. at   B. is   C. stadium

4   Jihun: Jian, this is _____ _____ time to come to the baseball stadium, _____ _____?
    A. isn't   B. first   C. it   D. your

5   Jian: Yes, I'm so _____. I _____ _____ _____ the game to start.
    A. wait   B. for   C. excited   D. can't

6   Dad: Look, the players _____ _____ _____ now!
    A. out   B. coming   C. are

7   Jian: _____ _____ is the Thunders?
    A. team   B. which

8   Jihun: _____ there, _____ _____ base.
    A. third   B. behind   C. over

9   They are _____ dark gray uniforms _____ they are the _____ team.
    A. wearing   B. visiting   C. because

10   Jian: Does the visiting team _____ _____ a _____ color?
    A. wear   B. always   C. dark

11   Jihun: Yes, _____'s the _____.
    A. rule   B. that

12   _____ teams have _____ uniforms and _____ teams have _____ uniforms.
    A. dark   B. bright   C. visiting   D. home

13   Jian: _____ is _____?
    A. that   B. why

14   Mom: _____ is an _____ story _____ that.
    A. about   B. interesting   C. there

15   In the _____, visiting teams could not _____ their uniforms after _____ game.
    A. every   B. past   C. wash

16   So they started _____ dark colors to _____ the _____.
    A. hide   B. dirt   C. wearing

17   Jian: Hahaha! That _____ a _____ _____!
    A. idea   B. was   C. good

---

1   야구 경기장에서의 하루

2   오늘 천둥 대 코브라 게임이 있다.

3   지훈이네 가족은 야구 경기장에 있다.

4   지훈: 지안아, 네가 야구 경기장에 온 건 이번이 처음이야, 그렇지 않니?

5   지안: 응, 나 아주 흥분돼. 나는 경기가 빨리 시작했으면 좋겠어.

6   아빠: 봐, 선수들이 지금 나오고 있어!

7   지안: 어떤 팀이 천둥이야?

8   지훈: 저기, 3루 뒤.

9   그들은 원정 팀이기 때문에 어두운 회색 유니폼을 입고 있어.

10   지안: 원정 팀은 항상 어두운 색을 입어?

11   지훈: 응, 그게 규칙이야.

12   홈팀은 밝은 유니폼을 입고 원정팀은 어두운 유니폼을 입어.

13   지안: 왜?

14   엄마: 그것에 대한 흥미로운 이야기가 있단다.

15   과거에는 원정 팀이 매 경기 후 유니폼을 세탁할 수가 없었어.

16   그래서 그들은 때를 숨기기 위해 어두운 색을 입기 시작했지.

17   지안: 하하하! 좋은 생각이었네요!

18 The players are _____ _____.
A. up   B. warming

19 Jian: Who's _____ _____ player?
A. favorite   B. your

20 Jihun: _____ _____.
A. 77   B. number

21 Jian: _____ _____ the number _____?
A. what   B. mean   C. does

22 Jihun: Hmm…. Players _____ a number _____ _____.
A. they   B. choose   C. like

23 Dad: You _____ _____?
A. what   B. know

24 In the past, the numbers were _____ _____ the players' _____ _____.
A. order   B. by   C. determined   D. batting

25 Jihun: That means _____ were _____ players _____ number 77!
A. with   B. there   C. no

26 Now, Jihun's favorite player _____ _____ _____ bat.
A. about   B. is   C. to

27 Jihun _____ _____.
A. anxious   B. looks

28 Jian: Your _____ player is _____ _____.
A. favorite   B. bat   C. at

29 Jihun: Yes. He _____ _____ 21 home _____ _____ this year.
A. already   B. hit   C. has   D. runs

30 If he _____ one _____ today, he will _____ the home run leader this _____.
A. more   B. season   C. hits   D. be

31 The _____ _____ _____ balls.
A. misses   B. several   C. batter

32 Now he _____ a _____ _____.
A. count   B. full   C. has

33 He is _____ _____ the next _____.
A. pitch   B. for   C. waiting

34 Jihun: HOME _____! _____ RUN!
A. RUN   B. HOME

35 _____! The ball _____ _____.
A. fast   B. flies   C. crack

36 It _____ _____, going, going, _____!
A. gone   B. going   C. is

18	선수들이 몸을 풀고 있다.
19	지안: 가장 좋아하는 선수가 누구야?
20	지훈: 77번.
21	지안: 그 숫자는 무엇을 의미해?
22	지훈: 음... 선수들이 원하는 번호를 선택해.
23	아빠: 그거 알아?
24	과거에는 번호가 선수들의 타순에 의해 결정되었단다.
25	지훈: 77번 선수가 없었다는 뜻이네요!
26	이제 지훈이의 가장 좋아하는 선수가 막 공을 치려고 한다.
27	지훈이는 불안해 보인다.
28	지안: 오빠가 가장 좋아하는 선수가 타석에 서네.
29	지훈: 응. 그는 올해 이미 21개의 홈런을 쳤어.
30	그가 오늘 하나를 더 치면, 그는 이번 시즌 홈런 리더가 될 거야.
31	타자는 여러 개의 공을 놓친다.
32	이제 그는 풀카운트가 되었다.
33	그는 다음 투구를 기다리고 있다.
34	지훈: 홈런! 홈런!
35	땅! 공은 빠르게 날아간다.
36	그것은 가고, 가고, 가고, 사라져 버렸다!

※ 다음 우리말과 일치하도록 빈칸에 알맞은 말을 쓰시오.

1 _____ _____ at the _____ _____

2 Today the Thunders and the Cobras _____ _____ _____ .

3 Jihun's family _____ _____ the _____ _____ .

4 Jihun: Jian, this is _____ _____ _____ to come to the baseball stadium, _____ _____ ?

5 Jian: Yes, I'm so _____ . I _____ _____ _____ the game _____ _____ .

6 Dad: Look, the players _____ _____ _____ now!

7 Jian: _____ _____ is the Thunders?

8 Jihun: _____ _____ , _____ _____ _____ .

9 They _____ _____ dark gray uniforms _____ they are the _____ _____ .

10 Jian: Does the _____ _____ always _____ _____ _____ _____ ?

11 Jihun: Yes, that's the _____ .

12 Home teams _____ _____ _____ and visiting teams have _____ _____ .

13 Jian: _____ is that?

14 Mom: _____ is _____ _____ _____ about that.

15 _____ _____ _____ , visiting teams could not _____ _____ _____ _____ _____ .

16 So they _____ _____ dark colors _____ _____ _____ _____ .

17 Jian: Hahaha! That was _____ _____ _____ !

1 야구 경기장에서의 하루

2 오늘 천둥 대 코브라 게임이 있다.

3 지훈이네 가족은 야구 경기장에 있다.

4 지훈: 지안아, 네가 야구 경기장에 온 건 이번이 처음이야, 그렇지 않니?

5 지안: 응, 나 아주 흥분돼. 나는 경기가 빨리 시작했으면 좋겠어.

6 아빠: 봐, 선수들이 지금 나오고 있어!

7 지안: 어떤 팀이 천둥이야?

8 지훈: 저기, 3루 뒤.

9 그들은 원정 팀이기 때문에 어두운 회색 유니폼을 입고 있어.

10 지안: 원정 팀은 항상 어두운 색을 입어?

11 지훈: 응, 그게 규칙이야.

12 홈팀은 밝은 유니폼을 입고 원정팀은 어두운 유니폼을 입어.

13 지안: 왜?

14 엄마: 그것에 대한 흥미로운 이야기가 있단다.

15 과거에는 원정 팀이 매 경기 후 유니폼을 세탁할 수가 없었어.

16 그래서 그들은 때를 숨기기 위해 어두운 색을 입기 시작했지.

17 지안: 하하하! 좋은 생각이었네요!

18 The players _____ _____ _____.

19 Jian: Who's _____ _____ _____?

20 Jihun: _____ 77.

21 Jian: _____ _____ the _____ _____?

22 Jihun: Hmm…. Players _____ a number _____ _____.

23 Dad: _____ _____ _____?

24 In the past, the numbers _____ _____ _____ _____ _____ _____ _____.

25 Jihun: That means _____ _____ _____ players _____ number 77!

26 Now, Jihun's favorite player _____ _____ _____ bat.

27 Jihun _____ _____.

28 Jian: _____ _____ player is _____ _____.

29 Jihun: Yes. He _____ _____ 21 home runs already this year.

30 If he _____ _____ _____ today, he will be the home run leader _____ _____.

31 The batter _____ _____ _____.

32 Now he _____ _____ _____ _____.

33 He is _____ _____ the _____ _____.

34 Jihun: _____ _____! HOME RUN!

35 _____! The ball _____ _____.

36 It _____ _____, going, going, _____!

18 선수들이 몸을 풀고 있다.

19 지안: 가장 좋아하는 선수가 누구야?

20 지훈: 77번.

21 지안: 그 숫자는 무엇을 의미해?

22 지훈: 음... 선수들이 원하는 번호를 선택해.

23 아빠: 그거 알아?

24 과거에는 번호가 선수들의 타순에 의해 결정되었단다.

25 지훈: 77번 선수가 없었다는 뜻이네요!

26 이제 지훈이의 가장 좋아하는 선수가 막 공을 치려고 한다.

27 지훈이는 불안해 보인다.

28 지안: 오빠가 가장 좋아하는 선수가 타석에 서네.

29 지훈: 응. 그는 올해 이미 21개의 홈런을 쳤어.

30 그가 오늘 하나를 더 치면, 그는 이번 시즌 홈런 리더가 될 거야.

31 타자는 여러 개의 공을 놓친다.

32 이제 그는 풀카운트가 되었다.

33 그는 다음 투구를 기다리고 있다.

34 지훈: 홈런! 홈런!

35 땅! 공은 빠르게 날아간다.

36 그것은 가고, 가고, 가고, 사라져 버렸다!

※ 다음 문장을 우리말로 쓰시오.

1 A Day at the Baseball Stadium

➡ _____

2 Today the Thunders and the Cobras have a game.

➡ _____

3 Jihun's family is at the baseball stadium.

➡ _____

4 Jihun: Jian, this is your first time to come to the baseball stadium, isn't it?

➡ _____

5 Jian: Yes, I'm so excited. I can't wait for the game to start.

➡ _____

6 Dad: Look, the players are coming out now!

➡ _____

7 Jian: Which team is the Thunders?

➡ _____

8 Jihun: Over there, behind third base.

➡ _____

9 They are wearing dark gray uniforms because they are the visiting team.

➡ _____

10 Jian: Does the visiting team always wear a dark color?

➡ _____

11 Jihun: Yes, that's the rule.

➡ _____

12 Home teams have bright uniforms and visiting teams have dark uniforms.

➡ _____

13 Jian: Why is that?

➡ _____

14 Mom: There is an interesting story about that.

➡ _____

15 In the past, visiting teams could not wash their uniforms after every game.

➡ _____

16 So they started wearing dark colors to hide the dirt.

➡ _____

17 Jian: Hahaha! That was a good idea!

➡ _____

18 The players are warming up.
➡ _____

19 Jian: Who's your favorite player?
➡ _____

20 Jihun: Number 77.
➡ _____

21 Jian: What does the number mean?
➡ _____

22 Jihun: Hmm…. Players choose a number they like.
➡ _____

23 Dad: You know what?
➡ _____

24 In the past, the numbers were determined by the players' batting order.
➡ _____

25 Jihun: That means there were no players with number 77!
➡ _____

26 Now, Jihun's favorite player is about to bat.
➡ _____

27 Jihun looks anxious.
➡ _____

28 Jian: Your favorite player is at bat.
➡ _____

29 Jihun: Yes. He has hit 21 home runs already this year.
➡ _____

30 If he hits one more today, he will be the home run leader this season.
➡ _____

31 The batter misses several balls.
➡ _____

32 Now he has a full count.
➡ _____

33 He is waiting for the next pitch.
➡ _____

34 Jihun: HOME RUN! HOME RUN!
➡ _____

35 Crack! The ball flies fast.
➡ _____

36 It is going, going, going, gone!
➡ _____

※ 다음 괄호 안의 단어들을 우리말에 맞도록 바르게 배열하시오.

1 (Day / A / at / Baseball / the / Stadium)
➡ _____

2 (the / today / Thunders / and / Cobras / the / game. / a / have)
➡ _____

3 (family / Jihun's / at / is / baseball / stadium. / the)
➡ _____

4 (Jihun: / this / Jian, / is / first / your / to / time / come / to / baseball / the / it? / isn't / stadium,)
➡ _____

5 (Jian: / I'm / yes, / excited. / so // can't / I / for / wait / the / to / start. / game)
➡ _____

6 (Dad: / look, / players / the / coming / are / now! / out)
➡ _____

7 (Jian: / team / which / Thunders? / the / is)
➡ _____

8 (Jihun: / there, / over / base. / third / behind)
➡ _____

9 (are / they / dark / wearing / uniforms / gray / they / because / team. / visiting / the / are)
➡ _____

10 (Jian: / the / does / team / visiting / wear / always / color? / dark / a)
➡ _____

11 (Jihun: / that's / yes, / rule. / the)
➡ _____

12 (teams / home / bright / have / and / uniforms / teams / visiting / uniforms. / dark / have)
➡ _____

13 (Jian: / that? / is / why)
➡ _____

14 (Mom: / is / there / interesting / an / that. / about / story)
➡ _____

15 (the / in / past, / teams / visiting / not / could / wash / uniforms / their / game. / every / after)
➡ _____

16 (they / so / wearing / started / colors / dark / hide / dirt. / the / to)
➡ _____

17 (Jian: / hahaha! // was / that / idea! / good / a)
➡ _____

1 야구 경기장에서의 하루

2 오늘 천둥 대 코브라 게임이 있다.

3 지훈이네 가족은 야구 경기장에 있다.

4 지훈: 지안아. 네가 야구 경기장에 온 건 이번이 처음이야. 그렇지 않니?

5 지안: 응, 나 아주 흥분돼. 나는 경기가 빨리 시작했으면 좋겠어.

6 아빠: 봐. 선수들이 지금 나오고 있어!

7 지안: 어떤 팀이 천둥이야?

8 지훈: 저기, 3루 뒤.

9 그들은 원정 팀이기 때문에 어두운 회색 유니폼을 입고 있어.

10 지안: 원정 팀은 항상 어두운 색을 입어?

11 지훈: 응, 그게 규칙이야.

12 홈팀은 밝은 유니폼을 입고 원정팀은 어두운 유니폼을 입어.

13 지안: 왜?

14 엄마: 그것에 대한 흥미로운 이야기가 있단다.

15 과거에는 원정 팀이 매 경기 후 유니폼을 세탁할 수가 없었어.

16 그래서 그들은 때를 숨기기 위해 어두운 색을 입기 시작했지.

17 지안: 하하하! 좋은 생각이었네요!

18 (players / the / up. / warming / are)
➡ _____

19 (Jian: / your / who's / player? / favorite)
➡ _____

20 (Jihun: / 77. / number)
➡ _____

21 (Jian: / does / what / mean? / number / the)
➡ _____

22 (Jihun: / hmm.... // choose / players / number / a / like. / they)
➡ _____

23 (Dad: / what? / know / you)
➡ _____

24 (the / in / past, / numbers / the / determined / were / the / player's / by / order. / batting)
➡ _____

25 (Jihun: / means / that / were / there / players / no / 77! / number / with)
➡ _____

26 (now, / favorite / Jihun's / is / player / bat. / to / about)
➡ _____

27 (looks / Jihun / anxious.)
➡ _____

28 (Jian: / favorite / your / is / player / bat. / at)
➡ _____

29 (Jihun: / yes. // has / he / 21 / hit / home / already / runs / year. / this)
➡ _____

30 (he / if / hits / more / one / today, / will / he / the / be / run / home / season. / this / leader)
➡ _____

31 (batter / the / several / balls. / misses)
➡ _____

32 (he / now / a / has / count. / full)
➡ _____

33 (is / he / for / waiting / pitch. / next / the)
➡ _____

34 (Jihun: / RUN! / HOME / RUN! / HOME)
➡ _____

35 (crack! // ball / the / fast. / flies)
➡ _____

36 (is / it / going, / gone! / going, / going,)
➡ _____

18 선수들이 몸을 풀고 있다.

19 지안: 가장 좋아하는 선수가 누구야?

20 지훈: 77번.

21 지안: 그 숫자는 무엇을 의미해?

22 지훈: 음... 선수들이 원하는 번호를 선택해.

23 아빠: 그거 알아?

24 과거에는 번호가 선수들의 타순에 의해 결정되었단다.

25 지훈: 77번 선수가 없었다는 뜻이네요!

26 이제 지훈이의 가장 좋아하는 선수가 막 공을 치려고 한다.

27 지훈이는 불안해 보인다.

28 지안: 오빠가 가장 좋아하는 선수가 타석에 서네.

29 지훈: 응. 그는 올해 이미 21개의 홈런을 쳤어.

30 그가 오늘 하나를 더 치면, 그는 이번 시즌 홈런 리더가 될 거야.

31 타자는 여러 개의 공을 놓친다.

32 이제 그는 풀카운트가 되었다.

33 그는 다음 투구를 기다리고 있다.

34 지훈: 홈런! 홈런!

35 땅! 공은 빠르게 날아간다.

36 그것은 가고, 가고, 가고, 사라져 버렸다!

※ 다음 우리말을 영어로 쓰시오.

1 야구 경기장에서의 하루

➡ _____

2 오늘 천둥 대 코브라 게임이 있다.

➡ _____

3 지훈이네 가족은 야구 경기장에 있다.

➡ _____

4 지훈: 지안아, 네가 야구 경기장에 온 건 이번이 처음이야, 그렇지 않니?

➡ _____

5 지안: 응, 나 아주 흥분돼. 나는 경기가 빨리 시작했으면 좋겠어.

➡ _____

6 아빠: 봐, 선수들이 지금 나오고 있어!

➡ _____

7 지안: 어떤 팀이 천둥이야?

➡ _____

8 지훈: 저기, 3루 뒤.

➡ _____

9 그들은 원정 팀이기 때문에 어두운 회색 유니폼을 입고 있어.

➡ _____

10 지안: 원정 팀은 항상 어두운 색을 입어?

➡ _____

11 지훈: 응, 그게 규칙이야.

➡ _____

12 홈팀은 밝은 유니폼을 입고 원정팀은 어두운 유니폼을 입어.

➡ _____

13 지안: 왜?

➡ _____

14 엄마: 그것에 대한 흥미로운 이야기가 있단다.

➡ _____

15 과거에는 원정 팀이 매 경기 후 유니폼을 세탁할 수가 없었어.

➡ _____

16 그래서 그들은 때를 숨기기 위해 어두운 색을 입기 시작했지.

➡ _____

17 지안: 하하하! 좋은 생각이었네요!

➡ _____

18 선수들이 몸을 풀고 있다.

➡ _____

19 지안: 가장 좋아하는 선수가 누구야?

➡ _____

20 지훈: 77번.

➡ _____

21 지안: 그 숫자는 무엇을 의미해?

➡ _____

22 지훈: 음... 선수들이 원하는 번호를 선택해.

➡ _____

23 아빠: 그거 알아?

➡ _____

24 과거에는 번호가 선수들의 타순에 의해 결정되었단다.

➡ _____

25 지훈: 77번 선수가 없었다는 뜻이네요!

➡ _____

26 이제 지훈이의 가장 좋아하는 선수가 막 공을 치려고 한다.

➡ _____

27 지훈이는 불안해 보인다.

➡ _____

28 지안: 오빠가 가장 좋아하는 선수가 타석에 서네.

➡ _____

29 지훈: 응. 그는 올해 이미 21개의 홈런을 쳤어.

➡ _____

30 그가 오늘 하나를 더 치면, 그는 이번 시즌 홈런 리더가 될 거야.

➡ _____

31 타자는 여러 개의 공을 놓친다.

➡ _____

32 이제 그는 풀카운트가 되었다.

➡ _____

33 그는 다음 투구를 기다리고 있다.

➡ _____

34 지훈: 홈런! 홈런!

➡ _____

35 땅! 공은 빠르게 날아간다.

➡ _____

36 그것은 가고, 가고, 가고, 사라져 버렸다!

➡ _____

※ 다음 우리말과 일치하도록 빈칸에 알맞은 말을 쓰시오.

Real-Life Zone B

1. A: _____ _____ do you _____? Basketball _____ soccer?

2. B: I like basketball. I'm _____ _____ play it _____ my

   friends _____ _____. I _____ _____.

1. A: 너는 어떤 운동을 좋아하니? 농구 아니면 축구?
2. B: 농구를 좋아해. 이번 주말에 친구들이랑 농구를 할 거야. 너무 기다려져.

Writing Workshop

1. Abebe Bikila _____ _____

2. _____: _____ 7, 1932

3. _____: Ethiopia

4. Speciality: He _____ _____ _____ a marathon winner at the

   Rome and Tokyo _____ _____ _____.

5. When he was _____ _____ _____ the marathon in Rome, he

   _____ _____ that his shoes _____ _____ _____ well,

   so he _____ _____ _____ the race _____ _____.

6. He _____ _____ _____ the race, but he finished the race

   _____ _____ _____.

7. He was _____ _____ the greatest runners in the world, _____

   _____?

1. Abebe Bikila   마라톤 선수
2. 생일: 1932년 8월 7일
3. 국적: 에티오피아
4. 특별 사항: 그는 로마 국제 스포츠 대회와 도쿄 국제 스포츠 대회의 마라톤 우승자로 알려졌다.
5. 그가 로마에서 달리기를 준비하던 도중에 자신의 신발이 잘 맞지 않는다는 것을 알고 그는 신발을 신지 않고 달리기로 결심했다.
6. 그는 경주 도중에 통증을 느꼈지만 우승자로 경주를 끝마쳤다.
7. 그는 세계에서 가장 위대한 달리기 선수들 중의 한 명이었어, 그렇지 않니?

Wrap Up

1. Sarang _____ _____ _____ _____

2. Sarang Middle School Sports Day _____ _____ _____ on

   the school playing field _____ _____, _____ 15.

3. There _____ _____ _____ games _____ _____ baseball

   and soccer.

4. There _____ _____ be _____.

5. It _____ _____ fun, _____ _____?

1. 사랑 중학교 운동회
2. 사랑 중학교 운동회가 학교 운동장에서 6월 15일 수요일에 열립니다.
3. 야구와 축구 같은 여러 가지 게임이 있을 것입니다.
4. 또한 탁구도 있을 것입니다.
5. 재미있게 들리지요, 그렇지 않나요?

※ 다음 우리말을 영어로 쓰시오.

Real-Life Zone B

1. 너는 어떤 운동을 좋아하니? 농구 아니면 축구?

➡ _____

2. B: 농구를 좋아해. 이번 주말에 친구들이랑 농구를 할 거야. 너무 기다려져.

➡ _____

Writing Workshop

1. Abebe Bikila   마라톤 선수

➡ _____

2. 생일: 1932년 8월 7일

➡ _____

3. 국적: 에티오피아

➡ _____

4. 특별 사항: 그는 로마 국제 스포츠 대회와 도쿄 국제 스포츠 대회의 마라톤 우승자로 알려졌다.

➡ _____

5. 그가 로마에서 달리기를 준비하던 도중에 자신의 신발이 잘 맞지 않는다는 것을 알고 그는 신발을 신지 않고 달리기로 결심했다.

➡ _____

6. 그는 경주 도중에 통증을 느꼈지만 우승자로 경주를 끝마쳤다.

➡ _____

7. 그는 세계에서 가장 위대한 달리기 선수들 중의 한 명이었어, 그렇지 않았니?

➡ _____

Wrap Up

1. 사랑 중학교 운동회

➡ _____

2. 사랑 중학교 운동회가 학교 운동장에서 6월 15일 수요일에 열립니다.

➡ _____

3. 야구와 축구 같은 여러 가지 게임이 있을 것입니다.

➡ _____

4. 또한 탁구도 있을 것입니다.

➡ _____

5. 재미있게 들리지요, 그렇지 않나요?

➡ _____

※ 다음 영어를 우리말로 쓰시오.

01 abroad _____

02 camel _____

03 cheerful _____

04 beginning _____

05 colorful _____

06 bright _____

07 sweet _____

08 enough _____

09 view _____

10 flight _____

11 capital _____

12 guest _____

13 modern _____

14 lamb _____

15 coastline _____

16 scared _____

17 language _____

18 magical _____

19 asleep _____

20 expect _____

21 whole _____

22 moment _____

23 amazing _____

24 culture _____

25 moved _____

26 tasty _____

27 once _____

28 wedding _____

29 rise _____

30 cozy _____

31 serve _____

32 imagine _____

33 chance _____

34 traditional _____

35 be full of _____

36 get used to _____

37 be made of _____

38 show A around B _____

39 be cooked with _____

40 Have you been (to) ~? _____

41 can't wait to _____

42 feel like+주어+동사 _____

43 wake up _____

※ 다음 우리말을 영어로 쓰시오.

01 기회 _____

02 화려한, (색이) 다채로운 _____

03 순간 _____

04 아늑한 _____

05 잠이 든 _____

06 ~할 만큼 (충분히) _____

07 낙타 _____

08 비행 _____

09 손님 _____

10 상상하다 _____

11 시작, 처음 _____

12 제공하다 _____

13 농담하다 _____

14 해외에 _____

15 경관, 전망 _____

16 양고기 _____

17 맛있는 _____

18 밝은 _____

19 아주 멋진, 마법의 _____

20 쾌활한, 유쾌한 _____

21 결혼(식) _____

22 현대의 _____

23 굉장한, 놀라운 _____

24 수도 _____

25 ~하자마자 _____

26 문화 _____

27 부분, 일부 _____

28 해안선 _____

29 (해가) 뜨다 _____

30 겁먹은, 무서워하는 _____

31 가슴 뭉클한 _____

32 전통적인 _____

33 기대하다, 예상하다 _____

34 전체, 모든 _____

35 잠에서 깨다 _____

36 A에서 B로 _____

37 ~인 것처럼 느끼다 _____

38 ~에 익숙해지다 _____

39 빨리 ~하면 좋겠다 _____

40 처음에는 _____

41 ~로 가득하다 _____

42 ~로 만들어지다(재료) _____

43 ~에 가 본 적 있니? _____

※ 다음 영영풀이에 알맞은 단어를 <보기>에서 골라 쓴 후, 우리말 뜻을 쓰시오.

1 _____ : shining strongly:: _____

2 _____ : not awake: _____

3 _____ : to make a joke: _____

4 _____ : noticeably happy: _____

5 _____ : appear above the horizon in the sky: _____

6 _____ : an opportunity to do something: _____

7 _____ : in or to a different country or countries: _____

8 _____ : seems to use special powers: _____

9 _____ : someone who is invited to visit you: _____

10 _____ : designed and made using the latest ideas or methods: _____

11 _____ : relating to Mongolia or its people: _____

12 _____ : believe or think that something will happen: _____

13 _____ : everything that can be seen from a particular place: _____

14 _____ : a place where planes take off and land with facilities for passengers:

_____

15 _____ : one of the pieces, sections, or elements that makes the whole of

something: _____

16 _____ : a place where trains or buses stop so that people can get on or off:

_____

보기			
part	station	magical	view
asleep	kid	bright	guest
Mongolian	expect	airport	rise
chance	abroad	modern	cheerful

※ 다음 우리말과 일치하도록 빈칸에 알맞은 말을 쓰시오.

Listen & Speak 1 A

B: _____ _____ _____ _____ Spanish food?

G: Yes, I _____. It's really _____.

B: 스페인 음식을 먹어 본 적 있니?
G: 응, 먹어 봤어. 매우 맛있어.

Listen & Speak 1 B

1. G: You _____ _____, Inho. What's _____?

   B: I'm _____ _____ Jejudo _____ my family this weekend. _____ you _____ _____ there?

   G: Yes, many times. I love the _____. _____ _____ _____ you?

   B: It'll be my first visit to Jejudo. I _____ _____ _____ this weekend!

2. B: _____ you _____ watched the sun _____ _____ the ocean?

   G: No. _____ _____ you?

   B: I _____ the sun _____ in Gangneung _____ New Year's Day. It was great.

   G: I _____ _____ _____, but I just couldn't _____ _____ _____ enough.

1. G: 인호야, 너 신나 보인다. 무슨 일이니?
   B: 이번 주말에 가족들과 함께 제주도에 가거든. 넌 가 본 적 있니?
   G: 응. 여러 번 가 봤어. 나는 그 해안선을 좋아해. 너는 어떠니?
   B: 난 이번이 제주도 첫 방문이야. 이번 주말이 빨리 왔으면 좋겠다!

2. B: 바다 위로 해가 뜨는 것을 본 적 있니?
   G: 아니. 너는?
   B: 나는 새해 첫날에 강릉에서 해돋이를 봤어. 멋지더라.
   G: 나는 몇 번 시도해 봤는데 일찍 일어나지 못했어.

Listen & Speak 1 C

1. A: _____ _____ _____ traveled to _____ _____?

   B: Yes, I _____. It was a wonderful _____.

2. A: _____ _____ _____ _____ a horse?

   B: Yes, I have. It was a _____ _____.

1. A: 다른 나라로 여행 가 본 적 있니?
   B: 응, 있어. 그것은 멋진 경험이었어.

2. A: 말을 타 본 적 있니?
   B: 응, 있어. 그것은 멋진 경험이었어.

Listen & Speak 2 A

G: _____ _____ _____ _____ your new house?

B: It's great. I have a _____ _____ now.

G: 새 집은 어때?
B: 좋아. 나는 이제 더 큰 방을 가졌어.

Listen & Speak 2 B

1. **G:** _____ was your _____?

   B: Great. I _____ _____ Dokdo _____ my family.

   G: _____ _____ you _____ it?

   B: It was _____. I want _____ _____ there again.

2. **B:** _____ _____ _____ _____ the new Chinese restaurant?

   G: Yes. I _____ _____ there last Saturday.

   B: _____ _____ _____ _____ it?

   G: The service was bad. I _____ _____ _____ there again.

Listen & Speak 2 C

1. **A:** _____ do you _____ this shirt?

   B: It's _____. I like it.

2. **A:** _____ _____ _____ _____ your ice cream?

   B: It's _____. I like it.

Real-Life Zone A

B: _____ _____ _____ _____ _____, Sujin?

G: Yes, I _____ to Cambodia _____ _____.

B: Wow. _____ _____ you _____ it?

G: It was really _____, but I _____ the trip.

B: Tell me some _____ _____ _____ you _____ _____ the trip.

G: Hmm... _____ me _____. I ate _____ spiders!

B: What? You're kidding. _____ did you _____ _____?

G: They were really big, _____ I was a little _____ _____ _____. But the taste was okay.

B: Really? I cannot _____ _____ _____.

Communication Task

A: _____ _____ _____ _____ tacos?

B: Yes, I have. They were _____.

   / No, I _____. I want to _____ some _____.

---

1. **G:** 방학 잘 보냈니?
   B: 좋았어. 가족과 함께 독도에 다녀왔어.
   G: 어땠어?
   B: 굉장했어. 다시 한 번 가 보고 싶어.

2. **B:** 새로 생긴 중국 음식점에 가 봤니?
   G: 응. 지난주 토요일에 거기서 저녁을 먹었어.
   B: 어땠어?
   G: 서비스가 형편없었어. 그곳에 다시는 가지 않을 거야.

1. **A:** 이 셔츠가 마음에 드니?
   B: 그것은 색이 화려하구나. 마음에 들어.

2. **A:** 너의 아이스크림은 어떠니?
   B: 그것은 달콤해. 마음에 들어.

B: 수진아 해외여행 가 본 적 있니?
G: 응, 지난여름에 캄보디아에 다녀왔어.
B: 와. 여행은 어땠니?
G: 날씨가 너무 더웠지만 여행은 즐거웠어.
B: 여행하면서 재미있었던 경험 좀 이야기해 줘.
G: 음… 생각 좀 해 볼게. 거미 튀김을 먹었어!
B: 뭐라고? 진짜로? 거미 튀김은 어땠는데?
G: 너무 커서 처음엔 조금 무서웠는데. 맛은 괜찮았어.
B: 정말? 난 내가 거미를 먹는 걸 상상할 수가 없어.

A: 타코를 먹어본 적 있니?
B: 응, 먹어 봤어. 맛있었어.
   / 아니, 안 먹어 봤어. 언젠간 한 번 먹어 보고 싶어.

※ 다음 우리말에 맞도록 대화를 영어로 쓰시오.

 해석

Listen & Speak 1 A

B: _____

G: _____

B: 스페인 음식을 먹어 본 적 있니?
G: 응, 먹어 봤어. 매우 맛있어.

Listen & Speak 1 B

1. G: _____
   B: _____
   G: _____
   B: _____

2. B: _____
   G: _____
   B: _____
   G: _____

1. G: 인호야, 너 신나 보인다. 무슨 일이니?
   B: 이번 주말에 가족들과 함께 제주 도에 가거든. 넌 가 본 적 있니?
   G: 응. 여러 번 가 봤어. 나는 그 해안선을 좋아해. 너는 어떠니?
   B: 난 이번이 제주도 첫 방문이야. 이번 주말이 빨리 왔으면 좋겠다!

2. B: 바다 위로 해가 뜨는 것을 본 적 있니?
   G: 아니. 너는?
   B: 나는 새해 첫날에 강릉에서 해 돋이를 봤어. 멋지더라.
   G: 나는 몇 번 시도해 봤는데 일찍 일어나지 못했어.

Listen & Speak 1 C

1. A: _____
   B: _____

2. A: _____
   B: _____

1. A: 다른 나라로 여행 가 본 적 있니?
   B: 응, 있어. 그것은 멋진 경험이 었어.

2. A: 말을 타 본 적 있니?
   B: 응, 있어. 그것은 멋진 경험이 었어.

Listen & Speak 2 A

G: _____

B: _____

G: 새 집은 어때?
B: 좋아. 나는 이제 더 큰 방을 가졌어.

Listen & Speak 2 B

1. G: _____

   B: _____

   G: _____

   B: _____

2. B: _____

   G: _____

   B: _____

   G: _____

1. G: 방학 잘 보냈니?
   B: 좋았어. 가족과 함께 독도에 다녀왔어.
   G: 어땠어?
   B: 굉장했어. 다시 한 번 가 보고 싶어.

2. B: 새로 생긴 중국 음식점에 가 봤니?
   G: 응. 지난주 토요일에 거기서 저녁을 먹었어.
   B: 어땠어?
   G: 서비스가 형편없었어. 그곳에 다시는 가지 않을 거야.

Listen & Speak 2 C

1. A: _____

   B: _____

2. A: _____

   B: _____

1. A: 이 셔츠가 마음에 드니?
   B: 그것은 색이 화려하구나. 마음에 들어.
2. A: 너의 아이스크림은 어떠니?
   B: 그것은 달콤해. 마음에 들어.

Real-Life Zone A

B: _____

G: _____

B: _____

G: _____

B: _____

G: _____

B: _____

G: _____

B: _____

B: 수진아 해외여행 가 본 적 있니?
G: 응, 지난여름에 캄보디아에 다녀왔어.
B: 와. 여행은 어땠니?
G: 날씨가 너무 더웠지만 여행은 즐거웠어.
B: 여행하면서 재미있었던 경험 좀 이야기해 줘.
G: 음… 생각 좀 해 볼게. 거미 튀김을 먹었어!
B: 뭐라고? 진짜로? 거미 튀김은 어땠는데?
G: 너무 커서 처음엔 조금 무서웠는데. 맛은 괜찮았어.
B: 정말? 난 내가 거미를 먹는 걸 상상할 수가 없어.

Communication Task

A: _____

B: _____

A: 타코를 먹어본 적 있니?
B: 응, 먹어 봤어. 맛있었어.
  / 아니, 안 먹어 봤어. 언젠간 한 번 먹어 보고 싶어.

※ 다음 우리말과 일치하도록 빈칸에 알맞은 것을 골라 쓰시오.

1 A _____ to _____
    A. Mongolia   B. Trip

2 This year, I had a _____ summer _____ I visited Mongolia _____ the first _____.
    A. because   B. for   C. special   D. time

3 _____ friend Altan _____ _____ Mongolia.
    A. from   B. is   C. my

4 His grandmother _____ me _____ Ulaanbaatar, the _____ of Mongolia.
    A. to   B. capital   C. invited

5 _____ a four-hour _____ from Seoul, Altan and I _____ _____ Chinggis Khaan International Airport in Ulaanbaatar.
    A. at   B. arrived   C. flight   D. after

6 It _____ thirty minutes _____ taxi _____ the airport _____ Altan's grandmother's house.
    A. by   B. took   C. to   D. from

7 _____ house is a *ger*, a _____ _____ house.
    A. traditional   B. her   C. Mongolian

8 It is a big _____, but it is _____ _____.
    A. tent   B. inside   C. cozy

9 When we _____, something _____ _____.
    A. wonderful   B. entered   C. smelled

10 It was _____ the *khorkhog* _____ she was _____ _____ us.
    A. from   B. cooking   C. that   D. for

11 *Khorkhog* is a _____ _____.
    A. barbecue   B. Mongolian

12 It is _____ _____ lamb and _____ _____ hot stones.
    A. of   B. with   C. made   D. cooked

13 I was _____ when Altan said Mongolians _____ *khorkhog* _____ special _____.
    A. serve   B. moved   C. to   D. guests

1 몽골 여행

2 나는 올해 몽골을 처음으로 방문해서 특별한 여름을 보냈다.

3 내 친구 알탕은 몽골 출신이다.

4 그의 할머니께서는 몽골의 수도인 울란바토르에 나를 초대하셨다.

5 서울에서 네 시간 비행 후 알탕과 나는 울란바토르의 칭기즈칸 국제공항에 도착했다.

6 공항에서 알탕의 할머니 댁까지 택시로 30분이 걸렸다.

7 할머니의 집은 몽골 전통 가옥인 게르이다.

8 큰 텐트이지만 내부는 아늑하다.

9 우리가 들어갔을 때, 뭔가 좋은 냄새가 났다.

10 그녀가 우리를 위해 요리하고 있던 호르호그에서 나는 냄새였다.

11 호르호그는 몽골식 바비큐이다.

12 그것은 양고기로 만들어졌으며 뜨거운 돌로 요리되었다.

13 나는 알탕이 몽골인들은 특별한 손님에게 호르호그를 대접한다고 말했을 때 감동을 받았다.

14 It was _____ delicious _____ I asked _____ more.
A. for   B. so   C. that

15 _____ dinner, Altan and I _____ _____ to see the night sky.
A. went   B. after   C. outside

16 The sky _____ _____ _____ bright stars.
A. full   B. of   C. was

17 I _____ _____ I was in a _____ place.
A. like   B. magical   C. felt

18 _____ the next three days, Altan _____ me _____ and helped me _____ Mongolian culture.
A. showed   B. during   C. around   D. experience

19 Every _____ was fun and _____, but I had the _____ fun when I _____ a camel in the Gobi Desert.
A. exciting   B. moment   C. rode   D. most

20 _____ first, I was _____ because the camel was taller _____ I _____.
A. expected   B. scared   C. than   D. at

21 But _____ I sat on its _____, I soon got _____ _____ its movement.
A. back   B. used   C. once   D. to

22 _____ the camel's _____, the _____ of the desert was truly _____.
A. view   B. amazing   C. from   D. back

23 My _____ to Mongolia was a _____ experience _____ many _____.
A. ways   B. visit   C. in   D. special

24 It _____ me a great _____ to _____ to know my friend's country and _____.
A. chance   B. get   C. culture   D. gave

25 I want to _____ Mongolia _____ _____!
A. again   B. visit   C. someday

14 그것은 너무 맛있어서 나는 더 달라고 했다.

15 저녁 식사 후, 알탕과 나는 밤하늘을 보기 위해 밖으로 나갔다.

16 하늘은 밝은 별들로 가득했다.

17 나는 신비한 장소에 있는 것처럼 느꼈다.

18 그 후 3일 동안, 알탕은 나를 구경시켜 주었고 몽골 문화를 경험할 수 있게 도와주었다.

19 매 순간이 재미있고 흥미진진했지만, 고비 사막에서 낙타를 탈 때가 가장 재미있었다.

20 처음에는 내가 예상했던 것보다 낙타의 키가 커서 무서웠다.

21 그러나 낙타 등에 앉자 곧 움직임에 익숙해졌다.

22 낙타의 등에서 보는 사막의 경치는 정말로 놀라웠다.

23 내가 몽골을 방문한 것은 여러 면에서 특별한 경험이었다.

24 내 친구의 나라와 문화를 알 수 있는 좋은 기회가 되었다.

25 나는 언젠가 몽골을 다시 방문하고 싶다!

※ 다음 우리말과 일치하도록 빈칸에 알맞은 말을 쓰시오.

1 A _____ _____ _____

2 _____ _____, I had a _____ _____ because I visited Mongolia _____ _____ _____ _____.

3 My friend Altan _____ _____ _____.

4 His grandmother _____ me _____ Ulaanbaatar, _____ _____ of Mongolia.

5 _____ _____ _____ _____ from Seoul, Altan and I _____ _____ Chinggis Khaan International Airport in Ulaanbaatar.

6 _____ _____ thirty minutes _____ _____ _____ the airport _____ Altan's grandmother's house.

7 Her house is a *ger*, a _____ _____ _____.

8 It is a _____ _____, but it is _____ _____.

9 _____ we _____, something _____ _____.

10 It was _____ the *khorkhog* that she was _____ _____ us.

11 *Khorkhog* is a _____ _____.

12 It _____ _____ _____ lamb and _____ _____ hot stones.

13 I _____ _____ when Altan said Mongolians _____ *khorkhog* _____ _____ _____.

1 몽골 여행

2 나는 올해 몽골을 처음으로 방문해서 특별한 여름을 보냈다.

3 내 친구 알탕은 몽골 출신이다.

4 그의 할머니께서는 몽골의 수도인 울란바토르에 나를 초대하셨다.

5 서울에서 네 시간 비행 후 알탕과 나는 울란바토르의 칭기즈 칸 국제공항에 도착했다.

6 공항에서 알탕의 할머니 댁까지 택시로 30분이 걸렸다.

7 할머니의 집은 몽골 전통 가옥인 게르이다.

8 큰 텐트이지만 내부는 아늑하다.

9 우리가 들어갔을 때, 뭔가 좋은 냄새가 났다.

10 그녀가 우리를 위해 요리하고 있던 호르호그에서 나는 냄새였다.

11 호르호그는 몽골식 바비큐이다.

12 그것은 양고기로 만들어졌으며 뜨거운 돌로 요리되었다.

13 나는 알탕이 몽골인들은 특별한 손님에게 호르호그를 대접한다고 말했을 때 감동을 받았다.

14 It was _____ delicious _____ I _____ _____ more.

15 After dinner, Altan and I _____ _____ _____ _____ the night sky.

16 The sky _____ _____ _____ _____ stars.

17 I _____ _____ I was in a _____ _____ .

18 _____ the next three days, Altan _____ _____ _____ and _____ _____ _____ Mongolian culture.

19 _____ _____ was fun and exciting, but I _____ _____ _____ _____ when I _____ a camel in the Gobi Desert.

20 _____ _____ , I was _____ because the camel was _____ _____ I _____ .

21 But _____ I _____ _____ its back, I soon _____ _____ _____ its movement.

22 From the camel's back, _____ _____ _____ _____ _____ was _____ _____ .

23 My visit to Mongolia was a special experience _____ _____ _____ .

24 It gave me a great chance _____ _____ _____ my friend's _____ and _____ .

25 I want to _____ Mongolia _____ _____ !

14 그것은 너무 맛있어서 나는 더 달라고 했다.

15 저녁 식사 후, 알탕과 나는 밤하늘을 보기 위해 밖으로 나갔다.

16 하늘은 밝은 별들로 가득했다.

17 나는 신비한 장소에 있는 것처럼 느꼈다.

18 그 후 3일 동안, 알탕은 나를 구경시켜 주었고 몽골 문화를 경험할 수 있게 도와주었다.

19 매 순간이 재미있고 흥미진진했지만, 고비 사막에서 낙타를 탈 때가 가장 재미있었다.

20 처음에는 내가 예상했던 것보다 낙타의 키가 커서 무서웠다.

21 그러나 낙타 등에 앉자 곧 움직임에 익숙해졌다.

22 낙타의 등에서 보는 사막의 경치는 정말로 놀라웠다.

23 내가 몽골을 방문한 것은 여러 면에서 특별한 경험이었다.

24 내 친구의 나라와 문화를 알 수 있는 좋은 기회가 되었다.

25 나는 언젠가 몽골을 다시 방문하고 싶다!

※ 다음 문장을 우리말로 쓰시오.

1 A Trip to Mongolia

➡ _____

2 This year, I had a special summer because I visited Mongolia for the first time.

➡ _____

3 My friend Altan is from Mongolia.

➡ _____

4 His grandmother invited me to Ulaanbaatar, the capital of Mongolia.

➡ _____

5 After a four-hour flight from Seoul, Altan and I arrived at Chinggis Khaan International Airport in Ulaanbaatar.

➡ _____

6 It took thirty minutes by taxi from the airport to Altan's grandmother's house.

➡ _____

7 Her house is a *ger*, a traditional Mongolian house.

➡ _____

8 It is a big tent, but it is cozy inside.

➡ _____

9 When we entered, something smelled wonderful.

➡ _____

10 It was from the *khorkhog* that she was cooking for us.

➡ _____

11 *Khorkhog* is a Mongolian barbecue.

➡ _____

12 It is made of lamb and cooked with hot stones.

➡ _____

13 I was moved when Altan said Mongolians serve *khorkhog* to special guests.

➡ _____

14 It was so delicious that I asked for more.

➡ _____

15 After dinner, Altan and I went outside to see the night sky.

➡ _____

16 The sky was full of bright stars.

➡ _____

17 I felt like I was in a magical place.

➡ _____

18 During the next three days, Altan showed me around and helped me experience Mongolian culture.

➡ _____

19 Every moment was fun and exciting, but I had the most fun when I rode a camel in the Gobi Desert.

➡ _____

20 At first, I was scared because the camel was taller than I expected.

➡ _____

21 But once I sat on its back, I soon got used to its movement.

➡ _____

22 From the camel's back, the view of the desert was truly amazing.

➡ _____

23 My visit to Mongolia was a special experience in many ways.

➡ _____

24 It gave me a great chance to get to know my friend's country and culture.

➡ _____

25 I want to visit Mongolia again someday!

➡ _____

※ 다음 괄호 안의 단어들을 우리말에 맞도록 바르게 배열하시오.

1 (Trip / A / Mongolia / to)
➡ _____

2 (year, / this / had / I / a / summer / special / because / visited / I / for / Mongolia / the / for / first)
➡ _____
_____

3 (friend / my / is / Altan / Mongolia. / from)
➡ _____

4 (grandmother / his / me / invited / Ulaanbaatar, / to / capital / the / Mongolia. / of)
➡ _____

5 (a / after / flight / four-hour / Seoul, / from / I / and / Altan / at / arrived / Khann / Chinggis / Airport / International / Ulaanbaatar. / in)
➡ _____
_____

6 (took / it / minutes / thirty / taxi / by / the / from / airport / to / Altan's / house. / grandmother's)
➡ _____
_____

7 (house / her / a / is / *ger*, / traditional / a / house. / Mongolian)
➡ _____

8 (is / it / a / tent, / big / it / but / cozy / is / inside.)
➡ _____

9 (we / when / entered, / smelled / something / wonderful.)
➡ _____

10 (was / it / the / from / that / *khorkhog* / she / cookinig / was / us. / for)
➡ _____

11 (is / *khorkhog* / a / barbecue. / Mongolian)
➡ _____

12 (is / it / of / made / lamb / and / with / cooked / stones. / hot)
➡ _____

13 (was / I / when / moved / said / Altan / serve / Mongolians / to / *khorkhog* / guests. / special)
➡ _____
_____

1 몽골 여행

2 나는 올해 몽골을 처음으로 방문해서 특별한 여름을 보냈다.

3 내 친구 알탕은 몽골 출신이다.

4 그의 할머니께서는 몽골의 수도인 울란바토르에 나를 초대하셨다.

5 서울에서 네 시간 비행 후 알탕과 나는 울란바토르의 칭기즈 칸 국제공항에 도착했다.

6 공항에서 알탕의 할머니 댁까지 택시로 30분이 걸렸다.

7 할머니의 집은 몽골 전통 가옥인 게르이다.

8 큰 텐트이지만 내부는 아늑하다.

9 우리가 들어갔을 때, 뭔가 좋은 냄새가 났다.

10 그녀가 우리를 위해 요리하고 있던 호르호그에서 나는 냄새였다.

11 호르호그는 몽골식 바비큐이다.

12 그것은 양고기로 만들어졌으며 뜨거운 돌로 요리되었다.

13 나는 알탕이 몽골인들은 특별한 손님에게 호르호그를 대접한다고 말했을 때 감동을 받았다.

14 (was / it / delicious / so / I / that / for / asked / more.)

➡ _____

15 (dinner, / after / I / and / Altan / outside / went / see / to / night / the / sky.)

➡ _____

16 (sky / the / full / was / of / stars. / bright)

➡ _____

17 (felt / I / like / was / I / a / in / place. / magical)

➡ _____

18 (the / during / three / next / days, / showed / Altan / around / me / and / me / helped / Mongolian / experience / culture.)

➡ _____

19 (moment / every / fun / was / and / exciting, / I / but / the / had / most / fun / I / when / rode / camel / a / the / in / Desert. / Gobi)

➡ _____

20 (first, / at / was / I / because / scared / camel / the / taller / was / I / than / expected.)

➡ _____

21 (once / but / sat / I / its / on / back, / soon / I / used / got / its / to / movement.)

➡ _____

22 (the / from / back, / camel's / view / the / of / desert / the / truly / was / amazing.)

➡ _____

23 (visit / my / Mongolia / to / a / special / was / experience / many / in / ways.)

➡ _____

24 (gave / it / me / great / a / to / chance / get / know / to / friend's / my / and / culture. / country)

➡ _____

25 (want / I / visit / to / again / Mongolia / someday!)

➡ _____

14 그것은 너무 맛있어서 나는 더 달라고 했다.

15 저녁 식사 후, 알탕과 나는 밤하늘을 보기 위해 밖으로 나갔다.

16 하늘은 밝은 별들로 가득했다.

17 나는 신비한 장소에 있는 것처럼 느꼈다.

18 그 후 3일 동안. 알탕은 나를 구경시켜 주었고 몽골 문화를 경험할 수 있게 도와주었다.

19 매 순간이 재미있고 흥미진진했지만. 고비 사막에서 낙타를 탈 때가 가장 재미있었다.

20 처음에는 내가 예상했던 것보다 낙타의 키가 커서 무서웠다.

21 그러나 낙타 등에 앉자 곧 움직임에 익숙해졌다.

22 낙타의 등에서 보는 사막의 경치는 정말로 놀라웠다.

23 내가 몽골을 방문한 것은 여러 면에서 특별한 경험이었다.

24 내 친구의 나라와 문화를 알 수 있는 좋은 기회가 되었다.

25 나는 언젠가 몽골을 다시 방문하고 싶다!

※ 다음 우리말을 영어로 쓰시오.

1 몽골 여행

➡ _____

2 나는 올해 몽골을 처음으로 방문해서 특별한 여름을 보냈다.

➡ _____

3 내 친구 알탕은 몽골 출신이다.

➡ _____

4 그의 할머니께서는 몽골의 수도인 울란바토르에 나를 초대하셨다.

➡ _____

5 서울에서 네 시간 비행 후 알탕과 나는 울란바토르의 칭기즈 칸 국제공항에 도착했다.

➡ _____

6 공항에서 알탕의 할머니 댁까지 택시로 30분이 걸렸다.

➡ _____

7 할머니의 집은 몽골 전통 가옥인 게르이다.

➡ _____

8 큰 텐트이지만 내부는 아늑하다.

➡ _____

9 우리가 들어갔을 때, 뭔가 좋은 냄새가 났다.

➡ _____

10 그녀가 우리를 위해 요리하고 있던 호르호그에서 나는 냄새였다.

➡ _____

11 호르호그는 몽골식 바비큐이다.

➡ _____

12 그것은 양고기로 만들어졌으며 뜨거운 돌로 요리되었다.

➡ _____

13 나는 알탕이 몽골인들은 특별한 손님에게 호르호그를 대접한다고 말했을 때 감동을 받았다.

➡ _____

14 그것은 너무 맛있어서 나는 더 달라고 했다.

➡ _____

15 저녁 식사 후, 알탕과 나는 밤하늘을 보기 위해 밖으로 나갔다.

➡ _____

16 하늘은 밝은 별들로 가득했다.

➡ _____

17 나는 신비한 장소에 있는 것처럼 느꼈다.

➡ _____

18 그 후 3일 동안, 알탕은 나를 구경시켜 주었고 몽골 문화를 경험할 수 있게 도와주었다.

➡ _____

19 매 순간이 재미있고 흥미진진했지만, 고비 사막에서 낙타를 탈 때가 가장 재미있었다.

➡ _____

20 처음에는 내가 예상했던 것보다 낙타의 키가 커서 무서웠다.

➡ _____

21 그러나 낙타 등에 앉자 곧 움직임에 익숙해졌다.

➡ _____

22 낙타의 등에서 보는 사막의 경치는 정말로 놀라웠다.

➡ _____

23 내가 몽골을 방문한 것은 여러 면에서 특별한 경험이었다.

➡ _____

24 내 친구의 나라와 문화를 알 수 있는 좋은 기회가 되었다.

➡ _____

25 나는 언젠가 몽골을 다시 방문하고 싶다!

➡ _____

※ 다음 우리말과 일치하도록 빈칸에 알맞은 말을 쓰시오.

Writing Workshop - Step 2

1. A _____ _____ Suncheon

2. My family _____ _____ _____ to Suncheon _____ _____.

3. We _____ the National Garden.

4. It was _____ large _____ _____ _____ _____ _____ _____
   the whole garden.

5. _____ _____ _____ _____, we were really hungry.

6. _____ _____, we had Gukbap _____ _____ _____
   _____.

7. Suncheon _____ _____ _____ Gukbap and we enjoyed it.

8. This trip was _____ good _____ I _____ _____ _____
   it for a long time.

Wrap Up 1-2

1. G: _____ _____ your _____, Tony?

2. B: It was great. I _____ _____ the International Food Festival
   _____ _____ _____.

3. G: _____ _____ did you _____?

4. B: I had a _____ _____ _____, *tangyuan*.

5. G: _____ _____ you like it?

6. B: I enjoyed it. It's _____ _____ sweet rice balls. Chinese
   people _____ _____ it to guests _____ _____ _____.

Wrap Up 7

1. _____ _____ the restaurant _____ just opened _____
   _____ _____ ?

2. The restaurant was _____ _____ _____ I had to _____
   _____ an hour _____ _____ _____.

3. The cheese cake _____ _____ _____ _____ _____
   _____ all of it.

4. The restaurant was _____ _____ _____ _____ _____
   talk with my friends.

1. 순천으로의 여행
2. 나의 가족은 작년 여름에 순천으로 여행을 갔다.
3. 우리는 순천 국가 정원을 방문했다.
4. 그곳은 너무 넓어서 우리는 정원 전체를 다 볼 수 없었다.
5. 세 시간 동안 걸은 후, 우리는 정말 배가 고팠다.
6. 저녁 식사로 우리는 부모님들이 좋아하시는 국밥을 먹었다.
7. 순천은 국밥으로 유명하고, 우리는 그것을 즐겼다.
8. 이번 여행은 너무 좋아서 나는 오랫동안 그것을 결코 잊지 않을 것이다.

1. G: 토니야, 주말 잘 보냈니?
2. B: 좋았어. 부모님과 함께 국제 음식 축제에 다녀왔어.
3. G: 무슨 음식 먹어 봤니?
4. B: 중국 전통 후식인 탕위안을 먹었어.
5. G: 어땠어?
6. B: 맛있었어. 그건 달콤하고 동그란 떡으로 만들었어. 중국 사람들은 보통 결혼식에서 손님들에게 이것을 대접해.

1. 모퉁이에 막 오픈한 그 식당은 어땠나요?
2. 그 식당은 매우 붐벼서 나는 안에 들어가기 위해 한 시간 동안 기다려야 했어요.
3. 그 치즈 케이크는 매우 맛있어서 나는 전부 먹어 치웠어요.
4. 그 식당은 매우 시끄러워서 나는 친구와 이야기할 수 없었어요.

※ 다음 우리말을 영어로 쓰시오.

Writing Workshop - Step 2

1. 순천으로의 여행
　➡ _____

2. 나의 가족은 작년 여름에 순천으로 여행을 갔다.
　➡ _____

3. 우리는 순천 국가 정원을 방문했다.
　➡ _____

4. 그곳은 너무 넓어서 우리는 정원 전체를 다 볼 수 없었다.
　➡ _____

5. 세 시간 동안 걸은 후, 우리는 정말 배가 고팠다.
　➡ _____

6. 저녁 식사로 우리는 부모님들이 좋아하시는 국밥을 먹었다.
　➡ _____

7. 순천은 국밥으로 유명하고, 우리는 그것을 즐겼다.
　➡ _____

8. 이번 여행은 너무 좋아서 나는 오랫동안 그것을 결코 잊지 않을 것이다.
　➡ _____

Wrap Up 1-2

1. G: 토니야, 주말 잘 보냈니?
　➡ _____

2. B: 좋았어. 부모님과 함께 국제 음식 축제에 다녀왔어.
　➡ _____

3. G: 무슨 음식 먹어 봤니?
　➡ _____

4. B: 중국 전통 후식인 탕위안을 먹었어.
　➡ _____

5. G: 어땠어?
　➡ _____

6. B: 맛있었어. 그건 달콤하고 동그란 떡으로 만들었어. 중국 사람들은 보통 결혼식에서 손님들에게 이것을 대접해.
　➡ _____

Wrap Up 7

1. 모퉁이에 막 오픈한 그 식당은 어땠나요?
　➡ _____

2. 그 식당은 매우 붐벼서 나는 안에 들어가기 위해 한 시간 동안 기다려야 했어요.
　➡ _____

3. 그 치즈 케이크는 매우 맛있어서 나는 전부 먹어 치웠어요.
　➡ _____

4. 그 식당은 매우 시끄러워서 나는 친구와 이야기할 수 없었어요.
　➡ _____

※ 다음 영어를 우리말로 쓰시오.

01 select _____

02 intelligent _____

03 teleport _____

04 burn _____

05 translate _____

06 animated _____

07 easily _____

08 sense _____

09 freeze _____

10 impossible _____

11 amusement _____

12 predict _____

13 without _____

14 machine _____

15 possible _____

16 cross _____

17 danger _____

18 mean _____

19 off _____

20 perfect _____

21 through _____

22 strange _____

23 replace _____

24 beat _____

25 check _____

26 situation _____

27 closet _____

28 space _____

29 chance _____

30 dictionary _____

31 translator _____

32 unbelievable _____

33 lucky _____

34 cloudy _____

35 not just _____

36 don't have to _____

37 in danger _____

38 no longer _____

39 based on _____

40 free from _____

41 by the way _____

42 be able to 동사원형 _____

43 slow down _____

Step2

※ 다음 우리말을 영어로 쓰시오.

01 동영상의, 생기 있는

02 기회

03 구름의, 흐린

04 가능한

05 행운의

06 번역가

07 기계

08 건너다

09 위험

10 즐거움, 오락

11 쉽게

12 선택하다

13 (휴대 전화로) 문자를 보내다

14 감지하다

15 의미하다

16 얼리다

17 ~ 없이

18 예측하다

19 불가능한

20 순간 이동하다

21 불타다

22 번역하다

23 사전

24 할인되어

25 옷장

26 완벽한

27 대체하다

28 똑똑한

29 ~을 통해, ~ 사이로

30 상황

31 이상한

32 믿기 어려운, 놀랄만한

33 확인하다, 점검하다

34 공간

35 그런데, 그건 그렇고

36 위험에 처한, 위험에 빠진

37 더 이상 ~하지 않다

38 ~할 수 있다

39 ~에 근거하여

40 속도를 늦추다

41 조심하다

42 ~의 염려가 없는

43 (사전 · 참고 자료 · 컴퓨터 등에서 정보를) 찾아보다

※ 다음 영영풀이에 알맞은 단어를 <보기>에서 골라 쓴 후, 우리말 뜻을 쓰시오.

1 _____ : to take the place of: _____

2 _____ : to defeat someone in a game: _____

3 _____ : the best possible: _____

4 _____ : to be destroyed by fire: _____

5 _____ : able to happen or be done: _____

6 _____ : to perceive or realize something: _____

7 _____ : to change words in another language: _____

8 _____ : to go from one side to the other side of an area: _____

9 _____ : having desirable things unexpectedly happen to you: _____

10 _____ : to say that an event will happen in the future: _____

11 _____ : to choose something from a number of things: _____

12 _____ : a large piece of furniture with a door used for storing clothes:
_____

13 _____ : when the sky is covered with a lot of clouds: _____

14 _____ : the enjoyment that you get from being entertained: _____

15 _____ : to create the sounds of powerful rhythm with the voice and the hands:
_____

16 _____ : a book that contains a list of words and phrases alphabetically with their
meanings or their translations in another language: _____

보기			
dictionary	select	amusement	closet
perfect	beatbox	lucky	translate
beat	replace	sense	burn
cloudy	cross	predict	possible

※ 다음 우리말과 일치하도록 빈칸에 알맞은 말을 쓰시오.

Listen & Speak 1 A

B: _____ _____ _____ _____ a new VR game?

G: That _____ interesting.

B: 우리 새로운 VR 게임을 해 보는 게 어때?
G: 그거 재미있겠다.

Listen & Speak 1 B

1. B: Do you _____ _____ ideas _____ our group _____?

   G: No. _____ _____ you?

   B: I'm _____ we should _____ _____ _____ jobs. _____ do you _____?

   G: That _____ _____ for our project. _____ _____ _____ some information _____ _____ _____.

2. G: The Robot Expo _____ next week. _____ _____ you go _____ me?

   B: Yes, I'd love _____. That _____ _____.

   G: We'll have a _____ _____ _____ _____ engineers.

   B: That'll be _____.

1. B: 우리 조별 프로젝트에 대한 좋은 생각이 있니?
   G: 아니. 너는 어때?
   B: 나는 미래 직업에 대해 이야기하면 좋겠다고 생각하고 있어. 너는 어떻게 생각해?
   G: 우리 프로젝트에 완벽한 것 같아. 인터넷에서 정보를 찾아보자.

2. G: 로봇 박람회가 다음 주에 시작돼. 나와 함께 가는 게 어때?
   B: 응, 가고 싶어. 그거 재미있겠는데.
   G: 우리는 로봇 공학자를 만날 기회가 있을 거야.
   B: 그거 아주 좋겠다.

Listen & Speak 1 C

1. A: I'm _____ _____ _____ a _____.

   B: That sounds _____ _____.

2. A: I'm _____ to _____ a model car.

   B: That _____ _____ _____.

1. A: 난 드론을 날릴 거야.
   B: 그거 재미있겠다.

2. A: 난 모형 자동차를 조립할 거야.
   B: 그거 재미있겠다.

Listen & Speak 2 A

G: Is _____ _____ for you _____ _____ _____ your smartphone?

B: No, it's _____ _____.

G: 네가 스마트폰 없이 사는 것이 가능할까?
B: 아니, 그건 불가능해.

Listen & Speak 2 B

1. **G:** This computer _____ nice. _____ _____ is _____?

 M: It's 500 dollars. It's _____ _____ one.

 G: _____ _____ _____ _____ _____ this coupon?

 M: _____ me _____. Yes, you can. So, you'll _____ 30 dollars _____.

 G: _____. I'll _____ it.

2. **B:** We _____ lots of _____ _____ our trip.

 G: We sure _____. We have _____ _____ 500 pictures.

 B: Is _____ _____ _____ _____ an _____ photo album _____ _____ them?

 G: Yes, it's _____. I _____ _____ _____ for that.

Listen & Speak 2 C

1. **A:** _____ _____ _____ for you _____ _____ _____ your eyes _____?

 B: _____. I _____ _____ that.

2. **A:** Is it _____ _____ _____ to _____ _____ Gangwondo _____ bicycle?

 B: _____. I _____ _____ _____.

Real-Life Zone A

G: _____ _____ those words on the board.

B: _____ do _____ _____? _____ _____ _____ _____ in the _____.

G: What _____ _____ the AI _____?

B: _____ do I _____ it?

G: You _____ your smartphone camera at the words and _____ AI _____ _____. You will _____ _____ _____.

B: Is it _____ _____ _____ _____ those words?

Speaker: Sure. I can _____ any language and _____ it.

B: Wow, that _____ _____. So, AI, _____ do those words _____?

Speaker: They _____ "Dreams _____ _____!"

B: That's _____.

1. **G:** 이 컴퓨터가 좋아 보이네요. 얼마예요?
 M: 500달러예요. 가장 최신 컴퓨터예요.
 G: 이 쿠폰을 사용하는 것이 가능한가요?
 M: 확인해 볼게요. 네, 사용할 수 있어요. 그러면, 30달러 할인돼요.
 G: 좋아요. 이걸로 살게요.

2. **B:** 우리는 여행 동안 사진을 많이 찍었어.
 G: 진짜 그랬어. 500장 넘게 있어.
 B: 그 사진들로 동영상 앨범을 만드는 것이 가능하니?
 G: 응, 가능해. 나는 그것을 위한 앱이 있어.

1. **A:** 눈 감고 문자 메시지 보내는 것이 가능하니?
 B: 물론이지. 할 수 있어.

2. **A:** 자전거로 강원도를 여행하는 것이 가능하니?
 B: 물론이지. 할 수 있어.

G: 저기 칠판에 있는 글자 좀 봐.
B: 무슨 뜻이지? 사전에서 찾아보자.
G: AI 번역기를 사용하는 게 어때?
B: 어떻게 사용하는 거니?
G: 스마트폰 카메라를 글자 위에 댄 후에 AI에게 번역해 달라고 해 봐. 아마 답을 해 줄 거야.
B: AI가 저런 글자를 읽는 것이 가능해?
Speaker: 물론이에요. 저는 어떤 언어도 읽을 수 있고 번역할 수 있어요.
B: 오, 정말 놀라워. 그럼 AI, 이 글자는 뜻이 뭐니?
Speaker: "꿈은 이루어진다."라는 뜻이에요.
B: 정말 대단하구나.

※ 다음 우리말에 맞도록 대화를 영어로 쓰시오.

Listen & Speak 1 A

B: _____

G: _____

B: 우리 새로운 VR 게임을 해 보는 게 어때?
G: 그거 재미있겠다.

Listen & Speak 1 B

1. B: _____

   G: _____

   B: _____

   G: _____

2. G: _____

   B: _____

   G: _____

   B: _____

1. B: 우리 조별 프로젝트에 대한 좋은 생각이 있니?
   G: 아니. 너는 어때?
   B: 나는 미래 직업에 대해 이야기하면 좋겠다고 생각하고 있어. 너는 어떻게 생각해?
   G: 우리 프로젝트에 완벽한 것 같아. 인터넷에서 정보를 찾아보자.

2. G: 로봇 박람회가 다음 주에 시작돼. 나와 함께 가는 게 어때?
   B: 응, 가고 싶어. 그거 재미있겠는데.
   G: 우리는 로봇 공학자를 만날 기회가 있을 거야.
   B: 그거 아주 좋겠다.

Listen & Speak 1 C

1. A: _____

   B: _____

2. A: _____

   B: _____

1. A: 난 드론을 날릴 거야.
   B: 그거 재미있겠다.

2. A: 난 모형 자동차를 조립할 거야.
   B: 그거 재미있겠다.

Listen & Speak 2 A

G: _____

B: _____

G: 네가 스마트폰 없이 사는 것이 가능할까?
B: 아니, 그건 불가능해.

Listen & Speak 2 B

1. G: _____

   M: _____

   G: _____

   M: _____

   G: _____

2. B: _____

   G: _____

   B: _____

   G: _____

Listen & Speak 2 C

1. A: _____

   B: _____

2. A: _____

   B: _____

Real-Life Zone A

G: _____

B: _____

G: _____

B: _____

G: _____

_____

B: _____

Speaker: _____

B: _____

Speaker: _____

B: _____

1. G: 이 컴퓨터가 좋아 보이네요. 얼마 예요?

   M: 500달러예요. 가장 최신 컴퓨터 예요.

   G: 이 쿠폰을 사용하는 것이 가능한 가요?

   M: 확인해 볼게요. 네, 사용할 수 있 어요. 그러면, 30달러 할인돼요.

   G: 좋아요. 이걸로 살게요.

2. B: 우리는 여행 동안 사진을 많이 찍 었어.

   G: 진짜 그랬어. 500장 넘게 있어.

   B: 그 사진들로 동영상 앨범을 만드 는 것이 가능하니?

   G: 응, 가능해. 나는 그것을 위한 앱 이 있어.

1. A: 눈 감고 문자 메시지 보내는 것이 가능하니?

   B: 물론이지. 할 수 있어.

2. A: 자전거로 강원도를 여행하는 것이 가능하니?

   B: 물론이지. 할 수 있어.

G: 저기 칠판에 있는 글자 좀 봐.

B: 무슨 뜻이지? 사전에서 찾아보자.

G: AI 번역기를 사용하는 게 어때?

B: 어떻게 사용하는 거니?

G: 스마트폰 카메라를 글자 위에 댄 후 에 AI에게 번역해 달라고 해 봐. 아 마 답을 해 줄 거야.

B: AI가 저런 글자를 읽는 것이 가능해?

Speaker: 물론이에요. 저는 어떤 언어 도 읽을 수 있고 번역할 수 있어요.

B: 오, 정말 놀라워. 그럼 AI, 이 글자는 뜻이 뭐니?

Speaker: "꿈은 이루어진다."라는 뜻이 에요.

B: 정말 대단하구나.

※ 다음 우리말과 일치하도록 빈칸에 알맞은 것을 골라 쓰시오.

1 A＿＿＿＿ ＿＿＿＿ the ＿＿＿＿ Expo
A. AI　　　　B. at　　　　C. Day

2 Jina and Suhan are ＿＿＿＿ the ＿＿＿＿ AI ＿＿＿＿.
A. World　　　　B. Expo　　　　C. at

3 They are ＿＿＿＿ the ＿＿＿＿ ＿＿＿＿.
A. home　　　　B. entering　　　　C. AI

4 Suhan: ＿＿＿＿ ＿＿＿＿ this! It's a house of the ＿＿＿＿.
A. at　　　　B. future　　　　C. look

5 Jina: Let's ＿＿＿＿ ＿＿＿＿ the bedroom first. Look, ＿＿＿＿ a smart ＿＿＿＿.
A. into　　　　B. there's　　　　C. go　　　　D. closet

6 Suhan: I'm standing in ＿＿＿＿ of this screen on the ＿＿＿＿ door and my clothes ＿＿＿＿ ＿＿＿＿.
A. keep　　　　B. front　　　　C. changing　　　　D. closet

7 Jina: The screen ＿＿＿＿ clothes that ＿＿＿＿ the ＿＿＿＿.
A. suit　　　　B. suggests　　　　C. weather

8 Suhan: That's amazing! We ＿＿＿＿ ＿＿＿＿ have to ＿＿＿＿ about ＿＿＿＿ for the weather.
A. longer　　　　B. dressing　　　　C. no　　　　D. worry

9 Jina: Right. Let's ＿＿＿＿ ＿＿＿＿ ＿＿＿＿ the living room.
A. on　　　　B. move　　　　C. to

10 Suhan: Oh, I like ＿＿＿＿ ＿＿＿＿ ＿＿＿＿.
A. speaker　　　　B. music　　　　C. this

11 AI Speaker: I'm ＿＿＿＿ ＿＿＿＿ a music ＿＿＿＿.
A. just　　　　B. speaker　　　　C. not

12 I can do ＿＿＿＿ ＿＿＿＿ you can ＿＿＿＿.
A. than　　　　B. imagine　　　　C. more

13 Jina: It's ＿＿＿＿ to ＿＿＿＿ that you can ＿＿＿＿ us. What can you do?
A. believe　　　　B. hard　　　　C. understand

14 AI Speaker: ＿＿＿＿ ＿＿＿＿ ＿＿＿＿ a movie?
A. watching　　　　B. how　　　　C. about

15 I'll ＿＿＿＿ ＿＿＿＿ for you.
A. one　　　　B. play

16 Suhan: Look, those ＿＿＿＿ windows are ＿＿＿＿ ＿＿＿＿.
A. getting　　　　B. smart　　　　C. darker

17 I ＿＿＿＿ ＿＿＿＿ I'm in a movie ＿＿＿＿.
A. like　　　　B. theater　　　　C. feel

1 인공 지능 박람회에서의 하루

2 진아와 수한이가 세계 인공 지능 박람회에 있다.

3 그들은 인공 지능 집으로 들어가고 있다.

4 수한: 이것 봐! 미래의 집이야.

5 진아: 침실 먼저 들어가 보자. 이거 봐, 스마트 옷장이 있어.

6 수한: 옷장 문에 있는 스크린 앞에 서 있으니까 내 옷이 계속해서 바뀌어.

7 진아: 스크린이 날씨에 적합한 옷을 제안하는 거야.

8 수한: 놀라워! 우린 더 이상 날씨 때문에 무슨 옷을 입을지 걱정할 필요가 없겠다.

9 진아: 맞아. 이제 거실로 가 보자.

10 수한: 오, 이 음악 스피커 마음에 들어.

11 인공 지능 스피커: 저는 그냥 음악 스피커가 아니에요.

12 저는 당신이 상상하는 것 이상의 것을 할 수 있어요.

13 진아: 네가 우리를 이해한다니 믿기 어려운 걸! 넌 뭘 할 수 있어?

14 인공 지능 스피커: 영화 보는 건 어때요?

15 하나 틀어 줄게요.

16 수한: 이것 봐, 스마트 창문이 점점 어두워지고 있어.

17 마치 내가 영화관 안에 있는 것 같아.

18 Jina: _____ _____ can you _____ ?
A. do　　　　　　B. else　　　　　C. what

19 AI Speaker: I can _____, _____ . _____ _____ , "cats and boots and cats and boots."
A. too　　　　　B. comes　　　　C. beatbox　　　D. here

20 Suhan: You're _____ . _____ _____ !
A. job　　　　　B. good　　　　　C. funny

21 Jina: _____ ! _____ a smart car station _____ !
A. outside　　　B. hurry　　　　C. there's

22 _____ go and _____ _____ that red car.
A. ride　　　　　B. let's　　　　　C. in

23 Suhan: This car is _____ _____ . Let's _____ _____ .
A. cool　　　　　B. in　　　　　C. so　　　　　D. get

24 AI Car: Welcome. Are you _____ _____ _____ ?
A. to　　　　　　B. ready　　　　C. go

25 Jina: Yes, _____ _____ we _____ now?
A. should　　　　B. what　　　　C. do

26 It's my first _____ to _____ _____ a smart car.
A. ride　　　　　B. time　　　　　C. in

27 AI Car: You don't _____ _____ do _____ .
A. need　　　　　B. anything　　　C. to

28 I will _____ and _____ you _____ the next station.
A. take　　　　　B. drive　　　　C. to

29 Suhan: Watch _____ ! I _____ a cat _____ the street.
A. out　　　　　B. crossing　　　C. see

30 AI Car: Don't _____ . I _____ just _____ it.
A. sensed　　　　B. have　　　　C. worry

31 When I _____ _____ situations, I _____ _____ or stop.
A. down　　　　B. dangerous　　C. sense　　　　D. slow

32 Jina: _____ _____ you do _____ ?
A. that　　　　　B. how　　　　　C. can

33 AI Car: I'm a very _____ _____ car.
A. robotic　　　　B. intelligent

34 I know _____ _____ _____ .
A. about　　　　B. all　　　　　C. driving

35 I can _____ danger _____ _____ knowledge and _____ .
A. on　　　　　B. predict　　　　C. experience　　　D. based

36 Suhan: _____ smart! You think and _____ _____ _____ a person.
A. like　　　　　B. how　　　　　C. act

37 You _____ really _____ a _____ .
A. like　　　　　B. human　　　　C. are

---

18 진아: 또 뭘 할 수 있어?

19 인공 지능 스피커: 비트박스도 할 수 있어요. "북치기 박치기 북치기 박치기."

20 수한: 넌 정말 재미있구나. 잘했어!

21 진아: 서둘러! 밖에 스마트 자동차 정류장이 있어.

22 가서 저 빨간 차를 타 보자.

23 수한: 이 차 정말 멋지다. 차에 타자.

24 인공 지능 자동차: 어서 오세요. 갈 준비 됐나요?

25 진아: 응, 우린 이제 뭘 해야 하지?

26 스마트 자동차에 타는 건 처음이야.

27 인공 지능 자동차: 아무 것도 하지 않아도 돼요.

28 제가 운전해서 다음 정류장까지 데려다줄 거니까요.

29 수한: 조심해! 고양이가 길을 건너고 있는 게 보여.

30 인공 지능 자동차: 걱정 말아요. 이미 감지했어요.

31 저는 어떤 위험 상황을 감지하면 속도를 늦추거나 멈춰요.

32 진아: 어떻게 그렇게 할 수 있어?

33 인공 지능 자동차: 전 아주 지능적인 로봇 차예요.

34 저는 운전에 대한 모든 걸 알고 있어요.

35 저는 제 지식과 경험을 바탕으로 위험을 예측할 수 있어요.

36 수한: 정말 똑똑하구나! 사람처럼 생각하고 행동하는구나.

37 정말 인간 같아.

※ 다음 우리말과 일치하도록 빈칸에 알맞은 말을 쓰시오.

1 A Day _____ the _____ _____

2 Jina and Suhan are _____ _____ _____ _____ _____.

3 They _____ _____ the _____ _____.

4 Suhan: Look at this! It's a house _____ _____ _____.

5 Jina: Let's _____ _____ the bedroom first. Look, there's a _____ _____.

6 Suhan: I'm standing in _____ of this screen _____ _____ _____ _____ and my clothes _____ _____.

7 Jina: The screen _____ clothes _____ _____ _____ _____.

8 Suhan: That's amazing! We _____ _____ have to worry about _____ _____ _____ _____.

9 Jina: Right. _____ _____ _____ _____ the living room.

10 Suhan: Oh, I like _____ _____ _____.

11 AI Speaker: _____ _____ _____ a music speaker.

12 I can do _____ _____ you _____ _____.

13 Jina: _____ _____ _____ _____ that you _____ _____ us. What can you do?

14 AI Speaker: _____ _____ _____ a movie?

15 I'll _____ _____ _____ you.

16 Suhan: Look, those smart windows are _____.

17 I _____ _____ I'm in a _____ _____.

1 인공 지능 박람회에서의 하루

2 진아와 수한이가 세계 인공 지능 박람회에 있다.

3 그들은 인공 지능 집으로 들어가고 있다.

4 수한: 이것 봐! 미래의 집이야.

5 진아: 침실 먼저 들어가 보자. 이거 봐, 스마트 옷장이 있어.

6 수한: 옷장 문에 있는 스크린 앞에 서 있으니까 내 옷이 계속해서 바뀌어.

7 진아: 스크린이 날씨에 적합한 옷을 제안하는 거야.

8 수한: 놀라워! 우린 더 이상 날씨 때문에 무슨 옷을 입을지 걱정할 필요가 없겠다.

9 진아: 맞아. 이제 거실로 가 보자.

10 수한: 오. 이 음악 스피커 마음에 들어.

11 인공 지능 스피커: 저는 그냥 음악 스피커가 아니에요.

12 저는 당신이 상상하는 것 이상의 것을 할 수 있어요.

13 진아: 네가 우리를 이해한다니 믿기 어려운 걸! 넌 뭘 할 수 있어?

14 인공 지능 스피커: 영화 보는 건 어때요?

15 하나 틀어 줄게요.

16 수한: 이것 봐, 스마트 창문이 점점 어두워지고 있어.

17 마치 내가 영화관 안에 있는 것 같아.

18 Jina: _____ _____ can you do?

19 AI Speaker: I _____ beatbox, _____. _____ _____, "cats and boots and cats and boots."

20 Suhan: You're _____. _____ _____!

21 Jina: _____! _____ a smart car station _____!

22 _____ _____ and _____ _____ that red car.

23 Suhan: This car is _____ _____. Let's _____ _____.

24 AI Car: Welcome. _____ you _____ _____ _____?

25 Jina: Yes, _____ _____ we _____ now?

26 It's _____ _____ _____ _____ _____ in a smart car.

27 AI Car: You _____ _____ _____ do anything.

28 I will drive and _____ _____ _____ the next station.

29 Suhan: _____ _____! I see a cat _____ the street.

30 AI Car: _____ worry. I _____ _____ _____ it.

31 When I _____ _____ _____, I slow _____ or stop.

32 Jina: _____ _____ you _____ that?

33 AI Car: I'm a very _____ _____ car.

34 I know _____ _____ _____.

35 I can predict danger _____ _____ knowledge and experience.

36 Suhan: _____ smart! You think and act _____ a person.

37 You are really _____ a _____.

18 진아: 또 뭘 할 수 있어?

19 인공 지능 스피커: 비트박스도 할 수 있어요. "북치기 박치기 북치기 박치기."

20 수한: 넌 정말 재미있구나. 잘했어!

21 진아: 서둘러! 밖에 스마트 자동차 정류장이 있어.

22 가서 저 빨간 차를 타 보자.

23 수한: 이 차 정말 멋지다. 차에 타자.

24 인공 지능 자동차: 어서 오세요. 갈 준비 됐나요?

25 진아: 응. 우린 이제 뭘 해야 하지?

26 스마트 자동차에 타는 건 처음이야.

27 인공 지능 자동차: 아무 것도 하지 않아도 돼요.

28 제가 운전해서 다음 정류장까지 데려다줄 거니까요.

29 수한: 조심해! 고양이가 길을 건너고 있는 게 보여.

30 인공 지능 자동차: 걱정 말아요. 이미 감지했어요.

31 저는 어떤 위험 상황을 감지하면 속도를 늦추거나 멈춰요.

32 진아: 어떻게 그렇게 할 수 있어?

33 인공 지능 자동차: 전 아주 지능적인 로봇 차예요.

34 저는 운전에 대한 모든 걸 알고 있어요.

35 저는 제 지식과 경험을 바탕으로 위험을 예측할 수 있어요.

36 수한: 정말 똑똑하구나! 사람처럼 생각하고 행동하는구나.

37 정말 인간 같아.

※ 다음 문장을 우리말로 쓰시오.

1 A Day at the AI Expo

➡ _____

2 Jina and Suhan are at the World AI Expo.

➡ _____

3 They are entering the AI home.

➡ _____

4 Suhan: Look at this! It's a house of the future.

➡ _____

5 Jina: Let's go into the bedroom first. Look, there's a smart closet.

➡ _____

6 Suhan: I'm standing in front of this screen on the closet door and my clothes keep changing.

➡ _____

7 Jina: The screen suggests clothes that suit the weather.

➡ _____

8 Suhan: That's amazing! We no longer have to worry about dressing for the weather.

➡ _____

9 Jina: Right. Let's move on to the living room.

➡ _____

10 Suhan: Oh, I like this music speaker.

➡ _____

11 AI Speaker: I'm not just a music speaker.

➡ _____

12 I can do more than you can imagine.

➡ _____

13 Jina: It's hard to believe that you can understand us. What can you do?

➡ _____

14 AI Speaker: How about watching a movie?

➡ _____

15 I'll play one for you.

➡ _____

16 Suhan: Look, those smart windows are getting darker.

➡ _____

17 I feel like I'm in a movie theater.

➡ _____

18 Jina: What else can you do?
➡ _____

19 AI Speaker: I can beatbox, too. Here comes, "cats and boots and cats and boots."
➡ _____

20 Suhan: You're funny. Good job!
➡ _____

21 Jina: Hurry! There's a smart car station outside!
➡ _____

22 Let's go and ride in that red car.
➡ _____

23 Suhan: This car is so cool. Let's get in.
➡ _____

24 AI Car: Welcome. Are you ready to go?
➡ _____

25 Jina: Yes, what should we do now?
➡ _____

26 It's my first time to ride in a smart car.
➡ _____

27 AI Car: You don't need to do anything.
➡ _____

28 I will drive and take you to the next station.
➡ _____

29 Suhan: Watch out! I see a cat crossing the street.
➡ _____

30 AI Car: Don't worry. I have just sensed it.
➡ _____

31 When I sense dangerous situations, I slow down or stop.
➡ _____

32 Jina: How can you do that?
➡ _____

33 AI Car: I'm a very intelligent robotic car.
➡ _____

34 I know all about driving.
➡ _____

35 I can predict danger based on knowledge and experience.
➡ _____

36 Suhan: How smart! You think and act like a person.
➡ _____

37 You are really like a human.
➡ _____

※ 다음 괄호 안의 단어들을 우리말에 맞도록 바르게 배열하시오.

1 (Day / at / A / AI / the / Expo)
➡ _____

2 (Suhan / and / Jina / at / are / World / the / Expo. / AI)
➡ _____

3 (they / entering / are / AI / the / home.)
➡ _____

4 (Suhan: / at / look / this! // a / it's / of / house / future. / the)
➡ _____

5 (Jina: / go / let's / the / into / first. / bedroom // look, / a / there's / closet. / smart)
➡ _____

6 (Suhan: / standing / I'm / front / in / this / of / screen / the / on / door / closet / and / clothes / my / changing. / keep)
➡ _____

7 (Jina: / screen / the / clothes / suggests / that / the / suit / weather.)
➡ _____

8 (Suhan: / amazing! / that's // we / longer / no / to / have / about / worry / for / dressing / weather. / the)
➡ _____

9 (Jina: / right. // move / let's / to / on / the / room. / living)
➡ _____

10 (Suhan: / oh, / like / I / music / this / speaker.)
➡ _____

11 (AI / Speaker: / not / I'm / a / just / speaker. / music)
➡ _____

12 (I / do / can / than / more / imagine. / can / you)
➡ _____

13 (Jina: / hard / it's / believe / to / you / that / understand / can / us. // what / you / can / do?)
➡ _____

14 (Speaker: / AI / about / how / a / watching / movie?)
➡ _____

15 (play / I'll / for / you. / one)
➡ _____

16 (Suhan: / look, / smart / those / are / windows / darker. / getting)
➡ _____

17 (feel / I / like / in / I'm / movie / theater. / a)
➡ _____

1 인공 지능 박람회에서의 하루

2 진아와 수한이가 세계 인공 지능 박람회에 있다.

3 그들은 인공 지능 집으로 들어가고 있다.

4 수한: 이것 봐! 미래의 집이야.

5 진아: 침실 먼저 들어가 보자. 이거 봐, 스마트 옷장이 있어.

6 수한: 옷장 문에 있는 스크린 앞에 서 있으니까 내 옷이 계속해서 바뀌어.

7 진아: 스크린이 날씨에 적합한 옷을 제안하는 거야.

8 수한: 놀라워! 우린 더 이상 날씨 때문에 무슨 옷을 입을지 걱정할 필요가 없겠다.

9 진아: 맞아. 이제 거실로 가 보자.

10 수한: 오, 이 음악 스피커 마음에 들어.

11 인공 지능 스피커: 저는 그냥 음악 스피커가 아니에요.

12 저는 당신이 상상하는 것 이상의 것을 할 수 있어요.

13 진아: 네가 우리를 이해한다니 믿기 어려운 걸! 넌 뭘 할 수 있어?

14 인공 지능 스피커: 영화 보는 건 어때요?

15 하나 틀어 줄게요.

16 수한: 이것 봐, 스마트 창문이 점점 어두워지고 있어.

17 마치 내가 영화관 안에 있는 것 같아.

18 (Jina: / else / what / do? / you / can)

➡ _____

19 (AI / Speaker: / can / I / too. / beatbox // comes, / here / and / "cats / boots / and / boots." / and / cats)

➡ _____

_____

20 (Suhan: / funny. / you're // job! / good)

➡ _____

21 (Jina: / hurry! / a / there's / car / smart / outside! / station)

➡ _____

22 (go / let's / ride / and / that / in / car. / red)

➡ _____

23 (Suhan: / car / this / cool. / is / so // get / in. / let's)

➡ _____

24 (AI / Car: / welcome. // you / are / to / ready / go?)

➡ _____

25 (Jina: / yes, / should / what / do / we / now?)

➡ _____

26 (my / it's / time / first / ride / to / in / a / car. / smart)

➡ _____

27 (AI / Car: / don't / you / need / do / to / anything.)

➡ _____

28 (will / I / drive / and / you / take / the / to / station. / next)

➡ _____

29 (Suhan: / out! / watch // see / I / cat / a / the / crossing / street.)

➡ _____

30 (Car: / AI / worry. / don't // have / I / sensed / it. / just)

➡ _____

31 (I / when / sense / situations, / dangerous / slow / I / down / stop. / or)

➡ _____

32 (Jina: / can / how / do / that? / you)

➡ _____

33 (Car: / AI / a / I'm / intelligent / very / car. / robotic)

➡ _____

34 (know / I / about / all / driving.)

➡ _____

35 (can / I / danger / predict / on / based / experience. / and / knowledge)

➡ _____

36 (Suhan: / smart! / how // think / you / and / like / act / a / person.)

➡ _____

37 (are / you / like / really / human. / a)

➡ _____

18 진아: 또 뭘 할 수 있어?

19 인공 지능 스피커: 비트박스도 할 수 있어요. "북치기 박치기 북치기 박치기."

20 수한: 넌 정말 재미있구나. 잘했어!

21 진아: 서둘러! 밖에 스마트 자동차 정류장이 있어.

22 가서 저 빨간 차를 타 보자.

23 수한: 이 차 정말 멋지다. 차에 타자.

24 인공 지능 자동차: 어서 오세요. 갈 준비 됐나요?

25 진아: 응, 우린 이제 뭘 해야 하지?

26 스마트 자동차에 타는 건 처음이야.

27 인공 지능 자동차: 아무 것도 하지 않아도 돼요.

28 제가 운전해서 다음 정류장까지 데려다줄 거니까요.

29 수한: 조심해! 고양이가 길을 건너고 있는 게 보여.

30 인공 지능 자동차: 걱정 말아요. 이미 감지했어요.

31 저는 어떤 위험 상황을 감지하면 속도를 늦추거나 멈춰요.

32 진아: 어떻게 그렇게 할 수 있어?

33 인공 지능 자동차: 전 아주 지능적인 로봇 차예요.

34 저는 운전에 대한 모든 걸 알고 있어요.

35 저는 제 지식과 경험을 바탕으로 위험을 예측할 수 있어요.

36 수한: 정말 똑똑하구나! 사람처럼 생각하고 행동하는구나.

37 정말 인간 같아.

※ 다음 우리말을 영어로 쓰시오.

1 인공 지능 박람회에서의 하루

➡ _____

2 진아와 수한이가 세계 인공 지능 박람회에 있다.

➡ _____

3 그들은 인공 지능 집으로 들어가고 있다.

➡ _____

4 수한: 이것 봐! 미래의 집이야.

➡ _____

5 진아: 침실 먼저 들어가 보자. 이거 봐, 스마트 옷장이 있어.

➡ _____

6 수한: 옷장 문에 있는 스크린 앞에 서 있으니까 내 옷이 계속해서 바뀌어.

➡ _____

7 진아: 스크린이 날씨에 적합한 옷을 제안하는 거야.

➡ _____

8 수한: 놀라워! 우린 더 이상 날씨 때문에 무슨 옷을 입을지 걱정할 필요가 없겠다.

➡ _____

9 진아: 맞아. 이제 거실로 가 보자.

➡ _____

10 수한: 오, 이 음악 스피커 마음에 들어.

➡ _____

11 인공 지능 스피커: 저는 그냥 음악 스피커가 아니에요.

➡ _____

12 저는 당신이 상상하는 것 이상의 것을 할 수 있어요.

➡ _____

13 진아: 네가 우리를 이해한다니 믿기 어려운 걸! 넌 뭘 할 수 있어?

➡ _____

14 인공 지능 스피커: 영화 보는 건 어때요?

➡ _____

15 하나 틀어 줄게요.

➡ _____

16 수한: 이것 봐, 스마트 창문이 점점 어두워지고 있어.

➡ _____

17 마치 내가 영화관 안에 있는 것 같아.

➡ _____

18 진아: 또 뭘 할 수 있어?

➡ _____

19 인공 지능 스피커: 비트박스도 할 수 있어요. "북치기 박치기 북치기 박치기."

➡ _____

20 수한: 넌 정말 재미있구나. 잘했어!

➡ _____

21 진아: 서둘러! 밖에 스마트 자동차 정류장이 있어.

➡ _____

22 가서 저 빨간 차를 타 보자.

➡ _____

23 수한: 이 차 정말 멋지다. 차에 타자.

➡ _____

24 인공 지능 자동차: 어서 오세요. 갈 준비 됐나요?

➡ _____

25 진아: 응, 우린 이제 뭘 해야 하지?

➡ _____

26 스마트 자동차에 타는 건 처음이야.

➡ _____

27 인공 지능 자동차: 아무 것도 하지 않아도 돼요.

➡ _____

28 제가 운전해서 다음 정류장까지 데려다줄 거니까요.

➡ _____

29 수한: 조심해! 고양이가 길을 건너고 있는 게 보여.

➡ _____

30 인공 지능 자동차: 걱정 말아요. 이미 감지했어요.

➡ _____

31 저는 어떤 위험 상황을 감지하면 속도를 늦추거나 멈춰요.

➡ _____

32 진아: 어떻게 그렇게 할 수 있어?

➡ _____

33 인공 지능 자동차: 전 아주 지능적인 로봇 차예요.

➡ _____

34 저는 운전에 대한 모든 걸 알고 있어요.

➡ _____

35 저는 제 지식과 경험을 바탕으로 위험을 예측할 수 있어요.

➡ _____

36 수한: 정말 똑똑하구나! 사람처럼 생각하고 행동하는구나.

➡ _____

37 정말 인간 같아.

➡ _____

※ 다음 우리말과 일치하도록 빈칸에 알맞은 말을 쓰시오.

Before You Read

1. _____ _____

2. AI _____ Human!

3. An AI program _____ _____ a human _____ a *baduk* _____.

4. The AI _____ _____ _____ _____ Lee Sedol, who is _____ _____ _____ _____ *baduk* _____.

5. *Baduk* is a board game, and the rules are _____ _____ _____.

6. Many people _____ it would be impossible _____ _____ _____ _____ _____ a human player.

7. However, the AI _____ _____ _____ _____ Lee's play, and it _____ _____ the game.

8. People _____ _____ that an AI can _____ _____ _____ a human.

1. 데일리 뉴스
2. AI가 인간을 이기다!
3. 바둑 대국에서 AI 프로그램이 인간을 이겼다.
4. AI가 이세돌과 대국을 벌였는데, 그는 가장 위대한 바둑기사들 중의 한 명이다.
5. 바둑은 보드 게임이고, 그 규칙은 이해하기 어렵다.
6. 많은 사람들은 AI가 인간 기사를 이기는 것은 불가능할 것이라고 믿었다.
7. 그러나, AI는 이세돌의 경기를 예측할 수 있었고, 그리고 마침내 경기에서 이겼다.
8. 사람들은 AI가 인간보다 더 똑똑할 수 있다는 것에 충격을 받았다.

Focus on Expressions

1. In 2099, people _____ _____ a flying car _____ _____ _____ the moon.

2. Kids _____ _____ _____ to the moon _____ the _____ _____ _____ is there.

3. _____ _____, horse-riding is _____ _____ _____.

4. They _____ _____ to _____ _____ the horses.

1. 2099년에 사람들은 달에 가기 위해 날아다니는 차를 탑니다.
2. 아이들은 가장 멋진 놀이공원이 그곳에 있기 때문에 달에 가는 것을 좋아합니다.
3. 다른 무엇보다도, 말타기는 그들이 가장 좋아하는 활동입니다.
4. 그들은 말에서 내리기를 원하지 않습니다.

Wrap Up 1-2

1. G: Minseok, there is a _____ _____ machine _____ _____. _____ _____ we _____ it?

2. B: That _____ interesting. We'll _____ _____ _____ easily and fast _____ _____ it.

3. G: I hope so. _____ _____ _____, do you think maybe _____ will be possible _____ _____ _____ _____ _____ humans someday?

4. B: I'm not sure. But we _____ _____ _____ _____ _____ danger _____ _____ robots.

5. G: _____ do you _____?

6. B: Robots can help people _____ _____. Robots can do the dangerous work _____ humans _____ _____ _____.

7. G: You're _____. We should _____ _____ _____ _____ _____ the bright side.

1. G: 민석아, 저쪽에 스마트 음식 주문 자판기가 있어. 가서 해 보지 않을래?
2. B: 재미있겠다. 저걸 사용하면 우린 쉽고 빠르게 주문할 수 있을 거야.
3. G: 그러길 바라. 그건 그렇고, 너는 로봇이 언젠가 인간을 대체할 수 있을 거라고 생각하니?
4. B: 잘 모르겠어. 하지만 우리는 로봇 덕분에 위험이 없어질 거야.
5. G: 무슨 뜻이야?
6. B: 로봇은 위험에 처한 사람들을 도울 수 있어. 로봇이 위험한 일을 할 수 있어서 사람들이 그 일을 하지 않아도 되지.
7. G: 네 말이 맞아. 우리는 항상 좋은 면을 보도록 해야 해.

※ 다음 우리말을 영어로 쓰시오.

Before You Read

1. 데일리 뉴스
   ➡ _____

2. AI가 인간을 이기다!
   ➡ _____

3. 바둑 대국에서 AI 프로그램이 인간을 이겼다.
   ➡ _____

4. AI가 이세돌과 대국을 벌였는데, 그는 가장 위대한 바둑기사들 중의 한 명이다.
   ➡ _____

5. 바둑은 보드 게임이고, 그 규칙은 이해하기 어렵다.
   ➡ _____

6. 많은 사람들은 AI가 인간 기사를 이기는 것은 불가능할 것이라고 믿었다.
   ➡ _____

7. 그러나, AI는 이세돌의 경기를 예측할 수 있었고, 그리고 마침내 경기에서 이겼다.
   ➡ _____

8. 사람들은 AI가 인간보다 더 똑똑할 수 있다는 것에 충격을 받았다.
   ➡ _____

Focus on Expressions

1. 2099년에 사람들은 달에 가기 위해 날아다니는 차를 탑니다.
   ➡ _____

2. 아이들은 가장 멋진 놀이공원이 그곳에 있기 때문에 달에 가는 것을 좋아합니다.
   ➡ _____

3. 다른 무엇보다도, 말타기는 그들이 가장 좋아하는 활동입니다.
   ➡ _____

4. 그들은 말에서 내리기를 원하지 않습니다.
   ➡ _____

Wrap Up 1-2

1. G: 민석아, 저쪽에 스마트 음식 주문 자판기가 있어. 가서 해 보지 않을래?
   ➡ _____

2. B: 재미있겠다. 저걸 사용하면 우린 쉽고 빠르게 주문할 수 있을 거야.
   ➡ _____

3. G: 그러길 바라. 그건 그렇고, 너는 로봇이 언젠가 인간을 대체할 수 있을 거라고 생각하니?
   ➡ _____

4. B: 잘 모르겠어. 하지만 우리는 로봇 덕분에 위험이 없어질 거야.
   ➡ _____

5. G: 무슨 뜻이야?
   ➡ _____

6. B: 로봇은 위험에 처한 사람들을 도울 수 있어. 로봇이 위험한 일을 할 수 있어서 사람들이 그 일을 하지 않아도 되지.
   ➡ _____

7. G: 네 말이 맞아. 우리는 항상 좋은 면을 보도록 해야 해.
   ➡ _____

MEMO

MEMO

영어 기출 문제집

적중100

2학기

정답 및 해설

시사 | 송미정

중 2

적중100

영어 기출 문제집

영어 기출 문제집

적중100

2학기

정답 및 해설

시사 | 송미정

중 2

Lesson 5

We Love Baseball

시험대비 실력평가   p.08

01 ⑤
02 I was about to call you when you called me.
03 ①
04 support, (1) 응원하다 (2) 지원하다 (3) 지원, 후원
05 ④
06 ③
07 ④

01 ⑤를 제외한 나머지는 동사와 동사의 행위를 하는 사람이다. 반면에 'cook'은 '요리하다'이나 'cooker'는 '요리 기구'라는 뜻이며, 요리사는 'cook'이다.

02 be about to: 막 ~하려는 참이다

03 order: 순서 / 그 문제들을 다른 순서로 살펴보자. ② class: 학급, 반 ③ lesson: 수업, 강의 ⑤ nature: 자연

05 in a hurry: 서둘러 / 이 일이 급하지 않기 때문에 서둘러 하지 않아도 된다. in the past: 과거에 / 과거에 의사들은 그 이유를 몰랐습니다.

06 <보기>의 miss는 '놓치다'의 의미로 사용했다. ③은 '그리워하다'의 의미로 사용되었고 나머지는 '놓치다'의 의미로 사용되었다. ① 나는 영화의 시작 부분을 놓치는 걸 싫어한다. ② 내년에는 이 신나는 축제를 놓치지 마세요. ③ 저는 여러분이 학창시절(학교 생활)을 그리워할 것이라고 확신합니다. ④ 과학을 배우고 경험할 수 있는 이번 기회를 놓치지 마세요! ⑤ 그 경기를 놓치다니 애석합니다.

07 thunder: 천둥 / 폭풍우 동안 번개가 번쩍인 후에 들리는 하늘에서 나는 큰 소리

서술형 시험대비   p.09

01 (1) batter (2) writer 02 can't wait
03 (1) stadium (2) home team (3) thunder (4) match
04 Why 05 come 06 up
07 (1) a big fan of (2) at bat (3) is about to (4) over there (5) twice a week (6) like to

01 주어진 보기는 동작과 동작의 행위자의 관계이다. act: 연기하다 actor: 배우 (1) bat: 공을 치다 batter: 타자 (2) write: 쓰다 writer: 작가

02 be looking forward to ~: ~을 기대하다, can't wait for ~: ~을 몹시 기대하다

03 (1) stadium: 경기장 / 이 경기장은 정말 거대해, 그렇지 않니? (2) home team: 홈팀 / 홈팀은 3대 0으로 원정 팀을 이겼다. (3) thunder: 천둥 / 경보음이 천둥 소리와 같다. (4) match: 경기 / 스페인 팀이 축구 경기에서 이기고 있어.

04 why don't we ~?: ~하는 게 어때?(제안, 권유) Why not?: 좋아.

05 come back to: ~으로 돌아오다, come out: 나오다

06 hurry up: 서두르다 / 서둘러 줄 수 있나요? 시간이 별로 없어요. warm up: (스포츠나 활동 전에) 몸을 천천히 풀다, 준비 운동을 하다 / 무거운 역기를 들기 전에 준비운동을 해라.

07 (1) be a big fan of: ~의 열렬한 팬이다 (2) at bat: 타석에 서서 (3) be about to 동사원형: 막 ~하려고 하다 (4) over there: 저기 (5) twice a week: 일주일에 두 번 (6) would like to 동사원형: ~하고 싶다

교과서 Conversation

핵심 Check   p.10~11

1 Which, or fish / meat
2 Which do you like better, dogs or cats
3 (B) → (D) → (A) → (C)
4 I can't wait for the trip. / I can't wait to take the trip.
5 can't , to

교과서 대화문 익히기

Check(√) True or False   p.12

1 F 2 T 3 F 4 T

교과서 확인학습   p.14~15

Listen and Speak 1 A
Which sport, or / more, twice, week

Listen and Speak 1 B
1 doing / I'm, at / Which country, or / to visit, like to
2 I'm thinking, getting, have / What, Which, better, or / Why don't, play with, can decide

Listen and Speak 2 A
Did / can't wait to watch

2   정답 및 해설

시험대비 기본평가   p.16

| 01 ③ | 02 ② | 03 ②, ④ | 04 ④ |

01 I can't wait.: 너무 기다려져.(희망, 기대 표현하기)

02 빈칸 다음에 일주일에 두 번 축구를 한다는 말로 보아 농구보다 축구를 더 좋아하는 것을 유추할 수 있다.

03 피터팬 아니면 마지막 잎새라는 말과 피터팬을 좋아한다는 말로 보아, 둘 중에 어느 것을 좋아하는지를 묻는다는 것을 유추할 수 있다. Which do you prefer?: 어느 것을 더 선호하니? Which story book do you like?: 너는 어떤 이야기책을 좋아하니?

04 '더 좋아하는 것에 대해 말할 때는 'I like A.', 'I like A better[more] (than B).'로 말할 수 있다.

시험대비 실력평가   p.17~18

01 ②	02 ④	03 ③	04 ④
05 ④	06 ④	07 I can't wait to see it.	
08 ②	09 ①	10 I'm going to go surfing.	

01 주어진 문장은 개와 고양이가 있다는 의미인데, 이것은 'Do you have a pet?(넌 애완동물을 기르니?)'의 대답이 될 수 있다. 그러므로 ②의 위치가 적절하다.

02 ⓓ의 문장은 '너의 애완동물과 놀 것이 매우 기다려져.'라는 기대의 말인데, 남자아이가 자신의 집에 와서 애완동물과 놀아 보는 것을 제안하기 전에 여자아이가 미리 말한 것이므로 어색하다.

03 ③ 여자아이가 개와 고양이 중 어떤 동물을 더 좋아하는지는 대화에서 언급되어 있지 않다. ① 남자아이는 애완동물을 기르는가? ② 왜 남자아이는 여자아이에게 자신의 집에 오라고 제안을 하는가? ③ 어떤 동물을 여자 아이가 더 좋아하는가? 개 아니면 고양이? ④ 얼마나 많은 개를 남자아이는 기르고 있는가? ⑤ 어떤 종류의 애완동물을 남자아이는 가지고 있는가?

04 무엇을 하고 있는지 묻는 질문에 (C) 지도를 보고 있다고 대답한다. (A) 두 나라에 표시한 것을 얘기하면서, 어느 나라를 먼저 방문하고 싶은지 묻자, (B) 미국을 방문하고 싶다고 대답하고 미국에서 농구 경기를 보고 싶다는 말을 한다.

05 선호에 대해 묻고 있는 질문에, 어느 것을 더 좋아한다는 답이 아닌 'Of course I do.(물론 나도 그래.)'는 어울리지 않는다.

06 '주어진 문장은 '오늘 오후에 우리 집에 올래?'라고 제안하는 말이다. 이에 대해 상대방이 거절이나 수락하는 것이 어울리므로, 'Of course.(당연하지.)'의 수락의 답과 연결될 수 있는 ④의 위치가 적절하다.

07 I can't wait: 너무 기다려져 'I can't wait.' 뒤에는 'for+ 명사'나 'to+동사원형'을 덧붙여 어떤 것을 기대하는지 쓸 수 있다.

08 지호에게 왜 그렇게 서두르는지 질문하자 (B) 천둥 대 코브라 경기가 6시에 시작한다며 6시 전에 집에 있어야 한다고 대답한다. (C) 코브라와 천둥 팀 중 어느 팀을 응원하는지 질문하자 (A) 코브라라고 대답한다. (D) 상대방도 코브라 팀을 응원한다고 말하며, 자신도 그 경기를 놓치고 싶지 않다고 말한다.

09 ① 다음 코브라 홈 경기가 몇 시에 시작하는가? ② 경기를 보면서 그들은 무엇을 먹을 수 있는가? ③ 다음 코브라 홈 경기가 언제 있는가? ④ 그들은 어느 팀을 더 좋아하는가, 코브라 아니면 천둥? ⑤ 지금은 몇 시인가?

10 be going to 동사원형: ~할 것이다. 빈칸 다음에 서핑을 하러 가는 것이 기다려진다는 말을 했으므로 방학에 서핑을 하러 갈 것이다.

서술형 시험대비   p.19

01 (A) that (B) about   02 forget

03 He can't wait to go rock climbing this weekend.

04 (C) → (A) → (B)   05 (A) → (C) → (B)

06 (A) Have (B) have

07 to see the game on Saturday

01 (A) 다음에 주어와 동사가 나와 있으므로 접속사인 that이 어울린다. (B) be excited about: ~에 신나다, ~에 들뜨다

02 대화의 흐름상 이번 주말에 암벽 등반하러 가기로 한 것을 잊지 않겠다고 말하는 것이 어울린다.

03 be looking forward to (동)명사: ~을 기대하다 can't wait to 동사원형: ~을 기대하다

04 지수에 대해서 들었는지 물어보는 질문에 (C) 그녀에 대한 뭐를 얘기하는 것인지 질문하며 그녀가 캐나다에 살고 있다고 말한다. (A) 그녀가 한국에 돌아왔으며, 그녀가 상대방을 보고싶어 한다는 것을 전해 준다. (B) 이에, 그녀를 빨리 보고 싶다고 기대를 표현하는 말을 한다.

05 테니스와 야구 중 어떤 운동을 하는 것을 좋아하는지 질문하자 (A) 테니스 치는 것을 좋아한다고 대답한다. (C) 오늘 오후에 같이 테니스를 칠 것을 제안하자. (B) 수락의 대답을 한다.

06 Have you heard about ~?: ~에 대해 들어본 적 있니? (현재완료의 경험적 용법) have: 가지다

07 'I can't wait.' 뒤에는 'to+동사원형'을 덧붙여 어떤 것을 기대하는지 쓸 수 있다.

Grammar 교과서

핵심 Check
p.20~21

1 (1) don't　(2) he　(3) doesn't　(4) didn't

2 (1) to　(2) in

시험대비 기본평가
p.22

01 ④　　　　02 ③

03 (1) was cleaned　(2) was written
　 (3) doesn't she　(4) can he

04 (1) built → was built　(2) Dorothy → she

01 능동태를 수동태로 만들 때는 수동태 문장의 주어 자리에는 능동태 문장의 목적어가 오고, 동사를 'be+pp'로 바꾸고 by 다음에는 능동태 문장의 주어를 목적격으로 쓴다.

02 앞 문장에 일반동사가 사용되고 현재시제이므로 do를 사용하며, 앞 문장이 긍정이므로 부정으로 쓰고, 인칭대명사 주어 they를 써야 하며, 축약형으로 쓴다.

03 (1) 수동태는 'be+pp'의 형태이다. (2) 책 이름은 단수로 취급한다. (3), (4) 부가의문문은 앞의 문장이 긍정이면 부정으로 하고 부정이면 긍정으로 한다. be동사나 조동사가 있으면 그 be동사나 조동사를 이용하고 일반동사일 경우는 do/does/did를 이용한다. 반드시 축약형을 사용해야 하고 주어는 인칭대명사로 바꿔 주어야 한다는 것에 주의해야 한다.

04 (1) 다리가 건설되는 것이므로 수동태가 적절하다. (2) 부가의문문에서 주어는 인칭대명사로 바꿔 주어야 한다는 것에 주의해야 한다.

시험대비 실력평가
p.23~25

01 ⑤　　　　02 ②
03 (1) to　(2) for　(3) of　(4) doesn't　(5) isn't　04 ④
05 ③　　　06 ①　　　07 ④　　　08 ⑤

09 ③　　　　10 ②　　　　11 ①　　　　12 ②

13 (1) Was this letter delivered by David?
　 (2) My uncle's house was destroyed by the flood.
　 (3) The table is made of wood.
　 (4) The teenagers will travel to Europe, won't they?
　 (5) Let's go to play tennis, shall we?

14 (1) doesn't she　(2) didn't you　(3) can she
　 (4) was he　(5) will[won't] you　(6) shall　we

15 (1) chosen to → chosen for
　 (2) is reduced → reduces
　 (3) be appeared → appear
　 (4) didn't Mina → didn't she
　 (5) will you → won't you
　 (6) does she → is she

16 ②　　　　　　17 will be held

01 The dirt가 숨겨지는 것이므로 수동태가 적절하다.

02 부가의문문은 앞의 문장이 긍정이면 부정으로 하고 부정이면 긍정으로 한다. be동사나 조동사가 있으면 그 be동사나 조동사를 이용하고 일반동사일 경우는 do/does/did를 이용한다. 반드시 축약형을 사용해야 하고 주어는 인칭대명사로 바꿔 주어야 한다는 것에 주의해야 한다.

03 직접목적어를 주어로 한 수동태에서 간접목적어 앞에 (1) give는 전치사 to를, (2) make는 전치사 for를, (3) ask는 전치사 of를 쓴다. (4), (5) 부가의문문은 앞의 문장이 긍정이면 부정으로, be동사나 조동사가 있으면 그 be동사나 조동사를 이용하고 일반동사일 경우는 do/does/did를 이용한다.

04 ④ A nice pen was given to me by Emily. ③ 능동태의 주어가 명확하지 않을 경우 생략할 수 있다.

05 ① isn't she ② isn't she ④ wasn't she ⑤ didn't she

06 4형식의 직접목적어를 주어로 하는 수동태에서 make는 간접목적어 앞에 for를 쓰는 동사이다. 또한 make, buy, read, write 등은 직접목적어를 주어로 하는 수동태만 가능하다

07 have가 일반동사 '먹다'의 뜻으로 쓰였으므로 do로 받는다. 앞이 과거이고 긍정이므로 didn't가 적절하다.

08 능동태의 목적어로 쓰인 the numbers를 주어로 하고 동사를 'be+pp' 형태인 'were determined'로 한 후 일반주어인 they를 'by them'으로 쓰거나 생략한다. by the players' batting order는 부사구로 쓰인 것이므로 그대로 둔다.

09 일반동사 긍정이므로 do를 이용하여 부정으로 하고 대명사 주어 she를 쓴다.

10 ② 수동태는 'be+과거분사'이다.

11 ①번은 be동사가 쓰였으므로 wasn't he를 쓰지만, 나머지는 일반동사의 과거형이므로 didn't he를 써야 한다.

12 be filled with: ~로 가득 차다, be pleased with: ~로 기뻐하다

13 (1), (2) 편지가 배달되고 집이 무너지는 것이므로 수동대가 적절하다. (3) be made of: ~로 만들어지다(물리적 변화) (4) 조

동사 will이 있으므로 won't를 쓰고 주어로 대명사 they를 쓴다. (5) Let's의 부가의문문은 shall we이다.

14 부가의문문은 앞의 문장이 긍정이면 부정으로 하고 부정이면 긍정으로 한다. be동사나 조동사가 있으면 그 be동사나 조동사를 이용하고 일반동사일 경우는 do/does/did 를 이용한다. 축약형을 사용해야 하고 주어는 인칭대명사로 바꿔 주어야 준다. 또한 명령문의 부가의문문은 will you? 나 won't you?를 쓰고 권유문(Let's ~)의 경우에는 shall we?를 쓴다.

15 (1) choose는 직접목적어를 주어로 한 수동태에서 간접목적어 앞에 for를 쓴다. (2) my stress가 목적어이므로 능동태가 적절하다. (3) appear는 자동사이므로 수동태로 쓰이지 않는다. (4), (5), (6) 부가의문문은 앞의 문장이 긍정이면 부정으로 하고 부정이면 긍정으로 한다. be동사나 조동사가 있으면 그 be동사나 조동사를 이용하고 일반동사일 경우는 do/does/did를 이용 한다. 축약형을 사용해야 하고 주어는 인칭대명사로 바꿔 주어야 준다.

16 그가 준비하는 것이므로 능동태 'was preparing'이 적절하다.

17 시제가 미래(next week)이므로 'will be+pp' 형태가 적절하다.

서술형 시험대비
p.26~27

01 (1) The big house is cleaned by Tino on Sundays.
(2) They will hold Sarang Middle School Sports Day on the school playing field on Wednesday, June 15.
(3) Delicious spaghetti was made for Judy by Jonathan.
(4) Are you satisfied with your job as a tour guide?
(5) By whom was Water Lilies painted in 1906?
(6) He will be made to take part in the science camp by Cathy.
(7) The animals are being looked after by them.

02 didn't he

03 (1) aren't they (2) can he (3) did he (4) is she (5) doesn't it (6) will[won't] you (7) shall we

04 (1) was repaired (2) was bought for (3) are made (4) was made to

05 doesn't she 06 was painted

07 (1) The pens were bought by the boy. 또는 The boy bought the pens.
(2) Soy sauce is made from soy beans and salt.
(3) Jack wrote Cloe a letter. 또는 A letter was written to Cloe by Jack.
(4) Vivian was heard to open the window by her son.

(5) Samgyupsal will be cooked for Emma by her husband next weekend.
(6) By whom was this table made?

08 (1) My bike was stolen last Friday.
(2) These cookies were made by my mom.
(3) His house is filled with books.
(4) Jenny wasn't at the party last night, was she?
(5) Let's talk about our favorite sport, shall we?

01 (1) 수동태는 능동태의 목적어를 주어로 하고 동사는 'be+pp'로 바꾸고 능동태의 주어를 'by+목적격'으로 바꾸어 쓴다. (2) 미래 시제의 수동태는 'will be+과거분사'이다. (3) make는 직접목적어를 주어로 하는 수동태만 가능하며 수동태에서 간접목적어 앞에 for를 쓴다. (4) be satisfied with: ~에 만족하다 (5) 의문대명사 who가 whom으로 바뀌는 것에 주의한다. 전치사 by를 문장 뒤로 보내 Who[Whom] was Water Lilies painted in 1906 by?로 바꿔 쓸 수도 있다. (6) 목적격보어가 원형부정사인 경우, 수동태 문장에서는 to부정사로 바뀐다. (7) 구동사의 수동태는 구동사를 하나의 동사처럼 취급한다. after나 by를 빠뜨리지 않도록 주의한다.

02 과거시제이며 일반동사 긍정이므로 didn't를 쓰고 인칭대명사 he가 적절하다.

03 부가의문문은 앞의 문장이 긍정이면 부정으로 하고 부정이면 긍정으로 한다. be동사나 조동사가 있으면 그 be동사나 조동사를 이용하고 일반동사일 경우는 do/does/did 를 이용한다. 반드시 축약형을 사용해야 하고 주어는 인칭대명사로 바꿔 주어야 준다. 또한 명령문의 부가의문문은 will you?나 won't you?를 쓰고 권유문(Let's ~)의 경우에는 shall we?를 쓴다.

04 (1), (2), (3) 컴퓨터나 스마트폰이 만들어지고 책이 구매되어지는 것이므로 수동태가 적절하다. buy는 간접목적어 앞에 전치사 for를 쓴다. (4) 목적격보어가 원형부정사인 경우, 수동태 문장에서는 to부정사로 바뀐다.

05 앞 문장이 긍정이고 현재이며 일반동사가 사용되었으므로 doesn't she가 적절하다.

06 샤갈의 '나와 마을'이란 작품이 샤갈에 의해 그려진 것이므로 수동태가 적절하다.

07 (1) The pens를 주어로 하면 수동태가, The boy를 주어로 하면 능동태가 적절하다. (2) be made of: ~로 만들어지다(물리적 변화), be made from: ~로 만들어지다(화학적 변화) (3) write는 직접목적어를 주어로 하는 수동태만 가능하다. (4) 목적격보어가 원형부정사인 경우, 수동태 문장에서는 to부정사로 바뀐다. (5) cook은 직접목적어를 주어로 한 수동태에서는 간접목적어 앞에 for를 쓰며 next weekend가 있으므로 미래시제인 'will be+과거분사'로 써야 한다. (6) 수동태에서 능동태의 주체가 'by+목적격'이 되므로 'By whom'으로 시작되는 의문문이 적절하다.

08 (1), (2) 수동태는 '주어+be동사+동사의 과거분사+by+행위자'의 형식이다. 행위자가 중요치 않거나 확실하지 않은 경우 'by+행위자'는 생략한다. (3) be filled with: ~로 가득 차다 (4) wasn't가 있고 주어가 Jenny이므로 was she?를 쓴다. (5) 권유문(Let's ~)의 부가의문문은 shall we?이다.

Reading 교과서

확인문제 p.28

1 T 2 F 3 T 4 F 5 T 6 F

확인문제 p.29

1 T 2 F 3 T 4 F 5 T 6 F

교과서 확인학습 A p.30~31

01 Baseball Stadium 02 have a game
03 is at 04 your first time, isn't it
05 can't wait for 06 are coming out
07 Which team 08 behind third base
09 visiting team 10 wear a dark color
11 rule
12 have bright uniforms 13 Why
14 interesting story
15 wash their uniforms 16 to hide the dirt
17 a good idea 18 warming up 19 favorite player
20 Number 21 What, mean
22 choose, they like 23 what
24 by the players' batting order 25 no, with
26 is about to 27 anxious 28 at bat
29 has hit 30 hits one more 31 misses
32 a full count 33 next pitch 35 Crack, flies
36 gone

교과서 확인학습 B p.32~33

1 A Day at the Baseball Stadium
2 Today the Thunders and the Cobras have a game.
3 Jihun's family is at the baseball stadium.
4 Jihun: Jian, this is your first time to come to the baseball stadium, isn't it?

5 Jian: Yes, I'm so excited. I can't wait for the game to start.
6 Dad: Look, the players are coming out now!
7 Jian: Which team is the Thunders?
8 Jihun: Over there, behind third base.
9 They are wearing dark gray uniforms because they are the visiting team.
10 Jian: Does the visiting team always wear a dark color?
11 Jihun: Yes, that's the rule.
12 Home teams have bright uniforms and visiting teams have dark uniforms.
13 Jian: Why is that?
14 Mom: There is an interesting story about that.
15 In the past, visiting teams could not wash their uniforms after every game.
16 So they started wearing dark colors to hide the dirt.
17 Jian: Hahaha! That was a good idea!
18 The players are warming up.
19 Jian: Who's your favorite player?
20 Jihun: Number 77.
21 Jian: What does the number mean?
22 Jihun: Hmm.... Players choose a number they like.
23 Dad: You know what?
24 In the past, the numbers were determined by the players' batting order.
25 Jihun: That means there were no players with number 77!
26 Now, Jihun's favorite player is about to bat.
27 Jihun looks anxious.
28 Jian: Your favorite player is at bat.
29 Jihun: Yes. He has hit 21 home runs already this year.
30 If he hits one more today, he will be the home run leader this season.
31 The batter misses several balls.
32 Now he has a full count.
33 He is waiting for the next pitch.
34 Jihun: HOME RUN! HOME RUN!
35 Crack! The ball flies fast.
36 It is going, going, going, gone!

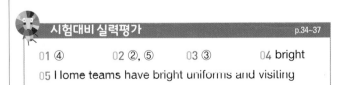

시험대비 실력평가 p.34~37

01 ④ 02 ②, ⑤ 03 ③ 04 bright
05 Home teams have bright uniforms and visiting

teams have dark uniforms.　　　　　06 ②

07 ①　　　　　　08 without

09 (A) to run　(B) to run　(C) during

10 ④　　　　　11 ⑤

12 The players are warming up.

13 과거: 선수의 타순이 7번째였다.

　현재: 선수가 좋아하는 숫자인 7을 등번호로 선택한 것이다.

14 ②　　　　　15 home run leader　　　16 ④

17 ③　　　　　18 wasn't she　　　19 ②

20 ②　　　　　21 Who do you think will win?

22 22nd　　　23 do　　　24 ②　　　25 ⑤

26 How → What

27 In the past, catchers stood about one meter behind home base and stopped the ball.

01 동의를 구하거나 사실을 확인하기 위해 '~해. 그렇지?'라고 되묻는 부가의문문 문장은 앞 문장이 긍정이면 부정으로 만든다. This는 it으로 바꾸는 것이 적절하다.

02 ⓐ와 ②, ⑤번: 형용사적 용법, ①, ④: 명사적 용법, ③: 부사적 용법

03 지안이가 야구 경기장에 온 건 이번이 처음이다.

04 dark의 반의어가 알맞다

05 '홈 팀은 밝은 유니폼을 입고 원정 팀은 어두운 유니폼을 입는 것'을 가리킨다.

06 '때'를 숨기기 위해 어두운 색을 입기 시작했다고 하는 것이 적절하다. ① (정형화된) 양식, 패턴, 무늬

07 ⓐ be known as: ~로 알려져 있다, ⓒ as the winner: 우승자로서

08 신발이 잘 맞지 않아서 '신발을 신지 않고(신발 없이)' 달리기로 결정했다고 하는 것이 적절하다.

09 (A) prepare는 목적어로 to부정사를 취하므로 to run이 적절하다. (B) decide는 목적어로 to부정사를 취하므로 to run이 적절하다. (C) 'during+기간을 나타내는 명사', 'while+주어+동사'이므로 during이 적절하다.

10 '도쿄'가 아니라 '로마'에서 신발을 신지 않고 달렸다.

11 ⓐ by: [척도·표준을 나타내어] …에 의거하여, …에 따라, by the batting order: 타순에 의해, ⓑ with number 77: 77번을 가진

12 warm up: (스포츠나 활동 전에) 몸을 천천히 풀다[준비 운동을 하다]

13 현재는 선수들이 좋아하는[원하는] 번호를 선택하지만, 과거에는 번호가 선수들의 타순에 의해 결정되었다.

14 ⓐ와 ①, ②, ④번은 완료 용법, ③ 계속 용법, ⑤번 결과 용법

15 지훈이의 가장 좋아하는 선수가 마침내 홈런을 쳤기 때문에 그는 이번 시즌 '홈런 리더'가 될 것 같다.

16 ④ 지훈이의 가장 좋아하는 선수가 오늘 몇 개의 파울 볼을 쳤는지는 대답할 수 없다. ① Jihun's favorite player. ② 21

home runs. ③ Yes. ⑤ Yes. / inning: (야구에서 9 =회 중의 한) 회

17 (A) 어렸을 때 학교 최고의 '아마추어' 골프 선수였다. (B) 1996년에 '프로' 골프 선수가 되었다. ② mature: 성숙한, immature: 미숙한, ④ expert: 전문가

18 부가의문문은 앞 문장이 긍정이면 부정으로 만든다.

19 골프를 시작한 나이는 알 수 없다. ① 프로 골프선수, ③ 1996년, ④ 1998년부터 2016년까지, ⑤ 2007년 11월

20 ⓐ와 ②번: 차례, ① 돌다, ③ (어떤 것이 다른 방향을 향하도록) 돌리다, 뒤집다, ④ (차량의) 방향 전환, ⑤ (…한 상태로) 변하다

21 Who를 맨 앞에 쓰는 것이 적절하다.

22 그는 올해 이미 21개의 홈런을 쳤다고 했으므로, 22번째 홈런을 친 것이다. twenty-second도 가능하다.

23 play를 받는 대동사 'do'를 쓰는 것이 적절하다.

24 A: newscaster(뉴스 프로 진행자) - B: 스포츠 기자의 관계이다.

25 위 글은 '스포츠 뉴스 대본'이다. ① 요약, 개요, ② (신문, 잡지의) 글, 기사, ③ 수필, ④ (책, 연극, 영화 등에 대한) 논평 [비평], 감상문

26 think의 목적어로 'What'을 쓰는 것이 적절하다.

27 앞 문장의 내용을 가리킨다. 과거에 포수들은 홈 베이스의 약 1미터 뒤에 서서 공을 잡았다.

🦉 **서술형 시험대비**　　　p.38~39

01 (1) wait　(2) dying

02 They are wearing dark gray uniforms because they are the visiting team.

03 (A) never　(B) excited

04 원정 팀은 항상 어두운 유니폼을 입는 것

05 in order / so as / in order that, might[could] / so that might[could]

06 take a shower → wash their uniforms

07 Players choose a number that[which] they like.

08 4

09 과거에는 번호가 선수들의 타순에 의해 결정되었는데, 한 팀의 야구선수는 9명이기 때문이다.

10 (A) has hit　(B) hits

11 Your favorite player is at bat.

12 Jihun's favorite player

01 I can't wait: 기다리기 힘들 정도로, 무엇인가를 너무나 하고 싶을 때 쓸 수 있는 표현, I'm dying to 부정사(for 명사): 몹시 …하고 싶어 하는, …하고 싶어 못 견디는

02 'visiting'을 보충하면 된다.

03 지안이는 전에 야구 경기장에 온 적이 '결코' 없어서 그녀는 아주 '흥분된다.'

04 바로 다음 문장의 내용을 쓰면 된다.

05 목적(~하기 위하여)을 나타내는 부사적 용법의 to부정사는 in order to, so as to, in order that ~ may[can], so that ~ may[can]로 바꿀 수 있다.

06 과거에는 원정 팀이 매 경기 후 '유니폼을 세탁할 수' 없었기 때문에 그들은 때를 숨기기 위해 어두운 색을 입기 시작했다. take a shower: 샤워를 하다

07 목적격 관계대명사 that[which]이 생략되어 있다.

08 과거에는 번호가 선수들의 타순에 의해 결정되었다고 했기 때문에 '4'번이라고 하는 것이 적절하다.

09 한 팀의 야구선수는 9명이므로, 등번호도 9번까지만 있었을 것이다.

10 (A) already가 있으므로 현재완료가 적절하다. (B) 조건의 부사절에서는 현재가 미래를 나타낸다.

11 at bat 타석에 서서

12 '지훈이의 가장 좋아하는 선수'를 가리킨다.

영역별 핵심문제
p.41~45

01 ④ 02 ④ 03 miss

04 ④ 05 ②

06 Which sport do you like? Soccer or table tennis?

07 ticket 08 ④

09 Which baseball player do you like?

10 more than Daniel Parker 11 ③

12 I'm looking forward to seeing it.

13 ④ 14 ③

15 (1) At last the thief was caught by the police last Saturday.

(2) We don't know exactly when the accident happened.

(3) Delicious galbitang is being made for him by Anna.

(4) Your love can be shown to your partner by saying "I love you."

(5) Mariel was seen to go out with her friend by Andy.

(6) The festival was put off by the city on account of the bad weather.

(7) She didn't say good-bye, did she?

(8) She can play soccer very well, can't she?

(9) Tino is wearing a blue shirt, isn't he?

(10) The hotel where we stayed was near the city hall, wasn't it?

16 (1) Tino likes eating ice cream, doesn't he?

(2) It was an interesting movie, wasn't it?

17 ②

18 (1) Where was your dog found yesterday?

(2) French is spoken in many countries in Africa. (

(3) Mr. Park goes shopping every Sunday, doesn't he?

19 (A) can't (B) is (C) visiting 20 ②

21 the Thunders 22 ③ 23 ②

24 ⑤ 25 ② 26 ③ 27 ⑤

28 gone 29 batting

30 it falls to the ground → it flies fast (and is gone)

01 ④ order: 순서 / 술을 섞을 때는 순서를 지키는 것이 중요합니다.

02 anxious: 불안한 ① excited: 신난, 흥분한 ② pleased: 기쁜 ③ bored: 지루한 ④ nervous: 불안한 ⑤ interested: 관심 있는, 흥미 있는

03 miss: 놓치다 / 타자는 여러 개의 공을 놓쳤다. 나는 이 경기를 놓치고 싶지 않아.

04 while+동사ing: ~하는 동안

05 축구와 탁구 중에 어떤 것을 좋아하는지 묻는 질문에 여자아이는 탁구를 좋아한다고 대답하고, 상대방은 어떤지 물어보는 질문이 들어가야 남자아이가 축구를 좋아한다고 대답할 수 있으므로 주어진 문장의 위치는 ②가 적절하다.

06 which 명사 do you like? A or B?: 어떤 ~을 좋아하니? A 아니면 B?

07 ticket: 티켓 / 어느 장소에 들어가기 위해 또는 어떤 것을 하기 위해 당신이 돈을 지불했다는 것을 보여 주는 공식적인 종이나 카드

08 ⓐ I looked at → I'm looking at ⓑ What country → Which country ⓒ would you like to visiting → would you like to visit ⓔ I'd like to seeing → I'd like to see

09 Which 명사 do you like?: 어떤 ~을 좋아하니?

10 더 좋아하는 것에 대해 말할 때는 'I like A.', 'I like A better[more] than B.' 또는 'I prefer A to B.'로 표현한다. 이때 비교대상이 되는 'than B'나 'to B'는 생략할 수 있다.

11 남자아이가 'When did you get it?(언제 생긴 거야?)'으로 물었으므로 때에 대한 정보를 대답해야 한다. ⓒYesterday my father bought it for me.

12 can't wait to 동사원형: ~하기를 기대하다, be looking forward to 동사명사: ~하기를 기대하다

13 ① James teaches math, doesn't he? ② She was great, wasn't she? ③ The door was opened by Tom. ⑤ The wall will be painted by the painters tomorrow.

14 첫 문장은 집이 청소하는 것이 아니라 청소되는 것이므로 수동태로 쓰인 is cleaned가, 두 번째 문장은 앞이 일반동사가 쓰였고 현재시제이며 긍정이므로 doesn't를 쓰고 주어가 Jejudo이므로 주어를 대명사 it으로 받는 것이 적절하다.

15 (1) 도둑이 경찰에 잡힌 것이므로 수동태 (2) happen은 자동사이므로 수 동태로 쓰이지 않는다. (3) 직접목적어를 주어로 한 수동태에서 make는 간접목적어 앞에 for를 쓴다. (4) 조동사가 있는 문장의 수동태는 '조동사 (7)- (10) 부가의문문은 앞의 문장이 긍정이면 부정으로 하고 부정이면 긍정 으로 한다. be동사나 조동사가 있으면 그 be동사나 조동사를 이용하고 일반 동사일 경우는 do/does/did를 이용한다. 반드시 축약형을 사용해야 하고 주어는 대명사로 바꿔 주어야 한다.

16 부가의문문은 '평서문(긍정문 또는 부정문)+반대 상황의 의문문'의 형태를 갖는다.

17 be interested in: ~에 흥미가 있다 be covered with: ~로 덮여 있다 be satisfied with: ~에 만족하다 be pleased with: ~로 기뻐하다 be filled with: ~로 가득 차다

18 (1), (2) 개가 발견되고 프랑스어가 말해지는 것이므로 수동태로 쓴다. (3) Mr. Park이 주어이므로 대명사 he로 받고 일반동사, 현재시제, 긍정이므로 doesn't를 쓴다.

19 (A) I can't wait: 기다리기 힘들 정도로, 무엇인가를 너무나 하고 싶을 때 쓸 수 있는 표현, (B) 'Which team'이 주어이므로 is가 적절하다. (C) visiting team: 원정 팀

20 ⓐ와 ②번: 형용사적 용법, ①, ④: 부사적 용법, ⑤ 명사적 용법

21 '천둥 팀'을 가리킨다.

22 과거에는 원정 팀이 매 경기 후 유니폼을 세탁할 수가 없었기 때문에 때를 숨기기 위해 어두운 색을 입기 시작했다는 말이 뒤에 나오므로, 홈팀은 '밝은' 유니폼을 입고 원정 팀은 '어두운' 유니폼을 입는다고 하는 것이 적절하다.

23 ⓒ와 ①, ④번은 동명사, 나머지는 다 현재분사

24 ⑤ 지안이는 그것이 '좋은' 생각이라고 말한다.

25 ⓐ와 ②번: 순서, ① (상품의) 주문, ③ 명령[지시]하다, ④ 정돈[정리](된 상태), ⑤ 주문하다

26 ③ 지훈이가 그 선수를 왜 좋아하는지는 대답할 수 없다., ① They are warming up. ② Number 77. ④ It means that the player likes the number 77. ⑤ They were determined by the players' batting order.

27 (A) at bat 타석에 서서, (B) wait for: ~을 기다리다

28 공이 '사라져 버렸다'고 해야 홈런을 치는 것이 된다.

29 be about to 동사원형 = be on the point of ~ing: 막 ~하려는 참이다

30 공이 땅에 떨어지는 것이 아니라, 빠르게 날아가서 사라진다.

단원별 예상문제
p.46~49

01 ③

02 (1) first base (2) competition (3) either (4) orders

03 (A) to take (B) wait **04** ③, ⑤ **05** ④

06 ③ **07** ② **08** ⓐ in ⓑ and ⓒ up

09 Which country would you like to visit first? The

U.S. or Mexico? **10** ②

11 There's a soccer match this weekend between Korea and Turkey.

12 ③ **13** ①

14 (1) will be read to his son by Simon tonight
(2) was fixed by Peter this morning

15 (1) didn't she (2) can't they (3) was it **16** isn't it

17 (A) excited (B) to start (C) third base **18** ⑤

19 ② **20** wash their uniforms, to hide

21 ②, ③, ④ **22** It is 77. **23** ①, ④ **24** ②

---

01 at bat: 타석에 서서 / 내가 아주 좋아하는 선수가 타석에서 있다. be about to 동사원형: 막 ~하려고 하다 / 영화가 막 시작하려 하고 있다. twice a week: 일주일에 두 번 / 그는 또한 일주일에 두 번 영어 수업을 듣는다.

02 (1) base: (야구의) 루, 베이스 (2) competition: 대회 (3) either: (부정문에서) ~도 (4) order: 순서

03 (A) take a boat ride: 보트를 타다 be going to 동사원형: ~할 것이다 (B) can't wait to 동사원형: ~을 기대하다

04 ① hide: 감추다, 숨기다 / 딸이 반지를 침대 밑에 숨겼다. ② fit: 맞다 / 헬멧이 잘 맞는지 확인하는 것을 잊지 마세요. ③ either: (부정문에서) ~도 / 그는 못 가고, 나도 못 간다. ④ decide: 결정하다 / 무엇을 먹을지 결정하는 것은 쉽지 않다. ⑤ support: (특정 스포츠 팀을) 응원하다 / 당신은 어느 팀을 응원하나요?

05 ④번은 visiting team(원정 팀: 경쟁하는 팀의 경기장이나 코트에서 경기를 하는 스포츠 팀)에 대한 설명이다.

06 주어진 문장에서 the game은 천둥 대 코브라의 경기를 의미한다. 지호가 그 경기를 보러 서둘러 집에 가고 있는 상황에서 알렉스가 놓치고 싶지 않다고 얘기하고 있다.

07 support: (특정 스포츠 팀을) 응원하다

08 ⓐ in a hurry: 서둘러 ⓑ between A and B: A와 B 사이에 ⓒ hurry up: 서두르다

09 would like to 동사원형: ~하고 싶다 visit: 방문하다

10 ② 남자아이는 멕시코에서 무엇을 하고 싶은가?

11 there is 단수명사: ~가 있다 between A and B: A와 B 사이에

12 ③ 윤호는 이번 주말의 축구 경기에 대해 들었다.

13 수동태 문장에서 행위자가 중요치 않거나 확실하지 않은 경우 'by+행위자'는 생략한다.

14 능동태의 목적어가 주어 자리에 있으므로 수동태로 쓴다.

15 부가의문문은 몰라서 질문하는 것이 아니고 상대방의 동의를 구하거나 사실을 확인하기 위해 사용된다.

16 동의를 구하거나 사실을 확인하기 위해 '~해, 그렇지?'라고 되묻는 부가의문문 앞 문장이 긍정이면 부정으로 만든다. This는 it으로 바꾸는 것이 적절하다.

17 (A) 감정을 나타내는 동사는 수식받는 명사가 감정을 느끼게 되

9

는 경우에 과거분사를 써야 하므로 excited가 적절하다. (B) to start가 wait의 목적어이고, for the game은 to start의 의미상의 주어이다. (C) '3루' 뒤라고 해야 하므로 third base가 적절하다. three bases: 세 개의 루

18 원정 팀의 선수들이 어두운 회색 유니폼을 입고 있는 이유는 대답할 수 없다. ① The Thunders and the Cobras do. ② At the baseball stadium. ③ No. ④ She feels so excited.

19 이 글은 '원정 팀이 어두운 유니폼을 입게 된' 이유에 관한 글이다. strong points: 강점, weak points: 약점

20 과거에는 원정 팀이 매 경기 후 '유니폼을 세탁할 수'가 없었기 때문에 그들은 때를 '숨기기 위해' 어두운 색을 입기 시작했다.

21 ⓐ와 ①, ⑤: 부사적 용법(목적), ②, ④: 명사적 용법, ③ 형용사적 용법

22 ③ 'Players choose a number they like.'라고 했기 때문에, 지훈이가 가장 좋아하는 77번 선수가 좋아하는 숫자는 '77'이다.

23 ⓐ와 ①, ④: (이야기 첫 머리에서) 재미있거나 놀라운 의견·소식 등을 말하려 할 때 씀. '저 있잖아, 내 이야기 들어봐'라는 뜻. ②, ⑤: 그것에 대해 어떻게 생각해? ③ 어떻게 (요리 를) 해드릴까요?

24 '지훈'이가 가장 좋아하는 선수가 77번 선수이다.

서술형 실전문제 p.50~51

01 will → won't   02 can → can't

03 I'm looking forward to watching the game.

04 (1) What was cooked for her family by her last night?

(2) Kimdaesung built Dabotap in the eighth century.

(3) Kevin waters the plants every morning.

(4) Some flowers were given (to) me by my friend two days ago. 또는 I was given some flowers by my friend two days ago.

05 (1) The light bulb was invented by Edison. 또는 Edison invented the light bulb.

(2) A dress was made for Sue by her mom.

(3) You aren't paying attention, are you?

(4) You forgot to bring your umbrella, didn't you?

06 (A) excited   (B) wearing

07 I can't wait for the game to start.

08 they are the visiting team

09 has come → has never come

10 (A) warming (B) Who's (C) what

11 A number they like is chosen by players. 또는 A number players like is chosen by them.

12 they determined the numbers by the players'

batting order.

13 In the past, the numbers were determined by the players' batting order.

01 암벽 등반하러 가기로 한 것을 잊지 말라는 말에 걱정하지 말라며 잊을 거라고 말하는 것은 어색하고 잊지 않을 것이라고 말하는 것이 어울린다. won't = will not: ~하지 않을 것이다

02 볼링과 야구 중 어떤 운동을 좋아하는지 묻는 질문에, 야구를 좋아한다며 이번 주말에 친구들이랑 야구를 하러 간다는 대답을 했는데 'I can wait.(나는 기다릴 수 있어.)'라는 말은 어색하다. I can't wait: 너무 기다려져

03 I can't wait to 동사원형.: ~하는 것이 너무 기다려져 = I'm looking forward to 동명사.

04 (1) 의문문의 수동태는 능동태의 의문문을 평서문으로 바꾼 후 이것을 수동태로 고치고, 다시 의문문으로 바꾸면 쉽다. (4) 4형식 문장의 수동태는 간접목적어와 직접목적어 각각을 주어로 하는 수동태가 가능하며 직접목적어를 주어로 한 수동태에서 give 동사는 간접목적어 앞에 전치사 to를 쓴다. 이 때의 to는 생략하기도 한다.

05 (1) 전구가 무엇을 발명할 수는 없으므로 수동태로 쓰거나 목적어로 쓰여야 한다. (2) make는 간접목적어를 주어로 하는 수동태로 쓰이지 않는다. 수동태에서 간접목적어 앞에 for을 쓰며 능동태(Her mom made Sue a dress.)로 고쳐도 좋다. (3) be동사가 쓰이고 있으므로 are you가 되 어야 한다. (4) 일반동사의 과거시제가 쓰이고 있으므로 did 를 써야 하고, 긍정이므로 부정으로 써야 하며 반드시 축약 형 didn't로 써야 함에 유의한다.

06 (A) 지안이가 흥분을 느끼는 것이므로 과거분사 excited가 적절하다. (B) 선수들이 유니폼을 입고 있는 것이므로 현재 분사가 적절하다.

07 I can't wait: 기다리기 힘들 정도로, 무엇인가를 너무나 하고 싶을 때 쓸 수 있는 표현.

08 '그들은 원정 팀이기' 때문에 어두운 회색 유니폼을 입고 있다. the Thunders가 팀 선수들을 가리키고 있기 때문에 복수로 취급하는 것이 적절하다.

09 지안이가 야구 경기장에 온 건 이번이 처음이라고 했기 때문에 has 'never' come으로 고쳐야 한다.

10 (A) warm up: (스포츠나 활동 전에) 몸을 천천히 풀다, 준비운 동 을 하다, 현재진행형으로 써야 하므로 warming이 적절하다. (B) 가장 좋 아하는 선수가 '누구야?'라고 해야 하므로 Who's가 적절하다. whose: 누구의, (C) You know what?: (이야기 첫 머리에서) 재미있거나 놀라운 의 견·소식 등을 말하려 할 때 씀.

11 능동태의 목적어인 a number they like를 주어로 하여 수동태로 바꾼다.

12 by the players' batting order가 행위자를 나타내는 것이 아니고 야구팀의 감독이나 팀 관계자들이 선수들의 타순에 의거하여 선수들의 번호를 결정한 것이므로 they를 주어로 하여 고쳐야 한다.

13 앞 문장의 내용을 가리킨다.

[모범답안]

01 (1) The dress was chosen for her by her mom.

  (2) Lots of money is donated to charity by me.

  (3) Lights should be turned off when you leave the room.

  (4) Chicken soup was made for him by her.

  (5) *Romeo and Juliet* was written by Shakespeare.

02 (A) amateur   (B) professional

  (C) LPGA Tours   (D) World Golf Hall of Fame

01 ①

02 (c)ompetition, (c)rack, (p)ast, (h)ide

  (1) hide   (2) cracks   (3) competition   (4) past

03 (1) over there   (2) in a hurry

  (3) come out   (4) waiting for

04 ④   05 more[better] than the red ones

06 I prefer the green ones to the red ones.

07 ⑤   08 ②   09 (A) starts (B) either

  (C) left   10 team   11 ②

12 more → better   13 ④   14 ③

15 (1) from → of

  (2) William was bought a new computer

    → A new computer was bought for William

  (3) are taken place → take place

  (4) don't → aren't

  (5) can't → will 또는 won't

16 ②

17 (1) don't you   (2) isn't she   (3) wasn't he

  (4) doesn't he   (5) won't you   (6) didn't you

  (7) will[won't] you   (8) shall we

18 ③   19 The Cobras.

20 wearing dark colors to hide the dirt   21 ④

22 the numbers were determined by the players' batting order

23 (A) players   (B) like

01 decide: 결정하다 determine: 결정하다 / 가격은 수요와 공급에 의해 결정된다.

02 (1) hide: 감추다, 숨기다 / 보이지 않는 곳에 무언가를 두다 / 그 개는 어제 뼈다귀를 땅속에 숨겼다. (2) crack: 찢어지는 듯한[날카로운] 소리 / 어떤 것이 떨어지거나 자체로 또는 다른 것과 부딪칠 때 나는 갑작스러운 큰 폭발음 / 밤새 큰 천둥 소리가 울렸다. (3) competition: 대회 / 사람들이 다른 사람들을 물리침으로써 어떤 것을 얻으려고 하는 행사나 경기 / 경쟁이 심해지고 있다. (4) in the past: 과거에 past: 과거 / 말하거나 쓰는 순간 이전의 시간 / 과거에 사람들은 말을 타고 여행을 다녔다.

03 (1) over there: 저기 (2) in a hurry: 서둘러 (3) come out: 나오다 (4) wait for: ~를 기다리다

04 go+동사ing: ~하러 가다 go surfing: 서핑하러 가다 go swimming: 수영하러 가다 play+운동 이름: ~하다 play soccer: 축구를 하다 play tennis: 테니스를 치다

05 더 좋아하는 것에 대해 말할 때는 'I like A.', 'I like A better[more] than B.' 이때 비교 대상이 되는 'than B'는 생략할 수 있다.

06 prcfcr A (to B): B보다 A를 더 좋아하다

07 다음 코브라 홈 경기를 함께 보자고 제안하고 있으므로 'Okay. (좋아.)'라고 수락하는 것이 어울린다.

08 어떤 팀을 더 응원하는지 선호를 묻는 문장이 나와야 하므로 의문사 'Which'로 질문해야 한다. support: (특정 스포츠 팀을) 응원하다

09 (A) The game이 문장의 주어로 3인칭 단수이기 때문에 동사에 s를 붙여야 한다. (B) either는 부정문에서 '~도'의 의미로 사용된다. (C) thirty minutes를 수식하므로 수동의 의미로 '남겨진'의 의미인 left가 어울린다.

10 team: 팀 / 다른 모임의 사람들에 대항해서 운동이나 경기를 함께 하는 사람들의 모임

11 ② watched → will watch 대화의 내용상 그들은 다음 코브라 홈 경기를 함께 보러 갈 것이다.

12 어떤 동물이 나에게 더 나은지 질문하고 있으므로, more(더 많은)보다 good의 비교급인 better(더 좋은)가 내용상 어울린다.

13 ① Cheesecake is baked for Scott every day. ② Mr. Lee wrote a letter. ③ My computer was fixed by my brother. ⑤ You have a pen, don't you?

14 ③ The plan was given up because of the heavy costs (by them). give up을 한 단어처럼 취급해야 한다.

15 (1) be made of: ~로 만들어지다(물리적 변화) be made from: ~로 만들어지다(화학적 변화) (2) buy는 간접목적어를 주어로 수동태를 만들 수 없으며 수동태로 바뀔 때 간접목적어 앞에 for를 쓴다. (3) take place는 자동사로 쓰이므로 수동태로 쓰이지 않는다. (4) 긍정의 현재시제 be동사가 쓰이고 있으므로 'be동사+n't'로 부가의문문을 만들어야 한다. (5) 명령문이므로 부가의문문은 'will you?'나 'won't you?'로 써야 한다.

16 ②번은 과거 동사로 쓰였고 나머지는 과거분사로 수동태를 만들고 있다.

17 부가의문문은 앞의 문장이 긍정이면 부정으로 하고 부정이면 긍

정 으로 한다. be동사나 조동사가 있으면 그 be동사나 조동사를 이용하고 일 반동사일 경우는 do/does/did를 이용한다. 반드시 축약형을 사용해야 하고 주어는 대명사로 바꿔 주어야 준다. 또한 명령문의 부가의문문은 will you?나 won't you?를 쓰고 권유문(Let's ~)의 경우에는 shall we?를 쓴다.

18 ⓐ와 ①, ④번은 현재분사, 나머지는 다 동명사

19 '코브라'가 홈팀이다.

20 '때를 숨기기 위해 어두운 색을 입기 시작한 것'을 가리킨다.

21 어떤 팀이 처음으로 어두운 유니폼을 입기 시작했는지는 대답할 수 없다.

22 'by'를 보충하면 된다. by: [척도·표준을 나타내어] …에 의 거하여, …에 따라

23 요즘은 '선수들' 자신에 의해 번호가 선택되는데, 그것은 그 들이 '좋아하는' 숫자이다.

New Places, New Experiences

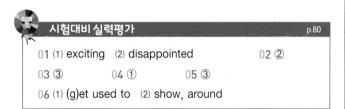
01 감정을 나타내는 동사에 '-ing'를 붙이면 '~한 감정을 일으키는'의 의미가 되고, '-ed'를 붙이면 '~한 감정을 느끼는'의 의미가 된다. (1) excited: 신이 난 exciting: 신나게 하는 / 어젯밤의 축구 경기는 정말 신났다. (2) disappointing: 실망시키는 disappointed: 실망한 / 그는 시험 결과에 실망했다.

02 ②에는 'interested(흥미를 느끼는)'가 어울리며, 나머지 보기들은 'interesting(흥미로운)'이 적절하다. ① 수학은 내게 가장 흥미로운 과목이다. ② 내가 관심 있는 과목은 컴퓨터공학이다. ③ 이 부분이 이 영화에서 가장 재미있는 부분이다. ④ 신문에 무슨 재미있는 기사라도 있나요? ⑤ 나는 지난 주말에 아주 재미있는 쇼를 봤다.

03 as soon as: ~하자마자 Once: ~하자마자 / 그는 자리에 들자마자 잠들었다.

04 expect: 기대하다, 예상하다 / 나는 그를 거기서 볼 거라고 예상하지 못했기 때문에 놀랐다.

05 ① 감독은 전체 팀원들을 불러 모았다. ② 그럼 내가 충분히 연습을 하지 않는다는 의미인가요? ③ moved: 가슴 뭉클한 / 많은 사람들이 그의 노래와 아름다운 목소리에 감동 받았다. ④ 이 같은 순간을 오랫동안 기다려 왔어. ⑤ 자동차는 우리의 현대 생활 양식에 중요한 부분이 되어 왔다.

06 (1) get used to: ~에 익숙해지다 (2) show A around B: A에게 B를 여기저기 안내하다

서술형 시험대비   p.61

01 (1) boring   (2) amazed   02 are used to

03 (1) shooting star   (2) so (s)cared that

     (3) asleep, (b)oring   (4) capital

04 with   05 (1) up   (2) At   (3) for   (4) like

06 (1) I hope this year will be full of joy.

     (2) This place is so magical that I want to live here.

01 (1) bore: 지루하게 만들다 boring: 재미없는, 지루하게 하는 / 그 영화는 너무 지루해서 보는 도중에 잠들었다. (2) amaze: 놀라게 하다 amazed: 놀란 / 우리 모두는 그가 일하는 속도에 놀랐다.

02 be used to: ~에 익숙하다(= be familiar to) / 나는 이제 네가 나의 억양에 익숙하다고 생각한다.

03 (1) shooting star: 유성 (2) so 형용사/부사 that 주어+동사: 매우 ~해서 …하다 scared: 겁먹은, 무서워하는 (3) asleep: 잠이 든 boring: 재미없는, 지루하게 하는 (4) capital: 수도

04 be made with: ~로 만들어지다 / 여러분은 팥, 우유 그리고 얼음으로 만든 음식이 무엇인지 알고 있나요? be cooked with: ~으로 요리되다 / 보통, 스파게티는 토마토소스로 요리된다.

05 (1) wake up: 잠에서 깨다 / 그녀는 시계를 맞추어 놓았지만 일어나지 못하였다. (2) at first: 처음에는 / 처음에 나는 네가 말하는 것을 이해했다고 생각했다. (3) can't wait for: 빨리 ~하면 좋겠다 / 그는 그 파티를 기대하고 있다. (4) feel like+주어+동사: ~인 것처럼 느끼다 / 내가 키가 큰 것처럼 느껴진다.

06 (1) be full of: ~로 가득하다 (2) magical: 아주 멋진, 마법의 so 형용사/부사 that 주어+동사: 매우 …해서 ~하다

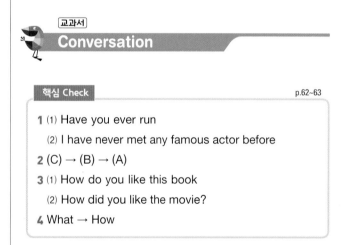

교과서
Conversation

핵심 Check   p.62~63

1 (1) Have you ever run

   (2) I have never met any famous actor before

2 (C) → (B) → (A)

3 (1) How do you like this book

   (2) How did you like the movie?

4 What → How

시험대비 기본평가　　　　　　　p.68

01 ④	02 ②	03 (C) → (B) → (A) → (D)
04 ②		

01 Have you ever+과거분사 ~?: 너는 ~해 본 적 있니? tasty: 맛있는

02 노래에 대한 만족 여부를 묻고 답하고 있다. How do you like ~?: ~는 어떠니? cheerful: 쾌활한, 유쾌한

03 (C) 인호가 신나 보여 무슨 일인지 이유를 묻는다. (B) 이유를 말하면서, 제주도에 가본 경험이 있는지 질문한다. (A) 여러 번 제주도를 가 봤다고 대답하며, 해안선을 좋아한다고 말한다. (D) 이번이 첫 제주도 여행이라며 주말이 빨리 왔으면 좋겠다고 얘기하면서 기대감을 표현한다.

04 'How do you like ~?'는 어떤 것에 대한 만족이나 불만족에 대해 물을 때 사용하며 '~는 어떠니?'라는 의미이다. 유사한 표현으로 'What do you think of[about] ~?'가 있다.

시험대비 실력평가　　　　　　　p.69~70

01 ②	02 ④	03 ③	04 ⑤
05 ⑤	06 ①	07 ④	08 ②
09 ④			

01 Have you ever+과거분사 ~?: 너는 ~해 본 적 있니? sun rise(= sunrise): 일출, 해돋이. 남자아이가 강릉에서 새해 첫날에 해돋이를 본 경험이 있다고 말하고 있으므로, 해돋이를 본 경험이 있는지 질문하는 것이 적절하다.

02 ① 여자아이는 일출을 본 적이 있는가? ② 남자아이는 일출을 본 적이 있는가? ③ 언제 남자아이는 일출을 봤는가? ④ 남자아이는 일출을 몇 번 본 경험이 있는가? ⑤ 어디서 남자아이는 일출을 보았는가?

03 피자를 만들어 본 경험이 있는지 물어보는 질문에 있다고 대답했는데 곧바로 피자를 오직 여러 번 먹어보기만 했다는 것은 어색하다.

04 'How did you like ~?(~는 어땠어?)'는 상대방의 만족여부에 대해 물어보는 표현이다. (C) 방학이 어땠는지 묻는 질문에. (D) 좋았다고 대답하면서, 가족과 독도를 다녀왔다고 얘기한다. (B) 독도가 어땠는지 묻는 질문에, (A) 굉장했다고 하며, 다시 한 번 가보고 싶다고 말한다.

05 Have you ever+과거분사 ~?: 너는 ~ 해 본 적 있니? 어떤 장소에 다녀온 적이 있는지 경험을 말할 때는 'have been to 장소'라는 표현을 사용함에 유의한다.

06 How did you like ~?: ~은 어땠어?

07 해외여행을 가 본 경험을 물어보니, (C) 지난여름에 캄보디아에 다녀왔다고 대답한다. (B) 여행이 어땠는지 물어보자, (D) 날씨는 더웠지만 여행은 즐거웠다고 대답한다. (E) 여행하면서 재미있었던 경험을 얘기해 달라는 말에, (A) 거미튀김을 먹었다고 대답한다.

08 (A) How was ~?: ~는 어땠어?(만족이나 불만족에 대해 묻기) (B) What ~: 어떤 ~ (C) How did you like ~?: ~는 어땠어?(만족이나 불만족에 대해 묻기)

09 친구가 아닌 부모님과 함께 다녀왔다.

서술형 시험대비　　　　　　　p.71

01 excited	02 Have you ever been there?
03 for	04 How do you like your new house?
05 ridden	06 How did you like it?
07 Have you ever traveled abroad	
08 ⓐ I have been to Cambodia → I went to Cambodia	

01 감정을 나타내는 동사에 '-ing'를 붙이면 '~한 감정을 일으키는' 의미가 되고, '-ed'를 붙이면 '~한 감정을 느끼는' 의미가 된다. excited: 신난

02 Have you (ever) been (to) ~?: ~에 가 본 적 있니?

03 can't wait for: 빨리 ~하면 좋겠다

04 How do you like ~?: ~는 어떠니?

05 현재완료(have/has+p.p)가 경험의 의미로 사용되면 '~한 적이

있다'라고 해석한다. ride-rode-ridden: 타다

06 How did you like ~?: ~는 어땠어?

07 Have you ever+과거분사 ~?: 너는 ~해 본 적 있니? travel: 여행하다 abroad: 해외에

08 'last summer(지난여름)'는 과거의 특정 시점을 나타내는 부사구이므로, 현재완료와 어울리지 않는다. 그러므로 과거 시제를 사용한다.

교과서
Grammar

핵심 Check
p.72~73

1 (1) so (2) that

2 (1) who[whom/that] (2) which[that]

시험대비 기본평가
p.74

01 ②, ⑤ 02 (1) which → that (2) very → so

(3) who → which[that]

(4) which I left it → which I left

03 (1) He spoke so fast that I could not understand him.

(2) The bike which[that] Eric wants to buy is very expensive.

04 ③

01 선행사가 the author로 사람이며 'I want to meet' 다음에 이어질 목적어 역할을 할 수 있는 목적격 관계대명사 who나 whom 그리고 that이 적절하다.

02 (1), (2) 'so+형용사+that+주어+동사'의 형태로 원인과 결과를 나타내야 한다. (3) 선행사 The mirror가 사물이므로 관계대명사는 which 또는 that으로 쓰는 것이 적절하다. (4) 목적격 관계대명사가 left의 목적어이므로 목적어 it을 또 쓰지 않는다.

03 (1) so를 추가하여 'so+부사+that+주어+동사'의 형태로 원인과 결과를 나타낸다. (2) 목적격 관계대명사 which나 that을 추가한다.

04 목적격 관계대명사 which 또는 that, 'so+형용사+that+주어+동사'이므로 공통으로 들어갈 단어는 that이다.

시험대비 실력평가
p.75~77

01 ⑤ 02 ⑤ 03 ⑤ 04 ①

05 The chair was so comfortable that she fell asleep.

06 (1) which (2) which (3) that (4) are

(5) clearly (6) so

07 (1) that (2) who is 08 ③ 09 ④

10 (1) ○ (2) ○ (3) X (4) ○ (5) X 11 ②

12 She is wearing the wedding dress which her mother left her.

13 He got up so early that he was sleepy all morning.

14 bags were, that, couldn't, them

15 (1) we can't, them (2) too slow to win

(3) cute enough, to

16 ④ 17 ⑤ 18 ③

19 (1) The boy band is BTS. + I like it most.

(2) This is the picture. + I took it three days ago.

(3) I know some people. + They work for Google.

01 모두 주격이나 목적격으로 사용된 관계대명사 that이 들어갈 수 있지만 ⑤번은 소유격 관계대명사 whose가 들어가야 한다.

02 주절이 과거이므로 that절의 동사도 과거로 쓴다. can't를 couldn't로 바꾸어야 한다.

03 ⑤번은 주격 관계대명사이고 나머지는 목적격 관계대명사이다.

04 ①번은 접속사이지만 나머지는 모두 관계대명사이다.

05 'so+형용사+that+주어+동사'로 '매우 …해서 ~하다'라는 의미를 나타낸다. fall asleep: 잠이 들다

06 (1), (2) 선행사가 사물이므로 which, (3) 선행사가 '사람+동물'이므로 that (4) 목적격 관계대명사가 꾸미고 있는 주어는 The boxes이므로 동사는 are를 쓴다. (5) 주절의 동사가 spoke이므로 so 다음에 부사를 쓴다. (6) 'so+형용사+that+주어+동사'로 '매우 …해서 ~하다'라는 의미를 나타낸다.

07 목적격 관계대명사와 '주격 관계대명사+be동사'는 생략할 수 있다.

08 enough는 부사일 때 형용사를 뒤에서 꾸며준다. 그러므로 easy enough로 쓰는 것이 적절하다.

09 ④는 'so+형용사+that+주어+동사'의 형태가 올바르고 주절의 주어가 that절의 목적어로 올바르게 쓰였다. ① Is he strong enough to lift it? ② The dinner yesterday was too awful to eat. ③ This watch is so expensive that I can't buy it. ⑤ I got up so late that I couldn't have breakfast this morning.

10 (1), (4)는 목적격 관계대명사로 생략할 수 있다. (2)는 주격 관계대명사이나 be동사와 함께 생략할 수 있다, (3)은 목적격 관계대명사이나 관계대명사가 그 앞에 전치사와 함께 있으므로 생략할 수 없다. (5)는 주격 관계대명사로 생략할 수 없다.

11 선행사가 사람이므로 who나 that을 이용하고 선행사 the woman이 두 번째 문장의 목적어이므로 목적격 관계대명사를 쓰고 목적어였던 her는 쓰지 말아야 한다.

15

12 목적격 관계대명사가 나올 자리이므로 '선행사+관계대명사+주어+동사'의 어순으로 쓴다.

13 'so+형용사+that+주어+동사'로 '매우 …해서 ~하다'라는 의미를 나타낸다.

14 남자가 가방을 두 개 들고 있으므로 주어는 the bags이고 'so … that ~' 구문을 이용하여 문장을 완성한다. 이때 주절의 주어가 that절의 목적어이므로 주절의 주어 the bags를 that절의 목적어 자리에 them으로 적절하게 써야 한다.

15 (1), (2) 'too+형용사/부사+to부정사'는 '원인과 결과'를 나타내는 'so+형용사/부사+that+주어+can't+동사원형'과 바꾸어 쓸 수 있다. (3) '형용사/부사+enough+to부정사'는 '원인과 결과'를 나타내는 'so+형용사/부사+that+주어+can+동사원형'과 바꾸어 쓸 수 있다.

16 주어진 문장과 ④에 쓰인 that은 선행사를 꾸며 주는 목적격 관계대명사이다. ① 지시대명사 ② 지시형용사 ③, ⑤ 접속사

17 주어진 문장과 ⑤의 that은 목적격 관계대명사로 쓰임이 같다. ①은 주격 관계대명사 ② 지시대명사 ③, ④ 접속사

18 첫 번째 문장에서는 to부정사가 있으므로 too와 enough 중에서 선택하는데, small 앞에 위치하므로 enough를 쓸 수 없다. 두 번째 문장에서는 접속사 that이 있으므로 so와 함께 쓰는 것이 적절하다.

19 (1), (2)는 모두 목적격 관계대명사가 있는 문장이므로 관계대명사 대신 선행사를 목적어로 해서 두 문장으로 쓴다. (3)은 주격 관계대명사가 있는 문장이므로 관계대명사 대신 선행사를 주어로 해서 두 문장으로 쓴다.

서술형 시험대비
p.78~79

01 (1) The story which she told me was surprising.
(2) This is the money which I really need.
(3) I have a friend who lives in Canada.
(4) This is the movie which has a sad ending.
(5) I met a person whose hobby is mountain climbing.

02 (1) This is the apartment which[that] she lives in.
(2) I like the jacket which[that] my wife bought for me.
(3) Aladdin is the movie which[that] I like best.
(4) Look at the cloud which[that] is floating in the sky.

03 (1) so, that, I can't   (2) which

04 (1) The boy has no toys which[that] he can play with. 또는 The boy has no toys with which he can play.
(2) He is the mechanic who[whom/that] I want to introduce to you.

(3) The girls who I took care of were my nieces.
(4) The pen that I'm writing with is Mike's.
(5) Everything (that) I told you was true.

05 (1) cooks so well that   (2) runs so fast that
(3) so smart that he, gets

06 (1) that you drink   (2) something that you listen to

07 (1) I was so tired that I could not work any more.
(2) The cat moved so quietly that no one noticed it.
(3) The stairs were so high and steep that I felt dizzy.

08 (1) This game console is so small that you can take it anywhere.
(2) The bags are too heavy for you to carry to the airport.

01 (1), (2), (4) 선행사가 사물이므로 관계대명사 which를 써야 한다. (3) 선행사가 사람이므로 관계대명사 who를 써야 한다. (5) 접속사와 소유격으로 연결해야 하므로 소유격 관계대명사 whose를 써야 한다.

02 목적격 관계대명사의 선행사가 사물이나 동물이면 관계대명사를 which 또는 that으로 쓰고 생략할 수 있다. 주격관계대명사는 be동사와 함께 생략할 수 있다.

03 (1) 'too+형용사/부사+to부정사'는 '원인과 결과'를 나타내는 'so+형용사/부사+that+주어+can't+동사원형'과 바꾸어 쓸 수 있다. (2) 관계대명사 that은 사물인 경우 which로 바꾸어 쓸 수 있다.

04 (1) 관계대명사 앞에 전치사가 함께 쓰인 경우 that을 사용하지 않는다. 사람은 whom, 사물은 which를 쓴다. (2) 선행사가 사람이므로 관계대명사 who[whom]나 that을 써야 한다. mechanic 정비사 (3) 선행사인 주어가 복수이므로 동사를 was가 아닌 were로 쓴다. (4) 관계대명사가 전치사의 목적인 경우 그 전치사를 빠뜨리면 안 된다. (5) what은 선행사를 포함한 관계대명사가 필요할 때 쓴다. that으로 고치거나 생략하는 것이 적절하다.

06 목적격 관계대명사에서 선행사가 something이면 주로 that을 쓰고 그 다음에 주어 동사가 나온다.

07 (1), (3) 'so+형용사+that+주어+동사'로 '매우 …해서 ~하다'라는 의미를 나타낸다. 주절이 과거이므로 that절의 시제도 과거로 쓴다. (2) that절의 주어와 주절의 주어가 다르기 때문에 noticed 다음에 목적어 it(=the cat)을 써야 한다.

08 (1) 'so … that ~' 구문은 두 개의 절로 되어 있으므로 주절의 주어가 that절의 목적어인 경우 생략하지 않고 반드시 쓴다. (2) 'too … to ~' 구문은 하나의 절로 구성된 문장이므로 주어 the bags(=them)를 carry의 목적어로 다시 쓰지 않는다.

확인문제　　　　　　　　　　　　　　p.80

1 T　2 F　3 T　4 F　5 T　6 F

확인문제　　　　　　　　　　　　　　p.81

1 T　2 F　3 T　4 F　5 T　6 F

교과서 확인학습 A　　　　　　　　　p.82~83

01 Trip
02 for the first time
03 is from
04 invited, to
05 a four-hour flight, arrived at
06 It took, by taxi
07 traditional
08 cozy inside
09 smelled wonderful
10 from, cooking for
11 Mongolian barbecue
12 is made of, with
13 was moved, serve, to
14 so, that
15 went outside
16 was full of
17 felt like
18 During, showed me around
19 had the most fun
20 At first, taller than
21 once, got used to
22 the view of the desert
23 in many ways
24 to get to know
25 again someday

교과서 확인학습 B　　　　　　　　　p.84~85

1 A Trip to Mongolia

2 This year, I had a special summer because I visited Mongolia for the first time.

3 My friend Altan is from Mongolia.

4 His grandmother invited me to Ulaanbaatar, the capital of Mongolia.

5 After a four-hour flight from Seoul, Altan and I arrived at Chinggis Khaan International Airport in Ulaanbaatar.

6 It took thirty minutes by taxi from the airport to Altan's grandmother's house.

7 Her house is a *ger*, a traditional Mongolian house.

8 It is a big tent, but it is cozy inside.

9 When we entered, something smelled wonderful.

10 It was from the *khorkhog* that she was cooking for us.

11 *Khorkhog* is a Mongolian barbecue.

12 It is made of lamb and cooked with hot stones.

13 I was moved when Altan said Mongolians serve *khorkhog* to special guests.

14 It was so delicious that I asked for more.

15 After dinner, Altan and I went outside to see the night sky.

16 The sky was full of bright stars.

17 I felt like I was in a magical place.

18 During the next three days, Altan showed me around and helped me experience Mongolian culture.

19 Every moment was fun and exciting, but I had the most fun when I rode a camel in the Gobi Desert.

20 At first, I was scared because the camel was taller than I expected.

21 But once I sat on its back, I soon got used to its movement.

22 From the camel's back, the view of the desert was truly amazing.

23 My visit to Mongolia was a special experience in many ways.

24 It gave me a great chance to get to know my friend's country and culture.

25 I want to visit Mongolia again someday!

시험대비 실력평가　　　　　　　　　p.86~89

01 ④
02 After a four-hour flight from Seoul
03 by a taxi → by taxi
04 ②
05 ⓐ a *ger*　ⓒ *khorkhog*
06 It was from the *khorkhog* that she was cooking for us.
07 filled with
08 ①, ④
09 ③
10 ⑤
11 ②
12 ③
13 flight
14 ②
15 ②
16 ⓐ so　ⓑ that
17 ②, ③, ⑤
18 ④
19 ①
20 taller
21 couldn't get → soon got
22 ③
23 ①, ④
24 forget → forget it
25 ①, ⑤
26 four thirty

01　ⓐ from: (출처·기원) … 출신의[에서 나온], ⓑ invited A to B: A를 B에 초대하다

02　'숫자+단위 명사'가 하나의 낱말로 형용사처럼 쓰일 경우에 하이픈으로 연결하고 four-hour처럼 단수로 쓰는 것이 적절하다.

03　교통이나 통신 수단을 나타낼 때: by+무관사 명사

04 ② Altan's 'grandmother' invited the writer to Ulaanbaatar.

05 ⓐ '게르', ⓒ '호르호그'를 가리킨다.

06 'from'을 보충하면 된다.

07 be full of = be filled with: ~로 가득 차 있다

08 get[come/learn] to 동사원형: ~하게 되다

09 ⓐ와 ③번: 한 번[일단] …하면, ~하자마자(접속사), ①, ④: 한 번(부사), ②, ⑤: (과거) 언젠가[한때]

10 이 글은 '몽골을 방문해서 겪은 특별한 경험'에 관한 글이다.

11 ⓐ와 ③, ⑤번: 관계대명사, ①, ②, ④번: 접속사

12 순천 국가 정원은 너무 넓어서 글쓴이의 가족은 정원 전체를 다 볼 수 없었다.

13 fly의 명사 flight를 쓰는 것이 적절하다.

14 ②번 다음 문장의 His에 주목한다. 주어진 문장의 My friend Altan을 받고 있으므로 ②번이 적절하다.

15 이 글은 글쓴이가 올해 몽골을 처음으로 방문해서 특별한 여름을 보냈다는 내용의 글이므로, 제목으로는 '내가 몽골에서 보낸 특별한 여름'이 적절하다.

16 so+형용사/부사+that: 매우 ~해서 …하다

17 ⓒ와 ②, ③, ⑤: 부사적 용법, ① 형용사적 용법, ④ 명사적 용법

18 호르호그가 뜨거운 돌로 요리되는 이유는 대답할 수 없다. ① It's a traditional Mongolian house. ② Altan's grandmother. ③ It is made of lamb. ⑤ They serve it to special guests.

19 ⓐ visit(명사)+to 장소, ⓑ 방법 앞에는 전치사 in을 쓰는 것이 적절하다.

20 처음에는 글쓴이가 예상했던 것보다 낙타의 '키가 커서' 무서웠다.

21 글쓴이는 낙타 등에 앉자 곧 움직임에 '익숙해졌다.'

22 ③ 만족한, ① 지루한, ② 실망한, ④ 자신감 있는, ⑤ 속상한

23 목적격 관계대명사 which나 that을 쓰는 것이 적절하다.

24 forget 다음에 목적어 it(=this trip)이 필요하다.

25 ⓐ와 ①, ⑤번: 완료 용법, ②, ③번: 경험 용법, ④ 계속 용법

26 half past/after four, thirty (minutes) past/after four도 가능하다.

서술형 시험대비 p.90~91

01 (A) special   (B) invited   (C) four-hour

02 It took four hours.

03 (A) Mongolia   (B) grandmother's   04 cozy

05 게르에 들어갔을 때 나던 좋은 냄새

06 (A) *khorkhog*   (B) night sky

07 to experience

08 I was scared because the camel was taller than I expected.

---

09 My visit to Mongolia   10 was moved

11 we could[might] / so that

12 (A) traditional Mongolian   (B) cozy

---

01 (A) '특별한' 여름을 보냈다고 해야 하므로 special이 적절하다. (B) 나를 '초대하셨다'고 해야 하므로 invited가 적절하다. visit: 방문하다, (C) '숫자+단위 명사'가 하나의 낱말로 형용사처럼 쓰일 경우에 하이픈으로 연결하고 단수로 써야 하므로 four-hour가 적절하다.

02 서울에서 울란바토르의 칭기즈 칸 국제공항까지 비행기로 '네 시간' 걸렸다.

03 올해 여름, 글쓴이는 '몽골'을 처음으로 방문했다. 알탕과 글쓴이는 알탕의 '할머니' 댁에 갔다.

04 cozy: 아늑한, 편리한

05 알탕과 글쓴이가 '게르에 들어갔을 때 나던 좋은 냄새'를 가리킨다.

06 알탕의 할머니는 알탕과 글쓴이를 위해 맛있는 '호르호그'를 요리해 주셨다. 그것을 먹은 후에, 알탕과 글쓴이는 밝은 별들로 가득한 '밤하늘'을 보기 위해 밖으로 나갔다.

07 help+목적어+to부정사 또는 원형부정사

08 'than'을 보충하면 된다.

09 '내가 몽골을 방문한 것'을 가리킨다.

10 감동을 받은 것이므로 수동태로 쓰는 것이 적절하다.

11 부사적 용법의 목적을 나타내는 to부정사는 'in order that 주어 can[may]' 또는 'so that 주어 can[may]'으로 바꿔 쓸 수 있다.

12 게르는 '몽골 전통' 가옥이다. 그것은 큰 텐트이지만 내부는 '아늑하다.'

영역별 핵심문제 p.93~97

01 ③

02 (1) is made   (2) show, around   (3) modern

03 ①   04 ①   05 ⑤   06 ⑤

07 guest   08 ⓑ, ⓒ, ⓓ, ⓔ   09 ②

10 ③   11 How did you like them?

12 ⑤   13 (1) warm enough   (2) so   (3) for

14 ①   15 ④

16 (1) The girls who[whom/that] I invited did not come to my birthday party.

(2) There was a TV program which[that] I wanted to watch.

(3) There are some cookies which[that] you can eat.

(4) The bag is so strong that I can carry a lot of books in it.

정답 및 해설

(5) I was so busy that I couldn't go shopping. 또는
I was too busy to go shopping.

(6) It is so easy that anyone can do it.

17 which

18 (1) I bought the radio. + It isn't working.

(2) That's the coach. + I saw him at the soccer match.

19 ⑤　　20 comes

21 It took thirty minutes by taxi from the airport to Altan's grandmother's.

22 ③

23 so it isn't cozy inside → but it is cozy inside

24 It was so delicious that I asked for more.

25 It gave me a great chance to get to know my friend's country and culture.

26 ①　　27 ④

28 (A) This is　(B) had　(C) to see　　29 ⑤

30 Welcome to Mongolia, a country full of the beauty of nature and culture.

---

01 satisfying 만족감을 주는 be satisfied with: ~에 만족하다. boring 재미없는, 지루하게 하는

02 (1) be made of: ~로 만들어지다 (2) show A around B: …에게 ~을 둘러보도록 안내하다 (3) modern: 현대의

03 from A to B: A에서 B로 / 이 그림을 오른쪽에서 왼쪽으로 살펴보아라.

04 chance: 기회 / 어떤 것을 할 기회

05 Have you ever+과거분사 ~?(너는 ~해 본 적이 있니?)는 상대방에게 경험을 묻는 표현으로 ever 다음에는 동사의 과거분사형을 써야 한다.

06 be made with: ~로 만들어지다

07 guest: 손님 / 당신을 방문하도록 초대된 사람

08 ⓐ 여자아이가 탕위안을 먹어 본 경험이 있는가? 토니가 국제 음식 축제에 가서 먹었다는 내용은 나오지만 여자아이가 탕위안을 먹었는지 안 먹었는지에 대한 언급은 없다. ⓑ 토니는 누구와 함께 국제 음식 축제에 갔는가? 토니는 부모님과 같이 국제 음식 축제로 갔다. ⓒ 탕위안은 무엇인가? 중국의 전통 후식이다. ⓓ 토니는 주말에 어디를 갔는가? 토니는 국제 음식 축제에 갔다. ⓔ 토니는 국제 음식 축제에서 무엇을 먹었는가? 토니는 국제 음식 축제에서 탕위안을 먹었다.

09 ⓑ No. → Yes. 새로 생긴 중국 음식점에 가 봤는지 질문하자 지난주 토요일에 거기서 저녁을 먹었다는 것으로 보아 간 경험이 있다고 대답해야 한다.

10 남자아이가 수진에게 여행하면서 재미있었던 경험을 이야기해 달라는 말에 생각해 본다고 대답하고 거미 튀김을 먹었다고 말해야 거미 튀김이 어땠는지 남자아이가 질문을 할 수 있으므로 ③이 적절하다.

11 How did you like ~?: ~는 어땠어?

12 수진이는 거미 튀김이 너무 커서 처음에 무서웠지만 맛은 괜찮았다고 했다.

13 (1) enough는 형용사/부사를 뒤에서 꾸며준다. (2) 'so … that ~' 구문으로 쓴다. (3) 'too … to ~'에서 의미상 주어가 필요할 때에는 'for+목적격'으로 쓴다.

14 ①번은 목적을 나타내는 'so that ~' 구문의 that이고, 주어진 문장과 나머지 ②~⑤는 모두 원인과 결과를 나타내는 'so … that ~'이다.

15 목적격 관계대명사가 전치사의 목적어인 경우 그 전치사를 반드시 써야 한다. 그러므로 'The road which he was driving on was not safe.' 또는 'The road on which he was driving was not safe.'로 쓰는 것이 올바르다.

16 (1), (2), (3) 관계대명사의 선행사가 '사람'이면 who나 that을 쓰고, 선행사가 '사물이나 동물'이면 which나 that을 쓴다. (4), (5), (6) 'so+형용사/부사+that+주어+동사'로 '매우 …해서 ~하다'라는 의미를 나타낸다. 주절과 that절의 시제를 일치하도록 쓴다.

17 첫 번째 문장의 빈칸에는 선행사 the skirt를 꾸며줄 목적격 관계대명사 which 또는 that이 필요하다. 두 번째 문장에서는 선택을 위해 사용되는 의문사 which가 나와야 한다. 그러므로 공통으로 들어갈 단어는 which가 적절하다.

18 관계대명사의 선행사가 '사람'이면 who나 that을 쓰고, 선행사가 '사물이나 동물'이면 which나 that을 쓴다.

19 ⑤ I got up too late to catch the bus. 또는 I got up so late that I missed the bus.로 쓰는 것이 적절하다.

20 be from = come from: ~ 출신이다

21 명사의 소유격 다음에 나오는 house는 생략할 수도 있다(소유격 다음의 명사가 무엇을 가리키는지 분명할 때).

22 주어진 문장의 It에 주목한다. ③번 앞 문장에서 말한 '좋은 냄새'를 받고 있으므로 ③번이 적절하다.

23 게르는 큰 텐트이지만 '내부는 아늑하다.'

24 so+형용사/부사+that: 매우 …해서 ~하다

25 gave 다음에 4형식 순서(간접목적어+직접목적어)로 쓰는 것이 적절하다.

26 이 글은 '글쓴이가 몽골을 방문한 것이 여러 면에서 특별한 경험이었다.'는 내용의 글이므로, 제목으로는 '특별한 경험, 몽골을 방문하기'가 적절하다.

27 글쓴이가 고비 사막에서 얼마나 오래 낙타를 탔는지는 대답할 수 없다. ① For three days. ② The writer experienced Mongolian culture with Altan. ③ It was when the writer rode a camel in the Gobi Desert. ⑤ The writer's visit to Mongolia.

28 (A) 기장이 방송으로 자신을 소개할 때는 This is가 적절하다. (B) 착륙할 때의 안내방송이므로 had가 적절하다. (C) hope는 to부정사를 목적어로 취하므로 to see가 적절하다.

29 위 글은 '기내 안내방송'이다. ① 생[실황] 방송, ② 탑승 안내 방송, ③ 기행문, ④ 교통 방송 안내[교통 정보]

30 Mongolia와 a country full of the beauty of nature and culture를 동격으로 처리하여 그 사이에 콤마(,)를 넣어야 한다. Welcome to ~.: ~에 오신 것을 환영합니다.

단원별 예상문제 p.98~101

01 (c)heerful 02 of 03 ⑤ 04 ④
05 Have you ever watched the sun rise over the ocean?
06 rise 07 ⑤ 08 ①
09 (A) How (B) How
10 (A) Yes, I have. (B) during
11 ⓐ interesting ⓑ scared 12 ③
13 (1) them 삭제
(2) in love → in love with / who → with whom
(3) who → which[that]
(4) which → who[whom/that] (5) it 삭제
(6) too → so (7) enough → so (8) very → so
14 ⑤ 15 so 16 ④
17 (1) This report is so difficult that you can't read it.
또는 This report was so difficult that you couldn't read it.
(2) I was too tired to finish my task.
(3) I was stupid enough to believe what you said.
(4) The rings that she was wearing were fantastic.
(5) I've found the dog which[that] you lost.
18 (A) visited (B) capital (C) took
19 though → because 20 ④
21 ⑤ 22 ③ 23 ④
24 Mongolian 25 ③ 26 ②, ⑤

01 cheerful: 쾌활한, 유쾌한 / 현저히 행복한

02 be full of: ~로 가득하다 / 그곳은 새로운 주인을 기다리는 동물들로 가득 차 있었다. be made of: ~로 만들어지다 / 이 핑크 드레스는 비단으로 만들어졌다.

03 ① bright: 밝은 / 어젯밤 달이 매우 밝았다. ② whole: 전체의, 모든 / 너는 완전한 그림을 보기 위해서 수많은 점들을 봐야만 한다. ③ modern: 현대의 / 고대의 건물부터 현대의 예술 작품에 이르기까지 당신은 그것들을 발견할 수 있다. ④ abroad: 해외에 / 나는 해외로 여행할 계획이다. ⑤ asleep: 잠이 든 / 그는 바쁜 하루를 끝내고, 잠이 든다.

04 expect: 기대하다, 예상하다 / 어떤 것이 발생할 것이라고 믿거나 생각하다

05 Have you ever+과거분사 ~?: 너는 ~해 본 적이 있니? rise: (해가) 뜨다

06 rise: (해가) 뜨다 / 지평선 위로 하늘에 나타나다

---

07 so → but

08 'Have you ever+과거분사 ~?'는 '너는 ~해 본 적이 있니?'의 뜻으로, 상대방에게 경험을 묻는 표현이다. 해 본 적이 있으면 'Yes, I have.'로, 해 본 적이 없으면 'No, I haven't.'로 답한다. 빈칸 뒤에 'It was a wonderful experience.(그것은 멋진 경험이었어.)'로 설명하고 있으므로, 긍정의 대답이 어울린다.

09 (A) How was ~?: ~는 어땠어? (B) How did you like ~?: ~는 어땠어?

10 (A) 해외여행을 한 경험을 묻는 질문에 지난여름에 캄보디아를 다녀왔다고 말하는 것으로 보아 긍정의 대답이 들어가야 한다. (B) during은 '특정 기간'이 이어지고, for는 보통 '숫자로 된 기간'이 이어진다.

11 감정을 나타내는 동사에 '-ing'를 붙이면 '~한 감정을 일으키는'의 의미가 되고, '-ed'를 붙이면 '~한 감정을 느끼는'의 의미가 된다. interesting: 흥미로운 scared: 겁먹은, 무서워하는

12 거미 튀김이 커서 처음에 조금 무서웠다. 하지만 맛은 괜찮았다는 내용이 어울리므로 But이 적절하다.

13 (1) 목적격 관계대명사는 접속사와 목적어의 결합이다. 그러므로 목적어 them은 삭제한다. (2) 목적격 관계대명사가 전치사의 목적어인 경우 그 전치사가 문장에 반드시 있어야 한다. 그러므로 전치사 with를 추가한다. be in love with: ~와 사랑에 빠지다 (3) 선행사가 사물이므로 관계대명사 which나 that을 써야 한다. (4) 선행사가 사람이므로 관계대명사 who나 whom, that을 써야 한다. (5) 목적격 관계대명사는 접속사와 목적어의 결합이다. 그러므로 목적어 it은 삭제한다. (6), (7), (8) 'so+형용사/부사+that+주어+동사'로 '매우 …해서 ~하다'라는 의미를 나타낸다.

14 ⑤의 관계대명사는 주격이므로 whom은 쓸 수 없다. who 또는 that으로 쓰는 것이 적절하다.

15 첫 번째 문장은 두 절을 원인과 결과의 관계로 연결해 줄 등위접속사 'so'가 필요하고, 두 번째 문장은 'so ... that ~'의 형태로 원인과 결과를 나타내는 문장이므로 'so'가 빈칸에 공통으로 들어간다.

16 ④는 목적격 관계대명사를 생략해서 쓴 올바른 문장이다. ① This is the video camera which he lent me. ② I'm listening to the music which you recommended. ③ I know a boy who speaks English very well. ⑤ I don't like people who tell a lie.

17 (1) 주절과 that절의 시제를 일치시켜야 한다. (2) too+형용사/부사+to부정사: 너무 …해서 ~할 수 없다 (3) 형용사/부사+enough+to부정사: 너무 …해서 ~할 수 있다 (4) 주어가 The rings이므로 were가 적절하다. (5) 선행사가 the dog으로 동물이므로 관계대명사 which나 that이 적절하다.

18 (A) 몽골을 처음으로 '방문했다'고 해야 하므로 visited가 적절하다. invite: 초대[초청]하다, (B) 몽골의 '수도'라고 해야 하므로 capital이 적절하다. capital: 수도, capitol: (미국) 주 의회

의사당, the Capitol: 미국 국회 의사당, (C) 30분이 '걸렸다'고 해야 하므로 took이 적절하다. It takes 시간: (얼마의 시간이) 걸리다, 행위자+spend+시간 ~ing/on 명사: ~하는 데 (시간을) 보내다[들이다]

19 몽골을 처음으로 '방문해서' 특별한 여름을 보냈다고 하는 것이 적절하다.

20 글쓴이가 울란바토르에 초대된 이유는 대답할 수 없다. ① This summer. ② No. ③ Altan's grandmother. ⑤ Thirty minutes.

21 'of'를 'for'로 고치는 것이 적절하다. ask for: 요청하다

22 이 글은 글쓴이가 경험한 몽골 전통 가옥인 게르와 몽골식 바비큐인 호르호그에 대한 내용의 글이므로, 제목으로는 '나는 게르와 호르호그를 즐겼다'가 적절하다.

23 몽골인들은 특별한 손님에게 호르호그를 대접한다.

24 'Mongolia'의 형용사형을 쓰는 것이 적절하다. Mongolian: 몽골의(형용사); 몽골 사람(명사)

25 주어진 문장의 But에 주목한다. ③번 앞 문장에 나오는 내용과 상반되는 내용이 뒤에 이어지므로 ③번이 적절하다.

26 ⓑ와 ①, ③, ④: 형용사적 용법, ② 명사적 용법, ⑤ 부사적 용법

🐱 서술형 실전문제   p.102~103

01 The service was good. → The service was bad.

02 I have been to Jejudo many times. / I have been there many times.

03 (1) What do you think of[about] your ice cream?
  (2) What's your opinion of[about/on] your ice cream?

04 (1) Jack was so sleepy that he couldn't work any more.
  (2) Mason is so short that he can't ride a roller coaster.
  (3) The man is so busy that he can't play with his daughter.
  (4) It was so hot that children couldn't play outside.

05 (1) I want a robot which[that] I can control.
  (2) Look at the picture which[that] my classmate drew.
  (3) Daniel is the boy who[whom/that] I met at the concert.
  (4) The cathedral which[that] we visited last year was beautiful.

06 (1) He is so honest that he can't tell a lie.
  (2) He is so old that he can enter a university.

07 like   08 (A) wonderful (B) cooked (C) so

09 (A) Mongolian barbecue (B) special guests

10 got used to

11 It gave a great chance to get to know my friend's country and culture to me.

12 (A) Mongolian culture (B) special experience

01 새로 생긴 중국 음식점의 서비스가 좋다고 말하면서 그곳에 다시 가지 않을 거라고 하는 것은 어색하다.

02 have been to 장소/장소 부사: ~에 가 본 적이 있다

03 'How do you like ~?'는 어떤 것에 대한 만족이나 불만족에 대해 물을 때 사용하며 '~는 어떠니?'라는 의미이다. 유사한 표현으로 'What do you think of[about] ~?', 'What is your opinion of[on] ~?' 등의 표현을 사용한다.

04 'so+형용사/부사+that+주어+동사'로 '매우 …해서 ~하다'라는 의미를 나타낸다. that절의 주어와 주절의 주어가 같으면 that절의 주어는 대명사로 쓰는 것이 두 문장을 연결했을 때 자연스럽다.

05 관계대명사의 선행사가 '사람'이면 who나 that을 쓰고, 선행사가 '사물이나 동물'이면 which나 that을 쓴다.

07 feel+like+주어+동사: ~처럼 느끼다

08 (A) 감각동사 smell의 보어로 형용사를 써야 하므로 wonderful이 적절하다. (B) 수동태 it is cooked에서 it is를 생략한 것이므로 cooked가 적절하다. (C) 뒤에 형용사가 나오므로 so가 적절하다. so+형용사/부사+that: 매우 …해서 ~하다

09 호르호그는 양고기로 만들어졌고 뜨거운 돌로 요리되는 '몽골식 바비큐'이다. 몽골인들은 '특별한 손님'에게 호르호그를 대접한다.

10 get used to: ~에 익숙해지다

11 give는 'to'를 사용하여 3형식으로 고친다.

12 알탕은 글쓴이가 '몽골 문화'를 경험할 수 있게 도와주었고, 몽골을 방문한 것은 여러 면에서 '특별한 경험'이었다.

🐰 창의사고력 서술형 문제   p.104

|모범답안|

01 A: Have you broken your arm?
  B: Yes, I have. / No, I haven't.

02 (1) was so small that, ride a roller coaster
  (2) was so shy that, say anything in public
  (3) was so young that, watch a movie for free
  (4) was so brave that, travel by myself

03 (A) Last summer (B) Ulleungdo (C) walked (D) the island

01 break one's arm: 팔이 부러지다

21

01 (1) of　(2) At, to　(3) of
02 (1) My friend is studying abroad now.
　(2) We expected to see each other again.
03 during　　04 ⑤　　　05 ⑤
06 (1) How was your vacation?
　(2) How did like your vacation?
07 amazing　　　　08 ③　　　09 ②
10 Have you been to the new Chinese restaurant?
11 ②　　　12 ③　　　13 ③　　　14 ③
15 (1) There is a shop which[that] sells good coffee in front of my office.
　(2) I like the game which[that] the boys are downloading now.
16 ①
17 (1) Tell me about the man whom you admire most.
　(2) She is the woman who lives next door.
　(3) Mandy swam so fast that she won the gold medal.
18 It's Ulaanbaatar.
19 It took thirty minutes by taxi from the airport to Altan's grandmother's house. 또는 It took thirty minutes from the airport to Altan's grandmother's house by taxi.
20 ②, ⑤　　　21 touched　　　22 ③
23 (A) experience　(B) scared　(C) amazing
24 ③　　　25 ④

01 (1) be full of: ~로 가득하다 / 방이 연기로 가득차서 창문을 열었다. (2) at first: 처음에는, get used to: ~에 익숙해지다 / 처음에는 그의 억양이 이해하기 어려웠다. 하지만 곧, 우리는 그것에 익숙해졌다. (3) be made of: ~로 만들어지다 / Feijoada는 브라질의 국민요리이다. 그것은 검정 콩과 고기로 만들어진다.

02 (1) abroad: 해외에 (2) expect: 기대하다, 예상하다

03 during: ~동안(내내) 쉬는 시간 동안 스노보딩에 대해서 더 이야기해 봅시다. 나는 겨울 방학 동안 여행을 했다.

04 ① get used to: ~에 익숙해지다 / 어떤 사람이나 사물과 친숙해지다 ② kid: 농담하다 / 농담을 하다 ③ station: 역, 정거장 / 사람들이 타거나 내릴 수 있도록 지하철이나 버스가 멈추는 장소 ④ part: 부분, 일부/ 어떤 것의 전체를 만드는 조각, 부분품 또는 요소들 중의 하나 ⑤ modern: 현대의. designed and made using the latest ides or methods / 가장 최신의 생각이나 방법을 사용하여 디자인되고 만들어진

05 late → early 해가 뜨는 것을 보려고 했는데 늦게 일어나지 못했다는 것은 내용상 어색하다.

06 'How did you like ~?'는 과거의 어떤 것에 대한 만족이나 불만족에 대해 물을 때 사용하며 '~는 어땠니?'라는 의미이다. 같은

의미로 'How was ~?'가 있다.

07 amaze: 놀라게 하다 amazing: 놀라운

08 토니에게 주말을 잘 보냈는지 물어보니 (C) 부모님과 함께 국제 음식 축제에 다녀왔다고 대답한다. (A) 무슨 음식을 먹어 봤는지 물어보니, (B) 중국 전통 후식인 탕위안을 먹었다고 대답한다. (D) 이어, 탕위안이 어땠는지 물어보니, 맛있었다고 대답하며 탕위안에 대해 설명해 준다.

09 How did you like ~?: ~는 어땠어?

10 Have you been to ~?: ~에 가본 적 있니? Chinese: 중국의

11 주어진 문장에서 it은 Cambodia를 의미한다. 캄보디아에 대한 상대방을 의견을 묻고, 날씨가 더웠지만 여행은 즐거웠다는 말이 나와야 한다.

12 누구와 캄보디아를 갔는지는 언급되지 않았다. ① 수진이가 캄보디아를 갔을 때 날씨는 어땠는가? ② 수진이는 지난여름에 어디로 여행을 갔는가? ③ 수진이는 누구와 캄보디아로 여행을 갔는가? ④ 수진이는 해외로 여행한 적이 있는가? ⑤ 수진이는 캄보디아에서 무엇을 먹었는가?

13 목적격 관계대명사와 '주격관계대명사+be동사'는 생략이 가능하다. 그러므로 ③은 The boy who is playing the violin is my son. 또는 The boy playing the violin is my son.으로 쓰는 것이 적절하다.

14 첫 번째 문장은 선행사가 사물이므로 목적격 관계대명사 which 혹은 that이 필요하다. 두 번째 문장은 선행사가 '사람+사물'이므로 주격 관계대명사 that이 필요하다. 그러므로 공통으로 들어갈 단어는 that이다.

15 선행사가 사물이나 동물이면 which나 that을 쓴다.

16 주어 The man을 'I sat next to'가 꾸며주는 형태이므로 ①이 목적격 관계대명사 who(m) 또는 that이 생략된 곳이다.

17 (1) 목적격 관계대명사 whom을 사용하여 선행사 the man을 뒤에서 수식한다. (2) 주격 관계대명사 who를 사용하여 선행사 the woman을 뒤에서 수식한다. (3) 'so+형용사/부사+that+주어+동사'의 어순으로 '매우 …해서 ~하다'라는 의미를 나타낸다.

18 몽골의 수도는 '울란바토르'이다.

19 'by'를 보충하면 된다. by taxi: 택시로

20 목적격 관계대명사 that이나 which가 적절하다.

21 be moved = be touched: 감동받다

22 이 글은 글쓴이가 경험한 몽골 전통 가옥인 게르와 몽골식 바비큐인 호르호그에 대한 내용의 글이다.

23 (A) 'help+목적어+to부정사/원형부정사'이므로 experience가 적절하다. (B) 감정을 나타내는 동사는 수식받는 명사가 감정을 느끼게 되는 경우에 과거분사를 써야 하므로 scared가 적절하다. scared: 무서워하는, 겁먹은, scary: 무서운, 겁나는, (C) 경치가 정말로 '놀라웠던' 것이므로 amazing이 적절하다. (감정을 나타내는 동사는 감정을 유발할 때 현재분사를 쓰는 것이 적절하다.)

24 ⓐ, ①, ④, ⑤: 명사적 용법, ②: 형용사적 용법, ③: 부사적 용법

25 낙타의 등에서 보는 사막의 경치는 정말로 '놀라웠다.'

Living in the AI World

01 ③	02 funny	03 ①	04 ③
05 ③	06 ②	07 (1) no longer[more]	
(2) don't (h)ave			

01　① 동물 중에는 지진을 예측하는 능력을 가진 것이 있다. ② 집의 수도관이 얼지 않기를 희망한다. ③ teleport: 순간 이동하다, 나는 시간과 공간을 통과해 순간 이동할 수 있습니다. ④ 암호를 확인한 다음 다시 시도해 보십시오. ⑤ 나는 아이를 위해 장난감을 골랐다.

02　fun: 재미 funny: 재미있는 / 너의 이야기가 너무 웃겨서 나는 웃음을 멈출 수가 없다.

03　translate: 번역하다 / 불어를 영어로 번역할 수 있는 사람을 아니?

04　beat: 이기다 / 그리스와의 첫 경기에서, 우리나라 팀은 그리스 팀을 이겼다.

05　③의 like는 '좋아하다'의 의미로 사용하였고, 나머지는 '~와 같이, ~처럼'의 의미로 사용하였다. ① 숲속에서 배우는 것은 재미있을 것 같지 않나요? ② 그 옷을 입으니 완전히 다른 사람처럼 보여요. ③ 왜 그렇게 좋아하시죠? ④ 그것은 약간 체스 게임 같이 보이지 않는가? ⑤ 그들은 사람들처럼 오랫동안 슬퍼한다.

06　strange: 이상한 unusual: 특이한, 이상한 / 실험 후에 사람들에게 어떤 이상한 것을 보았는지 물어봤다.

07　(1) no longe[more]: 더 이상 ~하지 않다 (2) don't have to 동사원형: ~할 필요가 없다(= don't need to, need not)

01 (1) greedy (2) funny (3) sunny, cloudy (4) lucky
02 (r)eplace
03 By, by
04 (1) translate (2) (p)ossible, finish
　　(3) (e)lse (4) (h)ave, perfect
05 (1) in (2) to (3) off
06 (1) I saw him crossing the street.
　　(2) He predicted that the GDP would go up.

01　(1) greed: 욕심 greedy: 욕심 많은 / Scrooge는 욕심 많은 노인이었다. (2) fun: 재미 funny: 재미있는 / 이야기가 재미있기 때문에 난 이 책을 좋아한다. (3) sun: 태양 sunny: 맑은 cloud: 구름 cloudy: 흐린 / 오늘은 날씨가 맑았지만 내일은 흐릴 것이

다. 너는 우산을 가져와야 할 것이다. (4) luck: 행운 lucky: 운이 좋은 / 나는 우연히 내가 좋아하는 영화 배우를 만났다. 운이 좋은 날이다! by chance: 우연히

02　replace: 대체하다(= take the place of) / 새로운 세포들이 오래된 세포들을 대신한다.

03　by the way: 그런데, 그건 그렇고 / 그건 그렇고, 아직도 공립 도서관에서 일하시나요? by 동사ing: ~함으로써 / 그것을 함으로써 시간 관리 기술을 배울 수 있습니다.

04　(1) translate: 번역하다 (2) possible: 가능한 Is it possible (for 목적격) to 동사원형 ~?: (…가) ~하는 것이 가능할까? (3) else: 그 밖의 (4) don't have to 동사원형: ~할 필요가 없다(= need not) perfect: 완벽한

05　(1) get in: ~에 타다 / 차에 당장 타, 안 그러면 늦을 거야. (2) get to: ~에 도착하다 / 내가 산 정상에 도착했을 때, 아주 어두워졌다. (3) get off: ~에서 내리다, ~에서 떨어지다 / 우리는 그를 곧 보게 될 것이다. 승객들이 지금 비행기에서 내리고 있는 중이다.

06　(1) cross: 건너다 (2) predict: 예측하다

1 Sounds
2 That sounds good / I think it's exciting
3 Is it possible that
4 Is it possible for him to finish this marathon?
　Can he finish this marathon?
5 Is it possible for you to make a cake?

1 F　2 T　3 F　4 T

don't / sounds

시험대비 기본평가 p.120

01 ③ 02 ① 03 ②

01 가능 여부를 나타내는 표현들로는 'Is it possible that 주어 동사 ~?', 'Is it possible for 목적격 to 동사원형 ~?', 'Can 주어 동사원형 ~?' 등이 있다.

02 여자아이는 남자아이의 의견을 좋아하면서, 인터넷에서 정보를 찾아보자고 제안하고 있다. sound 형용사: ~하게 들리다

03 로봇 박람회를 같이 가자고 제안하는 말에, (B) 제안을 수락하면서 박람회가 재미있겠다고 자신의 생각을 표현한다. (A) 로봇 공학자를 만날 기회가 있을 거라고 하자 (C) 그러면 좋겠다고 말한다. Why don't you ~?: ~하는 게 어때? exciting: 흥미진진한, 신나는 sound 형용사: ~하게 들리다 chance: 기회 look for: 찾다

시험대비 실력평가 p.121~122

01 ②	02 ④	03 ⑤	04 ④
05 ④	06 ⑤	07 ②	08 ③
09 ④			

01 sound 형용사: ~하게 들리다 exciting: 흥미진진한, 신나는

02 ① 남자아이는 로봇 박람회를 어떻게 생각하는가? 재미있을 것 같다고 생각한다. ② 그들은 로봇 박람회에서 누구를 만날 수 있을까? 로봇 공학자. ③ 여자아이는 남자아이와 어디를 같이 가기를 원하는가? 로봇 박람회. ④ 로봇 박람회를 가기 위해서 그들은 어디서 만날 것인가? 대화의 내용에 나와 있지 않으므로 대답할 수 없음. ⑤ 언제 로봇 박람회가 시작되는가? 다음 주에.

03 주어진 문장은 글자의 뜻을 물어보고 있는 질문이므로 글자의 뜻을 이야기해 주고 있는 'They mean "Dreams come true!"("꿈은 이루어진다!"라는 뜻이에요.)'라는 대답 앞에 오는 것이 적절하다.

04 사전을 찾지 않고 곧바로 AI 번역기를 사용하였다.

05 주어진 문장은 로봇이 위험에 처한 사람들을 도울 수 있다는 내용으로 ④번 다음 문장인 'Robots can do the dangerous work so humans don't have to.(로봇이 그 위험한 일을 할 수 있어서 사람들이 그 일을 하지 않아도 되지.)'가 주어진 문장을 좀 더 설명한 것으로 볼 수 있다.

06 스마트 음식 주문 자판기를 사용해 보자는 제안에, 쉽고 빠르게 주문을 할 수 있다고 말하고 있으므로, 제안에 대해 긍정하는 내용이 빈칸에 들어가는 것이 적절하다. sound 형용사: ~하게 들리다 interesting: 재미있는, 흥미로운

07 여자아이가 로봇이 인간을 대체할 수 있을 거라고 생각하는지 민석이에게 묻는 질문에 잘 모르겠다고 대답했다.

08 ③ Yes, I can. → Yes, you can. 또는 Is it possible that I keep a pet? → Is it possible that you keep a pet?

09 ④ 영화를 보자는 제안에 반대하는 말을 하고 재미있을 것 같다고 말하는 것은 앞뒤가 맞지 않는다.

서술형 시험대비 p.123

01 Can you

02 Is it possible to use this coupon?

03 She will pay 470 dollars.

04 (A) up (B) about

05 unbelievable

06 Is it possible for you to travel around Gangwondo by bicycle?

01 가능 여부를 나타내는 표현들로는 'Is it possible for 목적격 to 동사원형 ~?', 'Can 주어 동사원형 ~?' 등이 있다.

02 Is it possible (for 목적격) to 동사원형 ~?: (…가) ~하는 것이 가능할까?

03 컴퓨터 가격이 500 달러였는데 30달러 할인되는 쿠폰을 사용하였으므로 470달러를 낼 것이다.

04 (A) look ~ up: (사전·참고 자료·컴퓨터 등에서 정보를) 찾아 보다 (B) What about ~?: ~하는 게 어때?

05 unbelievable: 믿기 어려운, 놀랄만한

06 Is it possible (for 목적격) to 동사원형 ~?: (…가) ~하는 것이 가능할까? by bicycle: 자전거로

Grammar

핵심 Check   p.124~125

1 (1) doing   (2) sing   (3) washed
2 (1) to play   (2) to solve   (3) It

시험대비 기본평가   p.126

01 (1) sang → sing(또는 singing)
   (2) to fly → fly(또는 flying)
   (3) choose → to choose
   (4) That → It
02 (1) cry[또는 crying]   (2) cleaned
   (3) play(또는 playing)   (4) flow(또는 flowing)
03 ④
04 It is necessary for you to take a rest.

01 (1), (2) 지각동사의 목적어가 목적격보어의 행위의 주체가 될 때 목적격보어로 원형부정사나 현재분사를 쓰는 것이 적절하다. (3) 진주어로 to부정사가 적절하다. (4) 가주어로는 that이 아니라 it 을 쓴다.

02 (1) 지각동사의 목적격보어는 목적어와의 관계가 능동일 경우 원형부정사나 현재분사가 쓰인다. (2) 지각동사의 목적격보어는 목적어와의 관계가 수동일 경우 과거분사가 쓰인다. (3) 그들이 경기 하는 것이므로 play 또는 playing이 적절하다. (4) 물이 흐르는 것이므로 능동의 의미를 나타내 는 flow 또는 flowing 이 적절하다.

03 가주어로는 that이 아니라 it을 쓰며 진주어로 to부정사를 이용한다.

04 가주어 it과 진주어 to부정사를 이용하여 문장을 쓴다. 또한 의미상의 주어로 'for+목적격'을 써야 하므로 for를 추가한다.

시험대비 실력평가   p.127~129

01 ⑤   02 ③   03 ①   04 It is
good to ride bicycles for fun on weekends.   05 ④
06 (1) waiting (2) playing (3) played (4) listen (5) It (6) to
swim (7) of   07 ④   08 This → It   09 ③, ④
10 ④   11 him turn[turning] off the stove

12 ①, ⑤   13 ③   14 ②   15 ③
16 (1) It is not easy to make her laugh.
   (2) It is my plan to read 10 books during winter vacation.
17 (1) to paint → paint[painting]
   (2) wears → to wear
   (3) of → for
18 (1) Minsu hears a dog bark[barking] whenever he passes by the house.
   (2) I saw a bird fly[flying] high in the sky.
   (3) It is exciting for me to watch baseball games with my friends.
   (4) It is dangerous to put paper near the fire.

01 목적어와의 관계가 능동이므로 지각동사의 목적격보어로 원형부정사 혹은 현재분사가 적설하다. / It을 가주어로 하고 to부정사를 진주어로 쓰는 것이 적절하다.

02 feel은 지각동사이므로 목적격보어로 원형부정사 혹은 현재분사, 과거분사를 취한다. the dog이 his clothes를 끌고 가는 주체가 되므로 pull 또는 pulling이 적절하다.

03 가주어로는 that이 아니라 it을 쓰며 진주어로 to부정사가 적절하다.

04 가주어 it과 진주어로 to부정사를 이용하여 문장을 쓴다.

05 지각동사 feel의 목적격보어로 원형부정사 혹은 현재분사가 적절하다. At times, Nora felt him stare[staring] at her.

06 (1) 지각동사 see의 목적격보어로 원형부정사가 적절하다. (2) 지각동사 hear의 목적격보어로 현재분사가 적절하다. (3) the game이 play되는 것이므로 목적격보어로 수동의 의미를 갖는 과거분사가 적절하다 (4) make는 사역동사이므로 목적격보어로 원형부정사가 적절하다, (5) 가주어로는 that이 아니라 it을 쓴다. (6) 진주어로 to부정사를 쓰는 것이 적절하다. (7) to부정사의 의미상 주어를 나타낼 때 문장에 쓰인 형용사가 사람의 성질을 나타내는 말일 때는 'of+목적격'을 쓴다.

07 지각동사 watch의 목적격보어로 bake나 baking을 쓰는 것이 적절하다.

08 주어로 쓰인 'that'질의 경우에도 보통 가주어 'it'을 쓰고 'that' 절을 문장 뒤로 보낸다.

09 목적어와의 관계가 능동이므로 지각동사의 목적격보어로 원형부정사 혹은 현재분사가 적절하다.

10 it을 가주어로 하고 to부정사를 진주어로 쓰는 것이 적절하다.

11 Bill이 난로를 끄는 것을 보았다는 의미이다. 목적어와 목적격보어의 관계가 능동이므로 원형부정사 또는 현재분사로 써야 한다.

12 ② I saw a boy solve[solving] math problems. ③ By the way, do you think it will be possible for robots to replace humans someday? ④ Is it possible to fly through a rainbow?

13 (A) 지각동사의 목적어와 목적격보어의 관계가 능동이므로 현재분사가 적절하다. (B) 지각동사의 목적어와 목적격보어의 관계가 능동이므로 원형부정사가 적절하다. (C) 지각동사의 목적어와 목적격보어의 관계가 수동 (이름이 불리는 것)이므로 과거분사가 적절하다.

14 ②번은 인칭대명사이지만 나머지는 모두 가주어 It이다. 가주어는 해석하지 않지만 인칭대명사는 '그것'이라고 해석한다.

15 주어진 문장과 ③번은 목적격보어로 쓰인 현재분사이다. ① 분사구문 ② 진행형을 만드는 현재분사 ④, ⑤ 동명사

16 it을 가주어로 하고 to부정사를 진주어로 하여 쓰는 것이 적절하다.

17 (1) 지각동사의 목적격보어로 원형부정사나 현재분사가 적절하다. (2) it을 가주어로 하고 to부정사를 진주어로 쓰는 것이 적절하다. (3) to부정사의 의미상 주어로 사람의 성질을 나타내는 형용사가 쓰인 것이 아니므로 'for+목적격'이 적절하다.

18 (1)~(3) 지각동사의 목적격보어로 원형부정사나 현재분사를 이용한다. (4), (5) it을 가주어로 하고 to부정사를 진주어로 하여 'It ~ to부정사' 구문으로 쓰는 것이 적절하다. to부정사의 의미상 주어로 사람의 성질을 나타내는 형용사가 쓰인 것이 아니므로 'for+목적격'이 적절하다.

서술형 시험대비
p.130~131

01 (1) I saw them play[playing] soccer in the playground.
  (2) Barbara felt her heart beat[beating] faster.
  (3) Aaron looked at Sylvia come[coming] with Alex hand in hand.
  (4) A farmer bought 43 sheep at the market and saw them stolen 24 hours later.
  (5) It is hard to take care of a baby.
  (6) It is a lot of fun to go on a picnic.
  (7) It is difficult for me to learn a new language.

02 I heard Sam baking some cookies.

03 (1) It was very difficult to answer the math questions.
  (2) It was a great experience to swim in the blue sea.
  (3) It is good for your health to exercise regularly.
  (4) It is not easy for me to learn English.
  (5) It is true that a friend in need is a friend indeed.

04 (1) to stay (2) pulled (3) sing[singing] (4) take

05 to read 50 novels

06 (1) for me to pass the driver's test
  (2) to watch the view as we went higher and higher
  (3) of you to help that old woman
  (4) that Annabelle didn't tell him a lie

07 make[또는 making]

08 (1) He heard them playing te drums.
  (2) Suhan looked at AI Speaker playing a movie.

09 (1) It is very smart of her to solve that problem.
  (2) It is not safe to swim in this river as it is very deep.

01 (1)~(3) 지각동사의 목적어와 목적격보어의 관계가 능동이므로 목적격보어로 원형부정사 혹은 현재분사가 적절하다 (4) 지각동사의 목적어와 목적격보어의 관계가 수동이므로 과거 분사가 적절하다. (5) It ~ to부정사' 구문으로 쓰는 것이 적절하다. (6) 가주어로는 that이 아니라 it을 쓴다. (7) to부정사의 의미상 주어로 사람의 성질을 나타내는 형용사가 쓰인 것이 아니므로 'for+목적격'이 적절하다.

02 진행형의 문장이므로 목적격보어로 현재분사가 적절하다.

03 (1)~(4) 문장의 주어로 쓰인 to부정사를 뒤로 보내고 대신 주어 자리에 가주어 it을 쓴다. (5) 주어로 쓰인 that절의 경우에도 긴 that절을 뒤로 보내고 주어 자리에 가주어 it을 쓴다.

04 (1) ask는 to부정사를 목적격보어로 받는다. (2) 지각동사의 목적어와 목적격보어의 관계가 수동일 때 목적격보어로 과거분사가 적절하다. (3) 목적어와 목적격보어의 관계가 능동일 때 목적격보어로 원형부정사나 현재분사가 적절하다. (4) 사역동사 make는 원형부정사를 목적격보어로 받는다.

05 가주어로 it이 나와 있으므로 진주어로 to부정사를 쓰는것이 적절하다.

06 (1) '하는데 어려움이 있다'는 것을 '~하기 어렵다'는 문장으로, (2) Watching을 to watch로 바꾸어서, '가주어(it) ~ 진주어(to부정사) …' 구문을 이용하여 쓴다. (4) In fact는 '사실은'이라는 뜻이므로 It is true 다음에 that절을 진주어 로 쓴다.

07 지각동사 see의 목적어와 목적격보어의 관계가 능동이므로 목적격보어로 원형부정사나 현재분사가 적절하다.

08 지각동사의 목적어와 목적격보어의 관계가 능동이며, 진행형으로 쓰이고 있으므로 현재분사를 이용한다.

09 (1) to solve의 주어가 she이므로 of her로 의미상의 주어를 나타내야 한다. (2) 전치사 in의 목적어로 this river를 쓴다.

Reading

교과서

확인문제
p.132

1 T 2 F 3 T 4 F

확인문제
p.133

1 T 2 F 3 T 4 F

01 at
02 at the World AI Expo
03 entering
04 of the future
05 go into
06 on the closet door, keep changing
07 that suit the weather
08 no longer, dressing for the weather
09 move on to
10 this music speaker
11 I'm not just
12 more than
13 It's hard to believe
14 How about
15 play one
16 getting darker
17 feel like
18 What else
19 Here comes
20 Good job
21 Hurry
22 ride in
23 so cool, get in
24 ready to go
25 what should
26 my first time
27 don't need to
28 take you to
29 crossing
30 have just sensed
31 sense dangerous situations
32 How
33 intelligent robotic
34 all about driving
35 based on
36 How, like
37 like

1 A Day at the AI Expo
2 Jina and Suhan are at the World AI Expo.
3 They are entering the AI home.
4 Suhan: Look at this! It's a house of the future.
5 Jina: Let's go into the bedroom first. Look, there's a smart closet.
6 Suhan: I'm standing in front of this screen on the closet door and my clothes keep changing.
7 Jina: The screen suggests clothes that suit the weather.
8 Suhan: That's amazing! We no longer have to worry about dressing for the weather.
9 Jina: Right. Let's move on to the living room.
10 Suhan: Oh, I like this music speaker.
11 AI Speaker: I'm not just a music speaker.
12 I can do more than you can imagine.
13 Jina: It's hard to believe that you can understand us. What can you do?
14 AI Speaker: How about watching a movie?
15 I'll play one for you.
16 Suhan: Look, those smart windows are getting darker.
17 I feel like I'm in a movie theater.
18 Jina: What else can you do?
19 AI Speaker: I can beatbox, too. Here comes, "cats

and boots and cats and boots."
20 Suhan: You're funny. Good job!
21 Jina: Hurry! There's a smart car station outside!
22 Let's go and ride in that red car.
23 Suhan: This car is so cool. Let's get in.
24 AI Car: Welcome. Are you ready to go?
25 Jina: Yes, what should we do now?
26 It's my first time to ride in a smart car.
27 AI Car: You don't need to do anything.
28 I will drive and take you to the next station.
29 Suhan: Watch out! I see a cat crossing the street.
30 AI Car: Don't worry. I have just sensed it.
31 When I sense dangerous situations, I slow down or stop.
32 Jina: How can you do that?
33 AI Car: I'm a very intelligent robotic car.
34 I know all about driving.
35 I can predict danger based on knowledge and experience.
36 Suhan: How smart! You think and act like a person.
37 You are really like a human.

01 Jina and Suhan   02 ②, ④, ⑤   03 ②
04 ⑤   05 (A) one (B) What else (C) comes
06 I feel like I'm in a movie theater.   07 ①, ④
08 ②, ⑤   09 ③   10 changing   11 ②, ⑤
12 ④   13 ③   14 ①, ④   15 ⑤
16 (A) music speaker (B) beatbox   17 ①
18 ④   19 ①, ④   20 beaten[beat]
21 it   22 who is one of the greatest baduk
players   23 ④

01 '진아'와 '수한'이를 가리킨다.
02 ⓑ와 ②, ④, ⑤번: 현재분사, ①, ③: 동명사
03 '진아'가 침실에 먼저 들어가 보자고 말한다.
04 주어진 문장의 you에 주목한다. ⑤번 앞 문장의 내용을 말한 AI Speaker를 가리키므로 ⑤번이 적절하다.
05 (A) 'a movie'를 지칭하므로 one이 적절하다. 'a+명사'는 one 으로, 'the+명사'는 it으로 받는다. (B) '또 뭘 할 수 있어?'라 고 해야 하므로 What else가 적절하다. (C) "cats and boots and cats and boots."는 비트박스를 하는 한 예에 해당하는 말 이므로 comes 가 적절하다. 비트박스: 사람의 입으로 디제잉 (DJing)의 소리를 흉내 내는 일종의 모사이다.
06 feel like: …한 느낌이 있다

27

07 '고양이가 길을 건너고 있는게 보인다'고 해야 하므로, 지각동사 see의 목적격보어 자리에 동사원형이나 현재분사가 오는 것이 적절하다.

08 ⓐ와 ②, ⑤번: 멋진, 끝내 주는, ①, ④: (날씨·공기 따위가) 서늘한, 시원한, ③ 차분한, 침착한

09 이 글은 '인공 지능 자동차는 지능적인 로봇 차이기 때문에 운전에 대한 모든 걸 알고 있고 위험을 예측하며 운전할 수 있다'는 내용의 글이므로, 제목으로는 '걱정 말아요! 저는 운전에 대한 모든 걸 알고 있어요.'가 적절하다.

10 keep ~ing: 계속 ~하다

11 worry about = be concerned[worried, anxious] about: ~에 대해 걱정하다, ② be anxious for: 갈망하다, ⑤ be concerned with: …에 관계가 있다, …에 관심이 있다

12 수한이의 옷이 어떻게 계속해서 바뀌는지는 대답할 수 없다. ① They are entering the AI home at the World AI Expo. ② They enter the bedroom first. ③ He is standing in front of the screen on the closet door. ⑤ It suggests clothes that suit the weather.

13 ③은 진아(와 수한)를 가리키고, 나머지는 다 'AI Speaker'를 가리킨다.

14 ⓐ와 ①, ④번: ~처럼(접속사), ② 좋아하다(동사), ③ ~처럼(전치사), ⑤ 비슷한(형용사)

15 이 글은 AI Speaker가 그냥 음악 스피커가 아니라 사람들이 상상하는 것 이상의 것을 할 수 있다는 내용의 글이므로, 주제로는 '그것의 원래 역할을 하는 외에 AI Speaker가 할 수 있는 것'이 적절하다.

16 AI Speaker는 '음악 스피커'일 뿐만 아니라 영화를 틀어 주고 '비트박스'도 할 수 있다.

17 (A) take+사람+to+장소: ~를 …에 데리고 가다, (C) based on: ~에 근거하여

18 지식과 경험을 바탕으로 '위험을 예측할 수 있다'고 하는 것이 적절하다. ① safety: 안전(함), ⑤ generate: 발생시키다

19 ⓐ와 ②, ③, ⑤: 부사적 용법, ① 형용사적 용법, ④ 명사적 용법

20 'beat'의 과거분사형 beaten과 beat이다.

21 가주어 'it'이 적절하다.

22 one+of+the+복수명사: ~ 중의 하나

23 AI는 이세돌의 경기를 예측할 수 있었고, 그리고 마침내 경기에서 이겼다.

서술형 시험대비　　　　　　　p.142~143

01 entering into → entering

02 We no longer have to worry about dressing for the weather.

03 (a) closet door (b) the weather

04 than

05 What about / Why don't you

06 becoming 또는 growing

07 (1) 영화를 틀어 줄 수 있다.
　　(2) 비트박스도 할 수 있다.

08 Intelligence

09 (1) don't have to
　　(2) need not

10 AI Car가 이미 고양이가 길을 건너고 있는 것을 감지했고, AI Car는 어떤 위험한 상황을 감지하면 속도를 늦추거나 멈추기 때문이다.

11 a cat crossing the street

12 (A) Suhan (B) his clothes

13 amazed → amazing

14 suggests clothes

01 enter: ~에 들어가다, enter into: (논의·처리 등을) 시작하다

02 no longer: 더 이상 …아닌

03 그것은 스마트 '옷장 문'에 있는 스크린이고 그 앞에 서 있는 사람에게 '날씨'에 적합한 옷을 제안한다.

04 비교급 뒤에 'than'이 적절하다.

05 How about ~ing? = What about ~ing? = Why don't you+동사원형?: ~하는 게 어때?

06 get[become/grow]+형용사의 비교급: 점점 ~해지다

07 인공 지능 스피커는 그냥 음악 스피커가 아니라 당신이 상상하는 것 이상의 것을 할 수 있다고 하면서, 두 가지 예를 설명하고 있다.

08 intelligent의 명사형인 intelligence를 쓰는 것이 적절하다. artificial intelligence = AI: (컴퓨터) 인공 지능

09 don't need to = don't have to = need not: ~할 필요가 없다

10 바로 뒤의 내용을 쓰는 것이 적절하다.

11 '길을 건너고 있는 고양이'를 가리킨다.

12 '수한'이가 실제로 그의 옷을 계속 바꿔 입는 것이 아니다. 그는 단지 옷장 문에 있는 스크린 앞에서 있으면 '그의 옷'이 계속해서 바뀐다.

13 감정을 나타내는 동사는 감정을 유발할 때 현재분사를 쓰는 것이 적절하다.

14 옷장 문에 있는 스크린이 날씨에 적합한 '옷을 제안해주기' 때문이다.

영역별 핵심문제　　　　　　　p.145~149

01 look　　02 ①　　03 (1) on　(2) just
(3) longer　(4) if　　04 (1) (b)eat
(2) (i)ntelligent　(3) (r)eplace　　05 ④
06 ③　　07 ⑤　　08 ③　　09 for
10 ③　　11 ①　　12 (A) for (B) Sure
(C) do　　13 ⑤　　14 ⑤
15 (1) play(또는 playing)

(2) swim(또는 swimming)

(3) ride(또는 riding)

16 ②　　　　**17** ④

18 (1) I saw him riding[ride] a bike in the park.

(2) I smelled something burning in the kitchen.

(3) It is not possible to talk on the moon.

(4) It is exciting to play basketball with friends.

19 (1) danced → dance[dancing]

(2) burns → burning

(3) tearing → torn

(4) of → for

(5) beating → to beat

(6) make → to make

20 ①, ⑤　　　**21** ④　　　**22** closet　　　**23** I can do more than you can imagine.　　　**24** ②

25 Look out! 또는 Be careful!　　　**26** ④

27 slow down or stop when you sense dangerous situations　　　**28** called　　　**29** ⑤

---

01 look ~ up: (사전·참고 자료·컴퓨터 등에서 정보를) 찾아보다 / 그는 네가 그것들을 인터넷에서 찾을 충분한 시간을 줄 것이다. look for: 찾다 / 이 고래들은 무리지어 먹이를 찾는다.

02 free from: ~이 없는 / 그녀에게는 걱정거리가 끊이지 않는다.

03 (1) based on: ~에 근거하여 / 그 영화는 유명한 소설에 기반을 두고 있다. (2) not just: 단지 ~뿐이 아니다 / 그것은 단순히 돈의 문제만은 아니다. (3) no longer: 더 이상 ~하지 않는 / 그녀는 더 이상 아이가 아니다. (4) see if 주어 동사: ~인지 아닌지 확인하다 / 문이 잠겨 있는지 가서 확인해 보세요.

04 (1) beat: 이기다 (2) intelligent: 똑똑한 (3) replace: 대체하다

05 (A) '우리는 정말 그랬어.'란 의미로, did는 'took lots of pictures during our trip.'을 의미한다. (B) Is it possible (for 목적격) to 동사원형 ~?: (…가) ~하는 것이 가능할까?

06 사진으로 동영상 앨범을 만드는 것이 가능한지 물어보고 있으므로 가능한지 불가능한지 대답을 해야 한다. 또한 빈칸 뒤에 'I have an app for that.(나는 그것을 위한 앱이 있어.)'라고 말했으므로 가능하다고 대답하는 것이 적절하다.

07 (A) Why don't we ~?: ~하는 게 어때?(제안, 권유) (B) sound 형용사: ~하게 들리다

08 주어진 문장은 상대방의 생각을 물어보는 'What do you think?(너는 어떻게 생각해?)'이다. 그러므로 자신의 생각을 표현한 'That sounds perfect for our project.(우리 프로젝트에 완벽한 것 같아.)' 앞의 질문으로 어울린다.

09 (A) perfect for: ~에 완벽한, ~에 안성맞춤인 (B) look for: 찾다

10 여자아이는 남자아이의 의견이 프로젝트에 완벽하다고 생각한다. disagree: 동의하지 않다

11 로봇 박람회에 같이 가자고 제안하는 말에, 'That sounds exciting.(그거 재미있겠는데.)'이라고 했으므로 빈칸에는 제안에 긍정하는 말이 어울린다.

12 (A) to부정사의 행위에 대하여 행위를 하는 주체가 있을 때 to부정사 앞에 의미상 주어를 넣는다. 의미상의 주어는 일반적으로 'for+목적격'을 사용하며 주절에 사람의 '성질이나 성격 등'을 나타내는 형용사가 쓰였을 경우 'of+목적격'을 사용한다. Is it possible (for 목적격) to 동사원형 ~?: (…가) ~하는 것이 가능할까? (B) 'I can do that.(할 수 있어.)'으로 대답하고 있으므로, 가능하다고 말하는 것이 어울린다. (C) read를 의미하므로 do가 적절하다.

13 첫 문장에는 smell이 나왔으므로 목적격보어로 현재분사가 나와야 한다. 두 번째 문장에서는 지각동사이므로 목적격보어로 동사원형이나 현재분사가 나와야 한다.(사람들이 수영하는 것이므로 능동)

14 가주어로 it이 나와야 하며 진주어로 to부정사가 적절하다.

15 (1)~(3) 지각동사의 목적어가 목적격보어의 행위의 주체가 될 경우 목적격보어로 원형부정사나 현재분사를 쓴다.

16 that이 나오려면 뒤에 주어와 동사가 있는 절이 이어져야 한다. It was interesting to compare their situation and ours.

17 see가 지각동사이므로 목적격보어로 serve나 serving이 적절하다.

18 (1) 지각동사의 목적어와 목적격보어의 관계가 능동일 경우 목적격보어로 원형부정사와 현재분사를 모두 사용할 수 있으나 의미상 그 동작이 진행 중인 것을 나타낼 때에는 주로 현재분사를 사용한다. (2) smell은 목적격보어로 현재분사를 사용한다. (3)~(4) it이 나와 있으므로 '가주어(it) ~ 진주어(to 부정사)' 구문을 이용하여 쓴다.

19 (1), (3) 지각동사의 목적어와 목적격보어가 능동의 관계에 있을 경우 목적격보어로 원형부정사나 현재분사를 쓰고, 수동일 경우 과거분사를 쓴다. (2) smell은 목적격보어로 현재분사를 쓴다. (4) to부정사의 의미상 주어로 사람의 성질을 나타내는 형용사가 쓰인 것이 아니므로 'for+목적격'이 적절하다. (5) for an AI가 의미상의 주어로 나와 있으므로 to beat를 써야 한다. (6) it을 가주어로 하고 to부정사를 진주어로 쓰는 것이 적절하다.

20 주격 관계대명사 'that'이나 'which'가 적절하다.

21 이 글은 인공 지능 집에서 옷장 문에 있는 스크린이 날씨에 적합한 옷을 제안하는 내용의 글이므로, 제목으로는 '옷을 제안하는 스크린'이 적절하다. ⑤ suitable for: …에 알맞은[어울리는]

22 closet: 벽장; 보관 장소로 사용되는 작은 방이나 캐비닛

23 more than you can imagine: 당신이 상상하는 것 이상의 것

24 (A)와 ②번: 가주어, ①, ④: 비인칭 주어 <시간·날짜·거리·날씨 등에 대해 말할 때 동사의 주어 자리에 씀> ③ 가목적어 ⑤ 그것(앞에 이미 언급 되었거나 현재 이야기되고 있는 사물·동물을 가리킴)

29

25 watch out = look out = be careful: (특히 위험이 있을 때 경고하는 말로) 조심하다

26 ⓑ와 ①번: 완료 용법, ② 경험 용법, ③, ⑤: 계속 용법, ④ 결과 용법

27 앞 문장 '저는 어떤 위험 상황을 감지하면 속도를 늦추거나 멈춰요.'를 가리킨다.

28 "Alpha-Foot"이라고 '불리는' 축구 로봇이라고 해야 하므로, 과거분사로 쓰는 것이 적절하다.

29 ⑤ 위 글은 '학교 신문 기사'이다. ① (책, 연극, 영화 등에 대한) 논평[비평], 감상문, ② 독후감, ③ 수필

단원별 예상문제   p.150~153

01 (b)urn / burn   02 cloudy   03 ②
04 (1) in danger (2) based on   05 (t)ranslator   06 ⑤
07 Is it possible for AI to read those words?
08 dictionary   09 (C) – (D) – (B) – (A)
10 (D) – (A) – (C) – (B)   11 if   12 Is it possible to freeze fire?   13 ②
14 ②
15 ①, ③   16 ②, ⑤   17 ②   18 suits → suit   19 ⑤   20 ④   21 ②
22 ③   23 ②   24 ④
25 (A) robotic car (B) do anything

01 burn: 불타다 / 불에 의해서 파괴되다 / 불을 낮춰, 그렇지 않으면 그게 탈 거야.

02 cloud: 구름 cloudy: 구름이 낀, 흐린

03 ① freeze, freeze: 얼리다 / 얼음 한 판 얼리는 데 하루 종일 걸린다. ② slow, slow down: 속도를 늦추다 / 이것은 노화를 늦추는 데 널리 사용되고 있습니다. ③ texting, text: (휴대전화로) 문자를 보내다 / 친구들과 문자를 주고 받거나 온라인에서 말하는 것을 좋아하나요? ④ point, point (at/toward): 돌리다, 향하게 하다 / 공공장소에서 낯선 사람들을 손가락으로 가리키는 것은 예의 없는 행동이다. ⑤ take, take: 선택하다, 사다 / 어른 표 두 장을 사겠습니다.

04 (1) in danger: 위험에 처한, 위험에 빠진 (2) based on: ~에 근거하여

05 translate: 번역하다 translator: 번역가

06 AI 번역기를 사용하는 방법에 대해 묻고 대답하고 있다.

07 Is it possible (for 목적격) to 동사원형 ~?: (…가) ~하는 것이 가능할까? AI: 인공지능(artificial intelligence)

08 dictionary: 사전 / 알파벳순으로 그것의 의미 또는 다른 언어로의 번역이 있는 일련의 단어와 구를 포함하는 책

11 see if 주어 동사: ~인지 아닌지 확인하다

12 Is it possible (for 목적격) to 동사원형 ~?: (~가) ~하는 것이 가능할까? freeze: 얼리다

13 가주어로는 it을 쓰며 진주어로 to부정사를 이용한다. 또한 의미

상의 주어로 문장에 쓰인 형용사가 사람의 성질을 나타내는 말이 아니므로 'for+목적격'을 쓴다.

14 첫 번째 문장에서는 지각동사의 목적격보어로 원형부정사나 현재분사가 적절하다. 두 번째 문장에서는 it을 가주어로 하고 to부정사를 진주어로 하여 'It ~ to부정사' 구문으로 쓰는 것이 적절하다.

15 ② I heard my name called repeatedly. ④ Mick watched them fight[fighting] each other. ⑤ He was looking at the dog eat[eating] the bones.

16 ① It is necessary to come early in the morning. ③ It is helpful to read many kinds of books. ④ It was really boring for me to memorize English words.

17 (A) worry about: ~에 대해 걱정하다, (B) dress for: … 에 적합한 옷을 입다

18 주격 관계대명사 that의 선행사가 clothes이므로 'suit'로 고치는 것이 적절하다.

19 ⓑ와 ①, ③, ④번: 동명사(목적이나 용도), ②, ⑤번: 현재분사(동작이나 상태, 진행)

20 ⓐ: Suhan(과 Jina), ⓑ, ⓓ, ⓔ: AI Speaker, ⓒ: Suhan과 Jina를 가리킨다.

21 ⓑ와 ②, ④, ⑤번: 명사적 용법, ① 형용사적 용법, ③ 부사적 용법

22 스마트 창문이 점점 어두워지고 있다.

23 ②번 다음 문장의 do that에 주목한다. 주어진 문장의 내용을 받고 있으므로 ②번이 적절하다.

24 이 글은 '인공 지능 자동차는 운전에 대한 모든 걸 알고 운전한다.'는 내용의 글이다.

25 그것은 운전에 대한 모든 걸 알고 있는 아주 지능적인 '로봇차'이다. 사람들은 스마트 자동차에 타고 있는 동안 '아무것도 하지' 않아도 된다.

서술형 실전문제   p.154~155

01 Is that possible → Is it possible
02 I think that is perfect for our project.
03 Is it possible for you to text with your eyes closed?
04 (1) To save energy in our daily lives is important.
(2) It is important to save energy in our daily lives.
(1) To feel tired after work is natural.
(2) It is natural to feel tired after work.
05 riding a horse
06 enter
07 The screen suggests clothes that[which] suit the weather.
08 any longer

09 (A) what (B) How (C) based

09 (A) what (B) How (C) based

10 speed up → slow down

11 What a smart car (you are)!

---

01 가주어 it은 to부정사를 받고 있는 것이므로 that을 가주어 it 대신에 쓸 수 없다.

02 자신의 의견을 표현하는 말에는 'That sounds ~.', 'I think (that) ~.' 등이 있다.

03 Is it possible (for 목적격) to 동사원형 ~?: (…가) ~하는 것이 가능할까? text: (휴대전화로) 문자를 보내다 with+명사+p.p: ~가 ~된 채로

04 to부정사가 문장의 주어로 쓰일 때 주어 자리에 가주어 it을 두고 to부정사 부분(진주어)을 문장 뒤로 보낸다. 또한 to부정사가 문장의 주어일 때는 단수로 받는다.

05 지각동사의 목적어가 목적격보어의 행위의 주체가 될 때 목적격보어로 원형부정사나 현재분사를 쓴다. 목적격보어 자리에 원형부정사와 현재분사를 모두 사용할 수 있으나 의미상 그 동작이 진행 중인 것을 나타낼 때에는 주로 현재분사를 사용한다.

06 go into = enter: ~에 들어가다

07 주격 관계대명사 that[which]을 사용하는 것이 적절하다.

08 no longer = not ~ any longer: 더 이상 … 아닌

09 (A) 'do'의 목적어가 와야 하므로 what이 적절하다. (B) '어떻게' 그렇게 할 수 있냐고 해야 하므로 How가 적절하다. (C) 지식과 경험을 '바탕으로'라고 해야 하므로 based가 적절하다. based on: ~에 근거하여

10 어떤 위험 상황을 감지하면 '속도를 늦추거나' 멈춘다고 해야 하므로 'slow down'으로 고쳐야 한다. speed up: 속도를 높이다

11 How+형용사[부사]+(주어+동사)! = What+a/an+형용사+명사+(주어+동사)!

|모범답안|

01 A: Is it possible to fry an egg on the street[road]?

　 B: Yes, I think it's possible. / No, I don't think it's possible.

02 (1) singing　 (2) a girl eating　 (3) a boy looking at

03 (A) AI Cook

　 (B) vegetables and meat

　 (C) a delicious meal

　 (D) vegetables and meat

01 Is it possible (for 목적격) to 동사원형 ~?: (…가) ~하는 것이 가능할까? fry an egg: 계란을 부치다

---

01 getting　　 02 (1) to　 (2) on　 (3) of　　 03 ③

04 Is it possible for you to live without your smartphone?

05 impossible 06 ④　　 07 ①　　 00 ②

09 (A) interesting　 (B) to replace

10 (C) from　 (D) of　　 11 ⑤　　 12 possible

13 (1) It is good for your health to eat a lot of vegetables.

　 (2) It is possible that people may not want to talk to each other anymore.

14 ④　　　 15 ⑤

16 (1) Mina smelled onions frying.

　 (2) We heard them whispering[whisper] to each other.

　 (3) It is interesting to find and create new things.

　 (4) It is easy for you to send e-mails.

17 ③　　　 18 ③　　　 19 The screen suggests clothes that suit the weather.　　 20 ④

21 like　　 22 that → those　　 23 ②, ③

24 I can predict danger based on knowledge and experience.　 25 ⑤

---

01 get 비교급: 점점 더 ~해지다 / 이야기는 점점 더 재미있게 된다 get in: ~에 타다 / 그는 택시 앞좌석에 타고 있다.

02 (1) face to face: (~와) 서로 얼굴을 맞대고 / 그들은 마주보고 앉아 서로를 바라보고 있다. (2) move on: ~로 이동하다 / 자, 이제 다음 이야기입니다 (3) out of: (원천·출처) ~에서, ~으로부터 / 그들은 옥수수와 콩 같은 식물 재료를 사용하여 플라스틱 제품을 만든다.

03 off: 할인되어 / 개장일에 가구를 구입하시면 25퍼센트 할인해 드립니다.

04 Is it possible (for 목적격) to 동사원형 ~?: (…가) ~하는 것이 가능할까? without: ~ 없이

05 impossible: 불가능한

06 ⓓ는 가주어이며, 나머지는 this computer를 받는 대명사이다.

07 so: 그럼, 그러면

08 ② 현금으로 낼지 카드로 낼지에 대해서는 언급되지 않았다. ① 여자가 가진 쿠폰을 사용할 수 있는가? 사용할 수 있다. ③ 그들은 어디에 있는가? 컴퓨터 가게 ④ 그녀는 얼마나 할인을 받았는가? 30달러 ⑤ 여자는 무엇을 사기를 원하는가? 컴퓨터

09 (A) interesting: 재미있는, 흥미로운 (B) Is it possible for 목적격 to 동사원형 ~?: …가 ~하는 것이 가능할까? replace: 대체하다

10 (C) free from: ~이 없는 (D) because of 명사: ~ 때문에

11 ⓔ dark → bright 로봇이 위험한 일을 할 수 있어서 사람들이 위험이 없어진다는 내용은 좋은 면을 보고 있는 것이다.

12 possible: 가능한 / 일어나거나 발생할 수 있는

13 (1) 문장의 주어로 쓰인 to부정사를 뒤로 보내고 대신 주어 자

31

리에 가주어 it을 쓴다. (2) 주어로 쓰인 that절의 경우에도 긴 that절을 뒤로 보내고 주어 자리에 가주어 it을 쓴다.

14 지각동사의 목적어와 목적격보어가 능동의 관계에 있을 경우 목적격보어로 원형부정사나 현재분사를 쓴다.

15 to부정사의 의미상 주어로 사람의 성질을 나타내는 형용사가 쓰였으므로 'of+목적격'이 적절하다. It is very kind of you to help us.

16 (1) smell은 목적격보어로 현재분사를 쓴다. (2) 지각동사의 목적어와 목적격보어가 능동의 관계에 있을 경우 목적격보어로 원형부정사나 현재분사를 쓴다. 의미상 그 동작이 진행 중인 것을 나타낼 때에는 주로 현재분사를 사용한다. (3), (4) it을 가주어로 하고 to부정사를 진주어로 쓰는 것이 적절하다. to부정사의 의미상 주어로 사람의 성질을 나타내는 형용사가 쓰인 것이 아니므로 'for+목적격'이 적절하다.

17 ⓑ We heard Yena play(playing) the violin. ⓓ Jeniffer felt him come(coming) closer. ⓖ Is it safe to swim in this river?

18 ⓐ와 ②, ⑤번: 관계대명사, ①, ③, ④: 접속사

19 앞 문장의 내용을 가리킨다.

20 (That's) right.: 그렇습니다, ④ 괜찮아요. ① You got it. 맞습니다. ② You can say that again. 정말 그렇다[(당신 말에) 전적으로 동의한다]. ③ I agree with you. 당신 의견에 동의해요. ⑤ You said it. 맞습니다.

21 (A) like: 좋아하다(동사), (B) like ~처럼(접속사)

22 뒤에 복수명사(smart windows)가 나오기 때문에, 지시형용사도 복수형으로 고치는 것이 적절하다.

23 ⓐ와 ②, ③: 형용사적 용법, ①, ④: 명사적 용법, ⑤ 부사적 용법

24 'on'을 보충하면 된다.

25 인공 지능 자동차는 '자신의' 지식과 경험을 바탕으로 위험을 예측할 수 있다.

교과서 파헤치기

단어 TEST Step 1　　　　　　　　　　p.02

01 대회　　　　02 맞다　　　　03 감추다, 숨기다
04 찢어지는 듯한[날카로운] 소리　　05 규칙
06 놓치다, 그리워하다　　　　　07 홈팀
08 불안한　　　　09 반바지　　　10 결정하다
11 투구　　　　12 언젠가　　　13 먼지, 때
14 (부정문에서) ~도　15 경기장　16 (야구의) 루, 베이스
17 타자　　　　18 국제적인　　19 결정하다
20 잊다　　　　21 애완동물　　22 원정 팀
23 (good의 비교급) 더 좋은, 더 나은　24 티켓
25 경기, 성냥　　26 순서, 명령　27 그 뒤에, 그런 다음
28 휴가　　　　29 의미하다　　30 천둥
31 과거　　　　32 암벽 등반
33 (특정 스포츠 팀을) 응원하다, 지원하다　34 ~을 몹시 기대하다
35 A와 B 사이에　36 ~을 기다리다　37 ~의 열렬한 팬이다
38 서둘러 ~하다　39 ~을 기대하다　40 일주일에 두 번
41 ~에 신나다, ~에 들뜨다　　42 ~로 돌아오다
43 서둘러

단어 TEST Step 2　　　　　　　　　　p.03

01 hide　　　　02 either　　　03 ticket
04 vacation　　05 stadium　　06 base
07 rule　　　　08 visit　　　09 batter
10 match　　　11 order
12 determine, decide　　　13 pitch
14 rock climbing　15 mean　　16 thunder
17 crack　　　18 anxious　　19 competition
20 fit　　　　21 pet　　　　22 visiting team
23 shorts　　24 past　　　25 forget
26 international　27 miss　　28 sometime
29 dirt　　　30 get　　　31 better
32 support　　33 then
34 be about to 동사원형
35 between A and B　　　36 hurry up
37 be a big fan of 38 can't wait to 동사원형
39 twice a week　40 in a hurry　41 be excited about
42 look forward to (동)명사　　43 wait for

단어 TEST Step 3　　　　　　　　　　p.04

1 hide, 감추다, 숨기다　2 anxious, 불안한　3 fit, 맞다
4 home team, 홈팀　5 past, 과거　6 pitch, 투구

---

7 international, 국제적인　8 base, (야구의) 루, 베이스
9 determine, 결정하다　10 visiting team, 원정 팀
11 competition, 대회　12 order, 순서　13 thunder, 천둥
14 either, (부정문에서) ~도　15 crack, 찢어지는 듯한[날카로운] 소리　16 stadium, 경기장

대화문 TEST Step 1　　　　　　　　p.05~06

Listen & Speak 1 A
Which sport, or / more, twice a week

Listen & Speak 1 B
1 are, doing / I'm looking at / checked, Which country, to visit, or / to visit, like to
2 I'm thinking, getting, have / What do, think, Which, better for, or / Why don't you come to, play with, can decide

Listen & Speak 2 A
Did / can't wait to watch

Listen & Speak 2 B
1 want to see / When did / bought it for me, come to my house / course, can't wait to see
2 Don't forget that, rock climbing / worry, won't forget / excited about, I can't wait
3 hear about / about, lives in / came back, wants to see / can't wait to see

Real-Life Zone A
such a worry / have to, before, between, and, starts / Which team, support, or / to miss, either / Hurry up, left / Maybe, sometime / about going to, home game together / can eat fried chicken while watching, sounds, I can't wait

Wrap Up
which sport do you like, or / How about / big fan of / soccer match, between, Have, heard about / already have, I'm going to see, can't wait / fantastic

대화문 TEST Step 2　　　　　　　　p.07~08

Listen & Speak 1 A
M: Which sport do you like? Soccer or basketball?
G: I like soccer more. I play soccer twice a week.

Listen & Speak 1 B
1 G: What are you doing?
　B: I'm looking at a world map.
　G: You checked two countries. Which country would you like to visit first? The U.S. or Mexico?
　B: I want to visit the U.S. I'd like to see a basketball

33

game there.

2 G: I'm thinking about getting a pet. Do you have a pet?

B: Yes, I do. I have a dog and a cat.

G: What do you think? Which pet is better for me? A cat or a dog?

B: Why don't you come to my house someday and play with my pets? Then you can decide.

Listen & Speak 2 A

G: Did you get the tickets?

B: Yes! I can't wait to watch the game.

Listen & Speak 2 B

1 G: Do you want to see my new mountain bike?

B: Sure. When did you get it?

G: Yesterday my father bought it for me. Can you come to my house this afternoon?

B: Of course. I can't wait to see it.

2 B: Don't forget that we're going rock climbing this weekend!

G: Don't worry. I won't forget.

B: I'm excited about going. I can't wait.

3 G: Did you hear about Jisu?

B: What about her? She lives in Canada.

G: She came back to Korea last month. She wants to see you.

B: Oh, I can't wait to see her.

Real-Life Zone A

B1: Jiho, why are you in such a hurry?

B2: Hi, Alex! I have to be home before 6:00. The game between the Thunders and the Cobras starts at 6:00.

B1: Oh, are you a baseball fan? Which team do you support? The Cobras or the Thunders?

B2: The Cobras.

B1: Me, too! I don't want to miss the game either.

B2: Hurry up! We only have thirty minutes left.

B1: Okay. Maybe we can watch a game together sometime.

B2: That's a great idea! How about going to the next Cobras home game together?

B1: Okay. They have a game next Saturday. We can eat fried chicken while watching the game!

B2: That sounds great. I can't wait!

Wrap Up

B: Jimin, which sport do you like? Soccer or table tennis?

G: I love table tennis. How about you, Yunho?

B: I like soccer. I'm a big fan of James Hood. He's a

great soccer player.

G: Oh, really? There's a soccer match this weekend between Korea and Turkey. Have you heard about it?

B: Of course. I already have a ticket. I'm going to see the game on Saturday. I can't wait.

G: That's fantastic.

본문 TEST Step 1   p.09~10

01 Day, Baseball Stadium

02 and, have, game   03 is at, stadium

04 your first, isn't it

05 excited, can't wait for   06 are coming out

07 Which team   08 Over, behind third

09 wearing, because, visiting

10 always wear, dark   11 that, rule

12 Home, bright, visiting, dark   13 Why, that

14 There, interesting, about

15 past, wash, every

16 wearing, hide, dirt   17 was, good idea

18 warming up   19 your favorite   20 Number 77

21 What does, mean

22 choose, they like   23 know what

24 determined by, batting order   25 there, no, with

26 is about to   27 looks anxious

28 favorite, at bat

29 has hit, runs already

30 hits, more, be, season

31 batter misses several   32 has, full count

33 waiting for, pitch   34 RUN, HOME

35 Crack, flies fast   36 is going, gone

본문 TEST Step 2   p.11~12

01 A Day, Baseball Stadium

02 have a game   03 is at, baseball stadium

04 your first time, isn't it

05 excited, can't wait for, to start   06 are coming out

07 Which team   08 Over there, behind third base

09 are wearing, because, visiting team

10 visiting team, wear a dark color 11 rule

12 have bright uniforms, dark uniforms

13 Why   14 There, an interesting story

15 In the past, wash their uniforms after every game

16 started wearing, to hide the dirt

17 a good idea

18 are warming up

19 your favorite player　　　20 Number

21 What does, number mean

22 choose, they like　　　23 You know what

24 were determined by the players' batting order

25 there were no, with　　　26 is about to

27 looks anxious 28 Your favorite, at bat

29 has hit　　　30 hits one more, this season

31 misses several balls

32 has a full count

33 waiting for, next pitch　　　34 HOME RUN

35 Crack, flies fast　　　36 is going, gone

1 야구 경기장에서의 하루

2 오늘 천둥 대 코브라 게임이 있다.

3 지훈이네 가족은 야구 경기장에 있다.

4 지훈: 지안아, 네가 야구 경기장에 온 건 이번이 처음이야, 그렇지 않니?

5 지안: 응, 나 아주 흥분돼. 나는 경기가 빨리 시작했으면 좋겠어.

6 아빠: 봐, 선수들이 지금 나오고 있어!

7 지안: 어떤 팀이 천둥이야?

8 지훈: 저기, 3루 뒤

9 그들은 원정 팀이기 때문에 어두운 회색 유니폼을 입고 있어.

10 지안: 원정 팀은 항상 어두운 색을 입어?

11 지훈: 응, 그게 규칙이야.

12 홈팀은 밝은 유니폼을 입고 원정팀은 어두운 유니폼을 입어.

13 지안: 왜?

14 엄마: 그것에 대한 흥미로운 이야기가 있단다.

15 과거에는 원정 팀이 매 경기 후 유니폼을 세탁할 수가 없었어.

16 그래서 그들은 때를 숨기기 위해 어두운 색을 입기 시작했지.

17 지안: 하하하! 좋은 생각이었네요!

18 선수들이 몸을 풀고 있다.

19 지안: 가장 좋아하는 선수가 누구야?

20 지훈: 77번.

21 지안: 그 숫자는 무엇을 의미해?

22 지훈: 음... 선수들이 원하는 번호를 선택해.

23 아빠: 그거 알아?

24 과거에는 번호가 선수들의 타순에 의해 결정되었단다.

25 지훈: 77번 선수가 없었다는 뜻이네요!

26 이제 지훈이의 가장 좋아하는 선수가 막 공을 치려고 한다.

27 지훈이는 불안해 보인다.

28 지안: 오빠가 가장 좋아하는 선수가 타석에 서네.

29 지훈: 응. 그는 올해 이미 21개의 홈런을 쳤어.

30 그가 오늘 하나를 더 치면, 그는 이번 시즌 홈런 리더가 될 거야.

31 타자는 여러 개의 공을 놓친다.

32 이제 그는 풀카운트가 되었다.

33 그는 다음 투구를 기다리고 있다.

34 지훈: 홈런! 홈런!

35 땅! 공은 빠르게 날아간다.

36 그것은 가고, 가고, 가고, 사라져 버렸다!

1 A Day at the Baseball Stadium

2 Today the Thunders and the Cobras have a game.

3 Jihun's family is at the baseball stadium.

4 Jihun: Jian, this is your first time to come to the baseball stadium, isn't it?

5 Jian: Yes, I'm so excited. I can't wait for the game to start.

6 Dad: Look, the players are coming out now!

7 Jian: Which team is the Thunders?

8 Jihun: Over there, behind third base.

9 They are wearing dark gray uniforms because they are the visiting team.

10 Jian: Does the visiting team always wear a dark color?

11 Jihun: Yes, that's the rule.

12 Home teams have bright uniforms and visiting teams have dark uniforms.

13 Jian: Why is that?

14 Mom: There is an interesting story about that.

15 In the past, visiting teams could not wash their uniforms after every game.

16 So they started wearing dark colors to hide the dirt.

17 Jian: Hahaha! That was a good idea!

18 The players are warming up.

19 Jian: Who's your favorite player?

20 Jihun: Number 77.

21 Jian: What does the number mean?

22 Jihun: Hmm.... Players choose a number they like.

23 Dad: You know what?

24 In the past, the numbers were determined by the players' batting order.

25 Jihun: That means there were no players with number 77!

26 Now, Jihun's favorite player is about to bat.

27 Jihun looks anxious.

28 Jian: Your favorite player is at bat.

29 Jihun: Yes. He has hit 21 home runs already this year.

30 If he hits one more today, he will be the home run leader this season.

31 The batter misses several balls.

32 Now he has a full count.

33 He is waiting for the next pitch.

34 Jihun: HOME RUN! HOME RUN!

35 Crack! The ball flies fast.

36 It is going, going, going, gone!

구석구석지문 TEST Step 1   p.19

Real-Life Zone B

1. Which sport, like, or

2. going to, with, this weekend, can't wait

Writing Workshop

1. Marathon Runner

2. Born, August

3. Nationality

4. was known as, international sports competitions

5. preparing to run, found out, did not fit, decided to run, without shoes

6. felt pain during, as the winner

7. one of, wasn't he

Wrap Up

1. Middle School Sports Day

2. will be held, on Wednesday, June

3. will be various, such as

4. wil also, table tennis

5. sounds like, doesn't it

구석구석지문 TEST Step 2   p.20

Real-Life Zone B

1. A: Which sport do you like? Basketball or soccer?

2. B: I like basketball. I'm going to play it with my friends this weekend. I can't wait.

Writing Workshop

1. Abebe Bikila Marathon Runner

2. Born : August 7, 1932

3. Nationality: Ethiopia

4. Speciality: He was known as a marathon winner at the Rome and Tokyo international sports competitions.

5. When he was preparing to run the marathon in Rome, he found out that his shoes did not fit well, so he decided to run the race without shoes .

6. He felt pain during the race, but he finished the race as the winner.

7. He was one of the greatest runners in the world, wasn't he?

Wrap Up

1. Sarang Middle School Sports Day

2. Sarang Middle School Sports Day will be held on the school playing field on Wednesday, June 15.

3. There will be various games such as baseball and soccer.

4. There wil also be table tennis.

5. It sounds like fun, doesn't it?

단어 TEST Step 1 · p.21

01 해외에	02 낙타	03 쾌활한, 유쾌한
04 시작, 처음	05 화려한, (색이) 다채로운	
06 밝은	07 달콤한, 단	08 ~할 만큼 (충분히)
09 경관, 전망	10 비행	11 수도
12 손님	13 현대의	14 양고기
15 해안선	16 겁먹은, 무서워하는	
17 언어	18 아주 멋진, 마법의, 마술의	
19 잠이 든	20 기대하다, 예상하다	
21 전체, 모든	22 순간	23 굉장한, 놀라운
24 문화	25 가슴 뭉클한	26 맛있는
27 ~하자마자	28 결혼(식)	
29 (해가) 뜨다, 일어나다		30 아늑한
31 제공하다	32 상상하다	33 기회
34 전통적인	35 ~로 가득하다	36 ~에 익숙해지다
37 ~로 만들어지다	38 …에게 ~을 둘러보도록 안내하다	
39 ~으로 요리되다	40 ~에 가 본 적 있니?	
41 빨리 ~하면 좋겠다		42 ~인 것처럼 느끼다
43 잠에서 깨다		

단어 TEST Step 2 · p.22

01 chance	02 colorful	03 moment
04 cozy	05 asleep	06 enough
07 camel	08 flight	09 guest
10 imagine	11 beginning	12 serve
13 kid	14 abroad	15 view
16 lamb	17 tasty	18 bright
19 magical	20 cheerful	21 wedding
22 modern	23 amazing	24 capital
25 once	26 culture	27 part
28 coastline	29 rise	30 scared
31 moved	32 traditional	33 expect
34 whole	35 wake up	36 from A to B
37 feel like+주어+동사		38 get used to
39 can't wait to	40 at first	41 be full of
42 be made of	43 Have you been (to) ~?	

단어 TEST Step 3 · p.23

1 bright, 밝은　2 asleep, 잠이 든　3 kid, 농담하다
4 cheerful, 쾌활한, 유쾌한　5 rise, (해가) 뜨다
6 chance, 기회　7 abroad, 해외에　8 magical, 마법의

9 guest, 손님　10 modern, 현대의
11 Mongolian, 몽골의　12 expect, 기대하다, 예상하다
13 view, 경관, 전망　14 airport, 공항　15 part, 부분, 일부
16 station, 역, 정거장

대화문 TEST Step 1 · p.24~25

Listen & Speak 1 A
Have you ever tried / have, tasty

Listen & Speak 1 B
1 look excited, up / going to, with, Have, ever been / coastline, How about / can't wait for
2 Have, ever, rise over / How about / watched, rise, on / tried several times, wake up early

Listen & Speak 1 C
1 Have you ever, another country / have, experience
2 Have you ever ridden / wonderful experience

Listen & Speak 2 A
How do you like / bigger room

Listen & Speak 2 B
1 How, vacation / went to, with / How did, like / amazing, to visit
2 Have you been to / had dinner / How did you like / won't go back

Listen & Speak 2 C
1 How, like / colorful
2 How do you like / sweet

Real-Life Zone A
Have you ever traveled abroad / went, last summer / How did, like / hot, enjoyed / interesting experiences, had during / let, think, fried / How, like them / so, scared at first / imagine eating spiders

Communication Task
Have you ever eaten / tasty, haven't, try someday

대화문 TEST Step 2 · p.26~27

Listen & Speak 1 A
B: Have you ever tried Spanish food?
G: Yes, I have. It's really tasty.

Listen & Speak 1 B
1 G: You look excited, Inho. What's up?
B: I'm going to Jejudo with my family this weekend. Have you ever been there?
G: Yes, many times. I love the coastline. How about you?
B: It'll be my first visit to Jejudo. I can't wait for this weekend!

2 B: Have you ever watched the sun rise over the ocean?

G: No. How about you?

B: I watched the sun rise in Gangneung on New Year's Day. It was great.

G: I tried several times, but I just couldn't wake up early enough.

Listen & Speak 1 C

1 A: Have you ever traveled to another country?

B: Yes, I have. It was a wonderful experience.

2 A: Have you ever ridden a horse?

B: Yes, I have. It was a wonderful experience.

Listen & Speak 2 A

G: How do you like your new house?

B: It's great. I have a bigger room now.

Listen & Speak 2 B

1 G: How was your vacation?

B: Great. I went to Dokdo with my family.

G: How did you like it?

B: It was amazing. I want to visit there again.

2 B: Have you been to the new Chinese restaurant?

G: Yes. I had dinner there last Saturday.

B: How did you like it?

G: The service was bad. I won't go back there again.

Listen & Speak 2 C

1 A: How do you like this shirt?

B: It's colorful. I like it.

2 A: How do you like your ice cream?

B: It's sweet. I like it.

Real-Life Zone A

B: Have you ever traveled abroad, Sujin?

G: Yes, I went to Cambodia last summer.

B: Wow. How did you like it?

G: It was really hot, but I enjoyed the trip.

B: Tell me some interesting experiences you had during the trip.

G: Hmm... let me think. I ate fried spiders!

B: What? You're kidding. How did you like them?

G: They were really big, so I was a little scared at first. But the taste was okay.

B: Really? I cannot imagine eating spiders.

Communication Task

A: Have you ever eaten tacos?

B: Yes, I have. They were tasty. / No, I haven't. I want to try some someday.

01 Trip, Mongolia

02 special, because, for, time

03 My, is from   04 invited, to, capital

05 After, flight, arrived at   06 took, by, from, to

07 Her, traditional Mongolian

08 tent, cozy inside

09 entered, smelled wonderful

10 from, that, cooking for   11 Mongolian barbecue

12 made of, cooked with

13 moved, serve, to, guests

14 so, that, for   15 After, went outside

16 was full of   17 felt like, magical

18 During, showed, around, experience

19 moment, exciting, most, rode

20 At, scared, than, expected

21 once, back, used to

22 From, back, view, amazing

23 visit, special, in, ways

24 gave, chance, get, culture

25 visit, again someday

01 Trip to Mongolia

02 This year, special summer, for the first time

03 is from Mongolia   04 invited, to, the capital

05 After a four-hour flight, arrived at

06 It took, by taxi from, to

07 traditional Mongolian house

08 big tent, cozy inside

09 When, entered, smelled wonderful

10 from, cooking for   11 Mongolian barbecue

12 is made of, cooked with

13 was moved, serve, to special guests

14 so, that, asked for   15 went outside to see

16 was full of bright

17 felt like, magical place

18 During, showed me around, helped me experience

19 Every moment, had the most fun, rode

20 At first, scared, taller than, expected

21 once, sat on, got used to

22 the view of the desert, truly amazing

23 in many ways

24 to get to know, country, culture

25 visit, again someday

1 몽골 여행

2 나는 올해 몽골을 처음으로 방문해서 특별한 여름을 보냈다.

3 내 친구 일탕은 몽골 출신이다.

4 그의 할머니께서는 몽골의 수도인 울란바토르에 나를 초대하셨다.

5 서울에서 네 시간 비행 후 알탕과 나는 울란바토르의 칭기즈 칸 국제공항에 도착했다.

6 공항에서 알탕의 할머니 댁까지 택시로 30분이 걸렸다.

7 할머니의 집은 몽골 전통 가옥인 게르이다.

8 큰 텐트이지만 내부는 아늑하다.

9 우리가 들어갔을 때, 뭔가 좋은 냄새가 났다.

10 그녀가 우리를 위해 요리하고 있던 호르호그에서 나는 냄새였다.

11 호르호그는 몽골식 바비큐이다.

12 그것은 양고기로 만들어졌으며 뜨거운 돌로 요리되었다.

13 나는 알탕이 몽골인들은 특별한 손님에게 호르호그를 대접한다고 말했을 때 감동을 받았다.

14 그것은 너무 맛있어서 나는 더 달라고 했다.

15 저녁 식사 후, 알탕과 나는 밤하늘을 보기 위해 밖으로 나갔다.

16 하늘은 밝은 별들로 가득했다.

17 나는 신비한 장소에 있는 것처럼 느꼈다.

18 그 후 3일 동안, 알탕은 나를 구경시켜 주었고 몽골 문화를 경험할 수 있게 도와주었다.

19 매 순간이 재미있고 흥미진진했지만, 고비 사막에서 낙타를 탈 때가 가장 재미있었다.

20 처음에는 내가 예상했던 것보다 낙타의 키가 커서 무서웠다.

21 그러나 낙타 등에 앉자 곧 움직임에 익숙해졌다.

22 낙타의 등에서 보는 사막의 경치는 정말로 놀라웠다.

23 내가 몽골을 방문한 것은 여러 면에서 특별한 경험이었다.

24 내 친구의 나라와 문화를 알 수 있는 좋은 기회가 되었다.

25 나는 언젠가 몽골을 다시 방문하고 싶다!

1 A Trip to Mongolia

2 This year, I had a special summer because I visited Mongolia for the first time.

3 My friend Altan is from Mongolia.

4 His grandmother invited me to Ulaanbaatar, the capital of Mongolia.

5 After a four-hour flight from Seoul, Altan and I arrived at Chinggis Khaan International Airport in Ulaanbaatar.

6 It took thirty minutes by taxi from the airport to Altan's grandmother's house.

7 Her house is a *ger*, a traditional Mongolian house.

8 It is a big tent, but it is cozy inside.

9 When we entered, something smelled wonderful.

10 It was from the *khorkhog* that she was cooking for us

11 *Khorkhog* is a Mongolian barbecue.

12 It is made of lamb and cooked with hot stones.

13 I was moved when Altan said Mongolians serve *khorkhog* to special guests.

14 It was so delicious that I asked for more.

15 After dinner, Altan and I went outside to see the night sky.

16 The sky was full of bright stars.

17 I felt like I was in a magical place.

18 During the next three days, Altan showed me around and helped me experience Mongolian culture.

19 Every moment was fun and exciting, but I had the most fun when I rode a camel in the Gobi Desert.

20 At first, I was scared because the camel was taller than I expected.

21 But once I sat on its back, I soon got used to its movement.

22 From the camel's back, the view of the desert was truly amazing.

23 My visit to Mongolia was a special experience in many ways.

24 It gave me a great chance to get to know my friend's country and culture.

25 I want to visit Mongolia again someday!

Writing Workshop - Step 2

1. Trip to

2. took a trip, last summer

3. visited

4. so, that we could not see

5. After three hours' walking

6. For dinner, that my parents like

7. is famous for

8. so, that, would never forget

Wrap Up 1-2

1. How was, weekend

2. went to, with my parents

3. What food, try

4. traditional Chinese dessert

5. How did

6. made with, usually serve, at a wedding

Wrap Up 7

1. How was, that, around the corner

2. so crowded that, wait for, to get in

3. tasted so good that I ate

4. so noisy that I couldn't

구석구석지문 TEST Step 2   p.39

Writing Workshop - Step 2

1. A Trip to Suncheon

2. My family took a trip to Suncheon last summer.

3. We visited the National Garden.

4. It was so large that we could not see the whole garden.

5. After three hours' walking, we were really hungry.

6. For dinner, we had Gukbap that my parents like.

7. Suncheon is famous for Gukbap and we enjoyed it.

8. This trip was so good that I would never forget it for a long time.

Wrap Up 1-2

1. G: How was your weekend, Tony?

2. B: It was great. I went to the International Food Festival with my parents.

3. G: What food did you try?

4. B: I had a traditional Chinese dessert, *tangyuan*.

5. G: How did you like it?

6. B: I enjoyed it. It's made with sweet rice balls. Chinese people usually serve it to guests at a wedding.

Wrap Up 7

1. How was the restaurant that just opened around the corner?

2. The restaurant was so crowded that I had to wait for an hour to get in.

3. The cheese cake tasted so good that I ate all of it.

4. The restaurant was so noisy that I couldn't talk with my friends.

단어 TEST Step 1   p.40

01 선택하다	02 똑똑한	03 순간 이동하다
04 불타다	05 번역하다	06 동영상의, 생기 있는
07 쉽게	08 감지하다	09 얼리다
10 불가능한	11 즐거움, 오락	12 예측하다
13 ~ 없이	14 기계	15 가능한
16 건너다	17 위험	18 의미하다
19 할인되어	20 완벽한	21 ~을 통해, ~ 사이로
22 이상한	23 대체하다	24 이기다
25 확인하다, 점검하다		26 상황
27 옷장	28 공간	29 기회
30 사전	31 번역가	32 믿기 어려운, 놀랄 만한
33 행운의	34 구름의, 흐린	35 단지 ~뿐이 아니다
36 ~할 필요가 없다	37 위험에 처한, 위험에 빠진	
38 더 이상 ~하지 않다	39 ~에 근거하여	40 ~의 염려가 없는
41 그런데, 그건 그렇고	42 ~할 수 있다	43 속도를 늦추다

단어 TEST Step 2   p.41

01 animated	02 chance	03 cloudy
04 possible	05 lucky	06 translator
07 machine	08 cross	09 danger
10 amusement	11 easily	12 select
13 text	14 sense	15 mean
16 freeze	17 without	18 predict
19 impossible	20 teleport	21 burn
22 translate	23 dictionary	24 off
25 closet	26 perfect	27 replace
28 intelligent	29 through	30 situation
31 strange	32 unbelievable	33 check
34 space	35 by the way	36 in danger
37 no longer	38 be able to 동사원형	
39 based on	40 slow down	41 watch out
42 free from	43 look ~ up	

단어 TEST Step 3   p.42

1 replace, 대체하다   2 beat, 이기다

3 perfect, 완벽한   4 burn, 불타다   5 possible, 가능한

6 sense, 감지하다   7 translate, 번역하다

8 cross, 건너다   9 lucky, 행운의   10 predict, 예측하다

11 select, 선택하다   12 closet, 옷장

13 cloudy, 구름의, 흐린   14 amusement, 즐거움, 오락

15 beatbox, 비트박스를 하다   16 dictionary, 사전

대화문 TEST Step 1   p.43~44

Listen & Speak 1 A

Why don't we try, prefer

Listen & Speak 1 B

1 have any, for, project / What about / thinking, talk about future, What, think / sounds perfect, Let's look for, on the Internet

2 begins, Why don't, with / to, sounds exciting / chance to meet robotics / great

Listen & Speak 1 C

1 going to fly, drone / like fun

2 going, build / sounds like fun

Listen & Speak 2 A

it possible, to live without / not possible

Listen & Speak 2 B

1 looks, How much, it / the newest / Is it possible to use / Let, check, get, off / Perfect, take

2 took, pictures during / did, more than / it possible to make, animated, out of / possible, have an app

Listen & Speak 2 C

1 Is it possible, to text with, closed / Sure, can do

2 possible for you, travel around, by / Sure, can do that

Real-Life Zone A

Look at / What, they mean, Let's look them up, dictionary / about using, translator / How, use / point, ask, to translate, get an answer / possible for AI to read / read, translate / sounds unvelievable, what, mean / mean, come true / amazing

---

대화문 TEST Step 2   p.45~46

Listen & Speak 1 A

B: Why don't we try a new VR game?

G: That sounds interesting.

Listen & Speak 1 B

1 B: Do you have any ideas for our group project?

G: No. What about you?

B: I'm thinking we should talk about future jobs. What do you think?

G: That sounds perfect for our project. Let's look for some information on the Internet.

---

2 G: The Robot Expo begins next week. Why don't you go with me?

B: Yes, I'd love to. That sounds exciting.

G: We'll have a chance to meet robotics engineers.

B: That'll be great.

Listen & Speak 1 C

1 A: I'm going to fly a drone.

B: That sounds like fun.

2 A: I'm going to build a model car.

B: That sounds like fun.

Listen & Speak 2 A

G: Is it possible for you to live without your smartphone?

B: No, it's not possible.

Listen & Speak 2 B

1 G: This computer looks nice. How much is it?

M: It's 500 dollars. It's the newest one.

G: Is it possible to use this coupon?

M: Let me check. Yes, you can. So, you'll get 30 dollars off.

G: Perfect. I'll take it.

2 B: We took lots of pictures during our trip.

G: We sure did. We have more than 500 pictures.

B: Is it possible to make an animated photo album out of them?

G: Yes, it's possible. I have an app for that.

Listen & Speak 2 C

1 A: Is it possible for you to text with your eyes closed?

B: Sure. I can do that.

2 A: Is it possible for you to travel around Gangwondo by bicycle?

B: Sure. I can do that.

Real-Life Zone A

G: Look at those words on the board.

B: What do they mean? Let's look them up in the dictionary.

G: What about using the AI translator?

B: How do I use it?

G: You point your smartphone camera at the words and ask AI to translate. You will get an answer.

B: Is it possible for AI to read those words?

Speaker: Sure. I can read any language and translate it.

B: Wow, that sounds unbelievable. So, AI, what do those words mean?

Speaker: They mean "Dreams come true!"

B: That's amazing.

01 Day at, AI   02 at, World, Expo

03 entering, AI home   04 Look at, future

05 go into, there's, closet

06 front, closet, keep changing

07 suggests, suit, weather

08 no longer, worry, dressing

09 move on to   10 this music speaker

11 not just, speaker

12 more than, imagine

13 hard, believe, understand

14 How about watching   15 play one

16 smart, getting darker

17 feel like, theater   18 What else, do

19 beatbox, too, Here comes

20 funny, Good job

21 Hurry, There's, outside   22 Let's, ride in

23 so cool, get in   24 ready to go

25 what should, do   26 time, ride in

27 need to, anything   28 drive, take, to

29 out, see, crossing

30 worry, have, sensed

31 sense dangerous, slow down   32 How can, that

33 intelligent robotic

34 all about driving

35 predict, based on, experience   36 How, act like

37 are, like, human

22 Let's go, ride in   23 so cool, get in

24 Are, ready to go   25 what should, do

26 my first time to ride   27 don't need to

28 take you to   29 Watch out, crossing

30 Don't, have just sensed

31 sense dangerous situations, down

32 How can, do   33 intelligent robotic

34 all about driving   35 based on

36 How, like   37 like, human

1 인공 지능 박람회에서의 하루

2 진아와 수한이가 세계 인공 지능 박람회에 있다.

3 그들은 인공 지능 집으로 들어가고 있다.

4 수한: 이것 봐! 미래의 집이야.

5 진아: 침실 먼저 들어가 보자. 이거 봐, 스마트 옷장이 있어.

6 수한: 옷장 문에 있는 스크린 앞에 서 있으니까 내 옷이 계속해서 바뀌어.

7 진아: 스크린이 날씨에 적합한 옷을 제안하는 거야.

8 수한: 놀라워! 우린 더 이상 날씨 때문에 무슨 옷을 입을지 걱정할 필요가 없겠다.

9 진아: 맞아. 이제 거실로 가 보자.

10 수한: 오, 이 음악 스피커 마음에 들어.

11 인공 지능 스피커: 저는 그냥 음악 스피커가 아니에요.

12 저는 당신이 상상하는 것 이상의 것을 할 수 있어요.

13 진아: 네가 우리를 이해한다니 믿기 어려운 걸! 넌 뭘 할 수 있어?

14 인공 지능 스피커: 영화 보는 건 어때요?

15 하나 틀어 줄게요.

16 수한: 이것 봐, 스마트 창문이 점점 어두워지고 있어.

17 마치 내가 영화관 안에 있는 것 같아.

18 진아: 또 뭘 할 수 있어?

19 인공 지능 스피커: 비트박스도 할 수 있어요. "북치기 박치기 북치기 박치기."

20 수한: 넌 정말 재미있구나. 잘했어!

21 진아: 서둘러! 밖에 스마트 자동차 정류장이 있어.

22 가서 저 빨간 차를 타 보자.

23 수한: 이 차 정말 멋지다. 차에 타자.

24 인공 지능 자동차: 어서 오세요. 갈 준비 됐나요?

25 진아: 응, 우린 이제 뭘 해야 하지?

26 스마트 자동차에 타는 건 처음이야.

27 인공 지능 자동차: 아무 것도 하지 않아도 돼요.

28 제가 운전해서 다음 정류장까지 데려다줄 거니까요.

29 수한: 조심해! 고양이가 길을 건너고 있는 게 보여.

30 인공 지능 자동차: 걱정 말아요. 이미 감지했어요.

31 저는 어떤 위험 상황을 감지하면 속도를 늦추거나 멈춰요.

01 at, AI Expo   02 at the World AI Expo

03 are entering, AI home   04 on the future

05 go into, smart closet

06 front, on the closet door, keep changing

07 suggests, that suit the weather

08 no longer, dressing for the weather

09 Let's move on to

10 this music speaker

11 I'm not just

12 more than, can imagine

13 It's hard to believe, can understand

14 How about watching   15 play one for

16 getting darker

17 feel like, movie theater   18 What else

19 can, too, Here comes

20 funny, Good job

21 Hurry, There's, outside

32 진아: 어떻게 그렇게 할 수 있어?

33 인공 지능 자동차: 전 아주 지능적인 로봇 차예요.

34 저는 운전에 대한 모든 걸 알고 있어요.

35 저는 제 지식과 경험을 바탕으로 위험을 예측할 수 있어요

36 수한: 정말 똑똑하구나! 사람처럼 생각하고 행동하는구나.

37 정말 인간 같아.

1 A Day at the AI Expo

2 Jina and Suhan are at the World AI Expo.

3 They are entering the AI home.

4 Suhan: Look at this! It's a house of the future.

5 Jina: Let's go into the bedroom first. Look, there's a smart closet.

6 Suhan: I'm standing in front of this screen on the closet door and my clothes keep changing.

7 Jina: The screen suggests clothes that suit the weather.

8 Suhan: That's amazing! We no longer have to worry about dressing for the weather.

9 Jina: Right. Let's move on to the living room.

10 Suhan: Oh, I like this music speaker.

11 AI Speaker: I'm not just a music speaker.

12 I can do more than you can imagine.

13 Jina: It's hard to believe that you can understand us. What can you do?

14 AI Speaker: How about watching a movie?

15 I'll play one for you.

16 Suhan: Look, those smart windows are getting darker.

17 I feel like I'm in a movie theater.

18 Jina: What else can you do?

19 AI Speaker: I can beatbox, too. Here comes, "cats and boots and cats and boots."

20 Suhan: You're funny. Good job!

21 Jina: Hurry! There's a smart car station outside!

22 Let's go and ride in that red car.

23 Suhan: This car is so cool. Let's get in.

24 AI Car: Welcome. Are you ready to go?

25 Jina: Yes, what should we do now?

26 It's my first time to ride in a smart car.

27 AI Car: You don't need to do anything.

28 I will drive and take you to the next station.

29 Suhan: Watch out! I see a cat crossing the street.

30 AI Car: Don't worry. I have just sensed it.

31 When I sense dangerous situations, I slow down or stop.

32 Jina: How can you do that?

33 AI Car: I'm a very intelligent robotic car.

34 I know all about driving.

35 I can predict danger based on knowledge and experience.

36 Suhan: How smart! You think and act like a person.

37 You are really like a human.

Before You Read

1. DAILY NEWS

2. Beats

3. has beaten, in, match

4. had a match with, one of the greatest, players

5. difficult to understand

6. believed, for an AI to beat

7. was able to predict, finally won

8. are shocked, be more intelligent than

Focus on Expressions

1. get in, to get to

2. love to go, because, greatest amusement park

3. Above all, their favorite activity

4. don't want, get off

Wrap Up 1-2

1. smart food-ordering, over there, Why don't, try

2. sounds, be able to order, by using

3. By the way, for robots to replace

4. will be free from, because of

5. What, mean

6. in danger, so, don't have to

7. right, always try to look on

Before You Read

1. DAILY NEWS

2. AI Beats Human!

3. An AI program has beaten a human in a *baduk* match.

4. The AI had a match with Lee Sedol, who is one of the greatest *baduk* players.

5. *Baduk* is a board game, and the rules are difficult to understand.

6. Many people believed it would be impossible for an AI to beat a human player.

7. However, the AI was able to predict Lee's play, and it finally won the game.

8. People are shocked that an AI can be more intelligent than a human.

Focus on Expressions

1. In 2099, people get in a flying car to get to the moon.

2. Kids love to go to the moon because the greatest amusement park is there.

3. Above all, horse-riding is their favorite activity.

4. They don't want to get off the horses.

Wrap Up 1-2

1. G: Minseok, there is a smart food-ordering machine over there. Why don't we try it?

2. B: That sounds interesting. We'll be able to order easily and fast by using it.

3. G: I hope so. By the way, do you think maybe it will be possible for robots to replace humans someday?

4. B: I'm not sure. But we will be free from danger because of robots.

5. G: What do you mean?

6. B: Robots can help people in danger. Robots can do the dangerous work so humans don't have to.

7. G: You're right. We should always try to look on the bright side.

적중 100

영어 기출 문제집

정답 및 해설

시사 | 송미정